THE EMERGENCE OF

METROPOLITAN AMERICA

1915–1966

The Emergence of

1915-1966

METROPOLITAN
AMERICA

BY *Blake McKelvey*

RUTGERS UNIVERSITY PRESS   *New Brunswick, New Jersey*

To Jean

PREFACE

The urbanization of America had entered a new stage by 1915. Rapidly growing cities and towns, having multiplied several-fold in number during the preceding half century, had drawn fully half the nation's population into their busy affairs. For several decades, young men and women had been thronging from every section of the land to its urban centers. They had joined a great host of newcomers from abroad in building the expanding cities. Eager to better themselves, they had promoted the fortunes of their towns, whether large or small, knitting them progressively into the nation's economy. Spirited rivalries had developed between neighboring communities and also between more distant urban competitors. As some cities drew ahead, establishing commercial or industrial leadership over metropolitan regions, others achieved compensatory functions that enabled them too to share in the country's rapid progress.

Residents of all classes had contributed to this advance, and their achievements were not solely economic. So turbulent and at times bewildering had city life become that enterprising individuals in many places had banded together and founded a multitude of organizations to secure and safeguard their interests. In the process they had created a new and complex urban society in which economic, political, and social forces had conditioned the internal structure of each city and influenced the external relationship of one community to another. On the political level these developments had culminated in the Progressive Movement and brought the passage in 1913 of the Federal Reserve Act, which organized the nation's banking system into twelve reserve districts and gave tangible recognition to the emergence of a widespread pattern of metropolitan regions.

I have reviewed these developments in an earlier volume on *The Urbanization of America: 1860–1915*. Historians have generally come to recognize the importance of "The Rise of the City" in American history, yet some have concluded that, with the achievement of an urban-rural balance, the significance of the urban factor became diffused and requires little if any attention.

But the process of urbanization did not stop there; indeed, it had only commenced to take hold. And as the mushrooming metropolises increased in number and size, problems created by their growth posed crucial issues to the nation. The search for solutions was of course complicated by the outbreak of two world wars and a great depression, each of which helped, as we shall see, to project the metropolis into the mainstream of American history.

Even a cursory review of the nation's development over the last half century reveals the emergence of a number of basic internal dilemmas. Several of these involved changing relationships between the great cities, the states, and the federal government. We have, for example, witnessed an unprecedented growth of national power, with federal authority extending as never before into every city and hamlet. We have, at the same time, witnessed a multiplication of local community problems, especially in the big cities, and an incessant search by their leaders for the necessary power and proper means to cope with them. These simultaneous developments suggest the possibility that they may have been historically related. The detection and examination of such relationships are the major objectives of this book.

Several questions readily spring to mind. Has the expansion of federal power reflected in some degree the reluctance of the states either to grant sufficient power to their cities or to perform themselves the functions essential to an urban society? Have some of the perplexing civic and social problems that have plagued modern America been aggravated by the failure of growing cities to achieve effective leadership over their spreading populations? Did the staunch belief in free enterprise and reliance on voluntarism speed or retard urban growth and metropolitan adjustment? Is the sudden outburst of Negro rioting in several city slums hopefully a "revolution of rising expectations," or is it a tragic retribution for the nativism that slammed the door on foreigners only to accelerate the migration of Negroes to the cities?

These questions cannot be answered categorically. They serve, however, to uncover some of the basic historic dilemmas of the last half century. Many of these choices, between voluntarism and public action, between local, state, and national responsibility, between charity and public welfare, between home rule and consolidation, between segregation and integration, between elite and democratic standards and tastes, between the plans of experts and the decisions of the electorate, involved a choice between relative values. Some of the dilemmas had a moral quality that sorely tested the spirit of rival leaders; all had a historic character in that the decisions once reached helped to pose the issues for the next decade and inevitably influenced their outcome.

These questions have little relation to the probing internal analysis of metropolitan society that some sociologists have undertaken, or with the debate among political scientists over "who governs," or with the varied problems of urban form that have interested the geographers and planners. I will, however, take note of the contributions these and other students of the city have made to America's increasing awareness of its metropolitan character, for although I do not attempt to analyze the development of the American metropolis, I have endeavored to chart the emergence of metropolitan America.

My approach is historical and seeks to place the changing metropolitan and national relationships in a time and place perspective. All the basic dilemmas mentioned above were clearly and dramatically posed in the late teens, as my first chapter will reveal. The first tentative responses were partially forgotten in the postwar years as the prosperous twenties brought a burst of vitality to the emerging metropolises and engendered a degree of complacency in the states. For a brief moment in history it appeared possible that the great cities might master their dilemmas and create a decentralized America of more or less autonomous metropolitan regions; yet the obstacles proved too great and the rural opposition unyielding. These developments, reviewed in my second chapter, ill prepared either the cities or the states for the hardships of the depression that followed. The old choices between local, state, and national responsibility had to be faced anew in the thirties, together with other hard choices to be considered in the third chapter. Chief among these were the questions of public versus private responsibility and of voluntary as opposed to compulsory participation and compliance.

Since most of the programs formulated under the New Deal were designed to meet a specific crisis, they were generally regarded as temporary, and the slowed pace of metropolitan growth further encouraged procrastination over its basic problems. The outbreak of the Second World War reenforced that attitude in many places. But as that struggle progressed, most of the tentative relationships linking the cities to the federal government during the First World War and the depression revived. The postwar resurgence of growth sharply renewed many old metropolitan dilemmas and brought the long slumbering issue of racial integration dramatically to the fore. Together they present, with the Cold War, to which the last at least is closely linked, the major challenges to the Great Society.

Of course these and other dilemmas of urbanization did not alone explain the history of America in the last half century. They were more product than cause of the great wars and violent economic fluctuations. Yet it seems pertinent to inquire whether and in what respect the special character of America's metropolitan society influenced the development of these crises and helped to determine their outcome. I have tried in each chapter to relate the broader international and technological trends and the metropolitan responses to each other. I have endeavored, too, to identify the leaders who helped to make the choices, though the determination of who governs or who innovates is ever a moot one. But I have not attempted to write a fully rounded history of America's metropolitan society. That is a much broader subject and will require the attention of many historians as the years progress.

Fortunately, a host of scholars in other fields—political scientists, economists, sociologists—have progressively during the last half century increased our knowledge as to the nature of the city and its functions. I do not pretend to evaluate their findings except as they exerted a substantive influence on developments, but I have gratefully made use of those insights that pertain to a historical analysis. I hope that the attempt to view this broad development in perspective may contribute modestly to its comprehension.

BLAKE McKELVEY

Rochester, New York
December, 1967

ACKNOWLEDGMENTS

For support and backing in this study I am indebted to the City of Rochester, and specifically to Dr. Seymour Scher, City Manager, and Mr. Harold Hacker, Director of Libraries, whose keen interest in metropolitan research has encouraged me to fit this work over a number of years into the ongoing programs of the City Historian's Office.

I have received generous assistance in the preparation of this volume from many librarians and scholars. My colleagues on the staff of the Rochester Public Library have been most helpful, especially Miss Marion McGuire, Miss Sue Billings, and Mr. Robert W. Eames, and I wish to thank them and their associates for painstaking assistance in combing the shelves. Several librarians elsewhere have responded to requests for elusive materials, and Mr. John Russell of the Rush Rhees Library of the University of Rochester has kindly made its sources available.

A number of urban scholars have rendered generous assistance. I am grateful to Professor Richard C. Wade of Chicago and Professor Bernard A. Weisberger of Rochester who have read and offered helpful suggestions on the historical portions of my manuscript. I am especially indebted to Professor Walter C. Kaufman who, after reading the sociological and political science sections, supplied numerous bibliographical leads and made helpful criticisms that have served to sharpen my interpretation.

For aid in assembling the illustrations and for permission to use them I am indebted to the sources cited in each case. For her painstaking care in typing numerous drafts of this manuscript, I am most grateful to Miss Yolanda Ranches, my secretary throughout the period of writing; I am also indebted to Miss Sharon Palmer, a student assistant, for checking and rechecking references and bibliographical citations. And finally to my wife, Jean Trepp McKelvey, I give warm thanks for assistance in uncovering relevant materials and for aid and encouragement in bringing this project to completion.

B. McK.

CONTENTS

MAPS AND CHARTS

THE EMERGENCE OF
METROPOLITAN AMERICA
1915–1966

1. THE EMERGENCE OF METRO-POLITAN DILEMMAS: 1915-1920

The mushrooming cities of America had begun by 1915 to assume a new shape, to acquire new civic responsibilities, and to develop new interrelationships. The new shape was inescapable, as many observers testified. Most of the larger cities, more than two score in number, were sprawling horizontally, enveloping neighboring towns in ever-extending suburban ranges; at the same time each was sprouting a stem of towering skyscrapers at the center. Internally these inverted mushrooms faced, in addition to a host of traditional urban problems, a series of new crises in planning and housing, in employment and welfare, and most critical of all, in the absorption of a fresh wave of newcomers. Externally they were establishing new lines of communication, exploring new areas of competition, and seeking new sources of economic and political power to maintain their expanding functions. Inevitably they demanded increased attention from their respective states and the federal government.

Each of these developments and the problems they created were evident by the mid-teens. Thus a widespread housing shortage revived the search for responsible solutions and disclosed new planning dilemmas; sharp fluctuations in employment posed new challenges to public and private welfare; shifting population trends, coupled with new transport facilities, speeded the suburban migration and brought new problems to the central cores; mounting fiscal burdens in the aging metropolises spurred new efforts to broaden the tax base and precipitated legislative battles between the old cities and their suburban offspring. Intensified during the war years, these issues helped to awaken a new intellectual interest in the metropolis as the habitat of modern man and posed several crucial dilemmas for America during the next half century.

• The Metropolitan Regions Take Shape

The Federal Census of 1910 had for the first time identified twenty-five of the country's 2,400 urban places as metropolitan centers. These included all that had central-city populations in excess of 200,000, while nineteen others, with at least 100,000 in the central city, were listed as emerging metropolises. Together the forty-four numbered almost 20 million inhabitants. With another 7.5 million living in their suburban territories, they comprised 30 per cent of the nation's total. But more significant than the size of the metropolitan population, which exceeded by a ratio of almost 3 to 2 the residents of all lesser urban places, was the wide distribution of its units, with one or more located in each of twenty-three states.[1]

New York City still boasted a commanding numerical lead, more than the next three cities in size combined, yet its hegemony was less evident than in the past. In many fields it shared important functions with aggressive rivals. In banking, New York's earlier predominance was in 1915 apportioned among twelve Federal Reserve cities. Boston and Philadelphia as well as New York in the East, Chicago and St. Louis in the Midwest, had long been important banking centers; to these were now added Cleveland, Minneapolis, and Kansas City in the Midwest, Richmond, Atlanta, and Dallas in the South, and San Francisco in the Far West. As a port, New York had for decades shared portions of the foreign trade with Boston, Philadelphia, and Baltimore on the Atlantic, with New Orleans on the Gulf, and with San Francisco on the Pacific. These rivals and several new contenders were now bidding vigorously for that commerce.[2]

New contenders were arising in other special fields. As an industrial center New York was already overshadowed in many specialties, by Pittsburgh and Chicago in steel, by Detroit in automobiles, by Minneapolis and Buffalo in flour milling, to mention only a few. In the opinion of N. S. B. Gras, who first attempted, in 1922, to define a metropolis in functional terms, industrial activities were not germane to the analysis, yet each of the other major metropolises had its specialties. Cleveland and Milwaukee as lake ports were respectively machine-tool and brewing centers; Los Angeles, a haven for the retired, was becoming the headquarters of a new entertainment industry; Cincinnati, Indianapolis, Kansas City, Seattle, and Portland, Oregon, all regional trade hubs, each had manufacturing industries that added more than $100 million to the value of its products; Providence was a producer of textiles and silverware; Rochester manufactured photographic supplies and technical instruments; Washington was the administrative capital of the nation.[3]

But this loosely structured constellation of widely dispersed metropolitan centers was by no means static. Even the 1910 Census, which also listed sixteen places under 100,000 in size that experienced a growth of 100 per cent or more in the preceding decade, had foreshadowed the emergence of additional metropolises. Fourteen new ones appeared by 1920, five with strong industrial specialties: Reading in Pennsylvania, Akron and Youngstown in Ohio, Springfield and Hartford in New England. Six in three states not previously represented—Houston, Dallas, San Antonio, and Fort Worth in Texas, Salt Lake City in Utah, Des Moines in Iowa—were regional centers at the start and further dissipated the urban concentration and the metropolitan predominance of the Northeast.[4]

This wide dispersion of metropolitan centers justified the conclusion of Professor Gras that America had attained a "metropolitan economy" which was organized "by a system of exchange concentrated in the large cities." The output of farms and mines had long been surpassed by that of trade and industry, and now for the first time both the production gains and the population growth of the metropolitan districts exceeded that of the rest of

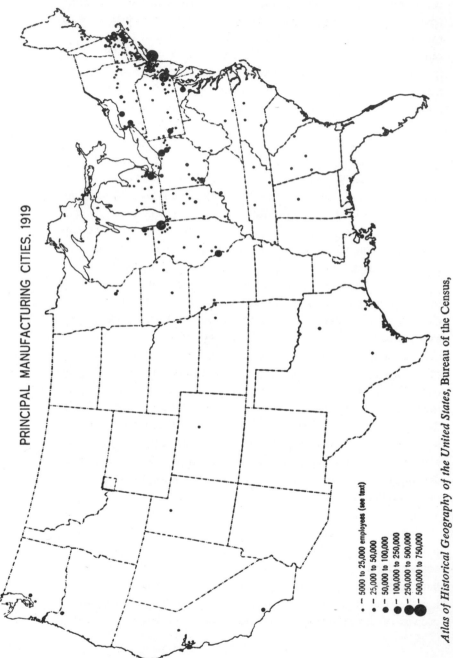

PRINCIPAL MANUFACTURING CITIES. 1919

- — 5000 to 25,000 employees (see text)
- — 25,000 to 50,000
• — 50,000 to 100,000
● — 100,000 to 250,000
● — 250,000 to 500,000
● — 500,000 to 750,000

Atlas of Historical Geography of the United States, Bureau of the Census,
U. S. Department of Commerce

the nation. With employment in industry rising 33 per cent between 1914 and 1919, the value-added mounted 150 per cent. Not only did the cities draw an increasing stream of migrants from depressed agricultural areas in the South, but they attracted migrants displaced from other farming districts by technological improvements of urban origin. With a dozen full-fledged metropolises serving the Deep South and the Prairie West, a dozen more were emerging there, including five of the country's ten most rapidly growing cities.[5]

These statistical and geographic trends had other portents. Although every metropolis had its central city and its neighboring suburbs, and all but two, Washington and New Orleans, boasted at least a few towering skyscrapers, regional and local contrasts in density and patterns of construction persisted. Despite complaints of their sameness, Boston, Philadelphia, and Baltimore were almost as distinct in the architectural style of their cores as was New York, and they differed from each other only less strikingly in their suburbs. Neither Chicago, Detroit, nor St. Louis; Cleveland, Cincinnati, nor Louisville; Pittsburgh, Washington, nor New Orleans; San Francisco, Seattle, nor Los Angeles, could be mistaken by an alert observer for any of the others.

Numerous visitors from abroad testified to this variety and to the creative vitality it engendered. Practically all of them exclaimed over the "spectacular" qualities of New York and admired its skyscrapers. One of its few critics, Paul d'Estournelles de Constant, a member of the French Senate, after deploring the monstrous character and disturbing effect of Manhattan's skyscrapers, viewed Philadelphia and Washington with appreciation; he later became ecstatic over San Francisco with its Chinatown and over the astonishing vitality of such new cities as Seattle and Kansas City. Each had its special qualities in his eyes, as did Denver and St. Paul, Milwaukee and Chicago; their differences sprang partly from their geographic settings and partly from their ethnic composition.[6]

Other visitors tended to confirm this classification; a few, however, added regional, historic, and functional differences to the analysis. Stephen Graham found Scranton a Slavic as well as a coal-mining headquarters; James O. Hannay found Memphis a cotton emporium thronged with Negroes; G. K. Chesterton noted the historic as well as the ethnic and functional contrasts of Philadelphia and Baltimore, St. Louis and Boston; Philip Gibbs among others found Chicago so richly endowed with functions and so cosmopolitan in its ethnic base as to challenge New York's economic and cultural predominance. None seriously questioned New York's leadership, but several, despite their somewhat hostile views of American materialism, took delight in the diversity they discovered. "Here is a country," concluded Clare Sheridan after a leisurely tour in which she saw many aspects of high and low life in a dozen cities, "that is composed of such widely different towns as Washington, Philadelphia, San Francisco, Los Angeles, all as different from one another as they are different from New York, and as different as New York is from Boston." [7]

Nevertheless, in their surge of expansion many of these large urban centers were losing some of their distinctiveness. A widely shared technology of transit and residential construction, coupled with a new speculative development of subdivisions, brought a measure of conformity to many suburbs. To some visitors the spacious suburban towns, especially those clustered in ranges along rapid-transit lines, with their privately owned homes standing in loose rows of unfenced yards, seemed, as Philip Gibbs put it, "a middle-class paradise." A few were appalled by the time required to drive to the nearest suburban station for the daily ride by trolley or steam train into the metropolis, but a visit to the slums quickly supplied an explanation for the exodus to suburbia. Only a few resident observers, such as young Alfred Kazin, sensed the threat this migration posed to the older neighborhoods. Yet Graham R. Taylor, in a pioneer study of *Satellite Cities,* saw many hazards as well as advantages in their development. [8]

Thus foreign visitors, as well as immigrants and natives seeking new opportunities, saw the promise of America in its great cities. Native intellectuals and creative artists likewise congregated there eager to share the urban benefits. "In all cases," as Professor Gras observed a few years later, "this [American] economic progress has been evolved in and around the metropolis. And so it is with the higher cultural pursuits." Many in all groups experienced disillusionment, and writers as dissimilar as Theodore Dreiser and Josiah Royce protested the impersonality and self-estrangement of the city and the leveling of the suburbs. Such complaints would soon become a familiar refrain as the imperfections of the metropolis were more consciously appraised. Yet, like many others, Dreiser, despite his ambivalent moods and bitter reverses, had long since found the metropolitan "quality of life and zest" irresistible and exultantly (if not finally) made Manhattan his home.[9]

• *Obstacles to Internal Metropolitan Order*

The civic achievements of the Progressive Era had given new vitality to many cities. Reform movements had brought able mayors to the fore in several places—John Purroy Mitchell in New York, Rudolph Blankenburg in Philadelphia, Newton D. Baker in Cleveland, James Couzens in Detroit—and had spurred campaigns for home-rule charters and strong-mayor systems in many others. Social surveys in a dozen communities had rallied public support for reforms in the civil service, in education and public health, in the regulation of utilities and the administration of other city functions. Bureaus of municipal research appeared under varied names in twenty-five metropolises, and the *National Municipal Review,* which surveyed this ten-year accomplishment in 1916, hailed it as a promise of future reforms. Richard S. Childs, advocate of the short ballot and of the council-manager system, happily reported their adoption in fifty cities by 1916. Walter T. Arndt recorded these and other hopeful advances in a book entitled *The Emancipation of the American City.*[10]

But if the state legislatures were becoming more responsive to requests for home rule, they were not ready to grant central cities the control they sought over their suburban regions. Eleven special metropolitan authorities, organized on a functional basis and generally appointed by the governors, had relieved the pressure for regional water, sewer, park, and port developments at New York, Boston, and Chicago, yet most efforts to establish similar authorities elsewhere were repulsed. Thus Cleveland and its encircling county, Cuyahoga, secured the passage in 1915 of a law creating

a metropolitan park commission only to have it declared uncon-
stitutional.[11] And when early in 1917 the Chicago Bureau of Public
Efficiency proposed a tentative scheme for the consolidation of all
local governments within the Chicago Sanitary District, it met a
chilly response at Springfield. Other consolidation moves advanced
by Cincinnati, Denver, Oakland, and San Diego encountered
similar rebuffs from their state legislatures.[12]

Cleveland got its park commission under a separate law, and
thinly disguised special legislation enabled other enterprising metropolises to tackle some of the problems that plagued them.
Among these the most significant in the long run would be housing,
and already in a dozen metropolises groups of concerned citizens
were seeking to inject public resources into this field.

The problem was twofold—inadequate supplies of low-priced
houses and apartments, and developing slum areas in many old
cities. New York, Boston, Chicago, and a few other metropolises
had for several decades been combating the latter situation with
regulatory measures but with discouraging results.[13] In a few
places private nonprofit groups were organizing to undertake the
construction of homes for workingmen. Boston, New York, and
Philadelphia already had a number of such projects, and in 1915
Pittsburgh, Akron, and Bridgeport launched similar efforts. In
January the National Conference on Housing, organized five years
before, drew a hundred delegates from New England cities to
Boston for its first regional institute. A year later, after reviewing
several reports of public housing projects in progressive cities
abroad, the Conference recommended similar efforts in America.
Only Massachusetts had a public housing body in operation, and
its Homestead Commission, created in 1915, had received a paltry
$50,000 to launch a demonstration project in Lowell.[14]

A closely related organization, the National Conference on City
Planning, took a broader approach to city problems. In addition
to housing, it included public buildings, parks, and highways, with
the last becoming its major concern. When delegates from sixty
cities gathered at the eighth conference in Cleveland, June 1916,
progress in the drafting of comprehensive street plans in at least
twelve metropolises was reported. One hundred cities and towns

in seventeen states had planning commissions by that time, and several of them had completed extensive studies; yet unforeseen, a new and explosive factor, the automobile, was to render much of their earlier planning obsolete.[15]

A few planners were already grappling with the new situation. In St. Louis they proposed a divided highway as a Central Traffic Parkway through the heart of the city; in Detroit and Los Angeles the authorities sought a solution with the introduction of traffic signals. Yet these pioneers scarcely grasped the proportions of the problem. A later tabulation would reveal that the annual output of passenger cars had jumped from 24,550 in 1905 to 895,930 in 1915, while the production of trucks had bounded from 450 to 74,000 in the same period; both virtually doubled in the next two years. The number of such vehicles on the roads increased threefold in five years, reaching 9,239,191 by 1920, and their traffic antiquated both urban and suburban highways.[16]

The revolutionary change in transportation presented challenging new opportunities to planners, but other problems pressed for attention in the great metropolises. Working under the leadership of Borough President George McAneny, formerly president for four years of the New York City Club, planners in New York City had achieved a new breakthrough in the spring of 1916 with the passage of a comprehensive zoning ordinance. The act, adopted after three years of careful study by a committee headed by Edward M. Bassett, a distinguished lawyer, incorporated height, area, and use standards in a three-pronged attempt to regulate the city's chaotic growth. Although Bassett's approach was legalistic and lacked a planner's conception of civic design, its bold advance over the hesitant provisions of earlier zoning acts in Boston, Washington, and Minneapolis encouraged new efforts in Newark and Philadelphia, St. Louis and Los Angeles, to achieve order in urban construction. The National Municipal League devoted an entire session to zoning procedures at its 1918 convention.[17]

But in achieving results, local associations were more useful than national conferences, and Charles M. Robinson, leader of the city-beautiful movement, undertook to gather reports from such bodies for periodic notices in the *National Municipal Review*.

Perhaps the largest and one of the most effective was the Greater Dayton Association, which enrolled 7,000 members in its first year, 1915, and completed 132 of the 194 projects its directors approved.[18] The Detroit Community Union, which published a local *Civic Search-Light* for many years, the municipal leagues, city clubs, and civic forums that thrived in a score of cities, all had similar objectives. Several of their leaders met at the annual convention of the National Municipal League in 1917 and formed a Civic Secretaries Association to coordinate their efforts.[19]

Of course the crux of the matter appeared in most instances to be finances. Here the new bureaus of municipal research performed a useful service by seeking economies through the central purchase of supplies and other efficiency measures. Some of the bureaus recommended tax reforms to eliminate inequities and increase the city's revenues for needed improvements, but except for the parent body in New York, headed by R. Fulton Cutting, one of the founders of its City Club, they seldom challenged the prevailing view of the citizen tax leagues that a reduction in taxes was a major goal.[20] Few were ready to endorse the proposal of Louis D. Brandeis, in *Other People's Money,* that cities should become their own bankers and should fund their own utilities. Indeed, only one major city, Milwaukee, had adopted that fiscal policy, although San Francisco, Seattle, St. Paul, and a few more were experimenting with other limited forms of municipal socialism.[21]

"No city will be able to work out its municipal destiny," wrote Walter Arndt in 1917, "until it has control over its own exchequer." Yet, in view of state curbs on the taxing and bonding powers of cities and other restrictions uncovered in his wide review of municipal developments, he could only hope that the mounting urban populations would soon effect a release from these restrictions. They reflected, he believed, the views of legislators "from rural districts and from villages and small cities . . . whose needs are smaller than the needs of their city colleagues." [22]

In fact the rural majorities had already disappeared by 1910 in thirteen states and would vanish in three more by 1920. Despite this historic shift, the leaders of a dozen metropolises were discovering the reluctance of the rural-dominated legislatures in their states to reapportion the districts. That reluctance played a major role in postponing the calling of a constitutional convention in Illinois in 1915.[23] It also blocked reapportionment in New York that year when the revised constitution was defeated by Gotham voters partly because it failed to correct inequities stemming from the 1894 constitution.[24] New York City was not as grievously underrepresented as Baltimore and Providence, for example, but its City Club and other reform groups were discovering that a great metropolis could not count on the support even of other cities within the state when issues involving its regional needs arose. To Richard S. Childs and his friends, the only hope appeared to lie in increased home rule, coupled with the safeguards of the short ballot and other democratic reforms; but already the principle of home rule, eagerly adopted by an increasing number of suburbs, was presenting a new obstacle to expansive metropolises.[25]

A new electoral device, first applied at Ashtabula, Ohio, in 1915, seemed for a time to promise a return to pure democracy. The theory of proportional representation was of course not new; it had had its advocates in America for two decades before a charter-revision committee in Ashtabula ventured to give it a trial. Despite some difficulty in training the voters and in persuading them to exercise their full range of choices, the new plan proved practical and useful. It quickly put its birthplace on the map and prompted Boulder, Colorado, and Kalamazoo, Michigan, to incorporate the system in their new 1918 charters.[26]

Most of the reformers who backed PR, the council-manager form, and other good-government schemes favored a nonpartisan approach in city elections. Yet Professor Charles A. Beard, though a frequent participant in the National Municipal League's conventions, could not agree with that view. He seized an opportunity at the 1917 meeting to blast the nonpartisan position by observing that no city government, however honest or efficient, could do much about the basic problems of the city. These he listed as poverty, overcrowding, unemployment, physical degeneracy, and low standards of life. To attack effectively any of these, he declared, urban leaders would have to seek state and federal assistance through political channels. Only a determined electorate could produce results.[27]

The solution of these basic urban problems, another group of reformers maintained, would not come through either local or national political action, but through a rejuvenation of the neighborhood community. This approach, which had inspired a social-center movement launched at Rochester a few years before, had its advocates in many cities, and more than a score of them gathered for their first national conference at New York in April 1916. Some of those present, like Clarence Perry of the Russell Sage Foundation, hoped by a planned reorganization of the neighborhood to promote social as well as architectural unity; others placed their faith in local associational effort and citizen participation.[28]

Prominent among the latter was Wilbur C. Phillips, who had evolved a special plan for organizing neighborhoods as social units. After securing the backing of Daniel Guggenheim and other philanthropists, Phillips persuaded his friends in Cincinnati to launch a drive in January 1917 for the organization of social units in a blighted district of that slum-ridden city. With his supporters he soon had thirty-one block units and two city-wide councils in active operation. The avowed object, following John Dewey's principles, was to encourage residents "to learn through doing." Most of the units agreed to tackle local health needs first and to provide wholesome activities for the children. Mothers of preschool children enrolled for special classes in family care, and many unit members attended tuberculosis clinics. But the task of maintaining attendance at the social-unit meetings became difficult after America's entry into the war, when conflicting ethnic loyalties brought the experiment to an end. Phillips tried to save his program by organizing a National Social Unit Movement, but the war soon diverted his backers.[29]

Many of the more traditional social agencies also were entering a new stage of development. Private welfare societies, established to meet specific needs, had proliferated in many cities to the point where services were sometimes duplicated and their most faithful backers overburdened. To correct this situation, Cleveland had organized a Federation for Charity and Philanthropy in 1913, and its successful operation, under a board appointed by the city officials, prompted twenty other cities to create similar bodies before

1917. Most of these boards assumed the task of raising each year the funds needed by the participating agencies; a few also undertook to maintain a central exchange in which the records of all relief applicants could be filed to forestall duplication.[30] Generous givers in several cities took the additional step of establishing a community trust to accept large sums for annual disposition as directed. When the Cleveland Community Trust received $30 million in its initial year, 1914, bankers in St. Louis, Chicago, Los Angeles, and Boston hastened to found similar trusts. Again, representatives of these varied bodies met in 1918 to form an American Association for Community Organization.[31]

A prime stimulus for the rapid growth of these cooperative efforts was the recession of 1914. One estimate put the number in American cities unemployed that winter at 2 million. A survey of thirty-six cities revealed that private charities expended almost $1.5 million, an increase of 73 per cent over their outlays two years before. In addition, fifty-six cities expended $3.6 million on hastily launched public works, giving at least part-time jobs to over 30,000 unemployed persons. All major industrial cities of the North and West established or reactivated free employment agencies under local or state laws; several achieved a high rate of efficiency, notably one in Cleveland, which filled nearly 15,000 positions during the six winter months. When some of these offices closed their doors after the upsurge of defense orders relieved the crisis, Professor John B. Andrews wrote an article for the *American City* in which he reviewed the limited accomplishments and urged advance planning by city, state, and national authorities to meet a possible return of unemployment. A shortage of labor not jobs soon developed, and within a year the federal government had reopened employment offices in all industrial cities and established local War Labor Boards to forestall work stoppages.[32]

• *Negroes Move to the Cities*

The outbreak of war in Europe also shut off or sharply reduced the flood of immigrants, thus contributing in two ways to the labor shortage. A sudden drop from 1,218,500 newcomers in 1914 to

326,700 the next year brought a new aspect of the labor situation sharply into focus, as for the first time in some cities employment offices began to register and serve Negro applicants. And as the influx of migrants from abroad continued to fall to a low of 110,000 for 1918, Northern industrialists, girding to fill war orders, took positive measures to stimulate a new migration of poor whites and Negroes from the South.[33] In the process they created a new problem for the cities that linked the fortunes of the metropolis inseparably with the history of the nation.

The migration of Negroes to the cities was not actually a new phenomenon. It had commenced several decades earlier and paralleled the movement of Southern whites from rural to urban areas. Together they had helped double the urban population of the thirteen Southern states within two decades; Negroes comprised 28 per cent of that total in 1910, which was only slightly less than their ratio of 29.8 per cent in the entire South. Lesser numbers of both whites and Negroes had migrated from the section, most of the whites to the West, most of the Negroes to Northern cities. Still the number of Negroes moving north had declined in the early 1900's and (because of the rapid growth of Northern cities from other sources) their ratio, too, had declined to 2.5 per cent of the urban total. Even Washington, which had the largest concentration of Negroes, 94,446, saw their percentage diminish slightly, to 28.5, as its other elements grew more rapidly. In New York City, where their second largest contingent dwelt, the Negroes slightly advanced their ratio, to 1.9 per cent in 1910; in Philadelphia and Cincinnati they made somewhat larger gains, but elsewhere they dropped or barely held their own.[34]

Although their percentages in Northern cities were low, when compared with those of the major immigrant groups, Negroes were sufficiently numerous in many places to achieve a sense of community. In nineteen Northern cities they numbered 5,000 or more and in seven of these the Negroes exceeded 25,000, as they did in all seven metropolises of the South. Like many of the immigrant colonies, these Negro subcommunities had developed an appearance of stability, supporting a number of religious, social, and educational institutions. A list of Negro weekly and monthly newspapers included 288 titles in 1910, and if many were short-lived, some like the *Afro-American* of Baltimore and the Chicago *Defender* were soundly established and ably edited. Negroes owned and operated a number of small business establishments in every major city, but few had amassed wealth, and generally the colored communities found their leaders among the clergy, doctors, lawyers, and educators, who formed the nucleus of a growing middle class.[35]

Despite a tragic record of lynchings and an appalling toll of crimes against and by Negroes, their contributions to the development of Southern cities was accepted almost in silence. There the migrants from hamlets and farms found lodging near their numerous relatives or former neighbors and maintained their accustomed relations with the whites, many of whom were recent arrivals too, and from the same rural districts. In some of the older towns whites and blacks lived in close proximity in widely scattered sections, but in growing cities, such as Birmingham and Memphis, each with 40 per cent nonwhite, separate Negro neighborhoods developed, some of them makeshift and poor, some reconversions of old residences, some modest but of new construction. Women outnumbered the men in these Negro quarters and supported their preachers and other professionals in maintaining congenial if often squalid communities.[36]

Negroes migrating to the Northern metropolises faced a different prospect and created a greater stir. Like other newcomers with rural backgrounds, they lacked the manners of urbanites and often encountered hostility from established residents even of their own race. Although the influx in the early 1900's was a moderate one, it was sufficient in several cities to overcrowd the former Negro districts and to exert pressure for their expansion. Surrounded as they had been for decades by the larger settlements of European immigrant groups, the Negro communities in the major cities of the North tended to buy out and displace the whites remaining in their districts and to assume a more self-conscious racial stance. The group of Negro leaders, led by W. E. B. Du Bois, who gathered in 1905 at Niagara Falls, Canada, and adopted resolutions demanding equality of opportunity, marked an early response to the growing tension.[37]

The Negroes, like the immigrants, attracted the interest and sympathy of urban progressives concerned for the well-being of the entire community. White social workers and philanthropists established the Frederick Douglass Center in Chicago and the Robert Gould Shaw House in Boston; they erected a block of model apartments for Negroes in New York, only three of many efforts. Frances A. Kellor established the National League for the Protection of Colored Women in 1905, a year before the Negroes themselves organized the Committee for Improving the Industrial Conditions of the Negro. Dr. William S. Buckley, a Negro school principal, headed that committee and five years later merged it with the League for Protection, and then with a third committee on urban conditions to form the National Urban League. Meanwhile, reports of a race riot at Springfield, Illinois, had prompted Oswald Garrison Villard and other progressives to convene a conference on the problem early in 1909 at the Henry Street Settlement in New York. A year later they brought leaders of the Niagara Movement and of other civil rights groups, both Negroes and whites, together to form the National Association for the Advancement of Colored People.[38]

The name of the NAACP weekly, the *Crisis,* first issued in 1910, forecast the spirit of the new movement; the real crisis did not develop, however, until the outbreak of war in Europe cut the flow of immigrants and prompted Northern industrialists to turn to the South for fresh labor recruits.

Many forces converged in 1915 to launch the new migration. A poor cotton crop in the South caused by the ravages of the boll weevil put thousands of cotton pickers out of work. The simultaneous development of a demand for unskilled labor in heavy-industry centers in the North prompted several firms to send recruiting agents into the South. Thus the Aluminum Ore Company in East St. Louis and a number of packing companies there and in Chicago paid trainmen on Southern roads to post notices and deliver handbills. The Chicago *Defender,* eager to expand its territory, secured ads from steel mills in Pittsburgh and Cleveland as well as Chicago, from ore carriers on the lakes, and from packing companies scattered from Cincinnati to Kansas City, and shipped thousands of free copies into the South, boosting its circulation from 10,000 to 90,000 in the process. Some of the first arrivals sent enthusiastic letters back home, and soon troupes of migrants converged on the railroad stations singing "Bound for the Promised Land." [39]

Jobs in abundance were awaiting them in 1915 and 1916, and better housing than they had left, but not in the latter case in sufficient supply. The newcomers soon jammed to overflowing the old Negro districts in a dozen cities. In Pittsburgh they crowded into the attics and cellars of an old commercial area; in Chicago they pressed south from their old quarters to the boundaries of Kenwood and Hyde Park. In St. Louis they were shunted across the river to East St. Louis, where they inundated an earlier Negro district and competed with immigrant workmen for nearby houses. When in May 1917 a strike at the Armour Packing Company yard in East St. Louis prompted the company to import a trainload of Negroes as strikebreakers, the tension mounted. A minor riot on the 28th was quickly suppressed with the aid of the militia, but hostilities festered and fighting erupted again in July when white gangs attacked Negroes leaving the dock area. Unable or unwilling to check the violence, the police and militia made few arrests except of armed Negroes; when the carnage stopped, thirty-nine Negroes and nine whites were dead and hundreds injured, but only four whites and eleven Negroes were convicted of homicide and sent to prison.[40]

Sobered by the East St. Louis outbreak, urban leaders elsewhere began to take precautions. Since the police had obviously been unprepared and the militia hostile to the Negroes, police chiefs in Washington, Chicago, and a few other cities scheduled training classes for their men. Many conscientious citizens sought to identify and remove the causes. In Philadelphia, which had the third largest resident population of Negroes, the Ministerial Union helped organize a Negro Migration Committee to find jobs and homes for the 50,000 newcomers who disembarked there; eighty Negro physicians volunteered their services in cases of emergency. Cleveland's Welfare Federation had called a state conference on the situation the year before at Columbus, where an Ohio Federation for the Uplift of Colored People was organized. It then established branches in six industrial cities to assist in the placement and housing of these newcomers ranging upward from 4,000 in Dayton to 20,000 in Cleveland.[41]

The Urban League, which had helped to direct the migration in a few cities—Detroit and Hartford, for example—seized the opportunity to organize branches in additional towns. It established offices in Chicago, St. Louis, Pittsburgh, and Philadelphia and sent its agents into some other cities where the NAACP was likewise developing local units. Many of the old Negro churches opened their doors, while "Holiness" preachers from the South staffed numerous "store-front" churches for their fellow migrants. Leaders of the Urban League invited representatives from industry and labor, as well as from housing companies and related governmental agencies, to a national conference in New York in January 1918 to discuss the plight of the Negro migrants to Northern cities.[42]

Meanwhile the great migration to the North had not slackened. Neither the East St. Louis riots nor the occasional bombings of Negro homes that occurred in other cities had checked it. A few Southern industrialists, alarmed by the emigration of so many workers, urged their local editors to speak out and expose the evils awaiting migrants to Northern cities. Humanitarian leaders in several Southern communities matched the record of their contemporaries in the North in efforts to improve the lot of their Negroes. Thus a Brotherhood House in Nashville, a Commission on Interracial Cooperation in Atlanta, and enlightened programs in Winston-Salem and Dallas received commendation from Negro writers.[43]

Southern Negroes, however, were looking for job opportunities, not welcoming committees, and the migration, once started, gained momentum during the war years. When, after the Armistice, the government canceled many war contracts, thousands of workmen, many of them Negroes, lost their jobs. Widespread fears of unemployment checked a further influx, but the effort in some cities to encourage idle Negroes to return to the South had little effect. The migration was to be a permanent one, as Dr. George E. Haynes, Negro executive secretary of the Urban League, had warned the delegates at a National Conference of Social Work meeting at Pittsburgh in 1917; Northern cities, he suggested, had a challenging opportunity to help release the Negro from the bondage of poverty and repression in the Deep South. Negroes, he said, were grateful for their new jobs and citizen rights and asked only for a chance to prove themselves. Prompted by that address, the Department of Labor created a Division of Negro Economics and appointed Haynes as its director charged with the task of organizing Negro advisory committees in the major industrial cities.[44]

Chicago, which received the largest influx of Negroes, an increase of 65,355 during the decade, was aware of its problems, but hoped to solve most of them. The old Negro community, by its long support of Mayor William Hale Thompson, had won political recognition with the election in 1915 of Oscar DePriest as alderman and the appointment of two Negro attorneys to the law department and of more than fifty Negroes to the police force. The Black Belt maintained a score of well-established churches and numerous social clubs; its residents shared with their white neighbors the facilities of several settlement houses, playgrounds, and schools. But the community also had representatives in the underworld, and its easy tolerance of commercialized vice and gambling speeded the deterioration of the area. Middle-class Negroes as well as whites were already moving out when the newcomers from the South arrived, yet the influx of over 50,000 in 1917 and 1918 quickly crammed and extended the former black belt and converted it into a black ghetto of unprecedented size.[45]

Several civic groups rallied to tackle the new problems. A housing committee of the Chicago Women's Club worked with settlement leaders, representatives of the Urban League, and volunteers recruited by the Cook County Sunday School Association in a protracted effort to find accommodations for the newcomers. Together these groups located jobs and shelter in nearby industrial towns for some 5,000 Negroes without appreciably relieving the pressure in Chicago. After the Armistice, when jobs became scarce, some Negroes, denied access to unions, accepted employment as strikebreakers, thus aggravating the situation. But it was the continuing demand for houses and the purchase of several on the western edge of the Black Belt that sparked a series of twenty-five bombings of Negro homes there in July 1919.[46]

Open fighting erupted on a hot Sunday afternoon on July 27 when a group of white bathers stoned a Negro swimmer who appeared off their section of the lake beach. Pelted and driven into deep water, the Negro lad drowned. As news of his death spread into the city, gangs of whites and Negroes began to roam the streets battling each other and the police for four terror-filled days and nights. Many homes and stores were wrecked or burned, and 575 persons were seriously injured, 38 of whom died. The victims included at least 23 Negroes and 15 whites, and the injured were similarly divided. Yet the police, unwilling or unable to check the white gangs, apprehended only 75 whites and 154 Negroes, and the mayor was finally compelled to call in the state militia. A cold rain on the fifth day helped to dampen the fury on both sides, though peace was not fully restored for another week.[47]

Chicago, however, was not the only scene of urban race riots in 1919. Both Washington and Omaha experienced serious anti-Negro outbreaks that summer, while lynchings, bombings, and mob attacks occurred in sixteen other places, North and South, before the year closed. This postwar violence marred the friendly relations that had developed in several cities between middle-class Negroes and whites; at the same time it brought resident and migrant Negroes closer together and made them more conscious of their racial bonds. Civil rights leaders felt challenged as never before to understand and correct the situation. The Chicago Commission on Race Relations, appointed by the governor to investigate the riots, made a probing study and issued a voluminous report of 672 pages. Its hearings and researches, conducted by a competent staff under the direction of Graham R. Taylor, son of the social-gospel leader, supplied documentation for a series of forthright recommendations that would provide direction for the civil rights cause during the next two decades.[48]

Yet bleak as the Negro's situation appeared in Chicago and in many industrial cities hard hit by unemployment, his position had somewhat improved in Southern cities and in several in the North as well. More than a third of all American Negroes were residents of urban centers by 1920, an increase of almost 900,000 in the decade. The advantages they enjoyed over rural Negroes in personal freedom, in higher wage rates, and in living accommodations were considerable, even when qualified by congestion. The benefits were most apparent in cities of slow growth, North and South. Even in New York City, where the Negro population mounted from 91,000 to 152,000, Manhattan shared the increased number with Brooklyn and other boroughs, so that congestion was not acute. And on Manhattan itself, the Negroes acquired a new area of settlement in Harlem, where speculative building promoters were eager to find tenants. One Harlem newcomer, James W. Johnson, would describe it a few years later as a "model American community." Moreover, a wide refusal by the courts to recognize the constitutionality of segregation ordinances held the way open in other cities for an expansion of Negro occupancy. Impressed by their recent gains, some Negro leaders such as Johnson and Haynes saw the migration to the cities, both North and South, as the best hope for their race.[49]

• A New City-Federal Alliance

The First World War, which had accelerated the migration of Negroes to the cities, provided an incentive for the development of important new relationships between the cities and the federal government. Although it diverted some urban leaders, notably Newton D. Baker, from urban to national careers, it drew many other local citizens more actively into community programs. Widely scattered city clubs found their public forums crowded as never before with men and women eager to hear and debate the war's challenge. The wartime emergency brought the formation of new clubs and relief agencies in many cities, and soon a number of war chests made their appearance. Indeed the citizen response in many places was so vigorous that the federal authorities, hastening to mobilize the nation's resources, turned increasingly to the urban centers for leadership in the organization of production and other war efforts. Some of the volunteer national bodies which had previously supplied a broader sphere for local officials and reformers, such as the National Municipal League, had a hard struggle to maintain their activities, but local urban leaders, both official and voluntary, acquired active new roles in the federal system.[50]

It was not only the gravity of the crisis, but also the spirited quality of the citizen response that sparked this transformation. When Baltimore met the pleas of the Red Cross and of numerous war-relief agencies by launching a drive in June 1917 for a three-year emergency fund of $1.5 million to cover these needs, and when Columbus, Ohio, topped that effort the next February in a campaign that raised $3,071,088 from 73,126 subscribers, the success of the new war chests was assured. A dozen cities conducted similar drives that spring, and many more were in the planning stage.[51]

Impressed by the effectiveness of these community-wide campaigns, the national treasury turned to the Federal Reserve Centers and their satellite cities to enlist the cooperation of local bankers in bond drives that proved equally successful. In similar fashion, the Council of National Defense, which had initially worked through similar state councils, began before the declaration of war to call on the city councils and other local bodies for assistance in developing war gardens, in promoting food and fuel conservation, and in launching other home-front programs. To speed these efforts, *The American City* sent a questionnaire to the civic and business heads of 1,200 cities requesting information on local projects under sixteen different categories. The replies received from 454 communities amply demonstrated the vitality of the urban response.[52]

Many local organizations vied in the performance of the new wartime functions. The Chambers of Commerce of sixty-two cities created special committees to launch or coordinate Americanization programs, while similar committees of local YMCAs performed that function in a dozen metropolises scattered from New York to Chicago, with notable results in the highly dynamic Detroit area.[53] The Detroit Chamber concentrated its efforts on combating a coal shortage, while its counterpart in Seattle launched a campaign to close the brothels that threatened the welfare of a nearby army camp. Marcus M. Marks, borough president of Manhattan, and Councilman Mahlon M. Garland of Pittsburgh vied for the honor of initiating the movement for daylight saving, which finally became a wartime measure after winning support from many leading Chambers of Commerce.[54]

The new federal-city relationship was most dramatically demonstrated in close cooperation under the Selective Service Act. Hugh S. Johnson later recalled the initial decision, to which he contributed as an assistant under General Enoch H. Crowder, when local authorities were organized to conduct the draft. In place of a national military bureaucracy, General Crowder charged groups of local citizens with the responsibility. By direct appeal to municipal officials across the land he achieved an effective organization of this crucial activity within the short span of sixteen days. More important than the speed was the sense of local participation in a stirring national response to an unprecedented emergency. No other action could have secured more widespread recognition of the new relationship between the cities and the nation.[55]

The local draft boards performed vital if somewhat symbolic functions, but the services rendered by the industrial leaders of some metropolitan centers were as practical as they were novel. The National War Industries Board, overwhelmed by the great volume of orders for arms and munitions and by the difficulty of parceling them out to competing firms, welcomed the offer of a group of Cleveland executives who proposed to coordinate that area's bids for contracts. Charles A. Otis, formerly president of the Cleveland Chamber, served as chairman of its War Industries Commission, which undertook early in 1917 to match the industrial potentialities of numerous small firms to the deficiences of major companies in order to enable them, backed by subcontracts, to bid for and fill large war orders. The efficiency achieved in Cleveland prompted the chief of the Division of Production to seek the aid of the U.S. Chamber of Commerce in dividing the country into industrial regions, the center of each, a metropolis whose leaders could supply the coordination demonstrated in Cleveland. Thus a list of ten, later twenty-one, ordnance districts came into being with the responsibiity delegated in each case to a key business association of an industrial metropolis, which was challenged to provide equitable and effective leadership to a wide region.[56]

As the volume of production mounted, vindicating the regional organization, the Army and other federal authorities adopted a similar zonal system for procurement purposes. State boundaries were blithely disregarded and state functionaries bypassed in the haste to get the job done.

In a similar but more significant disregard of traditions, the national ordnance department supplied funds to local firms not only to enlarge their factories or to erect new ones, but also to build houses needed to attract workmen to their plants. Again the federal authorities found in the cities able men, in this case architects and planners, ready to supply effective leadership. Frederick Law Olmsted, Jr., chairman of a committee appointed by the National Conference on City Planning to confer with the federal authorities on the planning of army camps, was able not only to place sixteen of the country's leading architects, serving as dollar-a-year men, in charge of that "wooden city" program, but also to bring the most advanced town planners into the work of supplying houses for essential war workers.[57]

Two newly established federal agencies had charge of the construction of these permanent houses. The Emergency Fleet Corporation launched home-building projects at a dozen shipbuilding centers, while the United States Housing Corporation started sixteen other projects near scattered industrial plants. Several of these were well-designed communities, reflecting the influence both of the British new-towns movement and of the neighborhood-organization program in America. Unfortunately, few of these projects were completed and several had barely commenced when the Armistice prompted a cancellation of most contracts. Advocates of housing reform—Olmsted, Robert W. De Forest, Samuel Gompers among others—met at Philadelphia and appealed to Washington for the creation of a permanent federal agency to complete and operate these projects and to promote and, if necessary, build adequate houses for workingmen. But the Wilson administration, eager to divest itself of wartime functions, was in no mood for such action.⁵⁸

The precipitate demobilization not only alarmed industrial, labor, and civic leaders, but also sparked a new debate over the extent and character of the federal government's responsibility for the national welfare. Howard L. McBain of Columbia University addressed the annual convention of the National Municipal League, at Rochester in January 1919, on this subject. The federal government could not in peacetime maintain all projects launched under wartime powers, yet some means should be found, he declared, to cooperate with state and municipal authorities on these essential programs. Other speakers urged that the United States should, like Britain, promote the development of garden cities to supply more adequate facilities for its working people.⁵⁹

Pressed for action to combat unemployment, President Wilson called a White House Conference of Governors and Mayors to encourage the launching of public works projects. Many people expressed disappointment when Congress failed to adopt an appropriation for the U.S. Employment Service, forcing the closing of most of the 750 local offices. Only a few cities were prepared to take prompt action. The mayor of Pittsburgh announced a $13 million improvement project, including some residential rehabilitation; Detroit and several other cities and a few states were preparing to launch public works projects to take up the employment slack. More significant than the number and size of these efforts was the fact that responsible civic leaders, in meeting for the first time to discuss these problems on a nationwide basis, were eager to explore possible areas of federal action.⁶⁰

• *Pioneer Urban Studies*

In the eyes of James Couzens, the first "strong" mayor of rapidly growing Detroit, the potentialities of American cities seemed in 1919 almost unlimited, but they posed some grave questions that called for courageous action. He thought in terms of Detroit's economic potentials, and of the responsibility he bore at the sudden drop in postwar employment, as well as the acute shortage of housing. "We must have [jobs and] accommodations for these people," he declared. "I do not see why we cannot float a $5,000,-000 bond issue . . . to aid workers in getting homes." When his legal advisers explained the constitutional limitations on the city's power, the former business partner of Henry Ford determined to carry his plea to the state and national legislatures.[61]

To young Lewis Mumford, writing for the *Nation* that September, the cities required not only greater powers but also a clearer understanding of their objectives. It seemed curious to him that problems such as housing, endemic in urban growth for several decades, had gained wide public attention only during the war. After reviewing the failure of three housing-reform programs in New York City, he concluded that these failures "are at bottom symptoms of deficient intellectual analysis and organization." [62]

The editors and writers of several urban journals vigorously endorsed this call for more adequate information and understanding. Harold S. Buttenheim, editor of *The American City,* and Richard S. Childs, who performed that function for the *National Municipal Review* in 1919, both welcomed candid discussion of urban problems and sought a wider sharing of municipal experience. With Paul U. Kellogg, editor of the *Survey* and former director of the monumental Pittsburgh Survey, they were eager to report the findings of local civic surveys and research bureaus and to promote regional institutes and national conferences on a host of urban questions. They persistently sought and publicized the views and programs of local officials and other leaders of civic institutions, in the realm of municipal art and adult education as well as in the more traditional fields of public safety, welfare, and convenience.[63]

A staunch backer of these efforts, the Russell Sage Foundation promoted training and research programs to upgrade the performance of the increasing number of professional civic and social workers. Several schools of civics and philanthropy, which had started independently under varied names in Boston, New York, Chicago, and elsewhere, affiliated in these years with nearby universities; Graham Taylor's school, for instance, became in 1910 the University of Chicago's Graduate School of Social Services.

Although these schools, which numbered seventeen in 1919, relaxed their former ties with urban settlement houses and reduced their dependence on resident training as participants, they offered new courses in the social sciences and endeavored to profit from the increased volume of printed materials available on the cities.[64]

Scholarly studies were appearing on several key aspects of the urban problem. Edith E. Wood published her Columbia doctoral dissertation, *The Housing of the Unskilled Wage Earner,* in 1919. Both Emmett Scott and George E. Haynes produced informative books on the migration of their fellow Negroes to Northern cities, while the thoroughly documented report of the Chicago Commission on Race Relations appeared in 1922. Nelson P. Lewis brought out the first edition of *Planning the Modern City* in 1916; Clarence Perry wrote *Ten Years of the Community Center Movement* in 1921; Graham R. Taylor produced a study of *Satellite Cities* in 1915; Charles Zueblin published an important book that displayed an early glimpse of some metropolitan aspects of municipal government. These and many other publications shed much light on the character of the emerging metropolis.[65]

Yet they did not exhaust the opportunities for urban analysis as envisaged by Professor Robert E. Park of the University of Chicago. Possessed of an omnivorous curiosity, he saw the city as the ideal "laboratory in which human nature and social processes may be conveniently and profitably studied." In a seminal paper, "The City: Suggestions for the Investigation of Human Behavior in the City Environment," published in the *American Journal of Sociology* in March 1915, he proposed a multiplicity of studies that would absorb the energies of sociologists for several decades. He wanted to determine the character and origins of slums, ethnic colonies, suburban dormitories, and a host of other "natural areas" and functional groups as a contribution to an understanding of the whole city and eventually the whole society. He wished also to probe the economic, political, and cultural forces that contributed to the urbanization process, which he saw as both constructive and disintegrating in effect.[66]

Park sought to discover the style and "milieu" of city life, not to savor it, as Dreiser and other creative artists or hedonistic residents might hope to do, but in order to distinguish the urban from the rural experience as an aid in formulating a science of man. He readily expressed his indebtedness to Jane Addams of Hull House, to Paul Kellogg of the Pittsburgh Survey, and to other reform-minded students of the city, with whom he frequently collaborated in these years, yet he sought to free his analysis from their motivation. Charles Beard, the economic historian, like most of the political scientists, felt less impelled to divorce his researches from his melioristic impulses and welcomed the chance to participate in the movements he studied. And in spite of its desire for objectivity, the Chicago school of sociologists was itself a product of a great metropolis at a turning point in the history of the nation, when metropolitan regions were becoming vital units in its development and, by raising new economic, political, and social issues, placed a premium on an increased understanding of the city.[67]

2. AN OUTBURST OF METRO-POLITAN INITIATIVE: 1920-1929

Americans, curious about the growing diversity and complexity of their society, found much to ponder in the 1920 Census. Not only did they now for the first time exceed 100 million in number, but a clear majority of them were urbanites, and more than two-thirds of these were residents of one or another of the fifty-eight metropolises that had absorbed over half the decade's population gains. Few observers could view the tabulation of that growth without projecting it forward to 1930 and beyond. Even *The New York Times* looked ahead with forebodings to 1950, when a predicted population of 194,208,566, most of it crowded into cities, would, its experts warned, face a diminishing food supply. In contrast, urban spokesmen throughout the country happily saw their towns soaring to new heights, both numerically and physically.[1]

A surge of vitality did in fact enliven most of the great cities. Thronging with newcomers from many sources, they progressively absorbed an ever-larger share of the nation's productive energies and brought it a new burst of prosperity. Although the status they achieved as statistical units in the census tables had no substance in administrative law, most of the fifty-odd metropolises developed a very real sense of their identity as communities. Citizen leaders in many places hastened in the early twenties to tackle the new problems that appeared on every hand. Undaunted by the mounting burdens, they strove to check the fragmentation of local government and to lay the foundations for metropolitan action.

• Accelerated Metropolitan Growth

Everybody knew, long before the preliminary census data appeared in November 1920, that the big cities were bursting their seams. A widespread housing shortage, advancing rents, overcrowded schools, and mounting congestion in the streets, all reflected the rapid population growth of the leading metropolitan centers. Yet these and other inadequacies failed to check the flood of newcomers from rural areas, North and South, as well as many again from abroad. Instead, the overcrowded central cities proceeded to disgorge and scatter an increasing number of their former inhabitants over the adjoining territory and into satellite towns. Thus the rapidity of their growth helped to determine the structural character as well as the problems of the emerging metropolises.

Accelerated indirectly by the war, the metropolitan movement acquired a new momentum. Servicemen, the majority of whom had hailed from rural districts, flocked by the thousands to the great cities, both adding to their problems and contributing to their vitality. Immigrants from abroad, reduced to a trickle during the war, bounded from a low of 110,000 in 1918 to 430,000 in 1920 and to 805,000 the next year, and most of these newcomers crowded into the big cities where their relatives and ethnic fellows could help them find shelter and jobs. War workers, recruited in great numbers from rural areas, many from the South, had acquired new urban tastes and skills and seemed more inclined to bring their younger brothers and sisters to the cities, even when jobs were scarce, than to return themselves to the farms.[2]

The old question as to which came first, jobs or people, was tentatively dodged by the metropolis as it drew newcomers from many sources and for a great variety of reasons, only one of which was the employment at higher wages that they hoped to find. Most newcomers had no specific jobs in view, and often weeks passed before they found any. All that the majority knew was that employment was depressed on the farms and the wages even more so. Fortunately the inrush of people itself created jobs and stimulated enterprising men to launch new ventures.

Los Angeles was the prime example of such a town. Profiting from the high repute of its southern California climate, from the glamour of its film studios, and from the recent discovery of oil in its soil, the mushrooming city ranked third in rate of growth by 1920, and second by 1930. In a few short decades it had become the fourth metropolis in size without developing a specialized industrial base or even a definable business center.[3]

In contrast, Akron and Detroit, first and second in rate of growth among the metropolises of 1920, were building on a plentiful supply of factory jobs. As the leading producers, respectively, of tires and cars, they prospered from the expanding demand for automobiles. Houston, Oklahoma City, and Tulsa, among other oil producers, benefited in another way from that industry. As Southern towns with vast hinterlands, they had the additional advantage of growing up with newly awakened regions; as a result they managed by diversification to maintain high growth rates for a longer period than, for example, more specialized and more constricted Akron.[4]

The cities that really captured the lead in the twenties, however, were the resort towns. Recreation centers, such as Atlantic City and St. Petersburg, had drawn crowds of visitors in earlier years and in sufficient numbers to maintain growing staffs of permanent residents. But it was in the twenties that retirees and other citizens began to settle in large colonies at these and other resorts, boosting them into the front rank in urban growth. Miami, with a 234.4 per cent increase in the twenties, outdistanced even Los Angeles, whose 133 per cent growth, partly due to the same factors, assured it second place. At least five of the top ten in metropolitan growth were resort cities or drew newcomers because of the attractions they offered as residential centers.[5]

Yet more important statistically to urban growth than either recreation or industry were the commercial and service functions that characterized the emerging metropolis. For the first time since the start of the industrial revolution in America almost a century earlier, the steady rise of that portion of the nation's employed who were factory workers was checked; after reaching a peak of 30.8 per cent in 1920, they dropped in the course of the decade to 28.9 per cent. Even in such predominantly industrial metropolises as Detroit and Pittsburgh, Milwaukee and Rochester, the largest gains were recorded in the trade, clerical, or professional categories. Of the seven metropolises with 50 per cent or more employed in industry in 1920, only Akron retained that ratio a decade later, and its growth was now the second slowest in the group.[6]

This diversity reflected a highly significant trend of the twenties —the increased productivity of industrial man-hours. Thus, while the number of persons engaged in manufacturing dropped between 1923 and 1928 from 96.3 to 90.0 per cent of the 1919 total, the volume of production increased from 122 to 136 per cent of the former level. Moreover, the output per person mounted in these years from 126.7 to 149.5 per cent of the 1919 rate despite a drop in the average number of hours per week. The increased output of the cities, accompanied by the increased leisure, created new jobs in distribution, in service, and in recreation. And since the real wages of all employed workers likewise rose in these years from 119 to 132 per cent of the 1919 base, the cities, especially the great metropolises, were better able to sustain the commercial, civic, and cultural functions that characterized the great central cities. These activities included the huge department stores and specialty shops, the banks and hotels and restaurants, the towering office blocks and civic administrative clusters, the theatres and museums and galleries, all of which competed for downtown space, as well as the parks and zoos and public and private sport arenas and other resorts that clustered around the outskirts of the affluent cities.[7]

Of course the importance of those functions most characteristic of the metropolis was more apparent in large centers already securely established than in cities still striving to gain admittance to that category. Among the latter, except for the half dozen resort cities and another half dozen state capitals whose administrative functions were increasing rapidly, an expanding industrial base was of prime importance. What was essential, in any case, was an activity that produced a surplus beyond the local need (the "export-base construct," as later economists would name it) either for export or to attract visitors or traders or new industries into town. A regional source of fuel for power could provide the means for a "takeoff," but in the densely urbanized Northeast, a basic industry serving outside markets generally supplied the chief ingredient of growth.[8]

The increased output per industrial man-hour, by boosting the return on capital, speeded technological developments that brought new industries and expanded old ones. Moreover, labor organizations, or the mounting fear that low wages would promote them, induced management, following Henry Ford's lead, to share the returns of the larger output with the workers in sufficient measure to create an expanding market for the consumer goods now in more plentiful supply. With the additional aid of new forms of consumer credit, the public not only absorbed the flood of cars and earlier products but also bought up the new radios and other items that helped to create new industrial opportunities.[9]

Many of the older metropolises benefited as the new industries swelled their local exports; several of the fourteen cities first included in the metropolitan tables in 1920 also demonstrated their industrial vitality. Some of the newcomers would thrive as regional centers, San Antonio and Salt Lake City, for example, but others, such as Akron and Youngstown, won a secure place among the leading industrial cities. Most of the thirty-five included in that group contributed to the increased output that added 26 per cent to the value of the nation's manufactured products during the twenties. And at the close of the decade, when a new census definition lowered the population requirement, most of the thirty-nine cities added to the metropolitan category had strong industrial specialties. Some like Canton, Ohio, Chattanooga, Tennessee, Flint, Michigan, and South Bend, Indiana, would have made it under the old definition.[10]

The optimism that mounting numbers engendered among a town's inhabitants often disappeared when the same citizens considered the threat that overpopulation posed to the nation. This concern, which overshadowed the opposing fear that cities, because

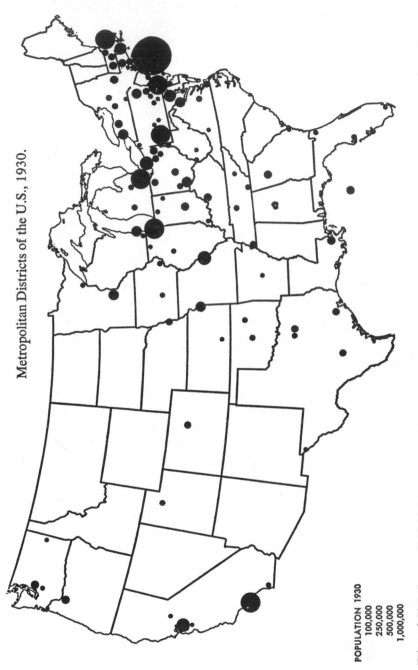

Metropolitan Districts of the U.S., 1930.

POPULATION 1930
100,000
250,000
500,000
1,000,000

Fifteenth U.S. Census, 1930, X:4

of their low birth rates, would deplete the nation's population, was aggravated in the early postwar years by sensational predictions of food shortages to come, as well as by the inadequate supply of housing and the unemployment that spread from city to city in 1920 and 1921. News reports of a rising flood of immigrants added to the alarm and helped to replace the Americanization movement of the war period with an exclusionist campaign.

Many forces contributed to the change in policy. Old and predominantly rural hostilities toward foreigners, especially those of the Catholic or the Jewish faith, were fanned into intense hatred by extremist groups such as the Ku Klux Klan and by nativist spokesmen such as Lathrop Stoddard and Henry Ford. The formerly strong opposition of some industrial leaders to a policy of immigrant exclusion had been shaken by the Red scare that swept the country after the Bolshevik revolution. Organized labor, alarmed in its turn by the wide extent of unemployment, moved for a temporary suspension of immigration. But neither these representatives of urban economic interests nor the progressive friends of the immigrants in many cities could support the extreme measures proposed by the exclusionists in 1920. After long debate a temporary quota system, advanced as a compromise, finally won adoption in 1921.[11]

Boston and New York quickly became aware of the hardships imposed by the new law. A crisis developed as the steamship lines, frantic to deliver their immigrant passengers before the quotas were filled, brought thousands of eager migrants to these principal ports. Soon the accommodations on Ellis Island were jammed to capacity, and several boatloads of disappointed immigrants had to be returned to Italy and Poland, whose quotas were most seriously overtaxed. Industrialists, ready late in 1922 to employ additional workers, joined many disinterested friends of the immigrants, as well as their ethnic societies, in protesting this inhuman policy. As recovery dispelled the fear of unemployment, labor leaders too became less opposed to immigration; in fact their success in forming laborers' unions in several cities in 1923 kindled a new interest in these unskilled newcomers.[12]

But if the major urban groups were ready to permit the 1921

law to expire, the nativists both rural and urban were girding to replace it with a stronger measure. Not only were they determined to cut the annual quota from 3 to 2 per cent, but they proposed to shift the census base from 1910 to 1890 in order both to reduce the size of the total and to alter its ethnic character. The earlier count, which antedated the great wave of immigrants from Southern and Eastern Europe, promised a selection of newcomers more in keeping, they declared, with the traditional American stock. This prospect attracted support from the South and the West and also from rural districts in the Northeast. In an effort to make it more palatable to representatives of the industrial states, Pennsylvania Senator David A. Reed introduced an amendment providing that a rationing system based on the national origins of the current population be substituted after two years for the 1890 base. That stipulation was accordingly adopted in the new Immigration Restriction Act of 1924.[13]

The new law sharply reduced the flow of immigrants, but it did not seriously check the growth of cities. When the migrants from abroad declined from 706,000 in 1924 to an average of 300,000 annually for the rest of the decade, the cities responded by drawing increased numbers from rural America. For the first time the farming population, despite its high rate of births, dropped almost a million in number as some 6 million left for near and distant cities. Migrants from the South to the North increased in number, both Negro and white, and again most of them headed for the great metropolises. Generally, as in the previous decade, they followed the principal rail lines into the North, overshadowing in the process the old east-west migration. But while the South sent over a million to Northern cities, its rural districts contributed more than twice as many to the cities and towns of the South.[14]

In some Northern cities such as Buffalo, not on a direct north-south route, the in-migrants hailed from widely scattered cities and towns, rather than from a restricted local or distant hinterland. Most Northern cities continued to attract immigrants from abroad, and in the twenties these newcomers still equaled natives of the state moving from the farms and outnumbered migrants from the South by approximately 4 to 1. Only the heavy-industry metropolises and a few others that had drawn a large influx from that region during the war years continued to pull strongly from that direction. As a result most cities, in the South as well as the North, received a more diversified mix of newcomers than ever before.[15]

In Chicago, Detroit, Pittsburgh and St. Louis, however, and a half dozen more, including New York, the migration from the South was accelerated. Indeed their dependence on it was strengthened after 1924 when the new immigration quotas drastically reduced the number admitted from Southern and Eastern Europe, which had for three decades supplied the unskilled labor their heavy industries required. In some, notably Detroit, new colonies of Southern whites also appeared; in others the already congested Negro districts overflowed their boundaries, occupying especially those tracts whose ethnic quotas were most drastically curtailed. In West Philadelphia, for example, they acquired homes sold by Jews moving up the ladder. In Chicago the black belt extended southward, and two new colonies of Negroes developed in former Jewish and Italian districts. In New York City, which attracted 170,000 additional Negroes, more than doubling its total, Harlem presented an ideal location. Not only were its accommodations relatively modern and its prospects in 1920 bright, but the Italian and Jewish colonies there, lacking sufficient replacements, offered little resistance to the mounting wave of newcomers. These included Spanish-speaking Negroes from the West Indies, over 50,000 in number, and other thousands from the cotton fields of the Deep South; by 1930 the nonwhite population of Harlem had reached 164,566, making it the largest community of Negroes in the land.[16]

Together the Northern cities absorbed during the twenties over 600,000 Negro migrants from the South. While some of these came from Southern cities, the urban centers of the South more than recouped their losses by attracting other Negro migrants from their hinterlands. Altogether the rural districts of the South sent some 1.5 million Negroes to Northern and Southern cities, and despite their high birth rates the rural Negroes dropped slightly in number. For the first time Negroes resident in urban centers exceeded those on the farms by at least a half million. With another two million resident in villages, chiefly in the South, the 5.2 million urban Negroes did not quite match the whites whose urban percentage was now 57.7, yet the Negro's urban gains during the twenties were more striking, and in fact they were most dramatic in the rapidly growing metropolises, which by 1930 numbered 96 places and included 54,753,645 residents.[17]

• *Expanding Metropolitan Patterns*

Whatever the sources of their growth, the big cities drew more newcomers than they could accommodate in traditional ways, and many for the first time disgorged more inhabitants than they attracted. The changing character of the in-migrants spurred the outward movement of former residents in some places, but changes in urban transportation, in industrial technology, and in housing standards were equally if not more responsible for the new suburban expansion that converted a score of growing cities into budding metropolises and spread the outer limits of several of the older ones to more than double their former size. This expansion, which was in some respects a flight from the city, helped to transform the prototype of the central city and gave shape to the larger community that surrounded it.

Of course the suburban migration dated back many decades in most cities, but it began in the twenties to acquire a new character. The streetcar suburbs and steam-train satellites of an earlier date had had an independent, small-town quality that gratified the nostalgic yearnings of many urbanites who romanticized the village community. Harlan Douglass described one as seen from an outlying hilltop in Union City, New Jersey, in 1925: "In the immediate foreground lies the Village. Its three spires lift their points, and one who knows can pick out the school, the Woman's Club building, the cluster of stores, and the plaza of the railway station. Its inhabitants, half-buried in foliage, are uncrowded." [18]

With the advent of the automobile as a commuting agent, the aspects of suburbia changed radically. Every side road drew its venturesome settlers, some of whom laid out spacious estates and erected villas to match, while others built their own houses in the

Interurban Trolley Lines of Indiana Area, 1920.

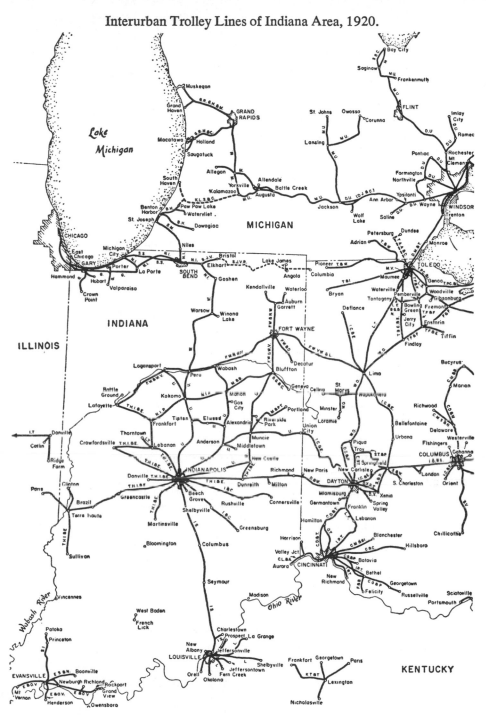

From George W. Hilton and John F. Due,
The Electric Interurban Railways in America (Stanford, 1960).
Stanford University Press

long evenings and newly acquired weekends that stretched out over a period of years and often saw the open spaces, which had drawn them there, gradually fill up with other escaping urbanites. As the number of auto registrations mounted from 8 to 17 million in the early twenties, and to 23,060,421 by the close of the decade, the number of families migrating to the suburbs also multiplied. The open spaces between the old villages and the satellite cities attracted a third of these migrants and grew more rapidly than any other urban category.[19]

Many of the older suburbs enjoyed an impressive growth, too. Around Atlanta, Cleveland, Milwaukee, and Buffalo, among other rapidly growing metropolises, the incorporated suburbs increased 100 per cent or more. Some of these were or now became industrial suburbs, and in the early twenties, during the heyday of the interurban trolleys, their prosperity seemed assured and their growth helped to boost the average for small cities above that of the large-city category. They were, however, integral and dependent parts of metropolitan districts, as became evident toward the close of the decade when collapsing interurbans seriously blighted their growth.[20]

Yet the central cities were still absorbing the largest share of the urban gains. Although their percentage of the increase dropped from 70.7 to 54.8 during the twenties, numerically their growth exceeded by a half million that of the same cities in the previous decade. In many places these newcomers occupied formerly vacant tracts or, in the South and West, newly annexed districts, but in some older cities a shift to high-density multiple dwellings was required to provide accommodations. Few of the apartment houses that began to appear in New York, Chicago, and other congested metropolises exceeded seven stories, for the great majority of the new "cliff dwellers," as they were sometimes called, still climbed to their floors. In the central business cores of these and many other cities, however, hotel and business blocks were soaring to twenty and more stories, with the result that problems of congestion, for both daytime and nighttime residents, were commanding attention.[21]

The human congestion was less acute, of course, than that of

traffic in the streets. In the early postwar years the increased number of private cars and motor trucks had cleared the streets of their
accustomed clutter of wagons, speeding the movement of trolleys
as well as of other traffic. The relief was of brief duration, however,
as the cars multiplied. Accidents also mounted alarmingly, prompting the organization of a new technology for traffic control.

"Traffic has increased several times faster than the population
in all our principal cities," declared Robert H. Whitter, a planning
consultant at Cleveland in 1920. The problem was more critical in
some cities than in others, and the response varied accordingly.
In Rochester, after an appalling year during which 164 fatal accidents were recorded, 24 caused by automobiles in the streets,
various groups joined to launch a safety campaign in 1918, the
first in the land, which was repeated for five successive years,
checking the mounting toll despite a twofold increase in the number of cars. This program inspired similar efforts under the direction of the newly formed National Safety Council, in St. Louis,
Kansas City, and elsewhere.[22]

Efforts to improve the flow of traffic were widespread. Control
towers and "wooden policemen" appeared at a few busy inter-
sections in several cities in the early twenties. In 1922 New York
installed a series of signal lamps at twenty-six street crossings along
Fifth Avenue rigged to be changed simultaneously by one officer.
Two years later the General Electric Company perfected a sim-
plified stop go signal light that could be operated by a time clock,
and Cleveland introduced a system that permitted traffic to flow
without a break along its principal arteries.[23] In order to clear the
roadway for more efficient use, New York and Philadelphia banned
parking along their major streets in 1922, and lesser cities began
to limit the blocks available for standing cars. Boston in 1926
moved to require fees for such parking. Many cities felt the need
for new and broader arteries, and several projected one or more,
but Detroit, the automobile capital, was the first in 1924 to propose
a system of divided highways and loops.[24]

Rapid growth encouraged innovation and spurred urban leaders
to seek technical solutions for their problems. Thus George H.
Herrold, the street superintendent in St. Paul, devised a traffic-

density map in 1923 that attracted wide use as a planning tool. Housing reformers too were perfecting new methods of measuring the need for additional dwellings; in 1920 they related housing demands for the first time to specific income levels. Few denied the urgency of the problems, but agreement often ended there as rival groups of experts promoted conflicting solutions.[25]

Such conflict was especially intense in the housing field. The aging Lawrence Veiller favored a reliance on regulatory measures that now seemed inadequate to the younger reformers who urged more forthright state action or, failing that, an appeal to the federal government to resume its housing program.

Nowhere was the housing crisis more acute than in New York State. To cope with it, Governor Alfred E. Smith had created a Reconstruction Commission in 1919 and named Clarence Stein as chairman of its housing committee. Stein, a young architect well acquainted, as a settlement volunteer, with the problems of poor slum dwellers, had highlighted their needs in his report. Governor Smith strongly endorsed Stein's proposals for a state housing agency and for local city housing boards empowered to acquire land and, if necessary, to construct houses with the aid of state housing credits. These measures required an amendment of the state constitution, and Governor Smith called a special session for that purpose in 1920. But the legislature, having previously adopted a rent-control measure supported by Veiller, was content to supplement that law with another granting tax exemption to stimulate new private construction.[26]

Civic leaders tackled the housing shortage in various ways in different cities. Hard-pressed New York and Washington maintained wartime rent controls longer than most other towns, and several followed New York's lead in granting tax exemptions on new construction. As director of the National Housing Association, Veiller promoted these and other regulatory measures through its monthly journal, *Housing Betterment,* in which he also publicized the activities of private and philanthrophic housing companies. In a review of fifteen such projects in 1922 he hailed Mariemont, a Cincinnati suburb designed by John Nolan, as America's outstanding garden city. Other projects in Louisville, New Orleans, and

Detroit attracted his favor, and Milwaukee received special praise for the cooperation achieved between city, county, and private developers. Veiller, who was also critical of the public-housing program in Britain, attacked successive proposals for subsidized housing in New York, Boston, Chicago, and Los Angeles. Private investors, if given proper encouragement, could, he maintained, meet the nation's housing needs.[27]

Home building did revive at a rapid rate in 1922 and succeeding years, not only in New York City but widely throughout the country. Mounting costs, however, priced the new houses far above the reach of the average urban workers and created a new differential between the suburbs, where most of the new construction occurred, and the central cities, where many old houses were remodeled as multiple dwellings for the poor. The new construction failed to relieve the pressure on the inner city slums, as several investigations revealed. Edith Abbott compiled a detailed survey of the wretched housing in a 33-acre slum district in Chicago; Bleeker Marquette, uncovering similar conditions in Philadelphia, spurred its Housing Association to debate the need for public assistance as well as for more diligent regulations. These and other surveys in Detroit and Cleveland, St. Louis and Boston, and a half dozen other metropolises, raised new questions as to the proper location for new housing and the difficulty of relocating the slum dwellers.[28]

Charles D. Norton, chairman of an Advisory Committee on a City Plan for New York (he had formerly been active in the planning movement of Chicago), became convinced in 1915 that the only hope for a solution of Manhattan's dilemmas lay in the adoption of a master plan for the entire metropolitan region. When the city officials refused to take the lead, he persuaded the Russell Sage Foundation to set up a research and planning staff to prepare a regional plan for Greater New York. With Frederick A. Delano, Robert W. De Forest, and John M. Glenn among its directors, it commanded wide respect and was able to engage as its director of research and planning Thomas Adams, a distinguished regional planner currently working in Canada who had formerly been president of the Town Planning Institute of Great Britain.[29]

The New York Regional Plan achieved unprecedented scope. It

studied not only highway and housing needs but also economic and population trends, the effects of proposed highway and rapid-transit improvements on land values, and the proper placement and density of residential and industrial developments. A former associate and staunch admirer of Ebenezer Howard in England, Thomas Adams sought to avoid the dangers of overcrowding that were inherent in the combination of rapid-transit with high-rise apartments. But he was also determined to make his plans so realistic and feasible that they would win acceptance by civic authorities concerned with assessment rates and municipal costs. He boldly attacked the overdevelopment of residential skyscrapers and joined with others in bringing Howard to New York in 1928 to help launch a drive for the construction of garden cities in America.[30]

The close relation between rapid transit and skyscrapers was widely debated in those years. Boston had to abandon the 5-cent fare in order to restore the solvency of its mixed system of elevateds, subways, and streetcars which fanned out to all points of the compass. Many cities abandoned the 5-cent fare on their transit lines, but New York battled fiercely to retain that fare throughout its vast system in order to assure the builders of the new towers that increasingly covered central and lower Manhattan a sufficient flow of daytime inhabitants. Philadelphia extended its rapid-transit lines to serve its skyscraper district. But Detroit, with 19 buildings of twenty or more stories and 100 of ten or more, rejected a proposed subway in 1929; as the automobile capital, it turned, with Los Angeles, to planning for the development of a superhighway system and a widespread suburban pattern.[31]

If the 5-cent fare seemed essential in New York City, so was economical housing. When private builders failed to supply new housing within the range of the average resident, Governor Smith appointed a State Commission on Housing and Regional Planning to seek a solution. Its reports, starting in 1924, documented the need and revealed the widening gap between the sale or rental price of new dwellings and the workingman's wage. Homeownership, though mounting in the suburbs, was declining in the inner city, where landlords were escaping rent controls by remodeling old houses into apartments. Governor Smith proposed the creation of a housing bank to spur construction by nonprofit corporations; the legislature, however, while ready in 1926 to create a State Housing Board to regulate limited-dividend corporations, refused to extend public credit for such ventures.[32]

Yet the reports did have some constructive results. Clarence Stein, chairman and most active member of the commission, took the lead in forming the City Housing Corporation in 1924 in which he joined with Henry Wright, a fellow architect, in a plan to build a housing project of high standards at minimum costs. Stein had helped the year before to organize an informal group sometimes called the Regional Planning Association of America, which drew into its circle such men as Lewis Mumford, Charles H. Whitaker, Clarence Perry, all writers and critics, as well as Alexander Bing, a realtor whose wealth and idealism made him an enthusiastic backer of Stein's model-housing projects.[33] Stein and Wright journeyed to England in 1924 to see its famous garden cities and to confer with Ebenezer Howard and Raymond Unwin, their principal founders. Unwin's oft-quoted precept, "Nothing gained by overcrowding," became the keystone of their plans as developed at Sunnyside in 1926 and at Radburn three years later.[34]

Sunnyside and Radburn represented a great advance over previous housing projects, both in America and abroad. They embodied many garden-city concepts brought from England as well as those of the American community center movement now championed by Clarence Perry. They were the first large housing projects designed for occupancy by families with automobiles, but they carefully restricted the channels of this traffic in order to preserve a park-like dwelling space throughout the community. The favorable publicity they received may have influenced the plans of some limited-dividend companies in other cities and provided a significant model for future housing developments.[35]

Planned at the start as low-cost housing, both Sunnyside and Radburn proved when completed to be much too costly for low-rental occupancy. Housing companies, seeking to reach low-income groups, turned instead to another architect whose higher density apartment groups nevertheless retained a park-like arrangement that traced its origin, too, to Howard and the British new towns. Andrew J. Thomas achieved recognition through his design of the Metropolitan Life Insurance Apartments, opened in 1924, and of various projects sponsored by John D. Rockefeller, Jr., and by the Amalgamated Clothing Workers of America.[36] The spacious courts and sunny gardens included in these high-density projects won praise from many planners, including Thomas Adams, who, however, favored the lower density of Sunnyside and Radburn for suburban developments. A survey by the Michigan Housing Association in Detroit in 1928 first devised an index of congestion to determine when and under what conditions housing was objectionable.[37]

Many critics, not least the editors of the *American City,* deplored the congestion created by the skyscraper, but in 1929, when that magazine published a survey of cities and their skyscrapers, it was the few it overlooked that protested, not those weighted down with tall buildings. Its first tabulation showed 4,778 buildings of ten stories or more, and 377 that soared twenty or more stories. Approximately half the total were located in New York City, but each of thirty other metropolises had 20 or more skyscrapers of ten or more stories. Washington with 20 still had a moderately unbroken skyline, but Chicago, with 384 over ten and 65 over twenty stories, was beginning to rival New York for mass congestion. San Francisco with 105 over ten stories, Atlanta with 31, Buffalo with 26, and Birmingham with 22 protested the article's inadequate recognition of their density; only Kansas City, with 37, modestly asked that its reported total of 60 be scaled down.[38]

• *Inner-City Concerns and Planning*

The skyscraper rivaled the automobile as the symbol of success in the twenties. One was the sign of a prosperous community, the other of an affluent family. Few even among the planners realized how opposed these two symbols were and how sharp their rivalry would become. Yet the tension they developed was evident in every city as the needs of the central district vied with the drawing power of the suburbs for the town's limited resources. Private

citizens and groups, enterprising companies, and municipal authorities championed first one and then the other side of this contest between urban centralization and diffusion, between the core
and the periphery of the metropolis.

Inner-city concerns predominated in the early postwar years.
The large numbers of the unemployed, both ex-service men and
discharged war workers, prompted many cities to launch public-
work programs in 1919. These included port improvements at St.
Louis, an extension of the waterworks at Denver and of the sewers
at Louisville, a vast program of street pavement at Boston, and
the construction of numerous public buildings, including more than
a score of community halls erected as war memorials, notably one
at Bridgeport and a larger one at Baltimore. Herbert Hoover
presided over a conference called by President Harding to promote
local efforts to supply jobs. When a poorly timed cut in federal
appropriations resulted in the closing of many employment offices,
local city councils or chambers of commerce rallied to reopen most
of them. Houston and its suburbs joined forces to launch the construction of inland docking facilities of such dimensions that the
federal government was finally impelled to send its dredges to
deepen a shipping canal from the Gulf.[39]

As industrial recovery eased the unemployment crisis, many
cities experienced a construction boom. New urban-dwelling starts
doubled in 1921 and doubled again in the next two years. A Committee of One Hundred in Cleveland laid the cornerstone in 1921
of an auditorium said to be the largest in the nation. Designed to
seat 13,000 and to accommodate big conventions and exhibitions,
it occupied one side of the civic center and spurred similar efforts
in Denver, Memphis, and other cities.[40] In like fashion, Houston's
ship canal stimulated inner-harbor navigation improvements at
New Orleans, and other harbor improvements at San Francisco,
Los Angeles, Seattle, and Portland that cost in the twenties over
$100 million. Philadelphia pressed forward with the demolition
of structures blocking the route of its projected Fairmont Parkway
on which it expected to spend $17 million. The completion in
1925 of the Holland Tunnel, linking Manhattan with New Jersey's
highways and permitting 2,000 cars to pass through each tube every

hour, was hailed as the decade's $48 million engineering master-piece; two years later a second tunnel, a mile in length, linked Detroit with Canada.[41]

The mounting flood of cars, rushing in and out of the cities every day, required new facilities at both ends of the drive. As one town after another limited parking on the streets, the conversion of empty lots in the central district for parking purposes introduced a new cause of inner-city blight. Nearby merchants nevertheless profited from the trade these lots brought, and several cities—Cleveland, Chicago, and Los Angeles among them—provided public parking courts in 1924. Sensing the commercial value of parking space, a Kansas City developer organized a Stop and Shop Company that autumn and constructed on the city's outskirts a retail shopping project which provided free and adequate parking space and supplied a model for suburban shopping centers in St. Louis the next year, and soon throughout the country. In 1928 Detroit opened the first large ramp garage, capable of holding 1200 cars.[42]

At the same time city folk out for a drive needed places to stop, too. Many towns, eager to attract visitors from afar, leased vacant fields on the outskirts and opened them as tourist camps. A few provided shelters with cookstoves and minimal sanitary facilities for the tourists who erected their own tents, built their own fires, and enjoyed a brief return to nature. Plagued by the problems these camps created, most cities quickly abandoned them to private operators, one of whom, in charge of a large "Camp Ground" near El Paso, Texas, in 1926, erected a number of wooden "bunga-lettes" for rent at $1.50 a night, and soon had a steady stream of tourists. Minneapolis established the first Gateway Tourist Bureau in 1928 with impressive headquarters on a major highway entering the city, where it supplied literature and answered questions for 54,900 tourists in its first eight-month season.[43]

The trolley companies still carried the major burden of resident travel in most of the large metropolises, but their passenger loads were dropping in the late twenties. The 5-cent fare so jealously guarded before the war had largely disappeared, and even the service-at-cost contracts so confidently promoted in the early twenties began to lose their charm by the end of the decade. John Bauer, the *National Municipal Review*'s expert on public-utility rates and services, urged city officials to restore a measure of competition in the transit field by chartering independent bus companies; by the late twenties, however, when the transit companies had bought up all such franchises in Buffalo and several other cities, the hope of developing competitive service dwindled. Only the competition of the private automobile was proving effective, and the result was not better but less frequent and more costly service. A proposal in 1929 that cities provide public parking lots at the suburban ends of their transit lines failed to attract wide application.[44]

The central cities continued to enjoy an advantage in most aspects of municipal engineering. Their water and sewer systems were more adequate and their police and fire departments more thoroughly organized. Most of the fire horses were retired in the early twenties, and the police horses soon after, as the two services turned rapidly to motor-driven equipment.[45] The fire departments perfected electric signaling devices and experimented with the use of chemicals, but they made no breakthrough comparable to that of the police with the introduction of radio, first at Berkeley, California, in 1929. Within a few months Detroit had thirty-five police cars equipped with radio receivers, and ten other cities hastily introduced similar equipment.[46]

In addition to the traditional public-safety functions, some cities were assuming new responsibilities. Pittsburgh and Chicago were among the first to recognize the need for forthright action to reduce the smoke nuisance. "Atmospheric sanitation" was the euphemistic phrase coined by a group of engineers at the University of Illinois in an endeavor to tackle this growing problem without stirring too much opposition from local boosters. Soon several cities, determined to protect their reputation for clear skies, such as Salt Lake City, New Orleans, and Kansas City, created municipal bureaus to promote the improvement of furnaces and the use of anthracite rather than soft coal. A dozen other cities joined the movement before the end of the decade—Cincinnati, Cleveland, and Akron in Ohio, St. Louis and Denver in the West, Rochester and New

York in the East; nevertheless, in 1929 only Cleveland was ad-
judged adequately staffed for the job.[47]

The age of the automobile also made it imperative that cities
in the snow belt clear their streets of snow in the winter. Rochester
and Buffalo, generally the hardest hit, had annually tackled their
drifts for a decade before the great blizzards of 1914 and 1920
alerted other cities to the problem. Straight-blade snowplows attached to dump trucks replaced the early horse-drawn V-plows
by the twenties, when mechanical snow loaders also made their
appearance, the first at Chicago in December 1920. Caterpillar
tractors, equipped with plow blades, joined the battle in New York
the next February when a record 12½-inch snowfall threatened
a $10 million loss in business. Since one freak storm could tie up
and inflict serious damage on a city like Philadelphia or Washington, far from the snow belt, most of the leading metropolises of
the North and Midwest had to equip themselves with snowplows
and enroll emergency crews to man them. The city engineer in
Duluth proposed the use of salt on the streets, but it did not win
favor in this decade except as an aid in clearing downtown cross-
walks.[48]

Improved snowplows arrived just in time to help keep the newly
established airways open throughout the year. In 1919, when the
federal government announced plans for an air-mail service, it
designated thirty-two cities as suitable stops if landing fields were
provided. When service was inaugurated a year later, twenty-one
cities had fields ready for use or in the course of preparation, most
of them as private promotions. Within another three years Chicago,
Philadelphia, Detroit, Boston, and Kansas City had opened municipal air terminals, and other large cities soon followed.[49] Cleveland,
which almost lost its air-mail service in 1924 because of the poor
condition of the two private landing fields, dedicated a 2000-acre
municipal port the next July, the largest in the country, and recorded 4,000 landings during the first year. As the number of air-
fields multiplied, approaching 5,000 by 1928, the urgent need to
bring this land use under the control of responsible city planners
focused new interest on that municipal function.[50]

Local airports made another contribution to city planning by supplying planes to take aerial photographs, which Nelson P. Lewis, a leading city planner, hailed in 1922 as a significant new tool for the profession. That latter term was becoming more truly appropriate as twenty-five colleges offered courses in city planning in 1925; Harvard, where James Sturgis Pray had delivered the first series of lectures in 1909, established a Graduate School of City Planning in 1930. Of the 150 cities with planning officials in 1923, twenty-five issued published reports. Every metropolis of 300,000 or more inhabitants had accepted planning as a municipal function by that date. Two years later the National Conference on City Planning launched its new quarterly, *City Planning*.[51]

Some of the early zoning laws were losing their force because of the numerous exceptions granted by the appeal boards. Conflicting political factions in New York City made the twenties a period of frustration for its zoning reformers. In Los Angeles the local Municipal League suspected the presence of graft. The courts, however, consistently upheld these laws, and 261 cities, including all the major metropolises, had zoned themselves by the close of 1924 when Boston finally adopted its law.[52]

If the major task of the early planners was, as Lewis put it, to correct "earlier mistakes" in the city's development, some real accomplishments were achieved in these years. The Chicago plan, launched with much fanfare in 1909, was now fulfilling its promise as the new Illinois Central terminal, a sports stadium, and the Field Museum approached completion on the lakefront, while the Wacker Drive, a two-level highway bordering the south bank of the Chicago River, built at a cost of $22 million, eased congestion in the central business district.[53] Camden's plan for a circular boulevard and a civic center, like the equally imaginative river development and civic center planned for Columbus, Ohio, was still in the paper stage, but Des Moines and Cleveland were now reaping the rewards of similar planning before the war.[54]

Cleveland's accomplishments rivaled those of any other city in the land. Malcolm B. Vilas, president for many years of the Citizens' League of Cleveland, had made it an effective proponent of practical planning. A civic-center plan, adopted in 1900, was now almost completed and adjoined the Union Terminal, a transit and transport focus. A cultural and educational campus, projected in 1919 five miles from the center, had by 1930 attracted a cluster of fourteen institutions including the Cleveland Art Gallery. The city had won its battle for a Metropolitan Park Board in 1918; it now had over 9,000 acres under development and secured the cooperation of Cuyahoga and neighboring counties and towns in the formation of the Cuyahoga Planning Congress, which supervised an extensive development of major highways throughout the metropolitan region. The League's success in these endeavors spurred Vilas and his associates to press for the establishment of a metropolitan government in 1929; when defeated in the legislature, they prepared to launch a new attempt the next year.[55]

Of the many civic-center plans submitted by citizen committees and other groups before the war, few had been developed. Arnold Brunner, who had helped to draft several of these plans, deplored the failure of American cities to carry them forward. The problem was in large part a fiscal one, for while some states were assisting their capital cities to develop civic centers, as at Denver, Harrisburg, and Des Moines, and others helped to bear the cost of their central parks, as at Boston, elsewhere the planners and their sometimes grandiose proposals had to compete with the traditional municipal services for the limited funds available.[56] The mounting costs of local government had prompted most states to place a top limit, generally of 2 per cent of the assessments, on the taxing powers, with another 2 per cent on the bonding powers of municipalities. When in 1927 the Detroit Bureau of Government Research made a thorough study of Detroit's expenditures over a period of years, it discovered that, contrary to the general belief, the city's per capita costs had in fact shown a drop that justified new expenditures for improvements. Detroit was encouraged to press forward with its loops and parkways; Dayton and St. Louis launched vast riverfront developments in the next year or two.[57]

In many places the desired improvements extended beyond the city limits and required negotiation with other municipalities. Baltimore established a metropolitan water district in 1925 in order to avoid competition for limited resources, and Washington organized a Suburban Sanitary Commission to plot and develop sewers and other facilities throughout the area. The successful performance of several earlier special-function metropolitan districts at Boston, New York, and Philadelphia, where water, sewer, or park authorities had linked otherwise independent municipalities in joint operations, encouraged the creation in 1923 of the New York Port Authority, the organization in 1926 of the National Capital Park and Planning Commission for Washington, and two years later the formation of a Metropolitan Water District that allied eleven neighbors of Los Angeles in a unified project.[58]

Thus in the twenties scattered cities, eagerly seizing their opportunities, sometimes evolved original programs that quickly won adoption elsewhere. Enterprising industrialists similarly developed technological innovations to meet urban needs, and their promotional efforts and advertisements helped to support such journals as the *American City,* which in its turn eagerly publicized each new advance. A stimulating diversity resulted, giving vitality to the material aspects of America's urban development in the twenties, and calling for an equally imaginative effort to devise administrative and governmental agencies capable of directing and supporting still larger metropolitan ventures.

• *The Search for Metropolitan Government*

Forced to stop at the city line, city planning seemed increasingly impotent in the twenties as the interdependence of the broader metropolitan community became apparent. Many civic clubs and research bureaus, long advocates of planning, urged the merits of metropolitan planning, even of metropolitan government. When the suburban passion for autonomy and the hostility of rural-dominated legislatures blocked these developments, the cities tried various compromises, but the difficulties inherent in fractured communities complicated many facets of urban government. As one reform after another met cool reception at the state capitals, leaders of the hard-pressed metropolises began to appeal through their national organizations for broader public support and, in a few instances, for federal assistance.

Richard S. Childs, the embattled reformer who had struggled

valiantly to keep the *National Municipal Review* afloat with the support of the League's 3,000 members, had a thrilling experience in April 1921. Invited to address the first convention of the newly formed League of Women Voters, he was astonished to find the hall crowded with 1,000 delegates and to learn that they represented local chapters that claimed over 2 million members. The confidence with which they approved an $80,000 budget convinced him that here was "a new civic army" whose leader, Mrs. Carrie Chapman Catt, sounded very much like a municipal reformer, and most of whose planks and resolutions had a very familiar ring.[59]

Despite the economic recession and the wave of intolerance, there was cause for optimism in the early twenties. Such obstacles actually strengthened the municipal reformers by providing new and challenging issues. As unemployment called forth some of the municipal improvements noted above, fears of ethnic radicals placed a renewed emphasis on nonpartisan elections and professional administration. As the recession and the Red scare faded, urban expansion acquired the boom proportions necessary to implement reforms; and civic leaders began again to express a friendly welcome toward newcomers. In Elizabeth, New Jersey, for example, a League of Neighbors conducted annual festivals for several years patterned after a Festival of Nations and Homelands Exhibit staged in 1920 by the Rochester Chamber of Commerce. Indeed in some cities, when the reformers finally awoke to the possibility of enrolling the revived ethnic associations in their civic leagues, they found the practical politicians already seated respectfully on their platform.[60]

If, on the national level, progressivism receded in the 1920's, on the urban level it enjoyed a new burst of vitality. Old established City Clubs in New York, Chicago, Cleveland, Milwaukee, and Portland, Oregon, took the lead in varied endeavors, and new clubs and municipal leagues appeared in numerous other cities. Even New Orleans, still basking in its Old South traditions, saw the formation in 1922 of a Civic Council which rallied thirty-five local organizations behind a concerted drive to clean up and improve the streets.[61]

The National Association of Civic Secretaries, soon renamed

the Government Research Council, drew the leaders of these varied groups together for mutual stimulation at the annual meetings of the National Municipal League. Of the fifty-five organizations represented at the League's thirteenth meeting in Philadelphia in 1923, eighteen were men's City Clubs, seven were Women's City Clubs, and fifteen of the others were research bureaus. A list of active research bureaus, compiled that year by the Detroit Bureau, reported the employment of almost a hundred professional staff members by civic organizations of this type in twenty-nine cities. Some of the City Clubs assigned research projects to volunteer citizen committees, and most of these, plus the Women's City Clubs and the local municipal associations, actively promoted the reforms their committees and staffs recommended. Few, however, matched the activity of the New York City Club under the leadership for many years of Raymond V. Ingersoll.[62]

Several of these bodies maintained or prompted their cities to establish municipal reference libraries. Efforts to persuade the federal government to create a national municipal bureau to collect and coordinate information on all cities, though frequently renewed in these years, failed to achieve success. The New York Bureau, reorganized in 1925 as the Institute of Public Administration, undertook many research projects in other cities and helped to launch independent bureaus in a dozen more places scattered from Newark in 1923 to Los Angeles five years later. After Dr. Frederick A. Cleveland, who directed much of this field work, resigned to enter industrial research, the broader activity of the New York Bureau dwindled, and in 1927 the Government Research Council cooperated with the National Municipal League in establishing a clearinghouse for information on cities. Russell Forbes, secretary of the Council, became director of the Municipal Administrative Service, which opened an office that February on Broadway.[63]

Most of the clubs and bureaus, having themselves accepted a nonpartisan approach to civic problems, sought to exclude politics from city government. Both the commission and city-manager plans had nonpartisan predilections, and the newly popular scheme for proportional representation, although it called for party nominations, sought to free the Council from partisan control. Most of the cities captured by the city-manager forces in this decade inserted nonpartisan provisions in their charters and several included proportional representation as well. Outstanding among the new city-manager cities were Cincinnati and Cleveland, Kansas City and Rochester, all larger than previous city-manager cities; the success of their campaigns encouraged advocates of city-manager charters in still larger metropolises, Philadelphia and New York among them, to hope briefly for similar victories. Yet the victories were not in every case lasting, as Cleveland discovered after five years and Akron after three, when, with several others, they repealed their city-manager charters.[64]

Generally the city-manager failures, relatively few in number, were political rather than administrative in character. Restrained from political activity themselves, the managers depended on their backers to supply such leadership, and when the latter failed to produce it, an opposing political faction sometimes seized control. In Cleveland they restored the strong-mayor system, which Boston had devised some years before. Both Detroit and Milwaukee clung to that system, and Buffalo, abandoning its commission form, was one of several metropolises that now elected a "strong" mayor.[65]

Cincinnati successfully combined the merits of the two systems. Possessing an abundance of leadership from the start, the Cincinnatus Association continued to supply political backing to successive city managers, enabling them to devote their full talents to administration. The Association, formed originally as a Sunday evening dinner club and forum, assumed an active role in local politics in 1921 when young Charles Taft, son of the former President, returned from Yale to practice law in the city. Taft, however, was only one of several in the Association who became indignant at the policies of the Republican boss. In order to break the boss's hold on the city, the Association drafted a city-manager charter and waged a triumphant campaign for its adoption; in the process it elected Murray Seasongood, one of its members, as mayor, and brought Colonel C. O. Sherrill from Washington to serve as city manager. Sherrill's administrative reforms, continued by his successor, Clarence A. Dykstra, won Cincinnati the reputation of best-governed city. The unique feature of its government was not the provision for proportional representation that some other cities shared but the continued leadership supplied by the Cincinnatus Association, which regularly ran a slate of candidates and, by an effective use of the radio and other campaign methods, won a majority in successive councilmanic contests. After four years, when Seasongood stepped down as mayor, Russell Wilson, assistant editor of the *Times-Star* and president of the Association, succeeded him and continued to provide vigorous leadership in the political arena.[66]

Of course Cleveland, Cincinnati's rival to the north, also had a group of dedicated reformers in the powerful Citizen's League and found an able administrator in its first city manager, William R. Hopkins. But Cleveland's more rapid growth raised problems that prompted its leaders to seek a merger of city and county functions. In the battle for consolidation they had to go to the state legislature, where the Republican boss in the Cincinnati region, fearful of a similar move by that city, rallied suburban and rural forces throughout the state to block the measure. Disillusioned with nonpartisanship and weakened by numerous resignations because of the city's constricted budgets, the city-manager candidates, despite a determined campaign in their behalf by the League of Women Voters, lost control of the council in 1929.[67]

Many city managers made their peace with the politicians, as Walter Lippmann advised at the Pittsburgh meeting in 1925, before the decade closed. As a result they were able to carry through important improvements and to introduce new technical advances. Improved water pumps and pipes, for example, increased the efficiency and reduced the cost of waterworks extensions; motorized equipment improved and speeded the collection of garbage, the cleaning of the streets, and the mixing and spreading of cement and other road surfaces. All could work together on these and other engineering reforms, reviewed in a special edition of the *American City* in 1930. But when a municipality had to reach beyond its borders to find a new water source, an outlet for its sewers, or some other regional objective, even a mayor with firm political ties could not always secure the necessary approval of the legislature, as New York's Mayor James J. Walker, among others, discovered. Thus Daniel W. Hoan, Socialist mayor of Milwaukee, though a favorite of many Wisconsin Progressives, saw his plans for city-county consolidation defeated in the rural-dominated legislature.[68]

The desire for consolidation or for some other form of city-county integration was beginning in the late twenties to dominate the thinking of many metropolitan leaders. In some states in the South and the West a city's power to annex adjoining territory that was not separately incorporated offered a workable solution, as Baltimore, Houston, and Los Angeles demonstrated. Although most attempts to consolidate the city and county governments failed in this decade (at Seattle in 1923, at St. Louis in 1926 and again in 1930, as well as at Cleveland in its two attempts), a few cities, notably Denver and Los Angeles, secured the passage of compromise measures.[69] For the larger metropolises this was no longer a major consideration, for the city limits in the case of New York and greater Philadelphia as well as greater Chicago encompassed more than one county. The persistence of separate county functions proved wasteful in their cases, but the real problem in these and other metropolises was to develop procedures for integrating the governmental activities of their expanding districts.[70]

Progress reports on the work of the New York Regional Plan Association prompted similar efforts in other major metropolises. The Chicago City Club submitted a proposal in 1923 for integrated planning by the 340 local governmental authorities active in the Chicago metropolitan district, but action was deferred. A Regional Planning Federation of the Philadelphia Tri-State District, organized in 1926 by its planners and supported by their corporate and other friends, raised $60,000 and engaged a staff to make a preliminary survey of the mutual problems affecting the residents of the 2000-square-mile tract within a 30-mile radius of Philadelphia. Boston and San Francisco soon had similar federations and engaged such able planners as John Nolan and Harlan Bartholomew to conduct their metropolitan surveys. Following the Cleveland pattern, Chicago finally got a Regional Planning Association, which brought officials of three states and two counties together for conferences on highways, airways, zoning, and other mutual concerns.[71]

Planners in a dozen other metropolises were soon holding conferences and projecting surveys. Two in particular made new forward steps. A New York State Conference on Regional and City Planning held at Buffalo in 1924 spurred the organization of a Niagara Frontier Planning Board, which was appointed by the officials of six cities, twenty-two villages, and two counties, with Chauncey J. Hamilton of Buffalo as its chairman. As the first official body engaged in regional planning, its successive reports attracted wide interest. Even the federal government, alerted at least to Washington's limited powers, authorized the creation of a National Capital Parks and Planning Commission to which President Coolidge named five members in April 1926 with Frederick Law Olmsted as chairman.[72]

Clarence Stein supplied the rationale of this movement when he declared, at the regional planning conference in Buffalo, that "No city is master of its own destiny." That wider planning was necessary, many agreed, but Professor Thomas H. Reed of the University of Michigan, after a study of metropolitan regions in Europe, concluded that regional planning commissions were only a temporary makeshift and that strong metropolitan governments were indispensable.[73] However, when Pittsburgh endeavored in protracted negotiations to bring its near neighbors together in a federated metropolitan government, its successive charter proposals met first a legislative block, then a legislative revision, and finally a defeat in 1929 when voters in several of the 120 polled cities and towns rejected it, although the total vote was 2 to 1 in favor. Professor Reed, who as director of the research staff had drafted the charter, urged that it be redrafted and resubmitted, but the onset of the depression diverted attention.[74]

The Pittsburgh experience raised again the problem of legislative reapportionment. While the charter's final defeat was at the local level, a stringent requirement of a two-thirds vote in two-thirds of the constituencies, irrespective of their size, had been inserted by a rural-dominated legislature. Similar frustrations in Chicago, which had almost half the population but less than a third of the legislators, and in Detroit, with a third of the population and less than a sixth of the legislators, prompted talk of secession and the formation of separate city-states. Baltimore got several additional representatives through a constitutional amendment it initiated and passed, but it had modestly asked for only a third of its numerical proportion. In Connecticut forty-one cities large and small, with five-sixths of the populations, had only one-third of the representatives in the legislature. Several state constitutions required a reapportionment after each decennial census, but in states such as New York, Illinois, Ohio, Michigan, and California, where entrenched rural representatives feared the dominance of rising metropolises, the legislatures repeatedly disregarded the constitutional provision. Only the governors, who represented the majority of the voters, spoke out for the cities, and their traditional stand in behalf of home rule was now proving a handicap to expanding metropolises.[75]

Frustrated by their repeated rebuffs from the state legislatures, municipal leaders made frequent appeals to public opinion. In articles and surveys they sought either to allay or to override the hostility of the rural representatives. Occasionally they took their cases to the courts, only to find them unwilling to infringe on the prerogatives of the legislatures, as in the *Fergus* v. *Marks* decision in Illinois in 1926, when the judge refused to order that body to fulfill its constitutional duty to reapportion the state. Appeals to the federal courts or to other federal authorities were infrequent, yet increasingly, throughout the twenties, this possibility was gaining attention.[76]

Federal aid to cities received occasional mention at National Municipal League conventions. Professor William Anderson of the University of Minnesota, who spoke on that subject in 1924, was not concerned with monetary assistance, of which the cities received very little and only indirectly through the states, but with the administrative services that benefited cities. Among these he included harbor improvements, postal services, weather reports, and many potential services under the commerce and general-welfare clauses. Secretary Herbert Hoover was more specific when he responded in 1927 to a request from the *American City* for a list of Commerce Department activities affecting cities. In addition to the recently established Division of Building and Housing, he cited the work of the Bureau of Standards in upgrading urban purchasing departments and utilities, the surveys of the Coast and Geodetic Offices, and the valuable information supplied by the Census Bureau to urban planners as well as to urban promoters and citizens generally. The Secretary's list, particularly that last point, was of keen interest and prompted editor Buttenheim to recall his repeated efforts since 1912 to persuade successive Presidents to establish a Federal Bureau of Municipalities; perhaps, he suggested, the Secretary, who had recently been elected President, will finally provide this essential source of information.[77]

• *Metropolitan Culture and Self-Analysis*

An increasing interest in the city, particularly in the metropolis, was apparent on all sides. Popular magazines devoted lengthy articles to the color and drama of urban life. The new media of radio and screen carried the city's dynamic and sometimes disturbing qualities into every hamlet and helped to spread its influence. The search for more and better information about the city became a concern of many officials, some in almost every department, and of students and critics of American society. Political scientists, sociologists, and economists began in the twenties to lay the foundations for important schools of thought. Even art and literature developed an urban temper.

Judgments on the city, particularly the great metropolis, differed so sharply in the twenties that they tell us chiefly about the character of the critics, most of whom were, of course, its products. An increased variety of journalistic outlets gave ample space to observers with divergent interests. These ranged from moralists to sophisticates, from promotional innovators to historical preservationists, from reformers to social scientists. Similarly dissident commentaries had appeared previously, but urban trends in the twenties served in some instances to reverse the roles. Thus the successful adoption of prohibition and the weight of many traditional restraints helped to alienate the sophisticates and made some moralists, at least in the early twenties, apologists for the cities. By the mid-decade prosperity was transforming old-family leaders into preservationists, differentiating them more sharply from those newcomers who became promoters and boosters. Many forces increasingly divided the reformers from the analysts, who stressed their objectivity and hoped thereby to develop a new science of man.

The sad and gloomy view of "Civilization in the United States," as portrayed by Harold E. Stearns and his Greenwich Village associates, generally attributed the aridity they found in America to the barbarism of the city. Yet one at least, Louis E. Reid, found it, on the contrary, to be "predominantly the civilization of the small town," and explicitly blamed villagers for foisting prohibition on the city. The youthful and precocious Lewis Mumford agreed with that last judgment in his lead article on "The City" where he displayed both the eloquence and the melancholy for which he was to become famous. Yet he had not lost hope for the metropolis: "With the beginning of the second decade of this century," he wrote in 1922, "there is some evidence of an attempt to make a genuine culture out of industrialism—instead of attempting to escape from industrialism into a culture which . . . has the misfortune of being dead." [78]

Whether the culture of rural and highly moralistic America was virile enough to impose prohibition on the cities was one of the crucial issues of the decade. The resort to legislative morality was on trial, and spokesmen for the Anti-Saloon League, the Woman's Christian Temperance Union, and the churches hopefully saw the cities benefiting and prospering under the benign influence of the Eighteenth Amendment. A steady decrease in arrests for intoxication in 300 selected communities between 1918 and 1920, and a moderate increase thereafter due to more vigorous enforcement, supported this view, they claimed, while mounting prosperity seemed to confirm it. [79] Some urbanites, opposed to prohibition and bemoaning their lost liberties, assembled equally convincing reports of the breakdown of law and order and of the spreading corruption of government agencies. Yet their evidence served only to assist the "drys" in persuading Congress to strengthen the enforcement program by sending federal agents in great numbers into the cities where local officers were failing to stamp out the illicit trade.[80]

The Prohibition Era had many effects on the cities as well as on the nation, but what chiefly interests us here is the influence it had on the development of urban-federal relationships. By bringing federal agents into the cities it provided new and direct contacts between local and national police and legal officials and placed many village moralists in seats of power. Frustrated by the loss of local autonomy, some urbanites clustered in sophisticated or romanticized bohemias; others, as "the lost generation," fled to Europe; but many rallied to carry their cause through political channels to the national arena, where the urban vote began to have a new importance by the close of the decade and ultimately routed the Prohibitionists.[81]

The heated debate over prohibition focused new attention on its chief battleground—the city. Crime statistics and the police came under closer scrutiny than ever before, and more citizens reflected on the causes of crime and the nature of political corruption. Chicago, widely dubbed the "crime capital of America" because of the sensational character of its gang warfare and the seemingly invincible power of Al Capone, head of its crime syndicate, attracted several probing studies. Many conscientious citizens and valiant officials in the reform administration of Mayor William E. Dever struggled to check the mounting tide of violence; yet, in spite of an increased rate of arrests and convictions, the number of homicides continued to rise. A forthright group of business leaders reported in 1927 that twenty-three lines of trade, from window cleaners to photographers, were subject to the control of racketeers. Two years later the Illinois Crime Survey detected no improvement.[82]

Other cities faced some of Chicago's problems, sometimes in greater intensity. Boston and Detroit, for example, experienced alarming increases in vice; New York and San Francisco suffered as ports of entry for dope smugglers. Yet the reformers who had battled for years against these evils could see some gains in the more candid recognition of the problems and in the development of techniques to cope with them. Not only were some Northern cities adding Negroes and other minority representatives to their police forces, but a few, such as Columbus, were appointing social-work consultants or creating crime-prevention bureaus, as in Dayton, while many more were establishing crime-detection laboratories and instituting officer-training programs. Finally in 1929 the appointment of the Wickersham Commission brought the weight of a federal investigation to bear on these troublesome urban problems.[83]

The bohemias, which had appeared in several of the major metropolises around the turn of the century, acquired a new character in the twenties. Their chief function as the nesting place for impecunious and often rebellious artists and intellectuals had made them the birthplace of many experiments in education, art, and literature. In some places, notably Greenwich Village in New York, the Latin Quarter in Chicago, and the Bohemian Grove in San Francisco, evidence of that vitality persisted; in some other places, however, the responsibility of absorbing all free spirits who applied made them a natural habitat for "speakeasies" and low dives that attracted a flood of visitors seeking opportunities for uninhibited excitement; as a result many of these communities succumbed to the commercialization their founders had abhorred.[84]

Yet some of the experiments they had launched were now producing results. In the field of education, for example, the Play School of Caroline Pratt and the Children's School of Margaret Naumberg, later renamed the City and Country and the Walden, respectively, both products of Greenwich Village in the preceding decade, provided laboratories and models for the progressive education movement launched in 1919 by Stanwood Cobb at Washington. These and other disciples of John Dewey soon had imitators and rivals in several of the older metropolises and inspired numerous articles and books, of which Harold Rugg and Ann Shumacker's *The Child Centered School,* published in 1928, was probably the most influential. A reaction against the formalized education offered in the large and overcrowded public schools of mushrooming cities, the progressive movement sought to nurture the creative potentials of each child as the surest basis for a genuine culture.[85]

Thus in education, as in many other fields, the metropolis harbored experimental innovations almost as readily as it demanded a measure of standardization. Not only did high schools and trade schools double in number during the twenties, but grade schools too, struggling to keep pace with the demand, welcomed new methods in the process. The progressive education movement in the private day schools had its counterpart in several urban school systems—in Gary and Rochester before the war, in Winnetka, a suburb of Chicago, and Denver among others in the postwar years. With their greater emphasis on learning to live in a community and on the creative involvement of the teacher as well as the child, these innovations developed aspects of Dewey's teachings neglected by the private schools and exerted a wider influence on the rapidly expanding profession. In similar fashion the Lincoln School, a demonstration center for Teachers College in New York, served during that decade as a training ground for thousands of teachers who carried the more social techniques into public school systems across the land. Special classes for handicapped and for talented pupils, as well as visual and other aids to instruction, appeared in progressive systems in a dozen cities. The full hearing these methods received before the conventions and in the *Journal* of the National Teachers Association, as well as in the publications of the United States Office of Education, extended that influence.[86]

Other national organizations, likewise the product of the urbanization process of previous decades, carried forward the crusade in behalf of women and children in the cities. When the Supreme Court struck down the Congressional bans against child labor previously secured by the National Child Labor Committee and its allies—the Women's Trade Union League, the Consumers League, and the Children's Bureau among others—Mrs. Florence Kelley rallied her forces to seek a Child Labor amendment. When that effort failed to win support in the state legislatures, Mrs. Kelley and her colleagues broadened the campaign to seek constructive advances in health and recreation programs on local and state levels.[87] Their accomplishments included child-guidance clinics with full-time staffs in thirty-five cities and such services on a part-time basis in a hundred other places, and the spread of the Boys' Club movement to a similar list of towns and of the mother's-assistance programs to all but four states. The Juvenile Court movement, with its conception of youthful delinquency as caused by social blocks to healthy outlets, now established special courts in all major metropolises. As head of the Children's Bureau, Julia Lathrop secured the adoption by Congress of a federal program of grants-in-aid in support of several of these programs in the states, thus supplying a precedent for more direct federal assistance to cities in the next decade.[88]

In the welfare field, local Councils of Social Agencies and Community Chests continued to provide constructive leadership. The movement spread to 134 cities by 1923 and reached 206 two years later, increasing the returns of their annual drives from $39.5 to $55.5 million. Probing surveys of community needs uncovered gaps in the local services, which new volunteer agencies hastened to fill—in mental hygiene, child placement, and family counseling in Rochester, in birth control and illegitimacy in Cleveland, to mention two of several more alert communities. Although this movement, dependent on volunteer support, faltered in some cities, such as Washington, which lacked a closely knit sense of community, its many achievements elsewhere fostered the development of the new profession of social workers, whose national associations, conferences, and publications helped to lay the basis for a new conception of public welfare.[89]

Washington had a longer experience than most metropolises in the effort to develop interracial cooperation. Since Negroes had for decades comprised its largest minority group, few social-welfare functions could be tackled without involving them, and separate facilities had generally been provided. Although a promising biracial Community Service program and an integrated Council of Social Workers had appeared in the late teens, both collapsed during the Red scare in the twenties, as did an attempt to create a biracial Citizens Advisory Committee in 1924. By the close of the decade, however, the founders of a Community Chest were ready to accept joint participation. Cincinnati went a step further and created an official Biracial Committee to advise its city manager, the first such body in a borderland metropolis.[90]

A questionnaire to the Chamber executives of more than a hundred cities brought replies in 1925 from a dozen Southern and border cities that had joint Negro and white committees to deal with race relations. Several other towns had committees composed of whites who maintained friendly personal contacts with Negro leaders. When the *American City* published the results of this survey, the secretary of the Chamber of Commerce in Orlando, Florida, wrote in to protest the omission of the accomplishments of his town, which boasted the best Negro high school in the South and was hastily constructing a beach for Negroes equal to one opened that spring for white residents. In most Northern cities public schools and beaches were generally available without discrimination, though residential patterns were modifying that situation in many places; the Hartford YMCA made quite a point in 1926 of opening its pool to Negroes on Saturday nights.[91]

The mayor of Detroit named an interracial committee, too, following the outbreak of serious rioting there in the summer of 1925. With the youthful Rev. Reinhold Niebuhr, pastor of a German church in the slum area, as its chairman, the committee made a probing study of the Negro in Detroit. The chief difficulty, the committee found, was overcrowding, an inevitable result of the 800 per cent increase of the city's nonwhite population within a decade. Yet Detroit, the committee noted, was keyed to rapid growth and depended in increasing measure on the Negro's labor. It could no longer, the committee declared, tolerate the discrimination in housing and private services that had contributed to the riot and should, in good conscience, take the lead in America in abolishing the color line.[92]

In Chicago the Negro had ceased relying on his white friends to procure his just rights. Having acquired a voice in politics, under the leadership of Oscar DePriest, a friend of Mayor William H. Thompson, they helped to return Thompson to power after a brief interval under the reform administration of Mayor Dever, and reaped many appointments in reward. Ralph J. Bunche, who wrote a stirring account of this triumph for the *National Municipal Review*, made even its reform-minded leaders see the political turnover in Chicago in a somewhat different and more objective light. A few months later Dr. Bunche received an invitation to address the annual meeting of the Government Research Association and presented evidence of the Negro's political achievements in seven Northern cities, though none rivaled the Illinois metropolis.[93]

Chicago, in fact, had become the center of a more objective approach to urban problems in general. The school of sociology, launched by Robert E. Park and Ernest W. Burgess at the University of Chicago in the war years, had focused its attention on the city. A joint course of "Field Studies," chiefly in the Chicago environs, attracted several able students who pressed their researches without financial support until 1923, when the newly formed Social Science Research Council gave the university a grant of $25,000 to back these community studies. The grant was renewed and enlarged in succeeding years and assured a concerted analysis by many scholars of life in the Chicago metropolis. Thus Clifford R. Shaw made a spot map, carefully locating the homes of juvenile court cases in order to uncover possible delinquency patterns; he also devised an interview technique for developing his case records. Nels Anderson spent several months living among the homeless men of Chicago to assemble materials for his book on *The Hobo.* Frederick M. Thrasher used a similar approach in preparing his study of *The Gang,* in the course of which he gathered information on 1,313 such groups in the city.[94]

These and other studies applied the ecological analysis favored by Park and Burgess. They accepted the Chicago community as a "natural entity," which was representative, they believed, of urban society. The enumeration and characterization of its inhabitants and the mapping of their spatial relationships supplied the basic data for a number of enlightening theories of urban growth. Burgess, for example, developed a concentric-ring thesis, which Harvey W. Zorbaugh's study, *The Gold Coast and the Slum,* helped to substantiate.[95] Burgess not only differentiated five concentric zones, but he also sought to relate them to aspects of urban growth in function and time. Scholars in other universities endeavored to apply the zone concept in their sociological and economic studies and city planners sought to take account of it in their projections. In similar fashion the researches of Shaw and

Thrasher inspired studies of delinquency patterns in other cities and attracted keen interest from the Wickersham Commission on crime.[96]

Zorbaugh's researches, probing the life of restricted urban neighborhoods, set a pattern followed by students of ethnics colonies and of small cities and towns. His data on the community-organization efforts in Chicago added new interest to the social-center movement, which now had its champions among planners as well as reformers. While the sociologists, despite their intense study of the "underside" of urban life, professed only a secondary interest in the practical use of their findings, Professor Louis Wirth, by compiling the first *Local Community Fact Book* for Chicago in 1930, supplied a convenient reference work for many responsible citizens and helped to promote the decision by the Bureau of the Census to extend the application of its census-tract reports, first compiled for Chicago and a few other metropolises in 1910, to a wide selection of cities.[97]

The publication of *Middletown* by Robert and Helen Lynd in 1929 represented a further extension of community analysis in economic and historic depth. Its significance in both respects awaited the appearance of a second volume eight years later, but the wide interest displayed in the first book as a vivid description of economic and social life in a small city reflected the increased emphasis on urban analysis in many fields. Not only did the *American Sociological Review* carry numerous articles on the city, but the American Sociological Society devoted its twentieth annual convention to that subject. Both the *Quarterly Journal of Economics* and the *Geographical Review* printed scholarly contributions pointing, as one title put it, "Towards an Understanding of the Metropolis." Mildred Hartsough's study of "The Twin Cities" and Robert M. Haig's volume in the *Regional Survey of New York and Its Environs* represented new advances in the analysis of metropolitan economy and a refinement of the concept of basic-nonbasic industrial activity. Alfred Weber drew some of these findings into his book, *Theory of the Location of Industry,* published in 1929.[98]

Political scientists, who had contributed most profusely to the literature on the city, continued with unabashed meliorism their cooperation with civic reformers and city planners in devising model charters, humane laws, and utopian plans. Although few attempted to define their basic tenets, they generally professed humanistic rather than rationalistic goals. Some in each group had moved far beyond the impulsive stage of the Good Government forces that had rallied three decades earlier against the evils exposed by the Muckrakers. Many were striving to develop and apply criteria of efficiency to their programs. The establishment of the School of Citizenship at Syracuse University in 1925 to train administrators and the organization three years later of the Institute of Local Politics at Chicago to educate citizen leaders represented complementary advances. Consciously or unconsciously most of them accepted the pragmatic philosophy of John Dewey, though a few, such as Lewis Mumford, were introducing concepts of an ideal culture as a basis for policy making.[99]

Of course the understanding of the metropolis desired by most citizens was of two orders—the information essential to participation on various levels in its life and the knowledge of self acquired through that experience. The urban dailies and assorted periodicals and books, long the chief source of the necessary information, continued with minor alterations to serve that function. New communications media, radio and motion pictures, entered the field of popular education in this decade, but their contributions were more in the order of a new experience than in the supply of additional information. Even the daily papers, which now reached into practically every home, were no longer content to supply news on current events and information concerning opportunities in local markets; the wartime experience had considerably extended their use of commentators on events, but of greater interest to most readers was the addition or expansion of entertainment features—pages of comics, crossword puzzles, and the fuller, sometimes sensational, use of photographs—which together made the reading of the daily paper an essential part of the urbanite's experience. Moreover, the fact that the leading dailies in each city progressively absorbed their rivals until, by the late twenties, most metropolises had two or three papers serving the entire region, while it reduced the diversity of opinion, strengthened the sense of unity throughout the community.[100]

Radio in its first decade contributed even more powerfully to that sense of community. Pittsburgh, pioneering in the establishment and operation of a radio station in the early twenties, set a pattern quickly followed in other metropolitan centers. Although the development of chain broadcasting commenced in 1926, such linkups remained the exception, and the radio stations in most metropolises retained their autonomy. As the number of broadcasting stations soared, however, a need for the regulation of wavelengths developed, and since neither local nor state action would suffice, the national government moved in 1927 to create a Federal Radio Commission. With a maximum of 89 wavelengths to distribute among 700 applicants, the commission divided each into ten kilocycles and assigned limited numbers of them, with some reference to the power of the sending stations, to 412 cities throughout the country, reserving a few for nearby Canadian stations.[101]

The importance of this medium increased rapidly as the sales of receiving sets mushroomed. By the close of the decade, when the number of families possessing radios exceeded 12 million the value of air time skyrocketed and cost advertisers some $20 million in 1930. Although such charges were only a small fraction of the sums paid to newspapers, area merchants could no longer meet the combined costs, and national advertisers commanded an increased share of the time and space. Inevitably they placed a greater emphasis on national programs, which brought a broader awareness of developments in other cities; in the twenties, however, the increased knowledge of other places also served to enhance the sense of community within each metropolitan region.[102]

The growing awareness of metropolitan identity was further strengthened in these years by a spirit of competition in several fields. Sports news from many cities spurred the backers of local clubs to seek winning teams in baseball and championship players in other contests. A similar rivalry in cultural fields encouraged the establishment of symphony orchestras in four additional metropolitan centers—Los Angeles in 1919, Indianapolis in 1921, Rochester in 1923, Oklahoma City in 1929—increasing the number of professional orchestras to fifteen. Genuine cultural aspirations contributed to these developments in each city, but appeals to local civic loyalty were necessary to sustain them. Seventeen large cities created official Art Commissions and forty new museums opened their doors. By the close of the decade every metropolis of 250,000 residents boasted at least one art museum. Many also had a museum of science, and all by this date supported public libraries, many with numerous branches. Several of the larger metropolises opened imposing new buildings for long-established institutions—a new library at Philadelphia, new art museums at Newark and San Francisco, a Museum of Arts and Sciences at Rochester, to mention only a few.[103]

Several metropolises achieved distinction in one or another field. Toledo's Art Gallery attracted wide fame for its collections and wider praise because of the crowds of local residents who attended its exhibits. Detroit, Boston, and Cleveland staged annual music festivals by drawing the choruses of several ethnic societies into collaboration with their orchestras; Chicago, Milwaukee, and San Francisco conducted annual community "sings," and Minneapolis featured a community pageant for many successive years. Several cities maintained bands and supported musical programs through their recreation departments; Baltimore created a Municipal Department of Music whose director scheduled an annual opera season in which he enlisted the talents of several local choruses, including one of Negroes. The outdoor musical theatre at St. Louis continued to supply free performances of a high quality to throngs of several thousand nightly during the summer months.[104]

In spite of the popularity of many of these highly acclaimed community programs, they did not match that enjoyed by several of less esteem, which Gilbert Seldes grouped together as "The Seven Lively Arts." He chose to celebrate such offbeat forms of entertainment as the slapstick comedians provided on the stage, as Charlie Chaplin, Mack Sennett, and a few others supplied on the screen, as the writers of popular songs and of ragtime music as well as the talented jazz players created in sound, and as the comic-strip artists rendered in ink. He included the Ziegfeld Follies productions, although they lacked the "frenzy" he admired in the others, with the comment that "we tend to a mechanically perfect society in which we will either master the machine or be enslaved by it." The popularity of these "arts," born of the metropolis, was unquestioned. They supplied almost a nationwide matrix for the new urban culture evolving in America. Yet despite his praise for their creativity and relaxing humor, even Seldes suspected, as he later came to see, that with the development of the mass media of radio and screen these popular forms could jell into a rather dull national mass culture.[105]

Lewis Mumford had a more immediate revulsion against the pretensions he found in the cities about him. He was appalled by the mechanistic tendencies in architecture, the commercialization of urban life, and the monotony and congestion that seemed the inevitable result not only in one or two big cities but increasingly in all metropolises as they approached the standard national pattern. Longing for the diversity that architects could achieve only by building freshly for each site, that cities could attain only by creatively representing their regions and their technology, Mumford idealized the regional city plans of Henry Wright and Clarence Stein as the last hope in an increasingly technological era for man to become the master rather than the slave of the machine.[106]

3. THE DISCOVERY OF METRO-POLITAN INADEQUACY: 1929-1939

Much to the surprise of some observers, American cities escaped the fateful decision seemingly posed for them in the late twenties. Instead of choosing between a course leading to mass conformity on a mechanistic level and a second course directed toward a revival of the ancestral village society, the mushrooming metropolises found themselves in the thirties battling for economic survival. Several of the more dynamic communities responded with vigor and confidence to the challenge of spreading unemployment only to find the task too large and far-reaching for their limited resources. When local efforts to relieve the situation faltered, and when the states too failed to find a solution, the leaders of one metropolis after another turned to the federal government for assistance.

A full analysis of the response from Washington to determine whether its hesitancy and moderation contributed to the duration of the crisis belongs, as does a study of the causes of the depression, to the economic historians. Some of them, using their new econometric techniques, may also test the possibility that economic strains in the transition from a rural-urban to a metropolitan economy set off the chain reaction that produced the breakdown. But what is of special interest here is the contribution the great depression made to American urban developments by forging a new working alliance between the cities and the federal government. The simultaneous appearance of a new intellectual awareness of the metropolis as a basic functional unit in American society also merits our attention.

• *The Challenge of Unemployment*

Whether or not excesses in the competitive schemes of commercial and industrial promoters in the mushrooming metropolises contributed to the economic breakdown that commenced late in 1929, the great cities, as corporate agencies of the states, lacked sufficient power to cope with the situation. The stock market crash in October occurred of course in New York City and flashed its shattering news through brokerage houses across the land, withering the fortunes of approximately nine million investors, chiefly urban residents. But mayors, councilmen, and city managers were no more responsible for the debacle than were the humblest citizens. Their chief responsibility only commenced as the number of workmen who lost their jobs increased, creating a demand for local relief.

Even the industrial and commercial leaders and the financial giants who variously influenced the economic fortunes of each town felt as innocent as they were bewildered in the face of the widespread collapse. The economy had long since become nationwide in character and, despite its occasional breakdowns, enjoyed such prestige that only a few regulatory devices had been assigned to the federal authorities, and some of these had been whittled away by court decisions.[1] The country had quickly recovered from a stock market slump in 1920, as from earlier setbacks in 1914 and 1907, and if the depression of the mid-nineties had been more severe, marvelous advances in the industrial field had made a repetition of that calamity appear unthinkable. By tightening their belts, business leaders hoped soon to enjoy a new burst of prosperity.

Unfortunately the two first responses effectively blocked either course. As speculators cut their losses and investors curtailed their outlays, businessmen disposed of their inventories and industrialists reduced their work forces, abolishing millions of jobs. A similar contraction of activity in earlier crises had prompted many unemployed immigrants to return to their homelands and drastically reduced the influx of newcomers. Some recent arrivals again departed, and the annual immigrant total dropped in 1931 to a third and the next year to a tenth of its average in the late twenties, but the number affected was small because of the new immigration policy and had little practical effect on the unemployment rolls. The war and the Americanization movement had absorbed most of the earlier immigrants into the community and gave them a claim on local public and welfare agencies that urban leaders could not disregard.[2]

Migrants from rural America were similarly stranded in the cities. Some of course returned to the farms, but hard times had depressed the rural districts increasingly in the late twenties, and although the migration to the cities was reduced, over two million moved from rural to urban areas during the thirties.[3] If some of these newcomers, including approximately a half million Negroes and another half million immigrants, found useful jobs, others less fortunate swelled the ranks of the unemployed. So many old residents lost their jobs in the early months of the depression that the presence of newcomers among the unemployed was not generally noted. As the months stretched into years, however, local objections to the support of needy migrants added still another argument to the plea for federal support.[4]

In the first throes of the depression it was not the federal or the state government but several of the more dynamic metropolises that accepted the new challenge with self-confidence. Cincinnati, awakened to its civic responsibilities by the vigorous campaigns of its Citizens Party, had responded with enthusiasm when, early in 1929, City Manager C. O. Sherrill announced a plan for stabilizing employment. Citizens appointed to that committee took their assignment seriously and organized subcommittees on public works, temporary employment, fact finding, job training and placement, among a half dozen others, each of which completed the preliminary study of its problems before the depression broke.[5] The example set by Cincinnati spurred the creation of similar committees in other cities—in Detroit and New York City as well as in Indianapolis and Boston, to mention a few that responded with vigor.[6]

Despite their earnest efforts to find and create jobs in that first harsh winter, the leaders in Cincinnati soberly admitted the following May that the unemployed, doubling in number during the year, had increased to 12,000. By November, when Sherrill saw the total reach 18,000, he was ready to lead his colleagues at the annual convention of City Managers in an appeal to Washington for an emergency loan to tide the cities over the depression. His successor, Clarence A. Dykstra, reviewing the needs of Cincinnati and other cities at the 1931 convention, asked for a federal appropriation, not a loan, and won the support of many delegates.[7]

President Hoover had in fact expressed concern as early as November 1929 when he addressed the governors urging them to enlist the aid of their cities in "the absorption of any unemployment which might result from the present disturbed conditions." Of course, in spite of a dearth of statistics, most mayors were already aware of the crisis. The editor of *American City,* endorsing the President's plea, assembled data on the public works launched in 320 municipalities during the winter. A year later he compiled a second report, recording the expenditure by 75 cities of over $420 million in that effort. Yet, despite the numerous jobs thus created, the unemployment rolls had lengthened and editor Buttenheim hastened now to endorse a plea by 58 mayors asking Congress to appropriate $1 billion for public works.[8]

New hope stirred in the fall of 1930 when Hoover appointed an Emergency Committee for Employment. But the President's rejection of the tentative proposal of its chairman, Colonel Arthur Woods, that the federal government undertake a program of public works and extend credit to cities for slum clearance and low-cost housing, brought the resignation of Colonel Woods and plunged responsible local officials into deeper gloom. As unemployment soared to new heights in 1931, Hoover revamped his committee as an Organization on Unemployment Relief and charged it with the task of spurring local communities to assume their full responsibility to the unemployed.[9] At the President's suggestion, the

National Association of Community Chests and Councils selected a week in October 1931 for the first concerted drive in 174 cities with organized chests and in some 200 more with cooperating committees. Despite some confusion as to whether the $83 million goal was exclusively for relief, as the President's message indicated, or included local agency support, most cities exceeded their quotas. When those towns, such as Rochester, that had previously conducted independent drives were included, the 1931 campaign was judged a success, though the $84,796,000 pledged soon proved hopelessly inadequate to meet the relief needs of 386 cities and towns.[10]

Most Community Chest leaders were proud of their accomplishments. Allen T. Burns, director of their National Association, boasted in 1930 that, while "stocks crashed, the community chests did not." Their response to the needs of the unemployed had been noteworthy. Yet they had responsibilities to their member agencies too, most of which were set up to help the poor help themselves and not to administer relief. The slogan for the 1932 drive, "Man Does Not Live by Bread Alone," expressed this wider commitment. In several cities, Chicago among them, the private agencies offered the services of their trained workers to assist the public welfare officials in sifting applicants for relief so that the able-bodied could be shunted into work-relief jobs and saved from the blighting effects of the dole.[11]

The difficulty everywhere was to find jobs. Even in cities bursting with self-confidence, such as Cleveland, Detroit, and Rochester, the problems proved insurmountable. In Rochester, where the city manager had appointed a Civic Committee on Unemployment in January 1930, its leaders had attacked the mounting problems on a broad front. Not only did the Rochester Community Chest raise its quota and run two successful drives to meet the emergency that year; it also lent its personnel to back a special "Spending Bee" drive that collected pledges from 10,771 residents to spend over $6 million on home repairs and other outlays that would create part-time employment. The city manager had requested and received a special work-relief appropriation of $250,000 early in 1930, expanding it to $800,000 before the year was out; the next year he requested $1 million to meet the increased demand.

The appropriation passed, and the city also created a local work bureau to comply with a new state law and thus secured the first grant of work-relief funds from Albany. Plans were under consideration for vast improvements recommended by a newly formed Civic Improvement Association when in January 1932 a Chamber address by Mayor Daniel W. Hoan of Milwaukee, describing the advantages of a city without debt, prompted the dispatch of a committee to Cleveland and Cincinnati to compare Rochester's relief measures with those of these self-respecting cities. Its findings, that Rochester had exceeded the efforts of these and other comparable cities, going deeply into debt without effecting recovery, brought a slowdown to local projects at Rochester.[12]

Other cities too were experiencing a resurgent demand for economy. To counter the movement, editor Buttenheim quoted the views of several economists, including John Maynard Keynes of England, warning against "a blind retrenchment of public spending" in the midst of a depression, when "we must collectively put into use enough currency and credit to restore" the economy. When Mayor Hoan published an article lauding the pay-as-you-go policy of Milwaukee, a political rival branded it a result of his Socialist suspicion of banks and noted that relief in Milwaukee had been borne by the county and with a generous use of its credit. C. A. Dykstra, new city manager of Cincinnati, spoke out in strong defense of public borrowing and, with former Mayor Murray Seasongood, urged that the federal government, too, take up the work.[18] Frederick L. Bird, on the other hand, writing for the *National Municipal Review,* marshaled evidence from 135 cities that reported serious fiscal difficulties. All but 21 had suffered increased delinquencies in tax payments. Over half had reduced their budgets for 1932, and Detroit had cut its outlays for improvements from $18 million to $400,000. Despite drastic retrenchments in salaries and services, by the end of the year 600 cities and towns had defaulted on their debts, bringing committees of bankers into control of many of them.[14]

Determined to avoid that result, Mayor Frank Murphy of Detroit invited the mayors of 67 large cities to gather at Detroit in May 1932 and draft an appeal to Washington. Mayors James M. Curley of Boston, James J. Walker of New York, and Daniel W.

Hoan of Milwaukee were among the 26 who answered the call, and when all but two endorsed a plea for a $5 billion construction program, these three with Mayor Murphy journeyed to Washington to present their case to Hoover in person. Although the President had blocked the more modest relief subsidies proposed in the LaFollette-Costigan bill that spring, he now approved the creation of the Reconstruction Finance Corporation (RFC) and the passage of the Home Loan Banking Act, which provided a minimal supply of credit for self-liquidating projects. The American Municipal Association, less committed to economy than the National Municipal League, supplied experts to help cities draft applications for such loans, but it was a slow process. Before the close of the year the bankers had taken over in Detroit, Chicago, and Philadelphia, as they would soon do in Rochester and several other cities.[15]

Yet the bankers, who had critical problems of their own in the black winter of 1932–33, had no solutions for the cities they took over. They ousted some incompetents and discredited a few others, such as Mayor Walker, who hastily resigned before the next election, yet in every case, after trying and sometimes costly delays, the bankers had to grant new extensions of credit. Moreover, since their policy of retrenchment had helped the business world reject Hoover's plea for renewed private investments, thus frustrating his hopes for national recovery, they now witnessed his defeat at the polls and, in the deepening gloom, saw the fall of one bank after another with such appalling speed that the only hope was for a bank holiday. Sparked by their own frugality, the crisis developed first in Detroit, but the temporary relief granted when the governor proclaimed a bank holiday in Michigan, and soon in twenty other states including New York, was not sufficient, and the bankers, like everyone else, looked forward with mixed hopes and fears for action by the new President.[16]

• Appeals for Federal Aid

Although the rebuffs received by urban delegations to Washington had been discouraging, the leaders had not become disheartened, for little was expected. Many, in fact, rejoiced when the RFC, despite its limited provisions, recognized the contractual independence of cities. Among the reformers, at least, the question of politics seemed irrelevant, especially in the 400 cities with city-manager or commission governments. The important point was to achieve a proper sharing of responsibility. Most cities with partisan administrations in the North and West had long been Republican, and most of them remained so in 1932. Yet, in spite of the ambiguities of the party platforms and the campaign speeches, many urbanites were impatient for a change that fall, and Roosevelt's occasional references to a "New Deal" were intriguing. At least 23 large metropolises voted Democratic for the first time since 1916, and six others gave Roosevelt such strong support that he was able to carry their states. Urban voters were awakening, and never again would their city leaders be so indifferent to a national election.[17]

Alerted at last to their new opportunities, the mayors of 50 cities gathered at Washington on February 17, 1933, to organize the U.S. Conference of Mayors and to prepare their strategy for a prompt appeal for aid from the new administration. The *American City* was out with a lead article entitled "Five Billions for Public Works and Housing," in which editor Buttenheim reported an interview he had had with Rexford G. Tugwell, one of the President-elect's "brain trust." Not all favored this course, however, and Buttenheim, in an effort to strengthen the urban demand, wrote an article urging enlarged governmental expenditures for the *National Municipal Review*, edited by the League's former secretary, Harold W. Dodds, who stressed the need for balanced budgets. A heated argument over retrenchment developed in that journal and may have contributed to a liberalization of its policy and the appointment of Howard P. Jones as editor that summer.[18] These urban spokesmen probably had little direct contact with the drafters of the National Industrial Recovery Act (NIRA), and yet their pleas no doubt speeded its adoption in June. In welcoming its provision of $3.3 billion for public works and housing, Buttenheim warned readers of the *American City* that only alert communities with soundly conceived projects could hope for a share of this assistance.[19]

The issue between the taxpayers and the tax spenders was not so easily settled, however, as a radio debate that July between Mayor Hoan and Dr. Luther Gulick of Columbia disclosed. A group of citizens summoned to Washington in January 1933 by President Hoover, in a last-moment effort to find a solution free of federal spending, had launched a drive for the organization of Citizens Councils for Constructive Economy in cities throughout the land. The first local council, formed at Dayton in April, started a campaign to persuade citizens to pay their delinquent taxes, which had mounted in that city since 1929 from $700,000 to $12 million. By August, when Des Moines, Iowa, announced the formation of its council, fifteen cities had fallen into line, and twenty-four more were preparing to take similar action. A debate was already raging in several of these councils, however, over what constituted true economy.[20]

Some hazards of retrenchment were already appearing. A self-employment scheme developed at Seattle had attracted wide praise until some of the neighborhood committees formed to implement the work voiced radical views, prompting the officials to seize control. To avoid that situation, the Citizens Councils in several places hastened to propose work-relief projects, for official control, even by federal agents, seemed preferable to the unchecked programs of committees of the unemployed. Almost a hundred mayors gathered at a second Conference of Mayors that September to hear Secretary of the Interior Harold L. Ickes explain the procedures necessary to secure a portion of the NIRA funds; a month later the American Municipal Association had 25 experts in the field helping cities draft suitable applications.[21]

The mayors of many cities were exceptionally busy that year. Several of them met with other municipal and state finance officials and interested bankers and professors at a special conference called in July at Chicago, where they adopted resolutions asking the federal government to establish a commission to examine the whole tax structure of the federal, state, and local authorities and to propose measures to enable them to carry on under their crushing debt burdens. Many applauded when Louis Brownlow, a former district commissioner in Washington and a city manager, declared that "what is sometimes mistaken for a breakdown in local government is in reality the result of a breakdown in a banking system that is suddenly unable or unwilling to advance . . . money." While awaiting action on this point, the Conference of Mayors met again in December and petitioned Washington for $2 billion more for local public works since most of the $3 billion previously voted had been committed to long-range projects and the cities faced another winter of desperation.[22]

The new Administration's most direct aid had been extended under a Federal Emergency Relief Fund (FERA) of $500 million administered through grants-in-aid to the states. As its director, Harry Hopkins, formerly a social worker in New York, had speeded the distribution of funds; he now secured a second appropriation of $400 million for Civil Works Administration (CWA) projects organized in cities and counties throughout the land. Only the persistent pleas of local officials increased the allotment and kept this costly program alive throughout the winter.[23]

Pressed from every direction, Roosevelt had from the first responded with reassuring if not always consistent action. In his initial week he had first closed the banks and then reopened them under the Emergency Banking Act that extended RFC credits in a more forthright fashion than Hoover had permitted, but with checks to ensure stability. After reassuring the bankers, he had given comfort to advocates of economy by pressing for the speedy adoption of a measure trimming federal salaries and other expenditures, thus freeing his hand for the establishment of the Civilian Conservation Corps to provide a useful outlet for unemployed youths and also to reassure the many social workers pressing for action in the welfare field. Most of the successive decisions in Roosevelt's first hundred days had touched the cities only as integral parts of the nation, but the FERA in May and the NIRA in June had directly tackled their relief problems, as we have already noted, and the Glass-Steagall Banking Act, also adopted in June, had further stabilized the banks by providing a federal guarantee of deposits. As Paul V. Betters, executive director of the U.S. Conference of Mayors, put it a few years later, "The year 1932 marked the beginning of a new era in federal-city relationships." [24]

The President's dramatic leadership had dispelled the worst

fears, yet it had not revitalized the economy. Many responsible leaders were encouraged to hope that more effective measures could soon be secured; it was, however, clear to many that they would have to press still harder for the programs they sought. Just as the mayors were striving to open new channels of cooperation between the cities and the federal government and to win increased national backing, so assorted groups of urban social workers were pressing through the leaders of their national associations for federal action not only in behalf of children and youths but also for social security for the aged, and with the support of some unions for collective bargaining for labor and housing for the poor. It soon became apparent that the essential legislative base for many of these efforts had already been provided in the National Industrial Recovery Act among other measures, and that the critical decision rested with the National Recovery Administration (NRA) and the extent of its responsiveness to urban needs.[25]

The most spectacular New Deal administrator was General Hugh Johnson, who as director of the NRA made it the focus of popular attention in cities throughout the land that summer and fall. As conservative businessmen were drawn into code-drafting sessions, dispirited citizens, even some of the unemployed, were marshaled into boisterous parades that spread an infectious sense of participating in the battle for recovery. Labor's charter, passed with some difficulty in Section 7(a), supplied new hope to the unions and created fresh stirrings among the workers in Minneapolis and a dozen other cities, bringing powerful new leaders into the political as well as the industrial arena in many metropolises and assuring them a voice at the nation's capital. Although these developments, like many other New Deal measures, such as the repeal of the Volstead Act, had their chief application in cities and towns, they were not essentially a part of metropolitan history, yet the spirit and leadership structure of many communities was considerably transformed.[26]

The pressure groups most directly interested in the transformation of the cities were concerned with housing; unfortunately their lack of agreement delayed action. President Hoover had called a Conference on Home Building and Home Ownership at Washington in December 1931 at which the problems of blighted areas and Negro housing were discussed, and also the problems and trends in homeownership, but much to the satisfaction of one of its group chairmen, Lawrence Veiller, the subject of public housing was carefully avoided. Veiller was accordingly "stupefied" several months later when the RFC provided federal credit to assist in slum clearance. Only New York State had a housing board equipped to make use of these funds, but Ohio, Massachusetts, and Texas hastened to adopt similar laws, and groups in Cleveland, Boston, and New York City were preparing to take action. Clarence Stein in New York maintained that the need was not for more housing but for better planned neighborhoods, and Veiller eagerly endorsed this view, emphasizing the excellent work previously done by Stein at Radburn and now at Chatham Village in Pittsburgh, as well as by other imaginative architects in a dozen projects elsewhere. Unfortunately, several of these privately sponsored ventures had been stalled by the depression, and to revive them, housing associations in Philadelphia and Pittsburgh, in Cincinnati and Cleveland, as well as in New York City, where former Governor Smith had accepted the chairmanship, began to press for a liberal grant of federal aid. Louis Brownlow, noting the introduction of new bills in eight state legislatures that winter, urged that they go beyond the New York statute and "recognize housing as a public utility." [27]

A group of social workers led by Mrs. Mary Simkhovitch in New York had convened a Public Housing Conference with that objective in 1931. A respected friend of Mrs. Franklin D. Roosevelt and of Senator Robert F. Wagner, Mrs. Simkhovitch persuaded the latter to include housing among the public works authorized by the National Industrial Recovery Act, adopted early in June 1933. Delighted by the new prospect, Ernest J. Bohn, head of a Housing Association in Cleveland, hastily called a National Conference on Slum Clearance to expedite the work. Boston, New York, and Queens soon received tentative approval of projects to cost over $3 million each, and shortly after Harold Ickes announced the formation of an Emergency Housing Corporation to administer the program Detroit secured the first grant for slum clearance. Veiller, bitterly critical to the end, not only saw the circulation of his journal, *Housing,* dwindle but read in November of the formation at Chicago of a National Association of Housing Officials, which superseded the National Housing Association that he had long dominated. The announcement in December 1933 of approval for a $12 million Cleveland Homes project, combining slum clearance with low-cost housing, marked the launching of the reorganized Housing Division of the PWA.[28]

In spite of the earnest efforts of local housing associations in several cities, the movement lacked comparative data on housing needs. To remedy the situation following a successful demonstration in Cleveland, the Civil Works Administration (CWA) organized a series of real-property inventories in sixty cities in January, and by May the first completed returns in ten leading metropolises disclosed serious shortages and widespread deficiencies in the existing supply of houses. The data gave new impetus to the adoption of state laws and the organization of local housing authorities. The inventories also spurred efforts to develop Subsistence Homestead projects on the outskirts of several cities. One of these, commenced near Dayton in the spring of 1932, was now partially occupied and had provided a model for eight other projects approved in February 1934, several of which were under construction in June when the passage of the National Housing Act created a fund (FHA) to extend credits to home builders in both urban and rural districts. In August Harold Ickes reported that construction was about to start on public housing projects in seven cities; the next month he launched one in person at Atlanta.[29]

A varied assortment of urban forces contributed to the new federal policy. The National Association of Housing Officials, headed by E. J. Bohn of Cleveland, had invited three European housing experts to visit American cities that fall and to report their findings at a special conference at Baltimore in October. After an extended tour of several weeks, during which they inspected the housing problems of fourteen metropolises, conferring with their mayors and housing reformers, Sir Raymond Unwin and his two associates addressed an impressive gathering of seventy-five Americans, including the chairmen or directors of all the principal housing and planning groups in the country. For the first time federal, state, and local officials and citizen leaders of varied views met together for a four-day discussion of the housing problems in American cities. A recently organized Labor Housing Conference was represented by Miss Catherine Bauer, its director, and the Russell Sage Foundation by Clarence Perry. Louis Brownlow, now director of the Public Administration Clearing House in Chicago, served as chairman of the conference, and with E. J. Bohn successfully arranged a visit by Sir Raymond Unwin and his lady to the White House, where they discussed the purposes and findings of the Conference with President and Mrs. Roosevelt.[30]

Experienced observers such as Charles E. Merriam could not help but marvel at the rapid development of city-federal relationships. Because of the emergency, "the Federal Government is deeply concerned," he declared in February 1934, "with housing and city planning, with child welfare, with the problems of commerce and labor." But to many mayors and other responsible urban leaders the federal concern did not seem adequately expressed. When the work-relief projects of the CWA terminated in April, neither the public works backed by the PWA nor private firms were ready to absorb the great host of the unemployed whose number hovered around ten million, approximately one-fourth of the labor force.[31] One reason perhaps was the inability of the impoverished cities to meet the commitments necessary to launch their PWA projects. Fortunately the passage of the Summers Bill in June 1934, providing a method for cities to negotiate with their creditors for a funding of their debts, promised to restore the solvency of some towns, but formidable tasks remained.[32]

Although the views of the budget balancers and of those opposed to federal subsidies seemed discredited in 1934, the limitations and slow implementation of the public-works and housing projects proved frustrating to many urban officials. Mayor T. S. Walmsley of New Orleans spoke out vigorously in May in support of a bill introduced by Senator Robert LaFollette to increase the PWA funds to $10 billion, and in October he journeyed to Hyde Park with eight other mayors, including Fiorello H. LaGuardia of New York, to present the needs of all American cities directly to the President. LaGuardia was a familiar figure in Washington; he had promptly, after his election, established close working relationships with both Ickes and Hopkins and had secured New York's full share of the funds available, but they were not sufficient.[33]

In November the cities strengthened their case by decisively defeating conservative Republican senators in Pennsylvania, Ohio, and Missouri and by adding nine new Democratic congressmen from metropolitan districts to the party's majority. When Roosevelt still seemed to hesitate, both the U.S. Conference of Mayors and the International City Managers Association adopted strong resolutions in support of increased PWA grants. Early in January the President responded, proposing an appropriation of nearly $5 billion for a new Works Progress Administration (WPA). Although the sum seemed inadequate to many urban leaders, the promise of a speedier attack on the unemployment problem and the naming of Harry Hopkins as director on its passage in April gave assurance.[34]

• *The New Deal Response*

If the creation of the WPA launched a second New Deal, as Arthur Schlesinger, Jr., contends, it also marked a turn in city-federal relationships. At the earnest recommendations of the Conference of Mayors, the federal authorities accepted the responsibility of supplying work-relief to the able-bodied, and turned the care of the unemployables back to state and local welfare. With this beginning, the division between local and federal responsibility was more clearly defined in other fields as the years progressed. Thus the cities, grateful for the aid of the Bureau of Air Commerce, which had spent $17.5 million on lighting and radio equipment at municipal airports, welcomed the creation of the Civil Aeronautics Authority to take over and expand the federal service, but they also asked and secured the right to a hearing before federal agencies planning projects that affected them. At the same time the federal government displayed a new flexibility in responding to the special interests of different communities.[35]

The new flexibility appeared as the WPA established a number of white-collar divisions to carry on projects launched independently in various cities or maintained from the CWA period. Writers' projects designed to give appropriate jobs to unemployed scholars, art and theatrical projects conceived in the same spirit, met the special needs of college towns as well as of great metropolises. The National Youth Administration enrolled needy high school students or graduates in part-time projects that gave them a sense of participating in useful community activities. Heartily endorsed if not in some cases inspired by the Conference of Mayors, these white-collar projects quickly caught on, and city after city fell into line until they became almost nationwide.[36] Yet the products in each case were local, required deliberate planning, and tended to enhance urban community values. Each of the state and city guidebooks, for example, almost a thousand in number, had its special qualities, as did the murals, sculpture, and paintings designed to decorate schools and other public buildings in hundreds of newly self-respecting places. The Federal Music Project gave jobs to thousands of unemployed musicians in numerous metropolises and free entertainment to millions of citizens, while the Federal Theatre Project, though concentrated in New York where the greatest need existed, reached out through seven regional headquarters to every community that could enroll twenty-five unemployed actors and sent its troupes into urban neighborhood centers and town halls to perform freshly written or adapted plays to some 30 million people in the course of the next three years.[37]

The federal government responded in still another way to a special demand rising out of the great metropolises when, in September 1935, Roosevelt created the Resettlement Administration to lay out a group of experimental new towns as model communities in rapidly growing districts. The development, prompted by the Regional Planning Association of America, incorporated the ideas of Stein, Mumford, and others who hoped to transform the planning concepts of American cities. Mumford had drawn Roosevelt into a round-table conference on regionalism in July 1931, and as President he retained a strong interest in the urban-rural environmental balance these reformers advocated. Tugwell, who became administrator of the project, was an admirer of both the

Garden City movement in England and the neighborhood-organization programs advocated by Clarence Perry. The fusing of these related reforms into the Greenbelt program resulted in the development over the next three years of Greenbelt, Maryland, thirteen miles from the center of Washington, Greenhills near Cincinnati, and Greendale on the outskirts of Milwaukee. Built by relief workers for low-income occupancy, they achieved a planned integration of residential community functions, and each attained a moderately high density in a spacious setting.[88]

Opposition to such imaginative experiments came from two directions. Intransigent advocates of free enterprise in housing, such as Veiller, found allies in this instance among the supporters of the Subsistence Homestead program and of FHA loans to private builders. Together they blocked the efforts of the Resettlement Administration to influence the planning of new towns in the great Tennessee Valley redevelopment project. That contest increased the tension between the two groups closest to Roosevelt—the social planners, such as Tugwell, and those associated with Justice Brandeis, who favored a larger measure of local independence and believed that only by such a policy could the housing program escape a Supreme Court ban. This tension was heightened in 1935 as the attack on the New Deal mounted from the right.[89]

When the Supreme Court struck down the NRA in May, Senator Wagner seized the occasion to salvage its labor provisions by pressing for the adoption of his National Labor Relations Act, which Congress finally passed two months later. Assured the right of collective bargaining, the unions, which had increased their membership under 7(a) from 2.9 to 3.8 million, proceeded to enroll another 5 million during the next four years. Although this rapid advance brought a split late in 1935 between the old AFL unions and the new industrial unions, the new Congress of Industrial Organizations (CIO), representing many metropolitan workers, brought fresh vitality to big-city politics and additional support for metropolitan demands in Washington. The great organizational drives in Chicago, Detroit, and a score of other cities occurred in 1937 and after, but labor's new self-confidence had been clearly evident at the polls in the preceding election.[40]

Part of that confidence sprang from the new federal instruments supplied for the protection of labor and from the sense of achievement acquired through the use and improvement of these instruments. When the National Labor Relations Board, strengthened by the appointment of experienced arbitrators, exposed unfair labor practices, such as the storing of arms at Youngstown and the use of labor spies at Pittsburgh, protracted court cases ensued, and the unions now had the Justice Department battling with them for the validation of the Wagner Act, which finally came in April 1937. Management opposition to plant elections, ordered and conducted by the Board, dwindled after that date, as did the violent organizational strikes that had disrupted production in many cities during the preceding two years.[41]

Local efforts to achieve harmony made a parallel advance. In Toledo, after a series of violent strikes in 1934 and 1935, a federal mediator, formerly from that city, promoted the creation of a local Industrial Peace Board to mediate disputes. Organized by labor and management late in 1935, it became an official agency of the city the next April and successfully terminated eight strikes and settled a score of other disputes in its first year. The Toledo Plan, as it was called, soon won adoption in Newark and Elizabeth among other cities in states lacking mediation boards. Even in New York, with an old but inactive board, LaGuardia established a local Industrial Relations Board, which settled 187 cases in a brief period in 1937, prompting a revival of the state board. Other states, too, revived earlier boards or established new ones, and the U.S. Conciliation Service, dating from 1917, considerably expanded its staff and services under the direction of Miss Frances Perkins, Secretary of Labor.[42]

Long suspicious of company pension plans, union leaders supported the more active drive of the social workers, notably settlement leaders, such as Lillian Wald, and those of the Women's Trade Union League, for old-age pensions and unemployment insurance. Pressed from the left by the agitation of Francis Townsend, Huey Long, and other share-the-wealth advocates, Roosevelt had named Miss Perkins, Harry Hopkins, and Henry Wallace as a Cabinet Committee on Economic Security in 1934. Under the

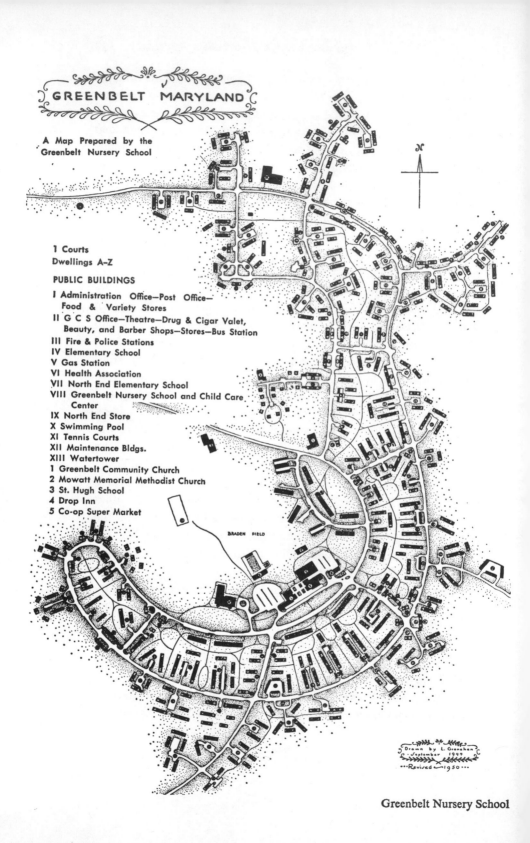

GREENBELT MARYLAND

A Map Prepared by the
Greenbelt Nursery School

1 Courts
Dwellings A–Z

PUBLIC BUILDINGS

I Administration Office—Post Office—
  Food & Variety Stores
II G C S Office—Theatre—Drug & Cigar Valet,
  Beauty, and Barber Shops—Stores—Bus Station
III Fire & Police Stations
IV Elementary School
V Gas Station
VI Health Association
VII North End Elementary School
VIII Greenbelt Nursery School and Child Care
    Center
IX North End Store
X Swimming Pool
XI Tennis Courts
XII Maintenance Bldgs.
XIII Watertower
1 Greenbelt Community Church
2 Mowatt Memorial Methodist Church
3 St. Hugh School
4 Drop Inn
5 Co-op Super Market

BRADEN FIELD

Drawn by L. Granahan
September 1944
···Revised 1950···

Greenbelt Nursery School

leadership of Miss Perkins it proposed the incorporation of both old-age pensions and unemployment insurance in one Social Security Act, which Congress passed in August 1935. Although the law covered only approximately half the country's employed workers, these included most unionists, as well as millions still unorganized, and represented a positive gain for most urban dwellers.[43]

When in the midst of these developments the U.S. Conference of Mayors sent another delegation to Washington in January 1936, it received a ready audience at the White House. Mayor La-Guardia, newly elected chairman of the Conference, could speak effectively of New York's needs and of the concern of Sidney Hillman and other union supporters there. Although the mayors did not get the $2,340,000 appropriation they sought, they did help to boost the President's new request for WPA from $1.1 million to $1.7 million. And a year later, when the depletion of its funds threatened the termination of the WPA, the Conference of Mayors made a hasty tabulation of the needs of a hundred cities and dispatched still another delegation to the Capital to report its findings in support of a plea for an additional $877 million to continue the program until June 30.[44]

Their views, when vigorously presented, now commanded attention, for the election of 1936 had more clearly demonstrated the power of the metropolitan vote. To observant analysts, the great landslide of votes, which gave Roosevelt all but Maine and Vermont, merited closer study. In populous New York State, the great metropolis had turned out a plurality that submerged the prevailing hostility to Roosevelt upstate, which moreover had been reduced by majorities in Buffalo, Rochester, and other cities. Chicago, Boston, Detroit, and Baltimore had each supplied over half the Democratic pluralities in their states, while the two leading metropolises in California and three in Pennsylvania had similarly produced the bulk of the party's support. And, on a closer look, later scholars have demonstrated that a significant portion of Roosevelt's strength in New York City and Chicago came from a shift in allegiance within the rapidly growing Negro districts.[45]

With the new Democrats in Congress from the cities, some representing slum areas, pressure for a more forthright housing program developed. The close control Secretary Ickes maintained over the PWA projects had frustrated housing reformers impatient for action in Chicago, Philadelphia, and especially in New York City where the Public Housing Conference again supplied aggressive leadership. Although Ickes was carefully investigating applications for housing projects from 37 cities early in 1935, only seven were under construction, and the $98 million earmarked for the rest seemed hopelessly inadequate. At the earnest plea again of Mrs. Simkhovitch, Senator Wagner introduced a bill that spring calling for an appropriation of ten times that amount for housing. Wagner had little hope of passing that original bill, but the Senate hearings on the measure afforded an opportunity to rally the support of housing reformers in many cities and brought Catherine Bauer of the Labor Housing Conference to Washington to help direct the campaign.[46]

When the first bill died in committee, Senator Wagner directed his research assistant, Leon Keyserling, to prepare a new draft, which was duly submitted in both houses the next spring. Roosevelt, however, was still preoccupied with other matters and, fearing a challenge in the courts, did not give the housing bill his full support until after the election. Determined opposition obstructed passage that winter, but petitions from several local housing councils and the earnest pleas of numerous mayors, ranging from La-Guardia in New York to R. E. Sherman of El Paso, Texas, helped to secure the housing law's adoption in August 1937. The proposed fund of $1 billion was cut in half in the final act, greatly disappointing some of its advocates; many, however, rejoiced to see that the initiative was now returned to the cities, 46 of which already had official housing authorities.[47]

Most of the major cities had not only housing authorities but also organized groups of citizens earnestly pressing for action in this field. Several, dating back a decade or more in Pittsburgh, Detroit, and Milwaukee, as well as still earlier groups in Boston, New York, and Philadelphia, had promoted first limited-dividend projects and then PWA projects; they now joined with new citizen housing councils in a dozen other cities, scattered from New Haven to Los Angeles, in pressing for a speedy implementation of the new program. In March 1938 the U.S. Housing Authority announced its approval of the first five projects, including one at Syracuse to provide 678 units at a cost of $4,360,000. By August it had contracts with 28 cities planning to build over 30,000 dwelling units at a cost of $154 million. By the end of the first year, when the number of local authorities had grown to 205, the U.S. Housing Authority had approved projects in 142 cities, slightly exceeding in its commitment the total appropriation, $7.5 million of which had already been spent.[48]

The impending exhaustion of the housing funds brought varied local responses. Harold Buttenheim, who had formed a new Citizens Housing Council in New York City representing all interested agencies, demanded a larger appropriation; the federal government has spent $12 billion in seven years on highways, he reported, and should not stop even at $800 million, as some proposed, for housing and slum clearance.[49] Herbert N. Nelson of the National Association of Real Estate Boards urged a cooperative effort by public and private agencies to restore blighted areas by removing and replacing only the worst structures and by aggressively remodeling the rest to renew the neighborhood. The Baltimore Housing Authority secured a grant from the Federal Home Loan Bank to undertake such a project in a 50-block area in collaboration with local investors. By June 1939 when the first small public housing project was nearing completion in Austin, Texas, 145 cities had such projects under construction, with 70 more approved and awaiting the authorization of more funds.[50]

Even the mayors were now encountering difficulty in procuring funds to complete important city projects. The PWA had backed the construction of hundreds of local hospitals, libraries, schools, and public halls, some of which still needed assistance to reach completion. WPA funds had improved local parks and playgrounds and even constructed public yacht basins in seventeen cities; now their councils faced the task of providing funds to maintain them and to continue some of the white-collar projects in the cultural field where an awakened public taste demanded it. While recognizing their local responsibility in this respect, the delegates at the May meeting of the U.S. Conference of Mayors, with LaGuardia

again its chairman, nevertheless petitioned Congress to appropriate
at least $725 million to fulfill the federal government's responsibil-
ity to supply jobs to all employables. Only the outbreak of war in
Europe in September, which started a rush of orders to American
factories, eventually brought this long effort to an end.[51]

• *The Desire for Metropolitan Autonomy*

The new alliance between the cities and the federal government
in relief and housing was only the most dramatic of the increased
city-federal relationships. In a 1936 study Frances L. Reinhold,
amplifying an earlier Brookings Institution survey, found that some
500 different types of services and relationships had been developed in the fields of planning, zoning, education, health, and internal improvements as well as in relief and housing. On contem-
plating the radical changes in governmental relationships under
the New Deal, Morton Wallerstein, a Richmond citizen planner,
predicted that, with 56 per cent of the population already concentrated in urban centers, pressure for increased federal assistance
would continue to mount. The findings of the National Resources
Committee, when published in 1939, compiled further evidence of
this trend toward the assumption of national responsibility.[52]

Some metropolitan leaders, however, were taking a second look
at these developments. Harold Buttenheim, who a few years before
had urged the formation of a "federal bureau of municipalities,"
became concerned in 1934 lest the development lead to national
centralization. In an article entitled "Uncle Sam or Boss Sam" he
noted that much of the coordination previously lacking was now
being provided by private organizations, thirteen of which had recently located their national headquarters in one building in Chicago, where some effective new cooperation was developing. Washington, he warned, should preserve its character as a federal capital
and not strive for national domination. On this point he agreed
with Harold W. Dodds, former editor of the *Review* and now
president of Princeton University, who declared, in December a
year later, "Under no circumstances must local government be
allowed to lose its position as a theatre for the citizen's active participation in public life." [53]

A British visitor to American cities, on a "World Tour in Search of Local Government," George M. Harris found ample evidence in 1934 of organized community effort. He was especially impressed by the municipal research bureaus he visited in Washington and Cincinnati among other places, by the leagues of municipalities he found in Minneapolis, Denver, and Seattle, by civic clubs in San Francisco, Portland, and elsewhere, and most of all by the convergence of these and other citizen bodies in the joint headquarters of their national organizations at Chicago, where Paul Betters, Walter Blucher, Carl H. Chatters, Coleman Woodbury, and other full-time executive secretaries supplied an informed leadership. Indeed their collaboration in the compilation of the *Municipal Year Book* under the editorship of Clarence E. Ridley of the City Managers Association, which published this volume annually after 1934, was most heartening. Somewhat overwhelmed by the wealth of professional talent developing in the field and by the reliance American cities placed on experts, Harris wondered whether they could not more adequately meet their major problem, finance, by a return for wider democratic support to the larger councils favored in England.[54]

Most students of urban government recognized that, if cities were to retain their autonomy, they would have to achieve a sounder fiscal base. The widespread drive to reduce tax delinquencies had restored confidence in Detroit and several other cities, but when Cincinnati and Cleveland appealed for a release from the 10-mill constitutional tax limit in Ohio, the special legislature convened by the governor produced such an outburst against increased taxes that the session adjourned without action, leaving the cities, whose plight was exposed, in a worse situation than before. Attempts to apply Milwaukee's hold-the-line policy brought retrenchment and civic apathy in Dayton, for example, as well as in Rochester.[55] LaGuardia's determined effort to find new sources of revenue in New York prompted the adoption in 1934 of a local income tax, which the state promptly rescinded, and then of a 2 per cent sales tax. These bold efforts, attacked from the right and the left, inspired no imitators, as most cities, fearful of stirring new hostility in rural-dominated legislatures, resigned themselves to dependence on federal assistance. Many did, however, adopt the installment plan of tax payments to ease the impact of their inescapable burdens.[56]

In some states the legislatures, whose revenues were growing more rapidly than those of the cities, assumed an increasing share of the burdens of local government, but at the price of reduced municipal autonomy. In Pennsylvania, for example, 425 local poor boards were abolished in 1935 as the state took over that function. Increased state supervision over urban finances, utilities, schools, and health programs had a similarly eroding effect on local government. Yet in such a costly function as highway construction, the states generally built only to the city line, although after 1933, when 25 per cent of a federal road subsidy was earmarked for cities, some states began also to apply part of their gasoline tax revenues to city streets. To avoid conflicts of jurisdiction, Indiana had developed a program of grants-in-aid that left administration more securely in local hands, a procedure that attracted wide and increasing application, resulting in a distribution of $973 million in grants-in-aid by all states in 1938.[57]

Second perhaps in importance in the long run, but of primary concern at the start, was planning. The traditional fears of planning had begun to disappear as one city after another saw the completion of pioneer projects. Earlier achievements in Chicago, Washington, and Cleveland had spurred ambitious plans in many places, and as some of these took shape, in Milwaukee and Denver among other places in the early thirties, more cities welcomed the opportunity to secure WPA funds for planning studies. As the decade advanced an increasing number of towns enjoyed a sense of accomplishment. Thus Columbus rejoiced as the work on its civic center and waterfront approached completion in 1938. Oklahoma City was as proud of the new civic center, which displaced an outmoded railroad yard, as Springfield, Massachusetts, was of its fifty carefully dispersed playgrounds, and Milwaukee of its newly improved lakefront. Most of the city planning commissions were busy enough with these and other matters, including the placement of public housing projects, but in the great metropolises the need to consider a broader area of planning was becoming increasingly insistent.[58]

The defeat of hopeful efforts to form metropolitan governments in the Pittsburgh and Cleveland areas in 1929 had focused attention on more modest attempts to develop regional plans. The completion and publication that year of the first volume of the comprehensive Regional Plan of New York, sponsored by the Russell Sage Foundation, spurred the Regional Planning Federation of the Philadelphia Tri-State District to finish the preliminary study of its 10-county area. Similar ventures in regional planning were attempted at Boston, Cleveland, and Detroit as well as at Chicago, which had an earlier, less comprehensive, metropolitan plan. None of these bodies had any real authority, although the cities and counties were frequently represented on the councils and sometimes supplied staff assistance in preparing reports. The two regional planning commissions with official status, at Buffalo and Washington, had limited powers and were chiefly engaged in highway and park planning. Both the New York and Philadelphia regional councils endeavored during the thirties to secure the establishment of county planning boards and to work with these and the official city planners within their districts to implement their master plans. At Milwaukee and six other one-county metropolises, the creation of a single county planning board seemed to offer a solution, though generally its powers were only advisory and failed to supply the desired coordination.[59]

In the opinion of Lewis Mumford, even these planners lacked a proper conception of regionalism. As expressed in his scathing review in the *New Republic* of Thomas Adams's summary volume on the New York Regional Plan, published in 1931, Mumford advocated planning for regional cities, not just planning of city regions. Neither the provisions Adams recommended for integrating the central city with its suburbs extending out to a radius of 40 miles or more nor the proposals he included to effect a distribution of future manufacturing as well as residential developments met Mumford's desire for regional cities equipped with a full complement of services and designed to fulfill all urban functions with a minimum of congestion and monotony and a maximum of individuality and beauty.[60]

Thomas Adams, in a spirited rejoinder, observed that his regional plan was drafted to serve a practical purpose and not to provide an ideal abstraction. The issue hinged somewhat on a determination of the optimal size of a metropolis, which sociologists soon began to debate at length, but the chief difference was between the realistic planner and the planner as a social philosopher and artist. Even Mumford's conception, following that of Henry Wright in his Regional Plan for New York State, differed radically from that of another artist and planner, Frank Lloyd Wright, who in 1935 first displayed his model of "Broadacre City," a design he hoped would displace the chaotic urban and rural wasteland he saw about him.[61]

Such criticisms were stimulating, but in the mid-thirties, when jobs and housing seemed more important, Clarence Stein, a colleague of Mumford in the Regional Planning Association of America, collaborated in designing the Greenbelt towns, although they lacked the balance of functions needed for a regional city. He also designed the fairly high-density Hillside Homes project, built with PWA funds in New York. Even these patterns seemed too costly or too rigid for adoption in the new public housing projects erected in the late thirties in cities across the land where a multitude of architects performed more or less independent roles. At least the defeat of the social planners, such as Tugwell, by the decentralists among Roosevelt's advisers replaced the authoritarian pattern of the National Planning Board, appointed by Ickes, with the research-minded and permissive National Resources Planning Board and kept the field open for regionalists and for metropolitan autonomy if local cooperation could be achieved.[62]

If the federal authorities were ready by the late thirties to promote metropolitan development, most state governments remained indifferent or hostile to that emergent local pattern. John S. Lansill of the Division of Suburban Resettlement under PWA urged cities to plan the proper use of all land within at least a 10-mile radius, citing Milwaukee for the start it had made, but few state legislatures would authorize such an extension of city powers. Yet the need for some control was emphasized by the completion of studies of the premature subdivision practices that had occurred on the periphery of Detroit, Rochester, and Syracuse on the eve of the depression, leaving vast areas blighted by delinquent tax claims. Cities in the West, with large areas of undeveloped land within their borders, could make model plans like that for Cerretos Park in Long Beach, California, by Charles H. Cheney, the architect of the nearby Palos Verdes Estates, where he had followed the Radburn tradition as adapted by J. C. Nichols in his Country Club District in Kansas City. In New York State, when the legislature granted city-planning commissions the power to set standards for subdivisions and to cancel those not developed within ninety days, the authority stopped at the city line and was not granted to county planners.[63]

The hostility of rural or at least nonmetropolitan legislators was increasingly evident. In Pennsylvania the repeated efforts of Philadelphia to consolidate its separate city and county governments in the interests of economy met stubborn resistance at Harrisburg. In Massachusetts the long-studied charter for Metropolitan Boston, drafted by Professor Joseph H. Beale of Harvard, and designed to create a federal city encompassing 43 adjoining communities, was rejected by the legislature. Attempts to rectify the situation by a reapportionment of the districts, as called for in most state constitutions, met a hostile silence in state legislatures or a moderate adjustment, as in Texas, where in 1937 the newly mushrooming metropolises were limited to one representative per 100,000, although smaller counties had one for every 38,831 residents. New York, Michigan, Illinois, and many more refused even to make the gesture of compliance.[64]

In spite of this resistance to their widening sway, the cities were extending their influence in a multitude of ways. The leading urban dailies as well as radio stations now reached beyond the metropolitan district to blanket whole regions. Moreover, as the great majority of families, urban and rural, acquired automobiles and telephones, the metropolitan district increasingly became the neighborhood. Suburbanites wanted not only water and sewers, gas and electricity, but also zoning and planning, even in some cases the efficiency supplied by a professional manager. As urbanization progressed and the sense of community deepened, the desire for consolidation revived. In 1935, when according to one observer over half the cities of 200,000 or more residents were considering some form of union with their suburbs, Cleveland and Milwaukee secured the adoption of metropolitan-county charters that consolidated several common functions.[65]

The older practice of creating independent metropolitan-district authorities to perform specific functions provided a partial answer to one or more pressing problems in a score of large cities. Among the 28 new special districts set up during the thirties were sanitary districts in Minneapolis-St. Paul and in Green Bay, a Regional Park District in Oakland, and district housing authorities in several metropolises.[66] The National Municipal League and several state and local municipal associations, hopeful of meeting some of these needs by strengthening the county governments, devoted repeated sessions to county problems. The League's *Review* hailed the charter of Los Angeles County, revised and "streamlined" in September 1938, as a model for the country and praised its council for being the first in the nation to adopt a budget larger than that of its central city. A census check the next year revealed that county government employees had increased 10 per cent in number during the decade. By this time, most of the 36 state leagues were conducting annual training seminars for county as well as municipal officials. Wayne University in Detroit was one of several urban-centered colleges to offer classes for government employees. The *Municipal Year Book* for 1940 listed 72 institutions that included two or more courses on municipal affairs in their programs of study.[67]

In spite of their moderate increase in number, from 97 to 108 old-style metropolises (over 100,000) and from 3165 to 3464 incorporated urban places, the cities had been forced, during the lean thirties, to reduce the total of their staffs and to curtail many services. This was accomplished in face of population increases by shifting many responsibilities to the counties and by a still larger diversion of tasks to federal relief agencies. As a result, few new advances were achieved, though the continued pressure from old and new municipal research bureaus and from a resurgent group of citizen tax leagues in a score of cities prompted new efforts for efficiency and economy.[68]

Operational improvements appeared in many different places. The progressive substitution of buses for trolleys on urban transit lines and the removal and salvaging of the rails with the aid of WPA labor in conjunction with repaving contracts modernized street surfaces and improved service in many cities. Police radios became standard equipment during this decade, and the new teletypewriter introduced in the police department of New York City in 1930 spread to 27 metropolitan counties within two years; Cleveland installed the first two-way radio in a police car in 1939. Most of those operations were strictly local in character, but in some cases a federal program, such as the building of Boulder Dam, which made a new water and power source available to Los Angeles, vitally affected a city's growth.[69]

Rapid improvements were occurring in air transport and largely as a result of federal subsidies. Although the Air Commerce Act of 1926 had authorized expenditures "to establish, operate and maintain . . . all necessary air navigation facilities except airports," many municipal airports, as public agencies, had applied for and received both PWA and WPA assistance; in fact, such funds represented 77 per cent of their combined capital outlays in the five years after 1933. As the desire to terminate these New Deal programs increased, the demands for direct federal aid to airports mounted, and both the Conference of Mayors and the American Municipal Association made strong pleas not only for the elimination of the "except airports" clause in the new Civil Aeronautics Act of 1938 but also for the inclusion of provisions for a comprehensive survey of the nation's airport needs. The adoption of both measures opened the way for important new developments in federal-city cooperation.[70]

In the meantime the depression, by reducing the number of cars on the roads, from 23 million to 20.5 million between 1929 and 1933 and of trucks from 3.4 million to 3.2 million, relieved pressure on the streets and highways and permitted the authorities to make needed repairs and improvements. Federal work-relief funds facilitated this task in every city and, since these resources were available only to public agencies, speeded the shift in many places from trolleys to buses, which jumped in number in these years from 33,900 to 44,900 and to 68,800 by 1939, when cars and trucks, again on the increase, reached 26.1 million and 4.4 million, respectively.[71]

In view of the population increase, no shift from public to private transportation occurred, but that fundamental decision had nevertheless been made. When in 1931 planning experts, meeting at the 23rd National Conference on City Planning in Rochester, discussed the choice between mass transit and private cars, they foresaw a different outcome. Charles Gordon of the American Electric Railway Association submitted a table showing that Washington and Kansas City, as cities of the third class, with respectively 53.3 and 51.1 per cent of those entering their business districts using private cars, would have to build up their mass-transit facilities if they wished to join the second class of cities, where the ratios were reversed; all first-class metropolises supplied mass transit for from 65.3 per cent in Los Angeles to 79.2 per cent in Philadelphia. Because of their straitened circumstances, Gordon argued, no city in the 500,000 bracket could supply the streets and parking facilities necessary to accommodate even a 50 per cent reliance on automobiles. Only one of a dozen commentators indicated mild disagreement, for none anticipated the huge funds for street improvements to be supplied from Washington.[72]

The years of slow traffic growth permitted the introduction of a number of technical improvements. The "cloverleaf" as a safe intersection, demonstrated in 1930 on the Lincoln Highway at a busy crossing near Jersey City, found increasing application throughout the country, as did the divided highway, a streamlining of earlier parkways, first perfected in 1932 in the freeway extension of Woodward Avenue in Detroit. Soon the freeways had to have limited access, no grade crossings, and service stations of their own, as on the Henry Hudson Parkway when finally commenced in 1934. By the end of the decade Pittsburgh and Cleveland were engaged in superhighway developments comparable to those of New York, Los Angeles, and Detroit.[73] Urban parking technology was improving too, as private ramp garages multiplied downtown and suburban shopping areas caught on around the outskirts of many cities following the completion of the Country Club

Plaza in Kansas City. Oklahoma City's experiment with coin-operated meters along downtown shopping streets in 1935 spread within four months to Dallas and within a year to 27 other cities.[74] Civic reform, especially the city-manager movement, lost some of its drive as the need for a stronger voice in political decisions became apparent. The manager system did find new applications in a few metropolitan counties and annually in a dozen or more additional cities, but Cincinnati remained the largest and most faithful to its nonpartisan principles. New York, however, voted to adopt proportional representation in 1936 and gave it a successful if somewhat turbulent trial that convinced some reformers as well as most politicians of the hazards involved. Only the dramatic leadership of LaGuardia staved off several moves for its repeal in those years.[75]

The outcome of such elections seemed almost as uncertain, even to conscientious officials, as the recommendations of the psychiatric clinics, with which juvenile courts in New York and a few other places were experimenting, seemed to many judges. Several crime clinics, now firmly established in all major metropolises, added a psychiatrist to the staff to provide possible leads, but his place in the administration of justice remained uncertain. Another decade would pass before political scientists began to probe the relationship between political power and justice as revealed by these and other civic dilemmas.[76]

Citizen leaders, proud of their accomplishments in many places, continued to vie for precedence in one field or another. Cleveland and Cincinnati, old rivals in Ohio, boasted respectively of the best municipal services and the best government, as Milwaukee, under Mayor Daniel W. Hoan until 1940, claimed the soundest fiscal system. The first attempt in 1929 to devise objective criteria with which to rate cities for services performed gave highest standing to such suburban towns as Oak Park, Illinois, Lakewood, Ohio, and Berkeley, California, but Springfield, Massachusetts, San Francisco, Seattle, and Cleveland all made fine showings. The U.S. Chamber of Commerce and the National Safety Council sponsored three intercity contests in fire prevention, health protection, and traffic safety, and the *Municipal Year Book* published the names of the winners in six urban categories each year throughout the thirties. Another effort to judge cities in special fields pronounced Boston and St. Louis as most adequately policed, Milwaukee as tops in public health and playgrounds, Minneapolis and Rochester in parks. More knowledge was needed and a clearer understanding of the desired qualities before the standards of a good city could be set, and Professor Edward L. Thorndike of Columbia University endeavored to supply both by rating some 310 places in *Your City,* published in 1939.[77]

• *Toward Metropolitan Self-consciousness*

Scholars were probing the secrets of urban society as never before. For one thing, the problems were becoming more insistent and more complex, demanding analysis before treatment. For another, the opportunities for rich profits from properly located real estate investments and properly chosen industrial bases, so spectacular in the twenties and so much more secure in the thirties, gave a high priority to land-use and other internal studies. Moreover, with urbanites now increasingly in the majority and with 51 per cent of all Americans residing in metropolitan districts by 1940, serious students of American society had to take account of the city.

Yet the intellectual ferment produced by the study of the city was more than a response to urban problems. It was part of a broader cultural adjustment to the emerging metropolitan society, expressed first in conscious recognition and then in various efforts to understand the new situation. Impressionistic descriptions, nostalgic or moralistic judgments, fact-finding surveys, ecological analysis of census data, even social-structure studies of natural areas no longer seemed adequate as the shock treatment of the depression brought an increasing awareness that cities too were in the throes of history.

The pioneer ecological studies at Chicago had by the late twenties produced the first tentative introductory texts in urban sociology. Although a few of the Chicago scholars, notably Nels Anderson, were drawn into administrative positions where they could apply their special knowledge to New Deal tasks, others pursued their researches, in some cases in other cities. Roderick D. Mc-Kenzie wrote a pioneer analysis of "The Metropolitan Community" for inclusion in the *Recent Social Trends* volumes, and several of his former Chicago colleagues contributed to the National Resources Committee's summary report on *Our Cities: Their Role in the National Economy,* published in 1937. Professor Louis Wirth, a member of its Urbanism Committee and director of its Urban Problems and Urban Ways of Life studies, published a significant paper on "Urbanism as a Way of Life" in the *American Journal of Sociology.* Here he not only proposed a more explicit definition of a city but also endeavored to formulate a general theory of urbanization.[78]

Critics of the Chicago school had already appeared, attacking its heavy reliance on ecological data and its assumption that the urban patterns found in Chicago were natural and therefore universal. Miss Milla A. Alihan of Columbia criticized the Burgess theory of concentric circles, which was based, she said, on the findings made by R. D. McKenzie at Columbus, Ohio, and imposed on a map of Chicago with evidence supplied by Zorbaugh and others. In her opinion the thesis not only misinterpreted a specific historical succession as an organic process but also obscured the truly natural areas. Maurice R. Davie of Yale had found a different pattern of residential areas and internal trends in his study of 1933 in New Haven, where urban growth followed natural or man-made radials. After comparing his findings with those of other land use surveys in Cleveland and elsewhere, Davie concluded that each city would have a different residential pattern and succession depending on its site, its functions, and other variables.[79]

Whatever the merits of these studies, they demonstrated the increased intellectual interest in the city, particularly the big city, as the dominant nucleus of modern life. The Lynds, however, had taken a small city—Muncie, Indiana—for their intensive study of urbanization in an industrial setting. By contrasting the life of its 35,000 inhabitants in 1924 with that of their 11,000 predecessors in 1890, they had achieved a time depth in their first *Middletown* volume, and in *Middletown in Transition* (1937) re-examined it under the impact of the depression. In addition to thus broadening the scope of urban sociological study, the Lynds reflected a new awareness of class and power groups that provided the major emphasis for another small-city study already under way at Newburyport in Massachusetts by W. Lloyd Warner and his associates.[80]

While these and other sociologists studied the internal social structures of cities large and small, several economists and geographers were analyzing the economic base and the internal and external technological relationships of cities and metropolises. H. H. McCarty's book on *Industrial Migration in the U.S.* launched a widespread study of the factors influencing industrial location. Richard Hartshone endeavored to show some of the links between cities on a "New Map of the Manufacturing Belt of North America"; Homer Hoyt's study of land values in Chicago and other cities opened lucrative opportunities for real estate consultants and prompted him to propose a pie-shaped sector theory as an alternative to the concentric circles of Professor Burgess. Robert Dickinson of the University of London developed a new functional classification of cities and refined earlier techniques for delimiting their metropolitan regions.[81]

Numerous studies in other fields reflected the growing scholarly interest in cities. Charles E. Merriam and his colleagues analyzed the government of the Chicago metropolitan region, and Harold Gosnell studied its political machine in operation. Caroline F. Ware's account of Greenwich Village and the studies of Allison Davis and associates, later published in *Deep South,* analyzed the character of urban subcommunities. Robert Faris and Warren Dunham made a pioneer effort to study rates of mental illness in an urban setting. Excited by the diversity of new approaches opening up, Miss Ware organized a session for the American Historical Association in 1939 on "The Cultural Approach to History" at which a paper by Ralph E. Turner on "The Industrial City: Center of Cultural Change" made a provocative contribution.[82]

Of course Arthur M. Schlesinger, Sr., had alerted American historians to the importance of the city as a meaningful theme six

Rival Concepts of Internal Urban Zones.

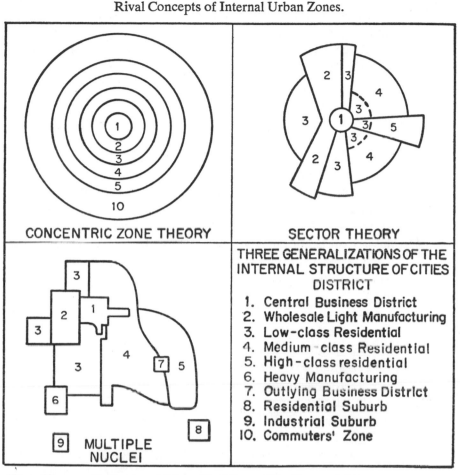

From Chauncey D. Harris and Edward L. Ullman, "The Nature of Cities,"
in Paul K. Hatt and A. J. Reiss, Jr., eds., *Cities and Society* (Glencoe, 1957).
Courtesy of Professor Harris

years earlier. His volume in "The History of American Life" series had depicted "The Rise of the City" as the dominant influence in the 1878–1898 period he covered. Several of his students at Harvard were already engaged in urban historical researches and produced scholarly books during the late thirties. Historians in at least two other graduate centers, Chicago and Johns Hopkins, were similarly engaged. In addition to several one-volume biographies of individual cities, two multivolumed studies had been launched, at Chicago and Rochester, and Professor Schlesinger had his paper on "The City in American History" ready for delivery that spring to the Mississippi Valley Historical Association.[83]

Paralleling the academic awakening to the city, a number of writers not associated with the universities were discovering the importance of the metropolis and producing books on the subject. Technical and journalistic publications were more numerous than literary works on the city in this period and in neither field was it the dominant theme, yet some of these contributions throw additional light on the place of the emerging metropolises in the nation.

Of course the tragedy of human suffering in a land of plenty largely absorbed the attention of creative writers during the thirties. In contrast with the twenties, when Sinclair Lewis flayed the small town in *Main Street* and the small city in *Babbitt* and when Scott Fitzgerald exposed the emptiness of the metropolis in *The Great Gatsby,* the leading writers now depicted the plight of the Okies in *The Grapes of Wrath* or the sores of rural "Yohnapatowpha County" in Mississippi. Some who voiced social protest placed their characters in urban slums, as in the "Studs Lonigan" trilogy by James T. Farrell and *Native Son* by Richard Wright. Their anger was in most cases directed toward the poverty and oppression of a system, not that of the city as such, yet part of the tragedy was the prevailing sense of rootlessness as one character after another failed to realize the promise now expected of the urban community.[84]

The theatre, abetted by the Federal Theatre Project of the WPA, gave the city more attention. The series of "Living Newspaper" dramatizations produced by that staff had a recurrent urban theme, and *One Third of a Nation,* perhaps its high point, reached a wider audience with its indictment of urban slums than most printed reports could hope for. Thornton Wilder's *Our Town,* which idolized the village, popularized the neighborhood spirit that inspired the community-center movement. Clifford Odets's *Waiting for Lefty* dramatized a strike scene in a metropolitan setting. And Charlie Chaplin in *Modern Times* presented his ironic portrayal of the machine age to the much wider cinema audience.[85] These and other urban-centered productions were only a fraction of the theatre's fare even in the depressed thirties, yet they represented an increased awareness of the metropolis.

If there was much lacking in urban society, as these and other critics maintained, it was not the same indictment hurled by H. L. Mencken in his *American Mercury* throughout the twenties. That journal in fact had lost its hold and in 1936 reduced its size, in contrast to the *Literary Digest,* which multiplied its circulation and topped all competitors. Its informative articles, designed for quick and easy reading, had an objective rather than a critical tone and served an educational purpose for millions of adults. Like the weekly *Life,* successfully launched in 1936, it reached into many homes formerly served only by the daily papers. These and other popular journals, crowded with details of everyday life, helped to develop a new sense of national community beyond that of the city or town. With the movies and, increasingly during the thirties, the radio they broadened the horizons of individuals in many communities.[86]

Most journalists were more intimately acquainted with the cities, and with a larger sampling of them, than were the scholars, and the books they now produced in increasing number generally displayed that familiarity. George R. Leighton's *America's Growing Pains* told the "romance, comedy and tragedy" of successive decades in five leading cities. Murray H. Leiffer wrote on the *City and Church in Transition;* Franklin Walker on *San Francisco's Literary Frontier;* Glen C. Quiett, *They Built the West: An Epic of Rails and Cities.* No other journalist, however, produced a book that rivaled *The Autobiography of Lincoln Steffens* as a revealing document on many cities and their urban trends over the previous three decades.[87]

More specialized writers were contributing to another class of books that supplied valuable information on the cities. Harland Bartholomew, head of a St. Louis firm of planners that consulted or drafted plans for many metropolises, compiled the results of his numerous detailed surveys in a manual for the aid of other city planners. Henry Wright, former partner of Clarence Stein, with a totally different conception of planning, wrote on *Re-housing Urban America,* and his friend Clarence Perry on *Housing for the Machine Age.* Edith E. Wood produced two more publications on that problem and Frank Lloyd Wright produced three describing his special views on architecture, another subject that received wide and fresh treatment in this period.[88]

Of course the architects and other graphic artists had additional ways of conveying their interpretations of the city. Although, because of the depression, few architects now had an opportunity to erect tall buildings, many could admire and take hope from the steady progress in this decade of Rockefeller Center. As a first attempt to place and coordinate high-rise buildings in a carefully planned setting that afforded street-level visitors an exciting sense of space, it stirred new interest in proper site planning. Most of the buildings erected with PWA aid displayed architectural mediocrity, in the judgment of Frederick A. Gutheim, writing for the *American Magazine of Art,* but he did single out a few in 1934 for commendation: a fire department building in East Orange, New Jersey, a hydro-plant in Eagle Pass, Texas, and the Ramsey County Court House in Minnesota. In residential community planning, the several projects of Clarence Stein, notably Baldwin Hills Village in Los Angeles, set a new standard of excellence. Only in the TVA dams did the New Deal, in the opinion of architectural historian John Burchard, achieve distinction.[89]

The efforts of the WPA Artists' Project to decorate the new public buildings with murals and sculpture gave some of them a new civic interest. Some of the artists, by including expressions of social criticism in their paintings, stirred bitter controversy, yet a few created memorable symbols for their cities, notably "The Bowery" by Reginald Marsh and "Nighthawks" among several others by Edward Hopper. Moreover, the popular quality of much of this product contributed to an awakening recognition of metropolitan America.[90]

The civic functions of many of the new buildings also helped to revive the community spirit of some cities. When Philadelphia staged a gala ceremony in September 1931 to dedicate its new Municipal Auditorium erected with local funds, a chorus of 1000 greeted the 14,000 citizens who packed the hall. San Francisco proudly dedicated its Opera House a year later, the only one in America municipally owned, though several cities welcomed opera companies to their municipal auditoriums. Pasadena also dedicated its auditorium in 1932, designed in the Italian Renaissance style, and six years later installed a pipe organ presented by a generous citizen. Los Angeles pressed the construction of a planetarium, the third in America, while St. Louis projected a fourth on a scale to rival those opened at Chicago and Philadelphia in the early thirties. Rochester was but one of many cities that built new public libraries with the aid of PWA funds and acquired a new center of civic vitality in the process.[91]

No city rivaled the civic rebirth enjoyed by New York under its explosive but warmly engaging mayor, Fiorello H. LaGuardia. With tireless energy he pressed the city's needs at Washington, securing, as his biographer Charles Garrett tells us, "in all more than $250 million in construction funds" from the PWA and almost $300 million in the first year of the WPA. With these and other resources, he pushed ahead with the construction of modern sewage plants, improvements on the water front, the completion of the long-delayed Bronx Terminal Market, the enlargement and rebuilding of the old North Beach Airport as LaGuardia Field, and the development of a comprehensive parkway and express-highway system. Benefiting in considerable measure from the completed studies of the New York Regional Plan and enlisting some of the leaders of that association for his City Planning Commission under the chairmanship of Rexford G. Tugwell in the late thirties, he also engaged the services of Robert Moses to direct an increasing portion of this construction activity. If that action and indeed each of his many forthright programs aroused criticism, LaGuardia's success in carrying them to completion gave the city a new sense of vitality and accomplishment.[92]

In the midst of these dramatic developments Mumford, a despairing critic, was preparing to brand New York, along with other great megalopises in America and abroad, as a colossal failure. Yet Lewis Mumford wrote his classic book, *The Culture of Cities,* not to damn New York, and certainly not LaGuardia, whose colorful vitality he could not help but admire, but (if we may judge from its organization) as a final rebuttal to Thomas Adams and the New York Regional Plan. A broadly learned and deeply committed scholar, he had absorbed much from the ecological school in Chicago as well as from Patrick Geddes in England, Spengler in Germany, and the American community-center movement rooted in John Dewey. From these and other sources he developed his own conception of the city as a cultural entity, almost organic in character, which, next to the family, was man's most important creation.

Mumford saw the city as a product of man's social needs developed in time and space with the skills and artistry he had achieved and from the earth in which it grew. Recognizing it as a form of life, ever in process of change and with a "capacity for renewal," Mumford sought, as he declared in his introduction, to determine "the possibilities for creating form and order and design in our present civilization." [93]

To establish a firm base for his criticism of modern man's mishandling of his heritage, Mumford pushed his researches back to the rebirth of towns in the Middle Ages. After describing the artistry and traditions of the medieval towns and of the capital cities of the emerging nations, he analyzed some of the mistakes of the "insensate industrial towns" from which the modern megalopolis had sprung. Although he had little faith in its regeneration without the establishment of a new and less materialistic social order, he did see in the regional city proposal of Henry Wright, the community-center movement of Clarence Perry, and the neighborhood designs of Clarence Stein some sociological and architectural components of a new urban order out of which a more creative and gratifying civilization might develop. [94]

Mumford's great contribution was his clear conception of the city as man's basic cultural nucleus. Although his criticisms had little effect on the practical proposals of the New York Regional Plan Association and less on the projects of Robert Moses, his eloquent book quickly became and remains a classic, winning more readers than any other book in the field. Dismissing the states almost as residual entities and the national government as a cluster of bureaucratic powers, he hailed the regional city as the vital unit in the national community and indeed in the Western world. It was perhaps ironical that as Mumford's book appeared the Resettlement Administration, whose Greenbelt towns were the closest approximation to his ideal, was being terminated by the New Deal faction that believed most heartily in decentralization and chiefly because of the unfavorable regional response.[95]

Few of the leading metropolitan statesmen participated in the debates over the ideal size of cities and other urban abstractions. They were, however, deeply involved in the struggle to secure responsible government in each metropolitan region and were greatly concerned lest the appeal for aid from Washington result in national centralization. Buttenheim's plea that Uncle Sam should not become "Boss Sam" sparked a series of annual reviews of "Federal-City Relations" in the *Municipal Year Book* by Earl D. Mallery of the American Municipal Association in which that advocate of federal assistance to cities warned of the dangers of centralization. Yet, despite the increasing number of state and national leagues and associations of municipal officials and reformers, the record of promising regional and state responses dwindled, while that of federal actions expanded. City Manager Dykstra of Cincinnati and Mayor LaGuardia of New York, confident that an alert local democracy could safeguard the city's independence, spearheaded the drive for still more federal programs and appropriations.[96]

4. THE METROPOLIS IN WAR
AND PEACE: 1940-1949

The outbreak of the Second World War, like the onset of the depression, renewed the alliance between the cities and the federal government tenuously formulated during the First World War. Fears and suspicions of national dominance, aroused by the centralizing trends of the New Deal, disappeared as urban leaders hastened to resume functions performed in that earlier war and patriotically assumed new tasks. The apathy and pessimism born of the depression likewise disappeared in the outburst of energy produced by the bombing of Pearl Harbor. With resurgent vitality the metropolises tackled problems they had previously neglected or sought to avoid. In many cases they received the eager support of the federal authorities, for now more than in any previous crisis the country's war effort depended on the productive capacity of its great cities. Moreover, the wide distribution of military contracts rejuvenated many old towns and spurred the rise of several new metropolises.

If in some respects the war reversed the earlier relationships, making the federal government the supplicant, eager to win a larger response from the cities, the return of peace restored the old situation. With renewed growth the mushrooming metropolises faced all the old problems in an intensified form. Central cities, surrounded by expansive suburbs, felt hemmed in as never before, prompting successive efforts to achieve metropolitan reorganization, regional planning, and reapportionment. As these struggles progressed in the state legislatures, other problems mounted to overshadow them. The housing shortage, aggravated by wartime restrictions and priorities, commanded first attention as the servicemen returned. Appeals to Washington brought assistance in their behalf and opened the door for further pleas in behalf of other poor families and for an attack on the central slums into which many Negroes, some of them also servicemen, were crowding. Efforts to dodge the issue, as beyond the scope of the federal government's peacetime responsibilities, proved unavailing as the latter problem became most aggravated at the very door of Congress in Washington itself. That metropolis had become the ship of state, a leader in a great urban armada that could never again be disengaged from the mainstream of the nation's history. Numerous scholars, recognizing that fact, were making the study of the metropolis their major concern.

• *Metropolitan War Efforts*

Having been saved from collapse by the federal government during the dismal thirties, the great cities were ready to play a significant role in the nation's "war for survival." Contacts and agencies developed during the depression proved useful in the new emergency. President Roosevelt, who had annually sent greetings to the U.S. Conference of Mayors, took the occasion in his 1940 letter to invite their cooperation in the newly announced defense program. LaGuardia as chairman reported that the WPA staff, rather than being phased out, would be directed into necessary defense work, that the housing program would be channeled into defense housing, and highway funds into defense roads. Indeed, almost the entire Conference that September was devoted to the defense program.[1]

The cities of course were vitally affected long before the country was actively engaged. First to reflect the outbreak of war in Europe on September 3 was the stock market, and cities that sought to float loans after that date had to offer higher premiums. Providence, for example, had to increase its bid from 2 to 3 per cent for 10-year bonds released the next day. Towns with munitions factories received huge rush orders, and delegations of engineers began to seek out and reappraise idle plants even in out-of-the-way places. Prospects brightened for the unemployed, and struggling communities of every size hastened to reassess their assets in light of the new emergency. Demands for increased production came from every direction, promising increased revenues, but the first effect on the local governments was the mounting cost of supplies.[2]

As reports from the battlefront brought news of the bombing of Warsaw and other cities, demands for local defense broke into the headlines. Alarmed by the hysteria, Howard P. Jones, editor of the *National Municipal Review,* warned in September 1940 that anti-aircraft guns were less needed in American cities than public health precautions, adequate housing, and alert police. All major cities rushed improvements on their airports; many staged training sessions for their police officers in the prevention of sabotage and for their firemen in the control of new fire hazards. Paul V. Betters, executive director of the Conference of Mayors, prepared a plan for civil defense, which gave the cities full responsibility but under federal direction. When LaGuardia, still chairman of the Conference, presented the plan to the President, Roosevelt promptly drafted the New York mayor as National Defense Director with former Mayor Hoan of Milwaukee as his deputy. The *Municipal Year Book* for that year published a list showing the origin and character of the defense councils in some 400 cities.[3]

Again, as in the First World War, local draft boards assumed the responsibility of selecting recruits for the armed services. Women as well as men were required, and the cities vied in filling their quotas.[4] Mounting defense orders from Washington followed quickly on the armament orders from abroad, and again industrial leaders in thirteen widely spaced metropolises accepted the responsibility of helping ordnance-district staffs coordinate the productive capacities of firms large and small to meet the inexhaustible demands.[5] Community chests, now widely established throughout the country, welcomed the opportunity, after a dramatic session at Cincinnati in June 1942, to raise war relief funds for various countries and, where possible, drew the Red Cross and other national agencies into United Fund drives. Urban bankers, responding to the call, conducted successive bond drives; urban schools and colleges hastened to offer training courses for reservists and technicians as well as for workers eager to acquire new skills.[6]

The most critical shortage in many cities was housing. Hastily erected munitions factories and army camps, springing up on the metropolitan outskirts, transformed some 300 cities into boom towns, crowding their schools and recreational facilities and burdening their police with security problems. Perhaps no metropolis faced these problems in a more acute form than Norfolk. There the rapid expansion of the Hampton Roads Navy Yard and other defense and munitions installations created a crisis situation. The population of the city mounted from 144,000 to an estimated 194,000 within two years, while an equivalent growth occurred in the adjoining area. The local defense council, in reporting 8293 new housing units completed or under construction, stressed the urgent need for 10,000 additional units. It soon became evident that this would not suffice and a campaign was launched to persuade private householders to absorb 20,000 additional roomers.[7]

Norfolk's critical educational, recreational, and police problems prompted an investigation of its situation and its needs by both state and federal commissions. Some of the stringencies there and in other war-boom towns could be relieved by recruiting more adequate staffs, but the job of supplying the necessary houses was more difficult and more costly. The passage of the Lanham Act in June 1941, making $150 million available for emergency defense housing, provided only temporary relief. All available PWA and FHA funds were soon redirected into the construction of permanent defense houses. One project at San Pedro, California, where Richard Neutra designed and grouped pairs of one-story houses on cul-de-sac roads, won commendation as outstanding among a half dozen that achieved distinction, but able architects seldom had an opportunity to plan these hastily conceived communities. Carl Feiss, professor of planning at the University of Colorado, warned that defense housing should not be placed too close to the factories but in residential neighborhoods where the amenities would be preserved.[8]

Of course the attack on Pearl Harbor intensified all defense programs and brought new wartime functions to the cities. An extension of the Lanham Act provided another $150 million for temporary war housing and $300 million for permanent houses at war camps and factories. Even these facilities were not adequate, and huge trailer camps appeared on the outskirts of a dozen cities. The January 1942 session of the National Municipal League drew a record-breaking attendance of 4700 delegates to St. Louis, many of them eager to learn how the cities could contribute to the war effort. Among the tasks assumed by urban communities as the war progressed were the scrap drives, the varied rationing schemes, the aircraft-spotting service, the war-bond drives, and a host of other functions that gave city residents an opportunity to participate in the struggle. Rural and small-town residents shared in these efforts, but the federal government looked to the metropolises for their initiation and implementation.[9]

As the prosecution of the war moved into high gear in 1942 and after, the national authorities, following the creation of the War Production Board, tended to assume a more centralized direction of contracts and priorities. In response to local protests of inadequate autonomy, twelve regional offices were set up—one in each of the Federal Reserve cities except Richmond, and one in Detroit. Even this effort to secure increased coordination and efficiency among the 120 field stations of the Office of Production Management soon gave way to a renewed practice of central control. Yet, if the war seemed to demand a unified command in production and other efforts, Roosevelt, LaGuardia, and Ickes among others constantly stressed the need for local cooperation and praised numerous specific efforts, such as Houston's success in staggering its working hours, Cleveland's vigorous action in establishing 36 child-care centers to release mothers for war work, and the campaign launched at Phoenix to clean up its vice districts in order to safeguard a nearby camp and airfield.[10]

The War Production Board, in an effort to tap all natural and manpower resources, placed orders in a number of small cities that effectively speeded their growth. Not only did Norfolk, Phoenix, Miami, and San Diego benefit and receive population gains ranging upward from 72 to 92 per cent, but lesser places such as San Bernardino, California, Lubbock, Texas, and Albuquerque, New Mexico, experienced similar gains and leaped into the metropolitan ranks. A score of other towns likewise achieved metropolitan standing during the forties, several of them with sudden increases based in part on war orders, notably Orlando, Florida, and Baton Rouge, Louisiana.[11]

Several rapidly expanding metropolises in the North attracted an increased number of Negroes to perform industrial and other jobs. This migration gained momentum after A. Philip Randolph, president of the Brotherhood of Sleeping Car Porters, took the lead in planning a march on Washington for July 1941. The prospect of such a march by unemployed Negroes, protesting discriminatory practices, prompted President Roosevelt to forestall it by issuing Executive Order No. 8802 banning discrimination in employment in government and in defense industries on the basis of race, creed, or color. As a result Detroit, Washington, Los Angeles, Chicago, Norfolk, and St. Louis among other cities experienced a rapid influx of Negroes in the early forties, and each community had difficulty in finding suitable accommodations for them. Chicago acquired an additional 60,000 Negroes in these years, but under the watchful eyes of a Mayor's Committee on Race Relations the large Negro community in that city was able to absorb them without serious incident. Similar interracial committees in Cincinnati, Cleveland, Boston, and Los Angeles helped to ease the situation there.[12]

In Detroit, however, where the arrival of 50,000 additional Negroes presented a greater strain on the existing community and its facilities, and where the competition with other ethnic groups for jobs was keen, serious friction developed. When the housing authority responded to white pressure and excluded Negroes from a new housing project built for them near a Polish district, hostilities mounted and finally erupted in a bitter riot on a hot Sunday in June 1943. The fighting broke out as an estimated 100,000 Negro and white picnickers jammed the bridge and other facilities leading to the public park on Belle Isle. Before it subsided a full week later many buildings in Paradise Valley, as the Negro settlement was called, and in portions of the Polish section as well, were demolished and 500 persons were injured. Thirty-eight deaths were attributed to the riot, and 1000 were left homeless, greatly adding to the housing as well as to the welfare problems of that troubled city.[13]

The housing problem was critical in every large city and demanded close cooperation between federal and local administrations. Even the centralized National Housing Agency, created early in 1942 to coordinate all federal programs in this field, had to negotiate agreements with local authorities before successful programs could be launched. Some 183,000 units were completed and 241,000 more were under construction in 125 cities by the close of the first year. One, called the city of Vanport, was being built to house 40,000 near two shipyards on the outskirts of Portland, Oregon. But several of these projects moved so slowly that many observers doubted that they would be completed before the war's end. A widespread fear of abandoned factories and unfinished houses added to the clamor for postwar planning.[14]

Advocates of postwar planning appeared even before the attack on Pearl Harbor. Memories of the severe local problems following the First World War and fresher memories of the hardships of the depression prompted many officials to look ahead to an impending emergency. This was a proper job for the cities, declared Frederick A. Delano, the President's uncle, in his 1941 report as chairman of the National Resources Planning Board. The bombing of Pearl Harbor focused attention for a time on the immediate war effort, but the emergency, as Walter Blucher of Detroit observed a few months later, actually strengthened the need for long-range planning. Before the close of the year Baltimore, Cleveland, Detroit, and seventy other cities had created postwar planning councils. By the next spring, when the National Resources Planning Board made its report to Congress, the number of cities responding to its prodding in this field had reached 108.[15]

The U.S. Chamber of Commerce, taking a slightly different course, urged cities to study postwar problems with the object of stimulating private action; following this lead, some metropolises, such as Rochester, created committees on postwar problems. When the editors of *Fortune* magazine decided in 1942 to promote this effort and chose Syracuse as one of two demonstration cities, their emphasis, too, was on the study of problems, not planning. But Sergei Grimm, executive director of the Syracuse Housing Authority, who organized the movement in that city, saw the need for broad-visioned public planning and won the support of Chancellor William P. Tolley of Syracuse University, who became chairman of the Syracuse-Onondaga Post-War Planning Council. The 77-member Council soon had a battery of sixteen committees enrolling 134 members who tackled their varied research and planning tasks with enthusiasm. Numerous experts visited Syracuse to give their counsel, and all proceeded smoothly until the extent of several of the proposals began to alarm some council members. Fears of a huge public-housing program prompted Mayor Thomas E. Kennedy to assert, in April 1944, "As long as I am mayor there will be no [more] public housing projects in Syracuse." In similar fashion disagreements developed between the planning experts and the businessmen over proposed changes in the central district; friction between city and town leaders created an additional impasse. The final report, when released in modified form in 1946, had lost its impact.[16]

Many other cities experienced similar difficulties, though few received such front-page treatment. Some metropolises, on the other hand, achieved real gains. In Pittsburgh, where Richard K. Mellon had become president of the Regional Planning Association in 1941 and helped two years later to found the Allegheny Conference on Community Development, their imaginative plans for new traffic arteries and river improvements enlisted unexpected support in 1946 from Mayor David F. Lawrence, who based his Democratic campaign on their program and vigorously carried it forward. New planning boards proposed ambitious schemes in Kansas City, Dallas, Detroit, and Cleveland among others, and several successfully weathered the political storms that followed. But everywhere the opposition was mounting, and in the late spring of 1943 Congress refused to extend the life of the National Resources Planning Board.[17]

The issue could not be dismissed that easily, however. Several cities had planning studies in process and urgent needs that committed them to action. Dallas was such a town and, with the aid of the Bartholomew Associates of St. Louis, was planning for twenty-five years of growth. Portland, Oregon, was looking ahead to an outlay of $60 million on projects selected by its special consultant, Robert Moses, who also released a schedule of postwar improvements for New York City to cost $100 million. The editors of the *National Municipal Review* deplored the blindness of Congress in abolishing the National Resources Planning Board, and Mayor LaGuardia in his annual address to the Conference of Mayors in 1944 strongly urged the federal government to plan and announce a program to spend $15 billion on public works to aid the cities combat unemployment at the war's end.[18]

Confident that the federal government would not fail them, many urban leaders began to move, as C. A. Dykstra, now president of the University of Wisconsin, put it in 1945, "from state-city to federal-city relationships." The American Institute of Planners reestablished its *Journal,* suspended at the outbreak of the war, and offered readers a critical evaluation of town and regional planning.[19] The Conference of Mayors devoted a full session in the spring of 1945 to reports from 75 cities that submitted detailed postwar plans. Philadelphia, with projects expected to cost $400 million, led the list. The Toledo planners prepared a huge model at a cost of $250,000 to depict the character and details of the new city to be built at the mouth of the Maumee River. Most of the financial sections of these plans indicated an expectation of generous aid from Washington. "It is up to Congress," declared Colonel Betters shortly after the collapse of the Japanese in August raised the specter of unemployment at home.[20]

• *Postwar Redevelopment*

Not Congress but the chief executive had been most concerned that the cities secure help in time of need. Now again in postwar America the old relationships were resumed; they were in many respects new and different relationships, however, for three years of crisis had brought many changes. Federal confidence was high, so high in fact that Congress could disregard problems until they hit, as it did with housing and planning and other metropolitan problems. The states too, if for different reasons and despite the postwar plans some had made, resumed their passive roles. Many cities that had enjoyed industrial expansion during the war now faced a threat of serious unemployment, yet their local bodies were also marking time, awaiting an announcement from Washington of federal aid for reconversion. Unfortunately, only $17.5 million had been appropriated, reported Alfred Willoughby, editor of the *National Municipal Review* in November 1945, as against the $500 million recommended as a start by the National Resources Planning Board.[21]

President Truman, however, was reassuring. Congress had made federal aid available for highways in cities, and he predicted early in 1946 that it would soon do the same for airports, hospitals, and health centers, water pollution, and housing. Several metropolises with superhighway plans ready for action, such as Los Angeles, Dallas, and Fort Worth, secured federal assistance and commenced construction. Cleveland voters approved a $35.5 million bond issue to help launch its postwar projects. Milwaukee and Kansas City as well as Philadelphia, among several others, pressed ahead with earlier projects. But it was the housing crisis created by the returning servicemen that demolished the old dikes confining the stream of federal revenues to traditional uses.[22]

The hasty emphasis on highways was unfortunate, indeed calamitous, from Lewis Mumford's point of view. Deploring the contemporary planner's obsession with "roads, highways, avenues, terminals, airports, shopping centers, factory districts," he demanded an end to urban expansion into formless and frustrating "conurbations" and called for a renewal of a "life centered environment" in regional cities. His new book, *City Development: Studies in Disintegration and Renewal,* published early in 1945, revived the old debate as to the proper size and character of cities. After surveying the accomplishments of the past two decades, he gloomily concluded that, rather than "humanizing the industrial city . . . we have dehumanized the population." In a review of that book, Miss Bauer, whose concern for the human needs of the metropolis was equally great, observed that Mumford "does not always recognize the forces on his side." She, in contrast, saw grounds for hope in the increased interest in urban redevelopment evident in the postwar plans of many cities.[23]

Seven state legislatures with large urban contingents had in fact followed the lead of New York and Illinois in adopting laws to permit the condemnation of blighted districts for redevelopment by nonprofit corporations. When in 1944 the U.S. Supreme Court upheld the New York law, in *Murray* v. *LaGuardia,* urban leaders in other states pressed anew for such legislation. The Urban Land Institute, established at Washington in 1936, drafted a "Proposal for Rebuilding Blighted City Areas" with federal assistance and persuaded Senator Wagner to introduce a bill providing federal credits and subsidies for this purpose. Although that bill failed to pass, the *Housing Year Book* predicted that it would be introduced again. The Federal Housing Agency issued a *Handbook for Urban Redevelopment for Cities.* The postwar plans of numerous towns already included such projects; those in Chicago, Cleveland, and a few others placed great emphasis on the objective of restoring the human scale to life in the metropolis by building planned neighborhoods to replace the slums.[24]

Many lauded these goals but disputed the merits of specific plans and wrangled over who should undertake the work. Harold Buttenheim and Mayors Wilson Wyatt of Louisville and Cornelius Scully of Pittsburgh discussed these questions at length before the Conference of Mayors that met at Montreal in June 1944. In New York City the Regional Plan Association, which in 1941 had claimed the accomplishment of half its proposals of two decades before, was now uncertain of its course and seemed eclipsed in the forties by Park Commissioner Robert Moses. Thus a heated debate erupted within its councils and throughout the city over the scheme of the Metropolitan Life Insurance Company to erect 35 apartment towers of 13 stories each on 61 acres to be cleared with state aid. If Stuyvesant Town, inspired by Robert Moses, with a projected density of 594 persons per acre, was the best that private enterprise could offer, Buttenheim for one preferred to experiment with public housing.[25]

A National Conference on Post-War Housing, meeting at Chicago in March 1944, raised more issues than it solved. Mrs. Samuel I. Rosenman of New York, chairman of the National Committee on Housing, had convened it with the hope that agreement could be reached by gathering the advocates of public and private housing, of federal, state, and local initiative, together in the same room. Although the attempt at conciliation failed, the Conference brought several new aspects of the housing problem into clearer focus. Jerrold Loebl, president of the Chicago Building Congress, stressed the need for broad greenbelts to separate the sprawling suburbs one from another and from the central city. Hugh Porter, head of the River Oaks Corporation, with a 1200-acre private redevelopment project on the outskirts of Houston, admitted the need for some federal assistance, chiefly in the form of guarantees on local bonds to assist in purchasing and clearing slum areas, but responsibility for their redevelopment should in most cases be given, he declared, to private enterprise. Professor Alvin Hansen of Harvard, who saw a greater need for public housing, suggested that federal aid be extended not in lump sums for its construction, but in annual grants to cover the losses on locally floated housing bonds. Herbert N. Nelson of the National Association of Real Estate Boards declared that the states should grant their cities sufficient powers to escape federal bondage; local governments, if properly constituted, could, he maintained, use tax incentives instead of grants to solve the problem.[26]

In the midst of the heated discussion that followed the formal papers, a new issue arose. A Negro delegate, identified only as Mrs. Valentine, posed the question by asking how the public and private redevelopers would treat the Negroes they displaced in the slums. Hugh Pomeroy of the National Association of Housing Officials assured her that any government would guarantee housing for all those displaced. Nelson, answering for the private developers, candidly replied that they would respect any covenants attached to the land. Miss Elizabeth Wood, who as chairman of the session on the second day had declared in her introductory remarks that "the fate of our cities lies in the postwar residential building programs," concluded the session with the remark that "Perhaps the only agreement among us is on the fact that a governmental role of some size and kind is necessary." [27]

The American Institute of Architects voted its approval of public housing, but carefully specified the type of assistance it favored. Locally directed and managed projects, aided by federal and state grants, won the support of most of its urban chapters, though many strongly opposed a federally controlled program. Carl Feiss stressed the merits of "urban esthetics" as a contribution to the human dimension in housing and deplored the lack of these qualities in most existing projects whether public or private. Architects may not be planning experts, Henry S. Churchill admitted, but their function is "to make the planner's abstractions real," "to breathe life into [his] ideas"; local chapters should therefore, he maintained, help to formulate general plans and enter the political arena if necessary to activate them.[28]

Political leadership was essential if Congress was to be persuaded to act. John B. Blandford, formerly director of the Civic Bureau of Government Research and now head of the National Housing Agency, estimated in 1945 that 12 million additional homes would be needed in the next ten years, a third of them for low-income families, yet he added that "the cities would have to handle their housing shortages." Mayor LaGuardia responded in indignation, "We ask for bricks and stones and plumbing, and they give us a mimeographed press release." The U.S. Conference of Mayors petitioned in December that $190 million be quickly appropriated to enable the National Housing Agency to make 100,-000 units of temporary housing available as emergency relief for hard-pressed cities. More substantial aid would soon be needed, the mayors maintained, since the estimated demand in New York City alone was for 250,000 units, in Chicago for 100,000, and loomed in similar proportions in a dozen other metropolises.[29]

Most of the states, too, relied on the cities to meet the problem. Eleven additional legislatures passed laws in 1945 for redevelopment purposes, but only two supplied funds or credits to facilitate the operation. Nevertheless, by October of that year seven cities had launched such projects—Philadelphia, St. Louis, Detroit, Minneapolis, Dallas, and Memphis as well as New York, which now commenced two new ones. Pittsburgh and Indianapolis soon joined this group, and in several other places nonprofit corporations erected veterans' housing projects, such as Fernwood Park in Rochester, on land supplied by the city.[30]

Most officials, local, state, and national, hoped that private builders would supply the needed houses and that philanthropists would build low-cost rental projects to replace the slums. Active citizens' housing associations in many cities were less sanguine and with local veterans' groups pressed for government support for low-cost rental projects. As the shortage became more acute, a half dozen metropolises followed New York's example and adopted rent-control ordinances to prolong the restrictions applied in these and some 300 other urban areas by the federal government in 1942. New housing starts increased in 1946 and rose to 854,000 the next year, many assisted by FHA- and VA-backed loans, but most were for sale at high prices and in the suburbs, thus sharpening the division between the affluent and the less fortunate.[31]

Despite the mounting pressure for federal action, a disturbing factor contributed to the delay. In addition to the old hostility to public housing as socialistic, a new fear that it would help expand the districts open to Negroes gripped white leaders in several metropolises. That issue was especially acute in Washington itself where a continuous influx of Negroes, alarming both the Board of Trade and the Real Estate Board, prompted efforts to tighten racial segregation with financial controls. These could be applied more readily under private construction, but in Washington even the members of the National Capital Park and Planning Commission and of the National Capital Housing Authority pledged the use of their powers to enforce segregation. In Louisville and Atlanta, where such action was taken for granted, public housing was supported as a benefit for both whites and blacks, but in some Northern cities federal housing assumed the character of an opening wedge for Negro invasion.[32]

Earnest groups in most Northern cities were unperturbed by this prospect. Adequate housing for all residents was the objective of the Better Housing Association in Rochester and of similar groups in a score of other metropolises. Several such bodies in

Ohio helped to persuade Senator Robert A. Taft to join with Senator Wagner of New York and Senator Allen J. Ellender of Louisiana in sponsoring a bill that authorized the construction of 500,000 low-rent dwelling units over a period of four years and appropriated $500 million to assist cities in launching urban redevelopment projects. Even *The New York Times,* concerned over the failure of private enterprise to supply low-cost rental housing, came out in support of the Taft-Ellender-Wagner Bill early in 1947.[33]

Although the bill again failed to pass, the publication of the findings of a Census Bureau survey of housing needs in all cities of over 50,000 rallied support. The redevelopment corporations in a score of cities eagerly added their endorsement, and several of them boldly ventured ahead with the limited resources available. Seven heavily urban states and New Hampshire now provided state credits for low-rental projects, while Indiana permitted the Indianapolis Redevelopment Commission to levy a tax in support of its programs. New York City and Milwaukee floated city bonds to speed the construction of low-cost housing, and in the absence of state laws Baltimore and Norfolk launched local projects in anticipation of early federal aid. Congress, which finally passed the Housing Act in July 1949, accepted the subsidy of low-cost housing as a national responsibility and extended the use of federal funds to back slum clearance and urban redevelopment. President Truman quite appropriately presented the pen with which he signed the act to the U.S. Conference of Mayors.[34]

The successful passage of the housing act reflected the skill of its drafters in accommodating dissident urban interests. If the demand for low-cost housing was the most urgent concern, the use of public funds in this field was made more palatable to others by providing federal backing for slum clearance and urban redevelopment of a nonresidential character as well. Local hostility to national housing projects was avoided by placing them under local authorities; and the fears of Negroes and other minorities that they would ruthlessly be displaced were quieted by a directive of the Solicitor General denying federal aid to any project that practiced discrimination on the basis of race, color, or creed. No position was taken for or against segregation within a city's program, but Congress did adopt a provision restraining state and federal courts from enforcement of the restrictive covenants often attached to urban property.[35]

Yet each of these dilemmas continued to plague the housing reformers. To assure success in the development of congenial neighborhoods it was not only desirable to give autonomy to local authorities, Lloyd Rodwin declared in 1948, but the views of local residents should also be considered. Yet the neighborhood-unit plan incorporated in the Michigan redevelopment law the next year stirred a bitter attack from Reginald R. Isaacs of Chicago, who labeled it a device for excluding undesirables and a cloak for racial segregation. The argument was by no means academic, as Chicago, with an expanding black belt, was already discovering; indeed the progress of its first redevelopment projects was creating a critical problem of relocation. This new dilemma would soon plague other Northern cities where the segregation of Negroes was increasing more rapidly than most citizens realized.[36]

Public housing officials, however, especially those handling applications for rentals, had ample warning of the new trend. Whether because of their color, their low seniority, or their lack of skills, Negroes were the first to lose their jobs in periods of retrenchment, and many with low wages at best were eligible for public housing. Projects erected in slums already dominated by Negroes raised few difficulties over admissions, but projects located in white areas presented a challenge to those who believed in integration. A probing study by Barry Bishop of the situation in ten cities early in 1945 revealed that, while many Negroes were indifferent to this issue, many, with Roy Wilkins of the NAACP, were protesting segregation and demanding full equality. The expiration of the Committee on Fair Employment Practices, created by Roosevelt's Executive Order No. 8802 as a wartime measure, brought new demands for a permanent FEPC. President Truman's Committee on Civil Rights recommended such legislation by Congress as well as by the states to assure fair employment to all.[37]

Negro and other civil-rights advocates were also waging a wide battle against the anti-Negro covenants embedded in many urban land titles. Finally, in *Shelley* v. *Kraemer,* the U.S. Supreme Court in 1948 reversed the traditional stand of lower courts and banned restrictive covenants that discriminated on the basis of race, color, or creed. Compliance, however, was spotty, even in official projects. Charles Livermore, director of Community Relations in Buffalo, warned housing authorities that "segregation is not the answer" and advised a search for sites on the outskirts where new and integrated communities could develop. Biracial commissions to assure fair employment practices and open housing appeared under varied names in a dozen metropolises by 1947, some with sizable budgets—$58,000 at Chicago, $38,000 at Detroit, $25,000 at Cleveland. Several New York State cities formed SCAD offices under the state's fair employment practices act of 1945. Yet despite these measures the income of most Negroes remained low, forcing them to seek shelter in the inner-city slums of many Northern metropolises.[38]

Downtown business leaders in some cities had received a warning, too. The Urban Land Institute, having completed detailed land-use studies for seven leading metropolises in the early forties, established a Central Business District Council in 1946 to tackle downtown problems. The spread of inner-city blight had alerted the central commercial interests of Washington and Baltimore, Philadelphia and Detroit, as well as St. Louis and Chicago, and made them receptive to varied schemes for urban redevelopment. Each of these towns (well over 10 per cent nonwhite), as well as Boston, Pittsburgh, and a few others, saw the formation during the mid-forties of a Central Council, as in Boston, or a Community Development Conference, as in Pittsburgh, and proceeded to establish a Redevelopment Corporation as soon as their state laws permitted. Their backing for the Taft-Ellender-Wagner Act reflected their desire for federal aid to halt the spread of inner-city slums that threatened the prosperity of the central business core. Their plans, when tentatively revealed in the late forties, envisaged open plazas to encourage the construction of new commercial properties and high-rise apartments, some in the luxury bracket to offset the emerging pattern of the poor inner city.[39]

These were in part cleanup and beautification projects, but they had other basic objectives. Pittsburgh and Detroit started with smoke-abatement campaigns, Baltimore and Philadelphia with historical restoration schemes. Boston conducted a Greater Boston Contest, which focused public interest on proposals for the architectural redevelopment of the decaying Scully Square area among other districts. Inspired by the enthusiasm of newly-elected Mayor Richardson Dilworth, Philadelphia prepared a Better Philadelphia Exhibition at a cost of $300,000 that drew 390,000 visitors and attracted nationwide attention. Dayton, as well as Indianapolis, Omaha as well as Milwaukee, New Haven as well as Providence, among other medium-sized metropolises, announced similar redevelopment plans that focused in part on the removal of the inner-city slums.[40]

The converse side of the slum problem was the wholesale migration to the suburbs, which now set in in earnest. The resurgence of urban growth saw the populations of twelve major metropolitan areas increase 50 per cent or more in the forties. San Francisco was the only one in this most-rapidly-growing group that exceeded a million in population (indeed its number was 2,193,000), but Washington with a 49.8 per cent growth and Los Angeles with 47 per cent were not far below. All of these and most of the 76 other metropolises over 200,000 in size saw their major growth in the suburbs; the few exceptions (all in the South) had again successfully annexed new tracts to provide or absorb their new residents.[41]

The best way to control this growth, according to Mumford and many other articulate planners, was by the promotion of new satellite communities, yet the few examples of such planning—on the outskirts of Chicago, Cincinnati, Cleveland, New York, and a few other big cities—were almost lost in the great rush to the suburbs. None of their patterns proved influential, and most of these projects were soon absorbed and lost their autonomy. Faced with a prospect of the migration of most whites from Manhattan, the directors of the Regional Plan Association of New York warned in 1948 that "the metropolis is at the crossroads." Only through more forthright regional planning could the situation be saved, declared Frederick J. Osborn, a British planner on a visit to America in 1948, yet "some means must be found," he declared, "to prevent the over-concentration and inordinate sprawl of [America's] urban development." [42]

One means, of course, was by the promotion of industrial and other functions in small cities or new towns. This policy received new support in the middle and late forties as the nation reacted to the Russian development of the atomic bomb. Renewed defense orders were again widely distributed, and a newly established National Security Resources Board strongly recommended further decentralization. The contracts, however, had to go to the lowest reliable bidders, and the most successful were generally located in established industrial centers. Fortunately, despite fears of a postwar recession, there were many thriving cities. The Census of Manufacturers for 1947 listed 24 that had enjoyed a threefold increase in the value of their manufactured products since 1939. Most of the thirty other industrial metropolises tabulated there reported gains that closely approached that rate of advance; Portland, Oregon, almost reached a fourfold increase. Since most of these manufacturing centers and many other thriving cities had enterprising industrialists and well-staffed bureaus, chambers, and industrial development committees eagerly pressing for new contracts, a wide diffusion of urban growth was assured. [43]

• Metropolitan Factionalism

The 140 Metropolitan Districts of 1940 increased to 168 Standard Metropolitan Areas by the close of the decade and numbered 84,500,680 residents, well over 55 per cent of the nation's total. Ninety exceeded 200,000 in population, and of these 14 exceeded a million. Their votes were amply sufficient to win national elections, and they held a more or less decisive majority in 30 states where they could at least elect the governors if they voted in unison. Of course such divisions seldom occurred, for rival parties attracted support in all cities and towns as well as in rural areas. The Democrats continued their hold, established in the New Deal era, over most central cities (Syracuse was one of the few exceptions) and the Republicans continued to dominate most suburban and rural areas in the North and West. [44] The alignment was no longer as clear-cut, but it was sufficiently marked to complicate the efforts of the cities to win support for their measures in the gerrymandered state legislatures and in Congress as well. The same alignment blocked repeated attempts to achieve either a unified government or effective planning within specific metropolises. Yet the pressures of urban life were incessant and left no factional compromise standing for long.

As the Conference of Mayors and other national associations of urban officials and reformers provided the chief spokesmen for metropolitan interests at Washington, so in each large city an assortment of citizen groups and official bodies championed a variety of reforms and endeavored to promote remedies for the community's problems. Most of the problems were old and familiar, and many of the embattled groups had become old and somewhat tired in the search for solutions. But with continued metropolitan growth many old problems became more acute, spurring the launching of new efforts to meet them either by a regrouping of the old forces or by the establishment of new organizations.[45]

Yet the problems of the forties were in many respects so greatly aggravated that old approaches were outgrown. Thus the city clubs and bureaus of municipal research that had provided leadership in the twenties and a sense of need in the thirties lost much of their effectiveness as the cities exploded into vast metropolises. Not only were the new and sprawling communities too large for easy participation in club forums and committees, but they were also too diversified to accept the findings of a bureau financed by a limited group as effectively representative of their civic interests. Several of the old bodies continued to perform vital functions, however, notably the City Club of Portland, Oregon, and the Research Bureau of Detroit, to mention only two. Some of the other clubs carried on only as lecture forums, and some of the bureaus became cost-accounting services, yet an informative "Researcher's Digest," published periodically in the *National Municipal Review* in the mid-forties, noted that 300 reports had been received in 1946 from local groups of this sort.[46]

With the local chapters of the League of Women Voters and the civic committees of some Chambers of Commerce, these citizen groups performed an indispensable educational function. In some cities the research bureaus received public support and official status, and 16 metropolises maintained municipal reference libraries by the mid-forties. Yet when these official bodies produced forthright reports on controversial questions, as for example the publication by the Detroit Bureau in 1940 of a booklet on "Detroit—A Tale of Two Cities," depicting the central city's increasingly unhappy plight, the effect was minimal. A more representative and more politically oriented body was needed to produce action. Mayor Frank Shaw's Citizens Committee on Government Reorganization, formed in Los Angeles in the mid-thirties, was such a body and helped to effect a considerable amount of consolidation of functions under the county. Similar attempts in Pittsburgh, Cleveland, and St. Louis among other places had generally failed in the past, but the publication of the 1940 Census, revealing a decline in the population of most core cities, spurred renewed efforts to achieve consolidation and a broader sharing of the tax burdens.[47]

The plight of the central city was widely experienced, as Albert Lepawsky pointed out in a study of Chicago and Professor Thomas H. Reed in a more general analysis of "The Metropolitan Problem."[48] The war diverted attention from these organizational problems for a time, but in California, where San Francisco and Los Angeles, the two most rapidly growing major metropolises, were bursting their seams, an official Metropolitan Areas Committee was organized early in 1944 with representatives from all 28 cities in the state. The urgencies of the war effort forced some urban utilities to extend their services beyond the city limits and, in John Bauer's opinion, justified an extension of city regulatory power to that wider service area. Yet the intergovernmental contract system, perfected in the Los Angeles area in the 1930's, provided a more acceptable method for the extension of services and supervision in many metropolises.[49]

The postwar years saw a revival of forthright efforts to achieve metropolitan consolidation. Professor Carl J. Friedrich of Harvard won a widely promoted Boston contest in 1944 with a plan for the consolidation of the governments of 66 cities and towns within its metropolitan area under a representative council to be elected by proportional representation. Although nothing came of this or of similar schemes in St. Louis and Pittsburgh, considerable success marked the efforts of other cities, such as Louisville, Milwaukee, and Atlanta, to annex extensive suburban areas that desired urban services. The U.S. Census listed over ninety special districts that performed single or multiple functions in 1947, but only one of the many attempts to achieve city-county consolidation reached fruition. That one, in Baton Rouge, succeeded only because Louisiana laws permitted the favorable majority in the city to override the opposing majority in the parish. Local commissions studied and proposed such schemes in Birmingham, Houston, and Miami as well as in Seattle among other places, only to suffer rejection by their villagers. Regional planning councils, however, increased to fifteen by 1945 and to thirty-four by 1949; although few of them achieved official status, several enlisted the cooperation of planning officials and produced studies and plans of educational value—at Louisville and Cleveland as well as at San Francisco and Los Angeles.[50]

One objection to consolidation, even to regional planning, was the ravages either action could inflict on existing neighborhoods. To answer that objection, some planners proposed the adoption of a borough system, as at New York and London. No city incorporated that proposal in its charter, but several metropolises did revive the neighborhood-unit scheme of Clarence Perry. Kansas City, for example, organized a number of community-service councils to give residents of urban neighborhoods a sense of participation in welfare development and city planning. Los Angeles carried this still further, decentralizing the administration of social welfare and other services and organizing citizen councils in numerous districts to safeguard the neighborhood's interests.[51]

Next to housing and planning, the crucial aspect of the metropolitan situation was fiscal. Many cities had greatly improved their financial positions during the war years when priorities on labor and materials forced a postponement of improvements. But as peace returned prices rose, and city officials needed new sources of revenue to tackle the backlog of jobs. Seattle, Denver, New

Orleans, and some forty California towns adopted sales taxes, following New York's example. St. Louis, Toledo, and several other Ohio and Pennsylvania cities adopted local income taxes patterned after that in Philadelphia. Yet several state legislatures refused to grant municipalities the power to levy such taxes, thus adding fuel to the urban desire for a reapportionment of legislative districts.[52]

The demand for reapportionment had moral and constitutional backing but little political support. When the U.S. Census of 1940 again revealed the disproportion between urban and rural legislative districts, movements developed in a dozen states to reapportion their legislatures. At least 23 states had taken such action during the thirties, but those failing to act included several that needed it most. Jealousy and fear of the big cities blocked reapportionment in California as well as New York, in Ohio, Michigan, Illinois, Minnesota, Texas, and several more where the issue arose in the forties. Even in Missouri, which adopted a reapportionment clause in its new constitution to assure fairer representation for St. Louis and Kansas City, the new law implementing the reform was so unequal that the courts held it invalid. After reporting a survey, which showed that 45 of 67 major cities were underrepresented and that 34 states penalized their largest cities, editor Willoughby of the *National Municipal Review* concluded, in December 1945, that "the states are inviting self-destruction." [53]

The disproportion was becoming more glaring with each decade, but now that urban growth was concentrating in the suburbs, the division between urban and rural representation was no longer clear-cut. Many suburban communities were also underrepresented and in the process of becoming more so. The complexity of the political tangle of interest was so great that when *Colgrove* v. *Green,* a Congressional districting case, reached the Supreme Court, Justice Felix Frankfurter declared in an influential obiter dictum that "the Courts ought not to enter this political thicket." That decision rendered in 1946 discouraged further appeals to the courts for relief.[54]

Blocked by weighted votes stacked against them in the legislatures and denied redress at the bar of justice, the cities took the only remaining course and appealed to the court of public opinion. The *National Municipal Review* published repeated attacks under such titles as "Home-grown Totalitarianism" and "Constitutional Tyranny." Only two states granted equal votes to their cities, one scholar concluded after a study of the 1950 Census data. Other students uncovered a similar discrimination in expenditures, though in this case eight states were found to have distributed a fair share of state revenues to the cities.[55]

It was little wonder that metropolitan leaders turned to the federal government when problems beyond their strength arose. Grants-in-aid for the construction of airports and hospitals were passed in 1946, to be followed two years later by subsidies for urban planning and for research on water pollution. In 1950 Congress appropriated funds to aid in the construction of schools. Some of these grants, as in the case of the schools, were justified as payments in lieu of taxes on federal property or federal activities within the cities, but at least the response in Washington was more encouraging than in most state capitals where even pleas for the right to levy increased local taxes were repeatedly rejected or only partially conceded. Milwaukee, having finally paid off all its debts, was discovered by Mayor Frank Zeidler in 1947 to be not only solvent but shabby. His proposal that the city float a $31 million bond issue to start its $216 million improvement program won support from 57 per cent of the voters that May. This was the proper solution, Mayor William F. Devin of Seattle declared, urging cities to unite in demanding more taxing powers rather than in pleading for larger handouts.[56]

Mayor Hubert H. Humphrey of Minneapolis and several others endorsed that view. But Humphrey, who had won as an independent in a nonpartisan election, and in a city with a weak-mayor system, had little political influence on the legislature. Although he declared in many speeches that "the cities lack power to govern themselves" and that they pay 90 per cent of the taxes but receive only a quarter of the revenues, his protests had little effect. Professor Luther Gulick, in an address on "The Shame of the Cities: 1946," contrasted the situation in Lincoln Steffens's day, when corruption gripped the cities, with that in the mid-forties, when filth, slums, traffic tie-ups, and deteriorating services presented a more serious threat in many metropolises. More powers and more resources were needed, but also more forthright leadership, declared Richardson Dilworth, leader of a reform faction in Philadelphia in the late forties.[57]

Citizen reform movements and action groups were stirring in many communities. A new day seemed to be dawning in Chicago, where the death of Al Capone and the defeat of Mayor Edward J. Kelly by Martin Kennelly raised citizen hopes in 1947 for an effective war on crime. In similar fashion Memphis ousted "Boss" Edward H. Crump. But these movements were not widespread, and New Orleans, which had enjoyed a progressive administration, saw it disrupted as Governor Earl K. Long sought to recapture its control for political advantage.[58]

In the case of airports, however, no mayor could resist the urge to seek federal assistance. This was a very special situation in which the cities provided the necessary bases for a nationwide system of transportation and communications and had maintained close collaboration with the federal government from the start in 1915 when the National Advisory Committee for Aeronautics was created. That relationship had developed through several stages until 1946, when, after a spirited contest with advocates of a return of local administration to the states, the cities again won full charge of their airport developments under federal supervision and with a greatly increased provision of federal funds. Mayor LaGuardia voiced the opinion of most of his colleagues when he declared, "The cities are paying the freight and providing the funds out of local revenues, [and] there is no place in the picture for an intermediary state agency." In adopting the Civil Aeronautics Act of 1946, Congress authorized its administrator to extend grants-in-aid to any public agency that met its standards in the planning and maintenance of airport facilities. Metropolitan airports quickly applied for and secured a major portion of the millions appropriated annually, and although more than a thousand cities and towns secured some assistance, only the major cities were able to match the 50 per cent grants on an ambitious scale, and they as a result were ready to accommodate the larger planes that increasingly dominated the airways by the mid-century.[59]

Several specific problems commanded major attention in the late forties. Delinquency and crime seemed everywhere on the increase, except perhaps in the South, where a few cities appeared to achieve some gains, at least when measured against their former records of violence. Several state legislatures were ready to help in the attack on this problem through the establishment of a State Youth Board, as in New York, and the extension of support to similar local bodies.[60] A few states granted their cities increased power for the control of the smoke nuisance, and Providence among other cities adopted measures patterned after those of Pittsburgh, Chicago, Detroit, and Salt Lake City, where earlier campaigns had demonstrated their merit. Los Angeles, once proud of its clear skies, was becoming known as a smog city, but public concern there was not aroused until 1948, when reports of the disaster at Donora, a steel town south of Pittsburgh, revealed the frightening potentialities of smog.[61]

As the study of smog progressed, its connection with the traffic problem emerged. In the forties, however, the automobile posed chiefly highway and parking problems with side effects on the transit question. As the number of passenger cars mounted from 25 million to 40 million in the five years following the war, and trucks from 5 million to 8 million, the traffic on city streets, particularly in the downtown districts, often became snarled at rush hours. Some cities sought to relieve the situation by improvements in their transit systems, as in Cleveland, Seattle, and San Francisco, where the trolleys and buses were publicly owned. Chicago debated an extension of its subway system, successfully opened in 1943 as the fourth in America, but underground systems found few advocates elsewhere. Several metropolises hastened to launch new highway programs, although construction would be a long-term operation. Either attack promised to be costly and prompted many city officials to turn again to the state and federal governments for assistance.[62]

President Truman responded in 1947 by calling a Conference on Highway Safety at Washington. Its sessions considered a wide range of problems, many of them centered in the cities. Most speakers looked there for solutions, but all agreed that the federal government should give its aid for safety research and that its highway funds should be shared more equitably with the cities. When, later that year, Congress authorized the construction of a national highway network of some 37,000 miles, at least 2800 miles were to be located in 182 large cities. This program would assist but not supplant the more vigorous superhighway projects under construction at Los Angeles, Philadelphia, Cleveland, and other metropolises. But when San Francisco announced the preparation of a freeway plan to cost $150 million in 1949, serious protests arose, not against its cost but against the damage the highways would inflict on a beautiful city. "Where is our city headed?" asked one critic, voicing a question widely debated in many metropolises in the late forties.[63]

• Urban Studies Intensified

The intellectual analysis of the metropolis had proceeded without letup during the war and acquired new depth as the decade advanced. Some scholars tabulated census data and other statistics with the hope of discovering the ecology of city growth and decay. Others prepared questionnaires and conducted sampling surveys to determine the class structure of urban communities. Still others, using newer techniques, compiled the findings of probing psychiatric interviews in an endeavor to uncover the sources of friction and cohesion in the metropolis. Many, espousing the objectivity of disengaged scientists, desired only an advance in knowledge and understanding; many others, more consciously participants, earnestly sought answers to the mounting problems of the great cities. Historians and geographers likewise gave increased attention to the cities.

But it was among the sociologists, more than in any other discipline, that the study of the city became a major concern. The demographers and ecologists, despite earlier criticism of their findings, continued their statistical researches confident that by a more precise definition of terms and a finer distinction of categories they could produce reliable formulae. Hope Tisdale advanced this effort by supplying a tidier definition of "The Process of Urbanization" in a widely quoted article published in 1942. Amos H.

Hawley and his student Don J. Bogue were perhaps the leading proponents of the use of ecological data in a social-structure analysis of America's increasingly urban society, and Bogue applied this technique effectively in a comprehensive study, "The Structure of the Metropolitan Community," published in 1950. Yet the progressive disappearance of distinctively different ethnic enclaves or colonies discouraged students trained by Hawley and others in that special field and strengthened the growing conviction that the urban world was basically a mass society.[64]

Some scholars nevertheless discovered enough differences between cities to justify a typological classification. Thus Calvin F. Schmid, in the course of preparing special surveys for Seattle, Minneapolis, and other metropolises, analyzed the social facilities of all major cities under numerous categories in order to rate objectively the communities he surveyed. Robert C. Angell employed a somewhat different statistical approach to measure and rate "The Social Integration of American Cities" and developed an interview technique to determine the "Moral Integration" of four selected cities. Syracuse, which as "Bellview" won top billing under the two studies, was unfortunately little impressed, partly, perhaps, because the high spirits engendered at the start of its postwar planning venture had been dissipated by its collapse.[65]

Some sociologists, influenced by recent anthropological studies of primitive communities, criticized the ecologists for a neglect of the historical or time dimension in their analysis. The wide contrasts between their approaches discouraged efforts to combine the two schools for a study of historical sociology, but increased knowledge of the resident surveys and interview techniques of the anthropologists stimulated some sociologists to explore another community dimension, that of social class. W. Lloyd Warner, experienced in anthropological research among the Australian aborigines, led his team of interviewers into Newburyport in the 1930's. The publication in 1941 of the first volume of the Yankee City series, *Social Life in a Modern Community,* by Warner and Paul E. Lunt, focused attention on class stratification in American cities and launched a new school of urban studies.[66]

The class analysis was not, of course, new, but the six-layered stratification was original and proved intriguing. Few scholarly students elsewhere detected the same divisions, yet numerous writers for the popular journals seized upon the analysis for surveys and stories, and many social evenings in parlors and on back porches throughout the land were devoted to the fascinating question of who belonged to the Upper Uppers, the Lower Uppers, and so on down the scale. Readers and reviewers of current and recent novels found a new standard of judgment, that of placing the various fictional characters in their proper stratification, and some writers rose to the occasion and produced books, such as *The Proper Bostonians* and, a few years later, *The Philadelphia Gentlemen,* that conformed closely to the analysis.[67]

The Warner school aroused criticism as well as emulation. Among sociologists, Pitirin A. Sorokin of Harvard, whose study of "Social Mobility" pointed in the opposite direction, enlisted support in an attack on the rigidities of the class-structure thesis. Yet many sociological teams, though often assured that no classes existed in the towns of their choice, soon found enough evidence to persuade them that important divisions existed and could with due effort be delineated. Warner, however, felt the need to refine his original ranking technique before the decade closed, taking advantage of some of the findings of August B. Hollingshead's study of *Elmtown's Youth*.[68] Other students devised additional ranking devices, and one team compiled an "Occupational Prestige Scale," rating ninety different types of employment from shoeshiners up to Supreme Court justices. Although their failure to reach agreement on the proper criteria of judgment cast doubt on the analysis, enough evidence was amassed to challenge the American "myth" of democratic equality.[69]

What it all signified was not clear. Some critics charged that the Warner school was creating a new and more stultifying myth of a class-bound society. Others, including the youthful C. Wright Mills, turned to the study of power groups, an approach destined to attract many followers in the next decade. In one study Mills depicted the American labor leader as "The New Man of Power," spurring further research in that field. Meanwhile his findings in another study on the origins of the American business elite,

Empire State Building under construction, 1930. Its partially completed state, with work progressing on the middle stories, is symbolic of the growth of American cities.

Empire State Building, 1931.

Jobless men on park bench in New York, 1930.

Photographs by Lewis Hine. Courtesy George Eastman House, Rochester, New York

President Roosevelt and Mayor LaGuardia in the late 1930's. *Courtesy USIA*

Meeting of the Workers Alliance Unemployed Council, 1937. *Photograph by Lewis Hine. Courtesy George Eastman House*

The United States Conference of Mayors, first panel of officers, February 17, 1933. From left: Mayor James M. Curley of Boston, Mayor Frank Murphy of Detroit, President, Mayor William Anderson of Minneapolis, Mayor Daniel Hoan of Milwaukee, and two delegates. *Courtesy Milwaukee County Historical Society*

Public Administration Center Building, 1313 East 60th Street, Chicago, opened in April 1938. The 13 national and international civic organizations that occupied this headquarters at the start have grown to 20 and a wing was added in 1962. *Courtesy International City Managers Association*

Groundbreaking ceremony, new Headquarters Building, 1313 East 60th Street, Chicago, January 1937. Front row from left, Louis Brownlow, Director of Public Administration Clearing House, Robert M. Hutchens, President of the University of Chicago, Clifford W. Ham, Executive Director, American Municipal Association, Charles E. Ridley, Executive Director, City Manager Association, Henry W. Toll, Executive Director, Council of State Governments. *Courtesy International City Managers Association*

Rush-hour traffic on 17th Street at Constitution Avenue in Washington, D.C., November 1945. *Wide World Photo*

Rush-hour traffic entering Brooklyn-Battery Tunnel leading to downtown Manhattan, January 1966. *Wide World Photo*

Eastern Expressway and Outer Loop Interchanges on outskirts of Rochester, N.Y., 1965. *Wahl's Photo Services, Pittsford, N.Y.*

Rockefeller Center, built 1930–39, comprised 15 buildings ranging in height up to the 70-story RCA Building. It occupied 12½ acres between 48th and 52nd Streets and fronted on Fifth Avenue.

Open space in congested metropolis. The Channel gardens and fountains and the sunken plaza or skating rink provided America's most exciting urban space. *Photographs courtesy Rockefeller Center*

View from Rockefeller Center Observation Roof atop the RCA Building in the 1940's. The Queen Mary is steaming up the Hudson to its berth. Spectacular views of metropolitan landscapes first became a common experience for urbanites in the 1920's.

Aerial view of upper Manhattan, 1956. *Courtesy Rockefeller Center*

Capitol Hill in Nashville before redevelopment, late 1930's.

Capitol Hill Project, Nashville, Tennessee, after completion in the 1950's.
Photographs courtesy Department of Housing and Urban Development

Harold S. Buttenheim, 1953, editor and publisher of *The American City. Courtesy* THE AMERICAN CITY

Luther Gulick, Columbia professor, author, city administrator of New York, 1954–56. *Courtesy Institute of Public Administration*

Clarence A. Dykstra, right, City Manager of Cincinnati and President of the National Municipal League, 1939, chatting with delegates at the convention in Indianapolis. *Courtesy National Municipal League*

Thomas H. Reed, Lieutenant Governor Frank C. Moore of New York, and Horace H. Edwards, City Manager of Richmond, at speakers' table at National Municipal League convention. *Courtesy National Municipal League*

Mayor LaGuardia, Clarence Stein and Frederick G. Frost in February 1941.
As president of the New York Chapter of the AIA, Frost is presenting the
Mayor with the Certificate of an Honorary Associate at the Chapter's 84th
annual dinner at which Mr. Stein received its Medal of Honor. *Courtesy
New York Chapter of the American Institute of Architects*

Central Business Mall, Kalamazoo, Michigan, late 1950's. *Courtesy
John M. Olin Research Library*

President Truman signing the National Housing Act, July 15, 1949. Looking on, left to right, Senators Burnet Maybank of South Carolina, Ralph Flanders of Vermont, and John Sparkman of Alabama, and Housing Administrator Raymond Faby. *Courtesy National Archives*

Past Presidents of the National Municipal League. Left to right, William Collins, 1960–62; Cecil Morgan, 1956–58; George H. Gallup, 1954–56; Richard S. Childs, 1927–31; and Alfred E. Driscoll, former Governor of New Jersey, being congratulated on his election as President of the League in 1962. *Courtesy National Municipal League*

The Pittsburgh Triangle area before redevelopment, 1940's. *Courtesy Department of Housing and Urban Development*

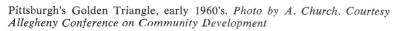

Pittsburgh's Golden Triangle, early 1960's. *Photo by A. Church. Courtesy Allegheny Conference on Community Development*

Hartford slum area before redevelopment. *Courtesy Department of Housing and Urban Development*

Hartford's Constitution Plaza after redevelopment in the mid-1960's. *Courtesy Department of Housing and Urban Development*

Oak Street area, New Haven, before redevelopment, early 1950's. *Courtesy Department of Housing and Urban Development*

Oak Street Redevelopment in process, 1966. *Courtesy Department of Housing and Urban Development*

President Kennedy receiving the report of the Committee on Juvenile Delinquency, May 31, 1962. The President flanked on his right by Mayor Wagner
of New York City and on his left by Senator Ribicoff of Connecticut. *Photo
by Abbie Rowe. Courtesy National Park Service, U.S. Department of the
Interior*

Mayor Richardson Dilworth, left, and Planning Director Edmund N. Bacon
on a radio program answering citizen questions concerning redevelopment
plans for Philadelphia. *Courtesy School District of Philadelphia*

Philadelphia's Washington Square, before rehabilitation. *Courtesy Department of Housing and Urban Development*

Washington Square, after rehabilitation. *Courtesy Department of Housing and Urban Development*

Gateway Redevelopment in Minneapolis, before and after views.

Photographs courtesy Housing and Redevelopment Authority of Minneapolis

President Johnson presenting a pen to Mayor Richard Lee of New Haven at the signing of the Housing and Development Act of 1965. *Courtesy Department of Housing and Urban Development*

Secretary Weaver and Vice-President Humphrey laying the cornerstone of the new HUD Headquarters Building in Washington, November 1966. *Courtesy Department of Housing and Urban Development*

March on Washington, August 28, 1963. Representative leaders of the organizations sponsoring the march may be seen with arms linked in the foreground. *Associated Press Wirephoto*

President Kennedy welcoming Leaders of the March on Washington at the White House. Left to right: Whitney Young, Jr., of the National Urban League; the Rev. Martin Luther King, Jr., Southern Christian Leadership Conference; John Lewis (face partially hidden), Student Non-Violent Coordinating Committee; Rabbi Joachim Prinz, American Jewish Congress; Dr. Eugene Carson Blake, National Council of Churches; A. Philip Randolph, AFL-CIO Vice-President; President Kennedy; Walter Reuther, United Automobile Workers; Vice-President Lyndon Johnson (in rear); Roy Wilkins, NAACP. *Associated Press Wirephoto*

Riot scenes in Rochester, New York. A proud and prosperous city, Rochester suddenly found itself a symbol of Negro revolt in the hot summer of 1964. *Photographs courtesy Gannett Press*

Hearing on the Issues of the Poor, 1966. Two years after the riots Rochester's antipoverty agency, Action for a Better Community, conducted hearings at which, on this occasion, leaders of FIGHT (Freedom, Integration, God, Honor, and Today) registered complaints. *Courtesy David A. Anderson of ABC*

Urban Renewal Projects in Washington. Capital Hill Twin Towers, above, completed in spring of 1963, 160 units. Capital Park Town Houses, below, summer 1963. *Photographs courtesy District of Columbia Redevelopment Land Agency*

Fresno Shopping Mall, an Urban Renewal project in a small-city business district. *Courtesy Department of Housing and Urban Development*

Rochester's Midtown Plaza Mall, 1962, constructed by two downtown department stores and housing thirty other commercial and community enterprises. *Courtesy Midtown Plaza*

St. Francis Square Renewal Project, San Francisco. *Courtesy Department of Housing and Urban Development*

First contingent of 600 new stainless steel cars acquired in September 1964 by the New York City Transit Authority. *Courtesy New York City Transit Authority*

The 15-story Heron House as seen from the terrace of a nearby town house. *Photographs by William A. Graham. Courtesy Reston Executive Office*

Town houses in Reston. *Photographs by William A. Graham. Courtesy Reston Executive Office*

President Johnson giving pen used in signing the Demonstration Cities Act in 1966 to Mayor Cavanaugh of Detroit. Vice-President Humphrey, former mayor of Minneapolis, and Mayor James H. S. Tate of Philadelphia attended this ceremony on November 3, 1966. *Courtesy the White House*

Senator Abraham A. Ribicoff's Subcommittee conducting the first full scale Senate hearings on the housing problems of cities. Senators Javits and Kennedy also attended most of the sessions. *Courtesy Senator Ribicoff's office*

prompted the economic historian William Miller to castigate the democratic assumptions of the entire school of American historians.[70]

While the profession as a whole remained unaware of the charge and indifferent to urban researches, a scattered group of historians continued the study of selected cities. More than a half dozen books appeared during the forties, full-length biographies of Milwaukee and Naugatuck, and period studies of the history of Charleston, Detroit, and Nashville as well as of Chicago, Baltimore, and Rochester. Duly warned of "The Dangers of an Urban Interpretation of History," none of them ventured to propound universal formulae of urbanization. Attacked as a result for their lack of conceptualization, as well as for their narrative approach, these scholars nevertheless demonstrated the separate identity and continuity of the urban communities they studied and brought the rise of the city and its problems into clearer historical perspective. Several comparative treatments of two or more cities explored intercity relationships neglected by other scholars and with a number of suggestive essays contributed to a fuller understanding of the emerging metropolitan society.[71]

Among the other social sciences only the economic geographers gave thought to an analysis of the city during the forties. Political scientists, absorbed with the problems of the metropolis, were little interested in theory, and few even took note of the challenge some urban sociologists were posing to their conception of democracy. Most economists, too, were preoccupied with other matters, but a number of economic geographers saw the rich possibilities of urban research. Chauncey D. Harris prepared "A Functional Classification of Cities in the U.S.," separating the 377 places of over 25,000 in 1930 into eight categories on the basis of occupation and employment. Robert E. Dickinson of England published a study of metropolitan regionalism in America that won close attention from regional planners. Rupert B. Vance and Nadia Danielevsky combined the demographic and geographic approaches in their monumental study of the character and migrations of the people of the South who were increasingly displacing the immigrant as the major source for expanding cities.[72]

As the study of the complexities of urban society progressed, some scholars made an effort to apply psychoanalytical techniques to the problem. John Dollard had the advantage of analytical training to aid in his researches for a pioneer study of *Caste and Class in a Southern Town,* and both August Hollingshead and Robert Faris endeavored to use these techniques in their urban researches. Several articles on delinquency and emotional break-downs in cities reported psychoanalytical case studies during the forties, and although their findings were not conclusive they proved sufficiently suggestive to encourage other scholars to project a further use of this method.[73]

The objective of most of these studies was a fuller understanding of the metropolis and of the broader urban society. The fact that few scholars, even within a single discipline, reached mutually supporting conclusions was disappointing to many. Yet this very diversity was symbolic of the plural character of the metropolis itself. At least the mounting scholarly interest spurred other more practical professionals to tackle special aspects of the metropolitan problem.

The social workers, whose professional training included in-creasing draughts of sociology, psychology, and other social sci-ences, began to view their problems in more academic terms. Many undertook research projects of their own, hoping to increase their understanding as well as improve their effectiveness on the job. Schools of Social Work fostered this development by establishing graduate departments to promote advanced study by workers in the field. In keeping with the division of responsibility worked out with the federal government during the New Deal, most community agencies specialized increasingly in the treatment of disadvantaged individuals, and both private and public agencies sought case-workers with some psychiatric training. The schools responded to this demand and the social-work journals gave it major attention. Yet the need for group workers in the juvenile field was not neg-lected, and the revival of the social-center movement in a few cities prompted articles and books on this subject too. Perhaps the most significant was Saul D. Alinsky's *Reveille for Radicals* in which he described his efforts to organize the Back of the Yards neighborhood in Chicago by encouraging its immigrant residents to assume full charge of their own welfare.[74]

Alinsky reflected or had an affinity with the power-structure theories of C. Wright Mills—both in fact had a common parentage in the struggle of organized labor for power under the New Deal. The Back of the Yards movement, like some other strongly organized neighborhoods, took as one of its objectives the exclusion of Negroes. As noted above, Reginald Isaacs attacked this discriminatory aspect of the community-center movement with great vigor, winning support from the NAACP and from CORE, the newly formed Committee on Racial Equality organized in 1942 by William Farmer and others. Several able Negroes wrote books dealing with racial segregation in the cities. But the most effective analysis was by Gunnar Myrdal, a Scandinavian scholar whose broad treatment of the *American Dilemma* questioned the Warner thesis of a class-structured society as an overstatement of socioeconomic differences. After reviewing a multitude of discriminatory practices, he found the Negro's greatest opportunity for advancement to lie in the cities. His moving account impelled readers to recognize that "the American Negroes, like the whites, are under the spell of the great national suggestion" of a land of opportunity.[75]

That viewpoint was of importance to planners, but in the forties they were concerned—at least the articulate ones—with a still more fundamental question, the purpose and character of the metropolis. Architects as well as planners participated in the discussions—several newcomers from abroad as well as old and new voices at home. Princeton established a new Bureau of Urban Research in 1941, joining several other universities in this respect, and excitement mounted at Harvard where Joseph Hudnut, the new dean of the School of Architecture, had brought Walter Gropius and Marcel Breuer from abroad to enrich his faculty in the late thirties. Mies van der Rohe from Germany became head of an architectural school in Illinois, and other European architect-planners, some of whom had arrived earlier, found a secure place in America. Several wrote books, including *Can Our Cities Survive?* by José Luis Sert, *The City* by Eliel Saarinen, and most notable of all, *Space, Time and Architecture* by Sigfried Giedion, an elaboration of a series of lectures he gave at Harvard in the late thirties. Several of these foreign-born architects received important commissions and with their students won a wide acceptance for the international style of architecture, effectively challenging the old classical and Victorian designs in urban construction.[76]

It remained for Americans to assess these contributions and to relate them to the planning needs of their expanding metropolises. Lewis Mumford's voice became familiar to thousands of radio listeners and his exciting assessments of the architectural merits of new buildings in New York, published in occasional "Sky Line" articles in *The New Yorker,* commanded wide attention. Though frequently devastating in his criticisms, he sometimes found occasion to praise, as in his two articles on the Fresh Meadows development opened in Queens in 1949. Built for the New York Life Insurance Company by Voorhees, Walker, Foley, and Smith, it not only contrasted with the Stuyvesant Town project of the Metropolitan Life Insurance Company, in both physical amenities and density, but won Mumford's praise as a fine example of large-scale community planning.[77]

Even Mumford's standards and preferences were subjected to analysis and criticism in a provocative book, *Communitas,* by Percival and Paul Goodman. Starting with a sketchy review of the leading architectural schools, the Goodman brothers, one an architect and one a literary critic, caustically assessed the merits of the garden-city designs, the cities planned for industrial efficiency, and the noncity of the Frank Lloyd Wright school. After demolishing them all, the Goodmans proposed three alternative plans of their own, one designed for efficient consumption, one for a minimum of regulation and security, and one that merged production with consumption, creativity with enjoyment, means with ends, in a spontaneous, diversified and yet harmonious community that obviously won their highest favor. Most readers recognized the alternatives and the whole presentation as fantastic if not preposterous, and yet in the late 1940's metropolitan trends and indeed the civilization they were producing seemed, in the opinion of David Riesman, to call for some such imaginative overhauling.[78] Unfortunately the planners to whom he looked for creative leadership succeeded only in raising new questions, and the first attempts to draw the varied scholarly analyses together produced at best only a kaleidoscopic view of metropolitan dilemmas.[79]

5. THE METROPOLIS AND THE "ESTABLISHMENT" IN THE 1950's

Editor Buttenheim invited a panel of experts to contribute brief articles for his mid-century issue of the *American City*. Unlike the previous fin-de-siècle, when many writers looked back to measure the century's accomplishments, these civic leaders in 1950 peered ahead to gauge the prospects for their programs. All the old problems remained, they reported; many indeed had become more pressing and patently more complicated. Perhaps the chief advance, as this symposium revealed, was the wide recognition of that complexity. Several of the contributors hopefully predicted an ultimate triumph for their favorite causes—home rule for cities, council-manager charters, governmental reorganization, fair apportionment, fiscal self-sufficiency, equal civil rights, better housing for all—but few of these embattled reformers could overlook the obstructions presented by uncooperative state legislatures, jealous local rivals, ethnic and racial hostilities, and an increasing array of other social and economic problems.[1]

Missing from that panel were the sociologists whose concepts of an urban mass society, whether governed by natural laws or by a stratified power structure, had failed to impress Buttenheim as relevant. As the decade advanced, however, the question of power and who should or would wield it became increasingly crucial, though not in the sense assumed by most sociologists. Edmund R.

Purves, executive director of the American Institute of Architects, observed "a fading away of the states," as the municipal and federal governments increased in importance, and predicted a co-operative union of these two vital centers of power. Although many urban leaders shared that expectation, several unforeseen developments soon made it appear less likely. Thus, when the federal government, under a new administration after 1952, displayed great reluctance in exercising its power, the leaders of many dynamic metropolises were impelled to restudy their positions.[2]

• *Metropolitan Revival in the Early Fifties*

Yet if, as the decade advanced, the awesome responsibilities of leadership obscured some of the attractions of the exercise of power, many cities experienced a rebirth of vitality and confidence in the early fifties. The U.S. Census brought assurance to most towns as their quickened growth rates dispelled lingering fears of stagnation. Even the great metropolises, whose central cities showed few gains, could take pride in the surprising increases of their broader regions, now for the first time designated as Standard Metropolitan Areas. Only a half dozen central cities, such as Scranton in Pennsylvania and Lowell in Massachusetts, had suffered a loss in population in the forties, and only in depressed industrial areas, such as the Pennsylvania coal fields, were the losses so severe and so persistent as to pull their metropolitan totals down in 1950 and again in 1960. The great majority of cities experienced a surge of growth that continued throughout the fifties, boosting the urban percentage to 64 in 1950 and to 69.9 by 1960. The proportion living in metropolitan areas likewise climbed to 56.8 and 62.9 per cent, respectively, at these dates as more than four-fifths of the country's gains accrued to its metropolises.[3]

But the number of urban places was likewise increasing and at an accelerating rate in all urban categories except the largest. The group of cities with populations over a million was limited to the five that had annexed sufficient territory at an early date. That limit did not hold for the metropolitan districts of course, and here the ranks of those over a million swelled from 11 in 1940 to 14 and 23 in the next two decades. Several ambitious core cities, especially in the South and the West, greatly expanded their territories—Dallas and Fort Worth in the forties, Atlanta, Houston, and Oklahoma City among others in the fifties.[4] But the annexation drive, though pressed with new vigor in the fifties, when 17 central cities added over 40 square miles each, did not keep pace with the birth of new towns. Most of the 507 new incorporations of the forties and the 943 of the fifties, over half in each group under 1000 in population were formed within or on the borders of metropolitan districts and presented new checks on the expansion of the core cities and new obstacles to the advocates of metropolitan consolidation.[5]

The rapidity of this metropolitan growth reflected a continuing migration from rural to urban areas and a renewed influx from abroad. Northern cities as before drew large numbers from the South, including almost 1.5 million Negroes, many of them from its cities, which in turn attracted replacements, plus a modest increment, from their rural hinterlands. Most of these Southern newcomers to Northern cities, and now to several large Western cities as well, settled in their aging central districts, more than doubling the nonwhite populations of a half-dozen major metropolises and speeding the migration of their earlier residents to the suburbs. The total population of the 212 central cities of 1960 showed an increase of 5.6 million during the decade, but most of it was the result of annexations that absorbed 4,851,483 suburbanites who were predominantly white. The nonwhite gains of the central cities, though slow in the largest Southern towns and in a few elsewhere, added 30 per cent or more in 36 of the 50 leading metropolises and raised their total to over 10 million, nearly a fifth of the 112,885,193 residents of the 212 Standard Metropolitan Statistical Areas as redefined in 1960. The suburban population, whose territory was greatly enlarged despite sizable losses to the cities, swelled in number from 36.9 million to 54.8 million in this decade and exceeded the central cities in many places, particularly in the Northeast.[6]

The dynamic but uneven quality of this urban growth upset many statistical assumptions and forced a reappraisal of most plans. Prognostications based on the 1940 Census had to be discarded as the wartime increase in birth rates persisted and the urban migration accelerated. The tensions of the cold war and the outbreak of hostilities in Korea in 1950, by reviving the draft calls and flooding many cities with new munitions contracts, accentuated both trends. Moreover, as these basic national policies tended indirectly to promote urban growth in general, the administration, by its placement of orders and distribution of functions, again pushed selected cities to the fore. San Diego, Miami, and Fort Worth, the most rapidly growing metropolises of the forties, made striking new advances in the fifties, while rising new towns, such as Phoenix and Fort Lauderdale, broke into the metropolitan ranks with high population gains based in part on war orders.[7]

The escalation of fighting in Korea had other effects on urban trends. Not only were idle munitions factories brought back into use and other plants pressed to increase their production in face of a tightening labor market that speeded automation, but civil defense again became a major concern and also a subject of controversy between city, state, and federal authorities. Renewed restrictions and priorities on materials and construction checked the building programs already launched in some metropolises and intensified the demand of many municipal leaders that the federal government's outlays, on highways, for example, be more equitably shared with the cities where congestion was most acute.[8]

Fear of an atomic attack by Russia heightened tension over civil defense. Metropolitan leaders protested when the Civil Defense Administration adopted a policy of working through the states, rather than directly with the cities. They deplored the easy recommendation, coming from several state capitals, that urban functions should be dispersed; they resented official directives concerning the type of air-raid shelters to be provided by the cities at their own expense. Civil defense was a federal responsibility, the Conference of Mayors maintained. When in 1951 Congress, responding finally to local demands, voted $31.7 million for this purpose, if matched by the states, Mayor Lawrence of Pittsburgh protested, as chairman of the Conference, that the appropriation was hopelessly inadequate; the cities, he declared, will need "at least $600 million" to do the job properly. They did not get it, however, and few responsible officials, local, state, or national, were satisfied with the shelters and other safety measures provided during the next few years. As a result, this mounting concern added to the pressure for a review of the relationship between the cities and the federal government.[9]

Civil defense was only one of several problems calling for a reassignment of responsibilities. After a review in 1951 of the federal services available to cities and towns, the American Municipal Association emphasized the urgent need for increased federal assistance in building urban highways, expanding metropolitan airports, combating air and water pollution, developing park and recreational facilities, and promoting public health and education. To document the need, editor Buttenheim distributed a questionnaire in which he posed various aspects of a leading question: "Is local government getting a square deal?" Yet many of his respondents agreed with Mayor William F. Devin of Seattle, who called for widespread efforts to halt and reverse the trend toward national control of municipal functions. A few months later the Conference of Mayors strongly recommended the formation of a commission to study intergovernmental relations.[10]

Despite or perhaps because of the general concern with the Korean crisis, several new federal-city relationships developed. In an expansion of its coverage, the Social Security Administration took municipal employees under its care in 1950, relieving each city's fiscal burdens in the process. In similar fashion the federal government's promotion of hospital construction under the Hill-Burton Act acquired new momentum and authorized construction at 766 such institutions in 1951, almost as many as had received aid in the previous five years of its operation. An alert municipal leader could often procure assistance from many sources, as City Manager L. P. Cookingham of Kansas City did in the wake of the great flood that ravaged that metropolis in July 1951. In addition to the emergency aid he mustered from thirty-two federal agencies during the height of the crisis, he secured the promise of a two-thirds reimbursement on the city's outlay of $1.4 million for the rehabilitation of its municipal services. Even this assistance, authorized under Public Law 875, was only a start, Cookingham declared, since the entire nation should assist local communities when stricken by a flood, a drought, or some other natural calamity.[11]

There was, in fact, no letup in the demands of struggling cities for state and federal assistance, but other aspects of the situation took precedence in the early fifties. The federal government, absorbed by the Korean conflict, was increasingly reluctant to assume new local responsibilities. Civic leaders were becoming more and more critical of federal directives and controls, and, with the housing and airport programs launched and other urgent needs at least partially met, many of them turned their attention to the reorganization of local governmental functions.

The shifting emphasis in metropolitan developments had its reflection in national elections. Although Truman, much to the surprise of most observers, had carried all the major cities in 1948, many swung into the Republican column in 1952. These included Newark and Buffalo in the Northeast, Louisville and Miami in the South, and all west of Kansas City. Barely a dozen large cities registered pluralities for Stevenson, and in most cases these were so small that the suburban vote for Eisenhower was sufficient to swing the metropolitan total into his column. Moreover, three of these Democratic strongholds, Baltimore, Milwaukee, and Providence, were to vote Republican in 1956.[12]

This dramatic political shift attracted considerable interest. Among other factors often noted by commentators was the rapid suburban growth, which in Southern and Western metropolises was more frequently reabsorbed through annexation into the city totals and helped to explain their Republican leanings. Many suburban residents, having escaped inner-city problems, were less concerned about federal-urban programs, while responsible civic leaders, many also living in the suburbs, were giving increased attention to varied plans for local reorganization. When President Eisenhower not only promised a relaxation of federal direction but also moved in 1953 to appoint a Commission on Intergovernmental Relations, all factions applauded.[13]

• *Attempts at Metropolitan Reorganization*

One aspect of the resurgent vitality of American cities was the establishment or reactivation of citizen associations and the confidence with which they prepared to tackle community problems. New charter revisions and new schemes for the expansion of municipal boundaries and the reorganization of neighboring jurisdictions enlivened the civic scene in many places. Despite the skepticism of many critics, especially those scholars who sought to identify a power elite, the citizen groups enjoyed an outburst of nonpartisan reform activity that considerably influenced the course of metropolitan developments.

Among the citizen associations, those of Kansas City and Minneapolis vied with the old established leagues or unions of New York, Chicago, and Cleveland. The new Citizens League of Greater Minneapolis, organized in February 1952 after a protracted cam· paign of "fireside" meetings in private homes, enrolled 1000 members within a few months and engaged a full-time director to coordinate its programs. The Detroit league still published its *Civic Searchlight,* and the newly launched *Kansas City Citizen* waged a successful campaign for the annexation of a suburban tract needed to facilitate a planned development of that metropolis.[14]

The quarterly journal of the American Planning and Civic Association featured reports from several of these volunteer organizations in each issue. Although the number of active participants was never very large and even the total membership, which sometimes exceeded 4000 in Minneapolis and Seattle, for example, seemed small when compared with the populations represented, these organizations focused public attention through their newsletters and other publications and their many committee meetings and civic forums, and sometimes they shed new light on urgent community issues. A few groups, notably those of Cincinnati, Kansas City, and Worcester, assumed the responsibility of nominating and conducting campaigns to elect the city officials. Although several of these citizen bodies subsided after a few years, perhaps as a result of a disillusioning defeat, many persisted and two at least celebrated their sixtieth and three their fiftieth anniversaries in this decade. A directory of civic organizations prepared by the American Planning and Civic Association in 1956 filled twelve closely packed pages.[15]

Impressed by the activities of some of these citizen groups, Harold Riegelman credited them in 1956 with taking over the function of leadership in the metropolis. Certainly the challenge was there, because of the fractured nature of metropolitan government, but that task was much too complex and too deeply entangled with rival political, economic, and neighborhood interests to be performed by loosely organized volunteer associations. They did, however, imprint their nonpartisan and good-government doctrines on the civic developments of the decade.[16]

One example of their influence was the revived popularity in this decade of the council-manager form of government. The disadvantages evident in the thirties, when a strong political voice seemed necessary to present a town's case at Washington, had faded as the city-federal relationships became institutionalized, and many new communities now adopted council-manager charters. Their number reached 1000 in December 1950, when Buena Vista received its charter, and approached 1500, well over half of all incorporated places, by July 1958, the fiftieth anniversary of the movement's birth. Most of the new adoptions were by small towns, and Cincinnati remained the largest in the group, but several progressive cities, including Miami and Kansas City, and numerous metropolitan counties were prospering under council-manager charters.[17]

In an effort to secure similar professional skills, several of the largest cities, following an example set by Louisville in 1948, appointed administrative assistants for their mayors. Boston, New York, Philadelphia, Los Angeles, and San Francisco each engaged skilled administrators at one time or another during the fifties. Few observers, however, doubted the superior advantages of a "strong" mayor when a happy choice won election, as occurred in Philadelphia, Pittsburgh, New Orleans, Detroit, St. Louis, Milwaukee, and New Haven in this decade. Yet Mayor Lawrence of

Pittsburgh, like City Manager Cookingham of Kansas City, needed the help of an active citizens' league to reach beyond the city limits and initiate measures of cooperation with the suburbs.[18]

Local efforts to achieve some form of metropolitan coordination multiplied during the fifties. After forthright attempts at city-county merger or federation had failed, at St. Louis and Pittsburgh, for example, these and other core cities experimented with the consolidation of common functions. Even Grand Rapids, with less than 300,000 residents in its entire area, worked out an urban-services district encompassing the suburban townships; Kansas City contracted to supply water to its suburbs as a start toward further metropolitan cooperation. That last announcement prompted a survey of similar practices in other metropolises, which revealed that 36 central cities provided fire protection, that 26 erected and maintained street lamps, that 24 collected garbage, and that 72 gave library services, in some cases free of charge, to residents beyond their borders.[19]

These, of course, were hardly ideal arrangements, either for a city or for its suburbs, and Paul Windel of the New York Regional Plan Association urged the states to create metropolitan-district commissions to promote more satisfactory adjustments, and new-town development boards to regulate their incorporation. California adopted a law in 1953 authorizing the formation of metropolitan service districts in urban counties, and Indiana created a broad urbanized area around Indianapolis in which further incorporations were prohibited without the approval of the city and county planners. Several of the regional planning associations proposed similar measures, but little was accomplished in other metropolises in the early fifties beyond the creation of additional special-function or general-service districts, some of them hastily established in suburban fringe areas, as at Los Angeles, to forestall central-city expansion.[20]

The formation of a metropolitan government at Toronto, in January 1954, revived the languishing movement in the States. All earlier arrangements appeared inadequate when compared with Toronto's provision of a metropolitan council representing the central city and each of its twelve suburbs, with full authority to levy taxes and perform an extended list of common functions. Civic delegations flocked to Toronto, from Seattle and Miami and a host of other places. President Eisenhower's action the previous year in appointing a Commission on Intergovernmental Relations had spurred eighteen states to create similar bodies and prompted Toledo among several other large cities to organize area-study committees to appraise their metropolitan needs.[21]

Another incentive for metropolitan studies came from the planning movement. Several of the delegates at the fiftieth annual meeting of the American Planning and Civic Association at Columbus, in May 1954, decided to form a separate Association of Metropolitan Regional Organizations. Its first convention in Philadelphia that September drew more than a hundred delegates from such bodies in a score of cities, and already its leaders, including Frederick Gutheim, president of the Washington Center of Metropolitan Studies, could report a significant achievement. By timely action they had secured the reinsertion in conference of a provision stricken from the Senate version of the new housing bill, which authorized grants-in-aid totaling $1 million to assist cities in preparing comprehensive plans as a prerequisite for the approval of their urban-renewal projects. The subsequent adoption of that provision assured support for this vital function in properly equipped metropolises.[22]

Everywhere the pressure for metropolitan reorganization was mounting. When the President's Commission on Intergovernmental Relations released its report in 1955, Patrick Healy, Jr., who had succeeded Carl Chatters as executive director of the American Municipal Association the year before, described its recommendations as "sobering." Not only did they call for a reduction of federal grants-in-aid and for "greater self-reliance at local and state levels," but they also urged the states to promote a reorganization of local governmental functions to enable urban communities to meet their responsibilities more effectively.[23] Although the Kestnbaum Commission, as it was popularly designated, did not explicitly endorse metropolitan government, its assertion that "the time is long overdue for a . . . study of the government . . . of metropolitan communities" rekindled the spirits of the metro proponents.[24]

Metropolitan studies multiplied in the late fifties. Several of the commission's fifteen supporting reports dealt with the subject, and the Governors Conference commissioned the Council of State Governments to make a comprehensive study of the governmental problems of metropolitan areas. Four states created commissions to conduct general studies in this field, and several metropolises organized official bodies representing all of their constituent communities to analyze their problems and propose action. These appointed boards and commissions usually engaged a local or national research bureau to conduct the study, as at Birmingham and Sacramento, respectively, or a university, as at St. Louis, Detroit, and Los Angeles. In some cases a citizens' association took the lead in launching a research program that stimulated or grew into an official study, as at Milwaukee. Local municipal leagues performed a similar catalytic service, in Seattle, for example. New organizations, such as Community Studies, Inc., of Kansas City and another with the same name at Dayton, undertook the work elsewhere.[25]

Both local and national foundations supported these studies in specific cities and backed long-range research programs on the problems of metropolitan government at university centers in Michigan, Pennsylvania, and Texas, among several other states. Paul Ylvisaker of the Ford Foundation was an active promoter of these studies. Perhaps the most prolific research institute was that at Los Angeles where the Haynes Foundation backed a series of sixteen studies on metropolitan problems edited by Edwin A. Cottrell and Helen Jones and conducted by the Bureau of Government Research and other appropriate agencies; the last and summary volume by the two editors, on *The Metropolis: Is Integration Possible?* appeared in 1955.[26] By far the most comprehensive metropolitan survey was that of St. Louis, backed by the Ford Foundation and a local trust fund and directed by a joint board created by St. Louis and Washington Universities; its research procedures, devised by Henry J. Schmandt and his associates, as well as its report, edited by John C. Bollens, became the models for other metropolitan surveys.[27]

As most of the reports called for action at both local and state levels, spirited contests erupted in many places. In Miami, where four earlier consolidation moves had been blocked by home-rule

advocates in the surrounding towns, a move by the rapidly growing core city to annex the entire county brought success to a new
effort in 1957 that assured autonomy to all municipalities, but
placed certain common functions under a new metro government
of Miami and Dade County.[28] The first moves for the organization
of metropolitan governments at Seattle, Louisville, and Nashville
met defeat in their suburbs in 1958, and the next year similar
measures lost in the same way at Knoxville and Albuquerque.[29]
Even in Canada, where provincial legislatures made the decision,
as for Toronto, without a local vote, moves in Montreal and Win-
nipeg were delayed by legislative fears of the political consequences.[30]

In several metropolises where earlier attempts at consolidation
had failed, the survey reports recommended more cautious steps
in that direction. After protracted study by research teams and
prestigious citizen bodies in Cleveland and St. Louis, where the
issue had been debated for two full decades, the voters in both
cities and their surrounding towns defeated new metro-district proposals in 1959. The district authority in each case seemed to some
in the cities too limited, and too threatening in the towns, and the
loss of local representatives in the projected small councils was
resented by political factions in all areas, including the Negro
slums.[01] In Seattle, after their first defeat, the reformers offered
and secured the adoption of a metro district with authority only
over the development of trunk sewers and water resources for the
area. The Illinois Metropolitan Area Local Government Services
Commission, created by the legislature to study Chicago's problems, recommended that continued functional integration would be
sufficient for that metropolis.[32]

In several states the municipal authorities had the power to
establish such special-function authorities, and in California urban-
service districts, by mutual agreement without resort to the polls,
and such action continued to relieve the pressure for metropolitan
reorganization in many places. Detroit, benefiting from the long-
range planning of its Regional Planning Commission, established
in 1948, was content to develop an intercounty supervisors' committee to promote cooperation throughout the metropolitan area.

In Milwaukee and Portland, Oregon, and in several other medium-sized metropolises, the recommendations of their study groups never reached the electorate.[33]

Several related developments helped check the drive for metropolitan reorganization. In New York, Philadelphia, and Boston, surrounded as they were by old-established cities, the only hope for area integration lay in the development of regional planning. That possibility had won precedence in several other metropolises, in some of which, notably Pittsburgh and San Francisco, economic-resources studies and area-development commissions seemed more important than governmental reorganization. In many old cities the community leaders were becoming increasingly absorbed with plans for urban renewal and housing, and a scholarly study by Edward C. Banfield and Morton Grodzins, published in 1958 by the American Council to Improve Our Neighborhoods, questioned the expectation that metropolitan government would be able to solve this and other controversial internal problems. Moreover, Congress, unwilling to grant home rule to Washington, could agree in 1959 only to strengthen the official status of the National Capital Metropolitan Conference as an instrument for regional planning.[34]

Interest in regional planning, dampened somewhat in the forties by its limited accomplishments at New York and elsewhere, revived dramatically in the middle fifties. The Philadelphia Citizen Council on City Planning, after reviewing the activities of metropolitan planning organizations in Pittsburgh, Cleveland, Boston, and New York, proposed the formation in 1951 of one for the Philadelphia region. That survey overlooked other regional planning councils, notably those at Washington, San Francisco, Cincinnati, and Detroit, as well as the earlier Regional Planning Federation of Philadelphia's Tri-State District, but the movement continued to lag until 1954, when Frederick Gutheim of Washington took leadership by forming the Association of Metropolitan Regional Organizations. Another year passed before a metropolitan study committee, appointed by the governor and including representatives from Philadelphia's five Pennsylvania counties, formed the nucleus for a regional council; soon it included official delegates from adjoining counties in New Jersey and Delaware.[35]

Other new councils appeared. Mayor Robert F. Wagner launched his New York Metropolitan Regional Council in June 1956 by drawing the chief elective officials of neighboring municipalities and counties together for occasional discussions of common problems. Disagreements abounded, but a three-day conference at Arden House, in September 1957, sponsored by the mayor and three governors, drew 60 officials from New York area communities and gave its Regional Council greater status. Similar councils were formed or revived at Boston, Chicago, Denver, and Minneapolis. In the South, where several large cities had relaxed the pressure for metropolitan reorganization by annexing vast suburban tracts, a few, such as Atlanta and Houston, formed regional councils to plan still wider developments.[36]

Numerous bodies contributed to regional planning at the national capital. These included the National Capital Regional Planning Council, the Washington Regional Conference, the Interstate Commission on the Potomac River Basin, a Joint Congressional Committee on Washington's Metropolitan Problems, a National Capital Metro Conference, and the Washington Center of Metropolitan Studies. In spite of the fact that Washington was now the second most rapidly growing metropolitan area in the country, this multiplicity of planning groups seemed to some a bit excessive, and its presence at the capital may have helped to prompt the suggestion that still another U.S. Council on Metropolitan Problems be created as a research aid to the President to assure him a firm grasp of the metropolitan situation not only in Washington but throughout the country.[37]

• *Urban Renewal and Redevelopment*

The suggestion in 1959 that the President needed a council similar to the Economic Advisory Council to keep him advised on urban affairs represented a complete switch of the viewpoint of the Eisenhower administration at its start and spelled out by his Kestnbaum Commission in 1955. The hope that metropolitan communities could, if properly reorganized, become self-sufficient was never fully tested, for confidence in that policy was lacking from the very beginning. In its argument before the Kestnbaum Commission, the American Municipal Association revived its old demand that the federal government make regular payments to reimburse communities for the nonleviable taxes on federal property within their borders. Increasing national programs made this a major consideration in many cities, and the Conference of Mayors adopted resolutions stressing the need for more revenues if cities were to assume full responsibility for their functions.[38]

Cities in states permitting local income taxes, and where local sales taxes had been authorized, escaped the plight of the great majority chiefly dependent on property taxes. Fourteen states in 1951 granted larger taxing powers to their municipalities; others made a larger and more equitable distribution of grants-in-aid, though most cities continued to pay a much larger portion of the state's taxes than they received in return. New York City, Philadelphia, and a few other large cities boosted the rates of their sales or income taxes to meet mounting needs, but studies balancing that gain against the loss of business concerns and residents fleeing into the suburbs, where they escaped the tax burdens of the metropolis, recommended restraint.[39]

Although committed to a retrenchment policy at the local level, the Eisenhower administration was not able to escape the mounting pressure for federal aid in urban matters. Successive study groups examined the varied needs of the cities: better sanitation, more adequate schoolhouses and recreational facilities, more ample tax resources, as well as governmental reorganization. Each group accepted the President's directives and endeavored to find areas for retrenchment, but the increasing demand among urban delegates for federal assistance could not be suppressed. The White House Conference on Education actually recommended federal assistance in the construction of schools, even in areas not heavily inundated with federal employees and their families. Long before this proposal was implemented, however, the backers of a Federal Water Pollution Control Act secured its adoption and the passage of a $50 million appropriation for use on a matching basis to assist small cities in this field.[40]

Once the Administration's ban on federal grants-in-aid was

broken, a host of programs demanded immediate attention. The federal highway program, calling for the construction of 41,000 miles of superhighways and an expenditure of over $32 billion during a period of thirteen years, was the largest. Not only would a third of this be spent within the borders of the nation's metropolises, but Congress earmarked part of the first appropriation to support the planning of the urban portions of this vast system. Assured of local autonomy, the officials in a dozen cities hastened to submit the plans they had already prepared to correct traffic congestion. The *American City* published several of these model plans, notably those of Kansas City, Wichita, and Columbus, but St. Louis secured the first federal grant for the construction of a part of the Mark Twain Expressway as a section of the Interstate System.[41]

Having accepted the principle of using federal grants-in-aid to promote local efforts, President Eisenhower, in his message to Congress in January 1957, endorsed federal aid for the construction of school buildings and two months later assured the Conference of Mayors that, although he could not grant all they asked, he would not reduce housing programs or curtail urban renewal. His increased interest in the city and its problems was perhaps stimulated by the response he had received from urban leaders for his People to People program the year before. The American Municipal Association had promptly endorsed the movement, and numerous mayors had appointed committees, in Rochester as an example, to develop Sister City alliances with foreign cities.[42]

In spite of this apparent reversal, the President created a Joint Federal-State Action Committee and directed it to seek out and recommend areas of federal action that could properly be returned to the states. After two years of conscientious research this distinguished committee, which included three Cabinet members, the director of the Bureau of the Budget, and ten state governors, recommended the transfer to the states of only two relatively minor federal programs, one of them providing grants-in-aid for cities to construct waste-treatment plants. Although the committee also proposed a diversion of part of the federal tax on local telephone calls, sufficient to cover the added cost to the states, and the President strongly endorsed the recommendations, Congress refused to move them from committee.[43]

Eisenhower, however, was not ready to abandon his objective of limiting the federal government "to its proper role" as he saw it. In 1958 he vetoed a bill granting increased aid to depressed areas and proposed cuts in the water and sewer aid programs. But Congress in turn then moved ahead of the Administration in its support of local programs and even included libraries (in small towns and rural areas); Congress considerably extended its aid to municipal airports and established seven regional headquarters and twenty-four district offices to expedite the development of this joint municipal and national program. Although the debate over aid for schools continued, the widespread spectacle of local districts voting down bond issues for new schools, while their enrollments mounted, convinced many congressmen as well as responsible civic leaders that "City problems have transcended municipal capacities," as the editor of the *Municipal Year Book* phrased it, and required federal action.[44]

By the late fifties urban redevelopment and public housing were major fields of federal action, but these programs had faced strong opposition at the opening of the decade. Opponents of public housing had rallied after the passage of the 1949 Act and petitioned Congress to terminate or reduce appropriations for these programs. With new housing starts at a record high in 1950 and holding close to that figure the next year, the need for public housing had disappeared, many home builders argued. "Practically all the new homes are built for sale at high prices," replied John D. Lange, executive director of the National Association of Housing Officials, "and the needs of the poor and even of middle-class renters are neglected." Since most of the new housing starts were in the suburbs, the Conference of Mayors, whose leaders were chiefly from the central cities, maintained its earlier support for urban redevelopment and public housing. The appropriations, it resolved in 1953, should be increased rather than diminished.[45]

Yet many congressmen were undecided. The dramatic start several private redevelopment projects were making at mid-century seemed to offer a free-enterprise solution. The attack in Pittsburgh on a wretched industrial slum and the construction in its place of its Golden Triangle was probably the most spectacular of several privately sponsored projects in Boston and Baltimore, Cincinnati and Chicago, to name only a few. Several economic-base studies by local bureaus reported the presence of strong regenerative forces —in Milwaukee and Detroit, among other dynamic cities. But, as these reports suggested, the leaders of the more promising redevelopment corporations, in Pittsburgh and Cincinnati, for example, worked closely with their mayors and launched their projects in full collaboration with major municipal improvement programs. Moreover, they desired official aid in assembling large parcels of land through condemnation proceedings, and they welcomed federal assistance in writing down the cost of such land.[46]

Torn between contending forces, Congress continued the housing program but included additional funds to encourage nonprofit corporations to build rental housing for veterans and other middle-income families. The organization of a National Association of Housing Cooperatives, with members from 175 such groups, reflected the vigor of this movement. Most of the locally established housing authorities had or promptly acquired redevelopment powers, and 32 of them applied for and secured federal approval of slum-clearance projects in 1951.[47]

That step, of course, was only the beginning, for every project faced local obstacles and delays that sometimes stretched into years. Political controversies over the selection of redevelopment areas and legal actions to forestall condemnation proceedings often consumed many months, as did the preparation of architectural plans, which now required the approval of the residents involved. Strong neighborhood associations, such as those in Cleveland and Kansas City, could sponsor or block proposed projects, and that possibility created a new incentive for the formation of these groups —a boon for local democracy if not always for the project designers. Finally, the search for a suitable developer and the negotiation of the contract consumed additional time.[48]

The most difficult problem, however, was that of finding homes for the displaced families. This task, mandated by the 1949 Act as a result of the unfortunate experiences of some cities with earlier housing developments, had become more formidable as the slum-clearance operations reached into Negro areas, as they did at Chicago, Detroit, and several other cities in the early fifties. Fear of an invasion by families displaced by redevelopment projects turned many residents of other districts against such programs and often deferred, if it did not finally obstruct, action.[49]

Nevertheless, a few cities pressed ahead and achieved promising beginnings. Philadelphia was the first to reach the construction stage under the 1949 Act with a 174-unit housing project in its East Poplar area. San Francisco soon started its much larger and more prolonged Diamond Heights redevelopment. Newark, with an aggressive director of its housing program and a responsive mayor, quickly launched one of the most active redevelopment programs in the country and won the cooperation of local and out-of-town promoters in a long-range effort to rejuvenate the inner city. Boston and St. Louis, Cincinnati and Providence, also made early starts.[50]

Mounting protests from many displaced residents soon prompted a closer look at these projects. It became apparent that the chief advantage in several instances had gone to the developers or to the commercial interests that acquired the cleared land, and not to the former inhabitants. Each city as a whole had benefited from redevelopment, but old communities had been disrupted and, if white, scattered throughout the metropolis or, if colored, crowded into other depressed areas. Catherine Bauer, writing in 1953 on "Redevelopment: A Misfit in the Fifties," refused to assess blame. Along with many others she had failed to anticipate the proportions of the housing shortage that had plagued inner-city residents since the close of the war. Although the 1949 Act contained authorization for development projects in open areas near the city center, the emphasis everywhere had been on slum clearance; moreover, despite their slow progress, some clearance projects had aggravated the housing shortage before adequate accommodations were provided elsewhere.[51]

Something more was needed to move the program into high gear and to safeguard the welfare of the residents for whom it was devised. Miss Bauer among others urged a broader approach, one that would take the entire community into consideration in order to plan a proper resettlement of the slum dwellers. The President in his 1954 message declared, "We shall take steps to insure that families of minority groups displaced by urban redevelopment operations have an opportunity to acquire adequate housing." The Act adopted that year sought to meet this and other objectives by its requirement that "a Workable Program," showing among other plans detailed arrangements for resettlement, be submitted before a new project was approved. It also provided funds for a new type of housing reform, called urban renewal, based on the Baltimore plan of upgrading sound houses and replacing only the most dilapidated in a concerted drive to renew an entire blighted area.[52]

The new law prescribed more exacting standards for local housing and renewal projects. Despite President Eisenhower's opposition in principle to an extension of federal intervention, both the housing and renewal administrations opened six regional offices to supervise these programs. Their staffs, however, were modest, for this was chiefly a local responsibility, the President maintained, and the numerous city authorities as well as the reform associations preferred to keep it decentralized. One of the established procedures was to call for a revision of the housing code, and several mayors made this their first objective before applying for a renewal program. The recently organized American Council to Improve Our Neighborhoods (ACTION) stressed this and other remedial efforts and endeavored to rally civic support for demonstration projects, notably one at Cleveland. By the end of the first year 76 cities had submitted and secured federal approval of Workable Programs under the new law. This brought the total of slum-clearance projects authorized under the 1949 and 1954 Acts to 340 in 218 cities. Demolition had started at 216 projects involving 108,000 substandard dwellings on 8,000 slum acres, but redevelopment was substantially completed only at relatively minor sites in nine cities.[53]

Since none of these new projects moved very rapidly, the American Municipal Association joined with ACTION in organizing a Community Improvement Clinic at St. Louis in July 1956 to expedite the work. That first clinic assembled officials from 55

Midwestern cities for a two-day discussion of their problems with the federal administrators. "City officials must take a bolder approach," declared Albert Cole, head of the renewal office, at a similar gathering a few months later, and he hastened to commend the pioneer work in upgrading blighted districts at Baltimore, Milwaukee, and Detroit. ACTION staged several additional clinics, one at Dayton; local housing associations and development commissions also undertook new housing surveys and economic-base studies to assist the officials of their cities in preparing Workable Programs. The Conference of Mayors sought and helped to secure two additional appropriations from Congress, increasing the urban-renewal fund to $1.35 billion by 1958, when slum-clearance or urban-renewal projects were under way in 221 cities.[54]

No city made a more vigorous attack on its problems than New Haven. Mayor Richard C. Lee, who had won his election in 1953 with a pledge to attack the city's slums, soon formed a Citizens Action Commission to assist in promoting that effort. He pressed successfully for local and national approval of a succession of slum-clearance and renewal projects that placed this small New England city sixth in the amount of federal grants authorized by the close of 1958 and first in per capita outlays. If some of the carefully prepared Workable Programs were blocked or permitted to lapse in other cities after federal approval had been granted, that was not the case in New Haven. Mayor Lee acquired a reputation for forthright action and pushed the work of relocation and demolition with such rapidity that he had a vast area near the heart of the city ready for reconstruction and promising plans for its development by the close of the decade.[55]

Although no other city matched New Haven's accomplishments, several made considerable progress in their attacks on the slums and some had more redevelopments completed. In volume of work completed and under way, New York and Chicago held a decisive lead by the close of the decade, yet a dozen other metropolises had spent more per person, with Norfolk and Washington itself pressing closest to New Haven's record in that respect. New applications were calling for a larger commitment of funds than Congress had yet authorized, but the actual expenditures remained small as efforts to speed up the work faltered. Objections from those displaced had measurably declined after the Act of 1956 authorized payments to cover the moving expenses and other losses of dislodged persons and firms. Administrative adjustments removed some other objections, and, although several remained, the Urban Land Institute proclaimed the renewal program in 1958 "the federal government's most significant and ambitious response . . . to the crisis of urbanism." [56]

Yet many of its staunchest friends realized that the urban-renewal projects had serious limitations and were producing some unfortunate results. The dislocation of old neighborhoods could in part be compensated for by developing carefully planned new communities, as in Cleveland's Longwood Redevelopment project. But the number of well-designed projects, either public or private, was limited, and debate continued over the respective merits of high- and low-rise apartments. Even when a satisfactory balance was achieved between density, living space, and rental values, with perhaps a measure of architectural distinction, as achieved in the Capitol Park Apartments in Washington, few if any of the former residents were able to enjoy it. And if some had found more suitable accommodations than before, many had been pushed into other wretched quarters which their numbers helped to depress. Neither the wider planning of the Workable Programs nor the rehabilitation of blighted areas had as yet fully corrected this situation.[57]

Friends and critics alike had different explanations. Some blamed the timidity and inadequacy of the provisions and called for the expenditure of the full sums required to rehabilitate the cities. A report by the Rockefeller Brothers Fund, after contrasting the current investment of some $9.5 billion of public and private funds annually with a candid appraisal of the housing needs, boldly recommended that these outlays be increased to $20 billion annually for at least a decade. Another study placed the urban-renewal needs of a typical metropolis of 300,000 at $2.37 billion over the next twelve years. The situation, these analysts concluded, demanded radical changes in governmental policies and vastly increased appropriations.[58] Other observers blamed the suburbs for refusing to join with their central cities in a metropolitan attack on the problem. Even the several urban counties with county housing authorities able to reach into the suburbs for sites for public housing had been stymied in that effort by social and political pressures. Governmental reorganization and political rejuvenation were needed to meet these problems, Mrs. Catherine Bauer Wurster concluded.[59]

Still other observers, equally aware of the political and economic dimensions of the job, were more concerned lest a crash program wreak havoc among the slum residents. They urged stepped-up efforts to rehabilitate salvageable areas and to increase the volume of low-cost housing prior to the bulldozing of additional slums. These of course were the objectives of the 1954 Act, and the major reasons for their failure, Robert C. Weaver concluded in 1960, were not only insufficient appropriations and poor timing but also the lack of a complementary program of social education both to develop the cultural potentialities of the slum residents and to combat the ring of prejudice that confined Negroes and other minorities in the inner-city ghettos. The dilemmas of class and race would have to be tackled simultaneously with those of urban renewal, he declared, to achieve success.[60]

• The Metropolis and Civil Rights

The dilemmas of urban renewal were the most acute of several that faced Americans in the 1950's because of their failure to accept Negroes into full and equal citizenship. The mushrooming metropolises, by drawing an increasing host of these suppressed people from the cotton fields to the cities, both North and South, had brought to light a number of shameful inequalities and confronted local, state, and national authorities with several disturbing issues—legal, political, and moral. All efforts to dodge them proved futile. The federal government, playing an increasing role in international affairs, could no longer afford to discriminate against Negroes in its military and civil services. Moreover, every attempt to dismiss other aspects of the problem as properly the concern of state and local authorities failed in this decade as the great urban migration pushed each issue to the fore in a succession of historic crises.[61]

Although the migration of Negroes and other nonwhites to the cities was numerically larger in the forties and fifties than the immigrant floods of an earlier period, proportionately, because of the increased urban population, it was not so great, and the traditional capacity of American cities to absorb newcomers could perhaps have met the new challenge but for the fact that the nonwhites retained their obvious color distinction. The visible evidence of its unique character assured this minority a cumulative growth that no former ethnic group, nor all combined, could match. Indeed, as the Negro's urban total surged past 9,393,000 in 1950, it exceeded the foreign-born in cities by almost a million. And ten years later, despite a renewed influx of immigrants that brought 2,515,-000 to America, some of them also nonwhite, the Negro's urban total, 13,792,000, exceeded that of the foreign-born by more than five million.[62]

Yet it was not their numbers, but the crowding of an increasing portion of them into the aging and decaying inner-city districts that created grave problems for every metropolis. Their general poverty coupled with a natural ethnic cohesiveness contributed to this concentration, as it had earlier with most immigrant groups, but now their distinctive identity discouraged efforts to escape from the constricted areas and thus progressively converted them into black ghettos. Although, because of the rapid increase in number, a scattering did occur in many cities in the fifties, most of it an "invasion" of nearby districts, the nonwhite percentages, which had reached the low 90's in many census tracts in 1950, approached 100 in a few places by the end of the decade.[63]

These vast communities of Negroes and other nonwhites posed new challenges not only to their metropolises but to the nation as a whole. As their numbers grew to more than a fourth of the central-city totals in fifteen metropolises and to a secure majority in Washington, new political complications emerged. Few whites objected when predominantly colored districts in New York City, Philadelphia, and Detroit, as well as Chicago, elected Negroes to Congress, but efforts to achieve home rule for Washington were

Demographic Maps of Rochester, New York, 1930, 1960.

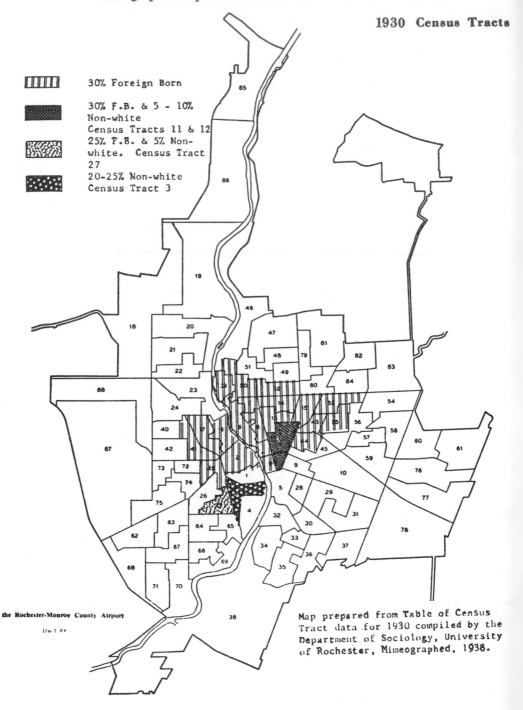

1930 Census Tracts

30% Foreign Born

30% F.B. & 5 - 10%
Non-white
Census Tracts 11 & 12

25% F.B. & 5% Non-
white. Census Tract
27

20-25% Non-white
Census Tract 3

the Rochester-Monroe County Airport

Map prepared from Table of Census
Tract data for 1930 compiled by the
Department of Sociology, University
of Rochester, Mimeographed, 1938.

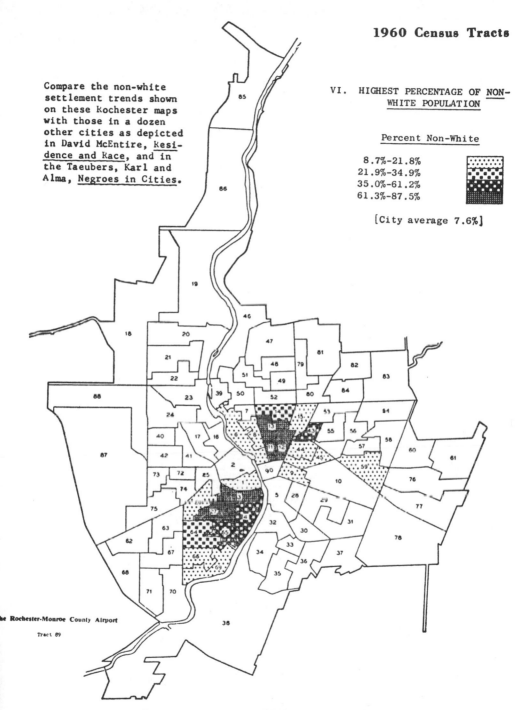

1960 Census Tracts

Compare the non-white
settlement trends shown
on these Rochester maps
with those in a dozen
other cities as depicted
in David McEntire, Resi-
dence and Race, and in
the Taeubers, Karl and
Alma, Negroes in Cities.

VI.   HIGHEST PERCENTAGE OF NON-
         WHITE POPULATION

Percent Non-White

8.7%-21.8%
21.9%-34.9%
35.0%-61.2%
61.3%-87.5%

[City average 7.6%]

Rochester Department of Urban Renewal and Economic Development checked in the mid-fifties when the Negroes attained a majority. Part of the opposition to metropolitan consolidation sprang in some places from a suburban aversion to the problems of the central city's mounting nonwhite population. In Dade County, Florida, however, this became one of several grounds for the formation of a metro federation to head off annexation by expansive Miami. And although scarcely mentioned in their reports, this divisive issue complicated the work of Eisenhower's intergovernmental commissions. Moreover, the schools, the recreational and welfare needs, as well as the housing of inner-city residents were also becoming a concern of the entire nation in this decade as a succession of civil rights crises alerted one and another branch of the federal government.[64]

Unaware of the old medieval maxim, "city air makes men free," Negroes, who now for three full decades had experienced its draughts, were becoming dissatisfied with their subordinate status and limited rights. The joint interracial committees formed in many metropolises had helped to prod civic leaders, particularly in the South, to provide equal facilities in the educational and recreational fields, as at Orlando, Florida, to meet the Supreme Court's separate-but-equal rule. In the North, several alert metropolises, such as Cleveland and Milwaukee, had adopted fair-employment-practices ordinances, while others banned discrimination in public-aided housing. Yet enforcement, many Negroes complained, was lax.[65]

Since few communities in the South attained the separate-but-equal goal, protests mounted there too. Dissatisfaction with the goal also was appearing, as the number of cases before the lower courts amply demonstrated. Protests against anti-Negro covenants in land titles, against discriminatory registration practices, and against segregated public services multiplied in the early fifties. The segregation doctrine, dating from the *Plessy* v. *Ferguson* decision of 1896, was modified by several Supreme Court decisions reinterpreting the Fourteenth Amendment as safeguarding the Negro's right both to register in a primary election and to enroll in a state university. If the great majority of the slum dwellers were unaware of and indifferent to these legal contests, a growing community of educated and sophisticated Negroes had developed in the large metropolis, and attorneys and other professionals were alert and responsive to the changing attitude of the courts.[66]

Attacks on the separate-but-equal doctrine as applied to public schools appeared in several Southern cities in the early fifties. A case from Topeka, Kansas, given priority on the court's docket after two extended hearings, provided the grounds for the historic decision delivered by Chief Justice Earl Warren in May 1954. Hailed generally as the most significant decision of the century, *Brown* v. *Board of Education,* recognizing that "in these days it is doubtful that any child may reasonably be expected to succeed in life if he is denied the opportunity of an education," concluded that "Separate educational facilities are inherently unequal" under the Fourteenth Amendment.[67]

With this dramatic reversal of its own earlier opinion, the Supreme Court took the lead in the exercise of authority during the decade in which President Eisenhower was endeavoring to restrict the field of federal power. Justice Warren, however, called on the local courts, not the central government, to enforce his decree, ordering desegregation with "all deliberate speed." A number of towns and cities in the border states soon began to desegregate. Washington, at the President's instigation, Baltimore, and more than a hundred school districts in the upper South complied with the order with little difficulty. But at Clinton, Tennessee, after the school board and town officials had jointly moved to desegregate, an outside agitator, John Kasper, was able to incite a mob of demonstrators whose riotous threats were only quieted by the courageous stand of the local police backed by the arrest and detention of Kasper in his second attempt to incite a riot. Farther south the reaction was much more hostile, and even supporters of integration sadly concluded that "it will take time." [68]

The school integration issue suddenly acquired national significance at Little Rock, Arkansas, in September 1957. After long deliberation the school board of this developing metropolis of 130,000 residents prepared to admit a few Negro children to its previously all-white Central High School. Numerous protests greeted the announcement of this plan, and Governor Orval

Faubus, in a heated television address, denounced the "forceful integration" at Little Rock. Subsequently he ordered a state contingent of the National Guard to surround the school and prevent this "unlawful" action. After hesitating for a day, the school board consulted and received an order from Federal District Judge Ronald N. Davis to proceed with its plan. When the nine Negro children selected for admission were blocked from entering the school by the troops, backed by a jeering throng of segregationists, Judge Davis promptly enjoined the governor from the use of troops to obstruct the integration order. The soldiers were withdrawn, but an enlarged mob of citizens maintained the blockade in defiance of the Supreme Court order. Appalled by the spectacle, President Eisenhower finally intervened and dispatched a contingent of paratroopers to Little Rock and mobilized the Arkansas National Guard, this time to control the mobs. The high school reopened on an integrated basis with troops patrolling its corridors for the rest of the year. When, however, tension failed to subside, one member of the school board requested and secured a suspension, by a federal district judge, of the integration plan. The matter sped to the Supreme Court, which set aside the suspension and again affirmed its integration decree. By the close of a second year token integration at least had won acceptance at Little Rock.[69]

Two basic principles of American government were contending for precedence, equal civil rights as defined by the Supreme Court and local autonomy as interpreted by the state governments. Few in the South doubted which would win, for the state-rights stand was a familiar one, and governor after governor arose to proclaim it. Yet in Georgia, where both legislature and governor hastened to enact anti-integration legislation, the state's chief metropolis, Atlanta, was more indignant over a recent refusal by the legislature to amend the county-unit rule, which seriously limited its representation in that body. Many of its civic leaders, who had long maintained friendly relations with the city's Negroes and boasted that Atlanta had the most prosperous Negro community in the South, were outspokenly reluctant to see their schools placed on the altar of a lost cause. When in 1961 the state university rather than the Atlanta schools became the first battleground, city representatives found sufficient support among the university's friends to repeal the anti-integration laws.[70]

The desegration decision had wide repercussions in other public-service fields. Alert NAACP attorneys in several communities filed charges in the lower courts protesting the exclusion of Negroes from city parks and playgrounds, in Atlanta and Memphis among other places, and demanding nondiscriminatory service from city-owned utilities. The lower courts generally granted these pleas and extended the ban against segregation to public housing, which raised the further question as to the court's policy in regard to public-supported housing under urban renewal. Park and interstate transportation cases, when carried to the Supreme Court, were formally included within the scope of its antisegregation doctrine. The Court refused to review a San Francisco decision upholding integration in public-aided housing, yet some developers continued to hope for an exception in the field of housing.[71]

The administrators of the FHA were equally troubled by this disturbing question. They had, over the years, made frequent revisions of policy in the granting of mortgage guarantees. The program as originally constituted in 1934 had denied applications that threatened a mixture of "incompatible racial and social groups." But in 1947, in response to mounting protests, the administrators had dropped that clause and two years later had specifically eliminated racial distinction in judging the merits of mortgage applications. Yet even this position, described as "neutral," aroused criticism from civil rights advocates, and in 1954 hoping to forestall further criticism, the FHA embarked on a policy of promoting "demonstration open-occupancy projects in suitable key areas." The urban renewal act of that year also provided for an extension of credit to individuals wishing to improve properties in blighted areas designated for restoration. Few Negroes took advantage of this provision, however, and none of their leaders spoke out in support of a measure proposed in 1957 to extend special assistance to members of minority groups; they did not, in the opinion of Davis McIntire, want minority housing projects or any other special assistance that might "confuse their campaign for integration." [72]

If the civil rights groups could not secure a forthright directive

that all public-assisted projects be open housing, they did head off
a movement in many cities to erect special projects for minority
groups. This movement, promoted in 1954 by the National Association of Home Builders, formed corporations in several metropolises—in Pittsburgh and Cleveland as well as in Dallas and
Houston—to speed the construction of homes and apartments for
minority families in "suitable," that is, segregated, districts in order
to eliminate any demand that might lead to more positive government action. The action chiefly feared at the start was more public
housing, but with the announcement of the school integration decision, the NAHB, sensing a new threat, endeavored to secure
FHA endorsement of its campaign. Hearing of that move, the
NAACP and the Urban League dispatched protests to the FHA
warning that "we do not want jim-crow dwellings whether they
are new or old." [73]

Their protests had the desired negative effect and may also have
given encouragement to an opposing movement to promote interracial housing in several cities. A survey a few years later identified
fifty projects of this type that started in the middle fifties and
numbered some 8000 units. The American Friends Service Committee, among other church bodies and a few labor unions, sponsored most of these experimental efforts in the vicinity of Philadelphia, Detroit, San Francisco, and several other metropolises,
but the reluctance of bankers to extend credit and the hostility of
real estate groups to the choice of suburban sites curbed the movement's expansion. Studies in seven cities of the effect of Negro
home purchases on the sale price of surrounding homes in previously all-white areas tended to refute the general expectation of
sharp losses, but failed to allay the fears. Only a few white neighborhoods whose residents included a high proportion of university
or other professional families seemed ready to welcome colored
neighbors in limited number, and much attention was given by
observers to speculation on the "tipping point." [74]

Impressed by the complexity of life in a metropolis and dis-
mayed by the obstacles to full integration, some aging Negro
leaders urged caution in order to preserve past accomplishments,
which represented, they declared, the best the Negro had ever

known. Advocates of restraint, sometimes called "Uncle Toms," appeared in every community, but the school decision of 1954 and its aftermath fired the imagination of many younger men and women who found a leader in 27-year-old Martin Luther King, Jr., an Atlanta-born Negro with a Ph.D. from Boston University.[75]

Dr. King's dramatic rise to leadership resulted from his handling of a revolt of humble Negro workers against the segregation of bus riders in Montgomery, Alabama. A weary Negro seamstress, tired also of humiliating oppressions, precipitated the revolt by refusing to surrender her seat near the front of a bus to a white man. Her arrest and trial, early in December 1955, on a charge of violating the segregation ordinance, prompted a gathering of fifty Negro leaders at Dr. King's church to call for a peaceful boycott of the Montgomery buses until "all citizens" could ride on them in full equality. Led by their clergy, most of the Negroes responded, and since a majority of the bus riders were Negroes, the buses soon became empty and plied the streets as a daily reminder of the effect of the boycott. Aroused by the economic loss and indignant at the "effrontery" of King and his associates in challenging an old established custom, the Montgomery authorities moved in February to indict Dr. King and the other Negro leaders on a charge of conspiring to conduct an illegal boycott. A Negro mass meeting responded by calling for a day of prayer and pilgrimage during which all Negroes would not only continue to stay off the buses but would also leave their cars at home and walk to work and shop in a city-wide demonstration of passive resistance. With chanted prayers and songs the movement spread and attracted sympathy and praise throughout the nation and abroad for its peaceful strategy. Dr. King was sentenced and forced to pay a $500 fine, but the boycott continued until December 1956 when a Supreme Court decision, holding bus segregation a violation of the Constitution, went into effect. In the jubilation that followed in Montgomery and among civil rights groups everywhere, many overlooked the vital link renewed here between metropolitan and federal forces.[76]

Dr. King's nonviolent protest movement accomplished for the Negroes of Montgomery, and later in some other Southern cities, what many social workers had long been striving to achieve—community organization in depressed areas. The neighborhood associations developed in several Northern metropolises, notably in Kansas City and Minneapolis, flourished most successfully in middle-class districts. They attracted principally the "joiners" and activists interested in improving the area or, sometimes, simply in fending off unwanted intrusions. Many old settlement houses continued to serve the poorer neighborhoods, but as nonwhites invaded and occupied them, the outward migration of old immigrant families quickened, and most of the adult programs eventually lapsed; the settlement staffs became increasingly absorbed in providing recreational activities for the children of the changing neighborhoods.

Despite fresh efforts by many old and new welfare institutions, the problems of the inner city continued to outpace them. To reach those teen-agers and young adults who found their excitement in street gangs and immoral and illegal activities, some settlement houses in New York City and elsewhere dispatched skilled workers to mingle with these youths, gain their confidence, and direct them to stable associations. These efforts, coupled with the counseling that absorbed the major attention of many other social workers, reached at best only a small portion of the inhabitants of the spreading slums of Northern cities. The vast majority of the disadvantaged remained adrift in a strange inhospitable world. Even the Negro churches, long the most successful of their institutions, generally failed to attract the new arrivals. The public schools, overburdened by the ceaseless enrollment turnover, were unable in many places even to maintain Parent-Teacher Associations.[77]

The tragic disintegration of slum communities contributed to the plight of their inhabitants and handicapped urban renewal officials. Those who conscientiously endeavored to follow legislative directives had difficulty in enlisting neighborhood participation in the planning and implementation of their projects. A few neighborhoods responded, one in Washington, where a group of social workers and neighborhood leaders worked closely with the renewal officials in a demonstration project that illustrated the value of community participation. Pittsburgh supplied another example. Its Homewood-Brushton neighborhood formed in 1954 a Community Improvement Association, which drew together the block clubs and other agencies of that lower middle-class district. The response was such from its struggling Negro homeowners that, when citizen leaders of the larger metropolis formed ACTION-Housing, Inc., three years later, they found one neighborhood partly organized and engaged in the rudimentary rehabilitative activities they sought to promote. Similar movements appeared in a few other metropolises; but none rivaled the success of Community Progress, Inc., of New Haven, where Mayor Lee and Edward C. Logue, his development administrator, worked closely with Father Ugo Cavicchi, pastor of the Wooster Square Church, in drawing the residents of that blighted district into active collaboration in its restoration and redevelopment. Lee soon enlisted the services of Mitchell Sviridoff, an experienced labor organizer who had become president of the Board of Education, as community organizer to promote the city's neighborhood redevelopment projects.[78]

Sviridoff's program, which would soon receive a Ford Foundation grant, demonstrated that neighborhood redevelopment could do more than restore housing. It attracted such eager participation by the slum residents in its retraining classes and other imaginative activities that nearby Hartford and other cities hastened to plan similar efforts. These constructive programs were, however, more difficult to launch than the combative approach, which rallied the oppressed against an obvious enemy or a threatened injury. Dr. King's movement, with its philosophy of nonviolence and its dedication to civil rights, developed a religious fervor and a social discipline that proved increasingly effective in Southern cities. In the North, where housing and job discrimination were the chief forms of oppression, the economic and educational deficiencies of many Negroes and other slum dwellers made dramatic accomplishments difficult and prompted community organizers to seek simpler goals that offered the possibility of achieving striking victories. Thus in St. Paul, the Rev. Floyd Massey, a Negro leader, organized the Rondo-St. Anthony Improvement Association to oppose the routing of the proposed Twin City freeway through the Negro community without adequate provision for resettlement. Massey failed to get the open-housing ordinance and other residence concessions he sought, but he did secure generous property evaluations and a depression of the highway to safeguard the rest of the community.[79]

Massey's problem was finding a responsible authority with which to negotiate. The city council lacked power to pass an open-housing ordinance; the housing authority could not pay the resettlement costs of persons displaced by highway projects; and the Twin Cities, with more than a third of the state's population but scarcely a fifth of the legislative seats, could not alter these drawbacks. Thus the Negro's battle for equal rights in Northern cities involved him not only in the struggle for metropolitan reorganization, as in Cleveland, but also in the reapportionment controversy.[80]

That old issue, although revived in many states during the fifties, seemed further from solution than ever. Because of the slower growth of central cities their underrepresentation had not substantially increased, but the lack of representation for metropolitan districts was seriously aggravated. A few states made moderate concessions to their cities, Texas and Michigan, for example; Ohio's rural precincts, however, defeated a proposed constitutional convention for fear it would redistrict the state. When a court in Wisconsin and a referendum in the state of Washington ordered reapportionment, their rural-dominated legislatures so "mangled" the redistricting that the courts had again to intervene. In Minneapolis a group of citizens brought suit in the federal district court and secured a decree mandating the state to adopt a fair-apportionment measure—an action hailed in the *National Municipal Review* as "a real milestone." [81]

The new self-confidence of the judiciary, following the lead of Chief Justice Warren, was matched in some respects by Congress, which had become more responsive to metropolitan problems than the Administration. It was not simply a shift in party control, although the Democrats who captured both houses in 1956 increased their hold in each successive election. Rather it was the appearance in the Senate and the House of strong new metropolitan spokesmen. Senators Joseph S. Clark and Hubert H. Humphrey previously had been mayors of Philadelphia and Minneapolis, respectively, and, with Senators John F. Kennedy from Boston, Paul H. Douglas from Chicago, and Jacob K. Javits from New York, they were much more favorably inclined toward urban-federal relationships. They considerably revitalized the programs of the Eisenhower administration, which in this field was sometimes called "The Establishment." [82]

The newly responsive Congress gave additional powers and funds to several earlier federal-city programs and legislated new ones. Public Law 660, adopted in 1956, amended the Water Pollution Control Act of 1948, which had supported research and planning and, as noted above, authorized an expenditure of $500 million on grants-in-aid for treatment plants, 200 of which were completed in two years. Congress passed its first Air Pollution Research Act in 1955 and four years later extended this technical program vital to every metropolitan region. Expanding support in housing and urban redevelopment, in airport and hospital construction, in health protection and crime detection, in river and harbor improvements, all focused on the cities; moreover, the federal highway program and a dozen other nationwide activities had special provisions designed to meet general or specific metropolitan problems.[83] The new Civil Rights Act of 1957, in support of which Dr. King staged his first march on Washington, conferred only limited safeguards on the use of the ballot. Yet it had a special relevance for the cities, where most Negroes now resided. Thus when President Eisenhower in a final gesture issued the report of his Commission on National Goals, one section of *Goals for Americans* dealt specifically with a suggested "Framework for an Urban Society." [84]

• *Toward a Theory of Urbanism*

Many scholars were busily searching, not for a framework but for *the* framework or social structure that would take into account the complexities of urban society and provide a resolution for both metropolitan and national dilemmas. This quest, commenced in previous decades, acquired new vigor as the resurgent cities spawned a host of social scientists and produced foundations to back their research. Zealous champions of rival schools subjected conflicting theories to a withering criticism in the scholarly journals. The light kindled by these controversies prompted further refinements in conceptualization and stimulated scholars in many fields to join the search for a theory of urbanism. As additional abstractions, however, disclosed new vistas rather than revealing the hoped-for synthesis, some scholars began, toward the close of the decade, to call for a return to the solid ground of urban experience where, meanwhile, other students had been grappling with mundane municipal problems and metropolitan trends.

The analysis that gained the widest following in the early fifties was that based on the belief that each city was controlled by a power structure. C. Wright Mills, who had helped to develop this thesis in the mid-forties, reviewed the findings of its many supporters in a comprehensive volume on local and national aspects of *The Power Elite,* published in 1956. Although the evidence, even of these like-minded scholars, was not entirely consistent, Mills was led to conclude that a relatively small group of business executives, military and political leaders, made up a power elite that controlled the nation's development. Despite evidence of the persistence of old-family hierarchies in some places and of resurgent enterpreneurial vitality elsewhere, he saw the proper law school and business trained executives and other staff men moving into a position of command. This nationwide elite structure, somewhat more "open," he believed, than its separate local antecedents had been in earlier decades, was also sometimes called "The Establishment"; it maintained control centers in a few leading metropolises, chiefly New York, Chicago, and Washington, where the key decisions of economic, military, and governmental policies were formulated.[85]

Yet that top command, which was supposed to control all subordinate divisions, was seldom mentioned by students of the power structure of individual cities. Floyd Hunter, whose volume on *Community Power Structure* described the situation his team of researchers had found in "Regional City" (Atlanta), identified a small group of business and professional leaders as its decision makers and suggested lines of command extending upward to the state capital. Hunter found a somewhat similar power structure, dominated in this case by the professions, in the town's large Negro district, but detected no links between the two power groups. That analysis supported the findings of Morton Grodzins and other scholars who noted a "great schism" or widening cleavage between the whites and blacks in American cities, but it supplied no hint of or direction for the contending forces already erupting in these years.[86]

The power-structure thesis, derived from the earlier multilayered class-stratification analysis of the Warner school, inspired numerous students to make similar studies of small and large cities, Baton Rouge and Seattle, for example. Most of them accepted the mass-society concepts of Ortega y Gasset and relied heavily on the pervasive influence of "anomie"—the enervating condition of social disequilibrium observed by Durkheim—to keep the great mass of men submissive to the decision makers. A widely read volume by David Riesman, *The Lonely Crowd*, published in 1950, seemed to many readers, despite his qualifications, to support this interpretation. Moreover, the power-structure thesis, as Robert Dahl, an early critic, observed, was "simple, compelling, dramatic, 'realistic' " and had "just the right touch of hard-boiled cynicism" to win acceptance in the fifties. Many citizens, disillusioned by repeated reform failures, were ready to see activity on civic committees and agency boards as "game playing," a layman's distortion of Norton E. Long's concept. Hunter in fact specifically cited the community chests of numerous cities as examples of organizational activities that had little if any power in decision making.[87]

Yet other scholars differed sharply with this interpretation. Professor Dahl at Yale led a team of political scientists in an intensive study of decision making in New Haven and uncovered evidence of a pluralistic society that did not lend itself to easy dominance by one power structure. Professor Long at Boston reached a somewhat similar conclusion for his article on "The Local Community as an Ecology of Games," and Edward C. Banfield at Chicago for an address before the American Political Science Association in 1958. Although the New Haven studies did not come out until the early sixties, Dahl's "Critique of the Ruling Elite," published in the *American Political Science Review* in June 1958, raised serious questions concerning the power-structure thesis. Most damaging was the failure of its proponents to cite specific evidence of significant decision making. This failure was the more surprising in view of the controversies currently raging in Atlanta, Baton Rouge, and Seattle, three of the cities studied, over metropolitan reorganization and legislative reapportionment, not to mention civil rights. Few power-structure analysts gave attention to these basic metropolitan questions of the fifties.[88]

Some sociologists, too, were skeptical of the monolithic power-structure and other mass-society concepts. Many were becoming convinced of the need to recognize the social and structural differences that size, scale, and function induced in cities and metropolises; many were also intrigued by the suggestion of Morris Janowitz that urban society was made up of numerous and sometimes overlapping "communities of limited liability." With the possibility of finding multiple structures the quest for new hypotheses quickened, and the publishing enterprise of the *Free Press,* established in 1947 under the editorship of Jerry M. Kaplan with a keen interest in this field, was timely.[89]

It is surely desirable, as Mills urged, to develop a "sociological imagination," Maurice R. Stein agreed, but scholars should be wary, he admonished in 1960, lest their findings be determined by the nature of their questions. "Perhaps," he added, "the depressing sense of uniformity [reported by some field workers], is at least in part an artifact of the research." By a careful restudy of the findings of earlier community studies, from the Chicago school and the Lynds down into the fifties, he demonstrated his thesis that "the processes of urbanization, industrialization and bureaucratization [had] shaped the social structure" of each community. Yet in the end Stein felt a twinge of regret that his abstractions had drained off all evidence of the vital human qualities he had hoped to find, and he concluded that "we [sociologists must] keep reminding ourselves that we are studying human communities." [90]

To Don Martindale at the University of Minnesota, on the other hand, "the contemporary American theory of the city is in crisis" because of its inadequate conceptualization. A great abundance of descriptive detail was at hand, but even the ecologists of the Chicago school of Park, Burgess, McKenzie, and Wirth had failed, as Wirth had observed in 1938, to produce a satisfactory theory of urbanism. After describing its major difficulties—its "geophysical" orientation, its "primitivism," and its neglect of social-structure institutions—Martindale placed the blame for the failure of American scholars on their neglect of the city's historical past. European scholars, in contrast, had, he declared, developed, by diligent use of their medieval antecedents, a more sophisticated urban theory. Most notable was that of Max Weber, which encompassed not only the formal institutional structure but also the web of informal social relations that differentiated the urban community from other societies. To make these insights more readily available, Martindale translated Max Weber's seminal volume on *The City* for an American publisher in 1958. Yet, interestingly enough, he concluded his lengthy "Prefatory Remarks" with a contemporary reflection. "The modern city," he observed, "is losing its external and formal structure. Internally it is in a state of decay while the new community represented by the nation everywhere grows at its expense. The age of the city seems to be at an end." [91] Some sociologists were, in any event, turning to the study of historical sociology and to the analysis of national rather than urban systems.

Other sociologists, however, were finding new and fruitful approaches to the city and opportunities to extract theory from observed experience. Eshref Shevky, Marilyn Williams, and Wendell Bell, for example, used new techniques of social-area analysis with the increasingly abundant census-tract data in developing a typology of urban subareas that enabled them to make comparative studies in time and space of similar neighborhoods in numerous cities. Scott Greer made an intensive study of four dissimilar neighborhoods in Los Angeles and found sufficient evidence of association and friendship patterns to discredit the application there of Durkheim's theory of anomie. Few observers failed to report a widespread civic apathy, but it was not so deep-seated as many assumed, Greer declared, even in the suburbs of which many scholars despaired.[92]

The dramatic growth of the suburban areas in these years made them a natural subject for intensive study. Again the slant of the questions often determined the answers and the character of the suburbs chosen contributed disproportionately to the patterns expounded. William H. Whyte's graphic description of the transient society of Park Forest on the outskirts of Chicago in *The Organization Man* assured it a place in many sociological readers and, together with predominantly Jewish Crestwood Heights near Toronto, described by John Seely and associates, and the "rat race" of New York's top executives, as depicted in *The Exurbanites* by Auguste C. Spectorsky, created a picture of several highly specialized suburban patterns that scarcely provided a representative analysis. Every metropolis might have its Levittown, as well as its Park Forest, but it also had several other suburban patterns, Wendell Bell maintained, offering a wide choice of life styles to the migrating urbanite and opportunities to participate in the changing character of his chosen location.[93]

Two special studies challenged the prevailing view of suburbs as middle-class retreats. Many of course were old villages brought within the sway of an expanding urban neighbor, and Samuel Pratt's account of the transformation of Linden, a town of some 2000 residents in 1900, seventeen miles from Flint and sixty from Detroit, provided a suggestive picture of such communities. He described the quickening experience of the residents of this isolated trade center as improved highways and automobiles more than doubled its population by mid-century and brought them within a half hour's drive of Flint and under the sway of Detroit's communication and banking facilities. Still another suburban pattern appeared on the outskirts of San Jose in California when the Ford Motor Company moved an old assembly plant to a nearby site and induced most of its former employees to settle in the new community. Bennett M. Berger's study of this neighborhood a year after the relocation discredited the assumption that migration to a suburb produces a transformation from working-class to middle-class patterns.[94]

Two comprehensive reviews of suburban trends appeared in the late fifties. One, edited by William M. Dobriner, assembled brief but pithy articles by more than a score of experts who analyzed suburban growth trends, described their economic, political, and domestic patterns, highlighted some of their basic problems, and concluded with a few pages by David Riesman on the "Suburban Sadness." In spite of their bright promises and the rosy dreams they inspired in prospective residents, the suburbs, in Riesman's view, had succeeded in making "visible the theme of conformity" in American life. He deplored the "massification of men in Levittown" and the aimlessness of suburbanites who tended their gardens rather than the civic affairs of the metropolis of which they were a part. Cherishing their automobiles as private chariots and their ranch houses as castles, suburbanites, according to Riesman, had substituted marketing for work as the focus of family life and sacrificed both individuality and community to a state of complacent isolation.[95]

Robert C. Wood's comprehensive study of *Suburbia: Its People and Their Politics,* published in the same year, concluded on a similarly despairing note, but for somewhat different reasons. He saw the ideology of suburbia as a modern embodiment of the traditional American "faith in communities of limited size" and regarded that nostalgic belief in the values of intimate neighborly association as the decisive factor in scattering millions of American urbanites into suburban retreats. The old "grassroots faith," in Wood's view, determined the sprawling shape of the American metropolis and called into being the multitude of small incorporated districts that persistently blocked the development of an integrated metropolitan government. Because the values of fraternity were highly regarded in small communities, conformity and nonpartisanship were fostered, he reported, and many suburbanites withdrew still further, not only from responsibility for the metropolitan community but also from an individual concern for the welfare of their neighborhoods or that of the nation at large. Aside from the school question, only a few minor issues commanded local attention, and the one that generally received the most vociferous and united support was the maintenance of local autonomy. Although the complexity of metropolitan life and the demands of affluent suburbanites created service needs far beyond the limited capacities of suburban governments, the development of administratively controlled special-function districts, financed in part by federal and state grants-in-aid, served, he declared, to relieve the pressure for metropolitan unity and permitted suburbanites to escape this last compulsion to rejoin the dynamic and invigorating world of the metropolis. Wood deplored the widening fissure between the central cities and their suburbs and saw it as a major inhibition on the creative development of America's metropolitan society.[96]

Some of these studies, by emphasizing the withdrawal of suburbanites from civic concerns, accentuated the alarm of many municipal reformers. Those who regarded the Democratic Party as the best spokesman for metropolitan interests saw the successive Eisenhower victories, aided by the swelling suburban vote, as the opening of a long era of Republican ascendancy during which the cities would progressively be denied federal assistance. The President's announced policy of federal restraint seemed to confirm this expectation. But the growing suburbs needed assistance, too, in some cases even more desperately than the cities, and congressmen representing these areas became increasingly generous with federal appropriations in the late fifties. And where Republican congressmen, failing to see the handwriting on the wall, helped to sustain the President's vetoes, Democrats took their seats, as in the cases of Timothy Sheehan, replaced by John McFall at Stockton, California, and Justin LeRoy Johnson by Roman C. Pucinski at Norwood Park in Illinois. A study by G. E. Janosik of the "Suburban Balance of Power" in Philadelphia's four suburban counties had detected evidence of this trend as early as 1955. After a review of the limited literature available, Wood concluded that suburban growth would not have as direct a bearing on the respective fortunes of the two parties as on the extent of outside aid for needed services.[97]

Interest in the suburbs prompted a renewed attempt to determine the outward reach of each metropolis. After a review of earlier efforts to map the regional boundaries of the great cities, Howard L. Green compiled a list of seven indicators based on available statistics concerning transportation loads and destinations, communications frequency, agricultural basins, recreation zones, manufacturing links, and banking controls. With the aid of such data he was able to divide southern New England into two major metropolitan regions, giving New York most of Connecticut and Boston eastern Massachusetts. Rhode Island and a narrow strip of eastern Connecticut and western Massachusetts comprised a border region in his analysis with its lesser metropolitan centers retaining only limited autonomy. A still broader study, backed by the Twentieth Century Fund, was already under way, headed by Professor Jean Gottmann on leave from the University of Paris, who was analyzing the web of interlocking relationships that seemed to be transforming the eastern seaboard from Boston to Washington into one vast megalopolis.[98]

Other economic geographers were refining earlier techniques to classify the economic characteristics of cities. In a review of their findings, Charlton F. Chate detected evidence of such close relationships among several small cities in each of nineteen urbanized regions that he proposed the inclusion in census tables of a new type of metropolis with multiple nuclei, such as the Durham, Raleigh, Winston-Salem, and Charlotte region in North Carolina. A Swedish scholar, Gunnar Alexandersson, supplied the most comprehensive treatment of *The Industrial Structure of American Cities* in a book full of maps and charts. Albert J. Reiss, Jr., developed a new socioeconomic classification, and Victor Jones proposed a tabulation of still other economic data to achieve a meaningful categorization of cities.[99]

Political scientists, too, were interested in the functional classification of cities, but most of the practitioners in this field were absorbed as consultants by the research bureaus and other agencies engaged in the many metro-reorganization studies noted above. Professor Gulick reviewed some of these developments in an address at Columbia University on the commemoration of its bicentennial. That address was but one of several on urbanism delivered on this occasion and later edited in a *Festschrift* by Robert M. Fisher. The University of Pennsylvania devoted a full issue of its *Law Review* to a Symposium on Metropolitan Regionalism in February 1957; nine months later the *Annals* of the American Academy of Political and Social Sciences published a similar list of distinguished articles on the "Metropolis in Ferment." [100]

Economists as well as political and other social scientists participated in these symposia. Indeed the longest and perhaps the most original contribution at the Columbia Conference was that on "Economic Efficiency" by Professor P. Sargant Florence, from Birmingham, England, whose analysis of the economic advantages that stemmed from a metropolitan environment merited, in editor Fisher's opinion, reproduction in full. Fiscal, transportation, and planning problems also received scholarly attention, as did urban aesthetics by Dean John Burchard of M.I.T., past president of the Academy. Moreover, several of these experts were deeply concerned by what some regarded as the decade's crucial questions: the relationships of the central cities to their suburbs and of the metropolises as real if not legal entities to the federal government.[101]

Numerous foundations and other bodies sponsored institutes and launched research programs to increase public knowledge of urban dilemmas. The Government Affairs Foundation in New York, which undertook in 1955 to make a synthesis of all metropolitan studies, soon found itself engaged in a long-term project, which it transferred the next year to the Kellogg Center of Michigan State University at Lansing, where Frank C. Moore, Luther Gulick, Frank Bane, and its other directors assembled a staff for a continuing National Conference on Metropolitan Problems. The Joint Center for Urban Studies at Harvard and M.I.T. formed in 1959 by a merger of their separate efforts in this field was one of a half dozen major university centers engaged in metropolitan studies at the close of the decade.[102]

These interdisciplinary ventures drew architects and planners as well as historians and philosophers into the concerted attack on the riddles of the metropolis. If not actually enrolled on their staffs, authors such as Christopher Tunnard, whose *American Skyline* provided an illuminating review of the development of urban architecture in America, and Wilfred Owen, whose books on the problems of metropolitan transportation were the best available, participated in frequent conferences at these centers. Although predominantly academicians and committed to scholarly research and professional training programs, the leaders of most of these institutions maintained a daily involvement in the metropolitan environment that gave a practical rather than theoretical flavor to their courses and to the books they produced, such for example as *Politics, Planning, and the Public Interest* by Martin Meyerson and Edward C. Banfield, who later became members of the Joint Center in Cambridge.[103]

Some regional research programs also focused on the city. Most notable was the prewar urban project of the Southern Regional Committee of the Social Science Research Council, which the Institute for Research in Social Science at the University of North Carolina later took over. The book finally produced under the editorship of Rupert B. Vance and Nicholas J. Demerath represented the contributions of many regional scholars and supplied a comprehensive interpretation of *The Urban South*.[104]

Architects and planners, journalists and technicians, even a few philosophers, contributed in these years to the study of the city. Clarence S. Stein's *Toward New Towns for America* placed his planning contributions in perspective and provided an inspiring model for city planners and tract developers. Robert A. Nisbet gave additional philosophical support to community organizers. John Rannells supplied technological guidelines to aid in a re-evaluation of land values and site selection in *The Core of the City*. Fred K. Vigman highlighted many of the mounting problems of the metropolis in his journalistic account of the *Crisis of the Cities*.[105]

Historians, too, and in increasing numbers, were pressing their study of the city's growth. New volumes appeared in the Chicago and Rochester series as Miss Bessie L. Pierce and I pressed into the metropolitan stages of our respective urban subjects. Carl Bridenbaugh published a second volume in his comparative analysis of colonial cities, and Richard C. Wade carried the new historical approach into the Old West with his perceptive account of *The Urban Frontier*. Bayrd Still supplied a richly detailed review of contemporary observations on the changing scene over many decades in New York City. Constance M. Green, after completing earlier studies of individual cities, made a first attempt to sketch the vast panorama of *American Cities in the Growth of the Nation*. Several scholars supplied historical reviews of significant urban developments, notably Frank M. Stewart's account of the activities of the National Municipal League during its first half century and John Higham's moving portrayal of *Strangers in the Land*. Other scholars contributed biographies of important urban leaders, among them Charles Garrett's account of *The LaGuardia Years*.[106]

But no academic scholar depicted the malaise of the contemporary metropolis as graphically as Frank P. Zeidler, mayor of Milwaukee, did in his contribution to the symposium *Metropolis in Ferment*. His assignment was to peer into the future and assess the prospects for urban government during the next two decades. Oppressed by the frustrations of the middle fifties, he did not see much hope for a resolution even of current dilemmas. Smarting from recent repulses, he could expect little from the states except increased aid and comfort for urbanites who fled to the suburbs to escape responsibility for metropolitan ills. From the federal government he expected a further retreat from the solicitude for the cities expressed, even if ineffectively, under the New Deal. From the social scientists (though he did not mention them) he expected a further refinement of ideology to justify the segregation of Negroes and other unfortunates in more securely bounded inner-city ghettos. From the technical scientists he expected the development of new machines to pollute the air and water and create such a crescendo of noise and confusion as to make the final atomic holocaust seem a merciful release.[107]

Wallace S. Sayre, a Columbia professor engaged in a study of the New York metropolitan region, ventured to respond to Mayor Zeidler's grim prophecy. But rather than make a frontal attack, he chose to regard each of the mayor's predictions of doom as hints of where, by a slight reversal or shift of forces, a way out of current dilemmas could be found. Thus the cities might "form an alliance with the national government in a political contest against the state governments and the suburbs." Or urban leaders could frustrate the "aggressive determination on the part of the state legislatures and the suburban governments to 'isolate' the central cities" by playing down "the urban-suburban hostility" and drawing the suburbanites into renewed partnership in revitalized metropolitan communities. Even the threat of "a rising tempo of ethnic and racial politics" and of increased turmoil by unemployed youths in the streets could, he too believed, be averted by a more vigorous promotion of urban renewal and redevelopment, "as in [Mayor] Clark's Philadelphia." And if the states continued to refuse or delay reapportionment, the new "Metrogovernors" will, he predicted, have overshadowed, before 1977, the antiquarian state executives as well as the occupants of "the Citadel of the U.S. Senate." [108]

6. FEDERAL-METROPOLITAN CONVERGENCE IN THE 1960's

The gloomy forebodings of metropolitan leaders in the late fifties disappeared in the election of 1960. Seldom, indeed, has a full decade brought such a convergence of trends as those linking the fortunes of American cities and the nation in the early and middle sixties. Developments considered far distant at the start, such as reapportionment, or undreamed of, such as the Negro revolution, occurred in quick succession as though in a chain reaction. If the causal connections remain obscure, the basic interrelationships are inescapable, as numerous interdisciplinary seminars and scholarly compilations have demonstrated. All the controversies and dilemmas of the previous half century have reappeared and several have come finally to a head. Their convergence has revived or accelerated old programs and spurred the launching of new efforts— federal, state, and local—in a historic play of events that has had two opposing themes—revolution and consensus.

• The "New Frontier" and the Metropolis

The action of course commenced in the national election of 1960. Whereas the Republican platform, adhering to the Eisenhower policy, pledged to "leave to the state and local governments those programs and problems which they can best handle," the Democratic platform promised federal support for schools, medical care, depressed areas, urban transportation, housing, planning, and urban renewal among other matters that directly concerned the cities. Although neither candidate dealt specifically with many of the major issues posed by the metropolis, John F. Kennedy's stirring allusions to the "New Frontier" of American opportunity had a quickening appeal to millions of urbanites who saw new hope for a responsible federal attack on their problems. Of the ninety leading cities, all but twelve gave him sizable pluralities, sixty of them sufficiently large to carry their counties into the Democratic column.[1]

Civic leaders watched with keen interest as President Kennedy formulated his program. Their hopes rose when he declared, in his message on the economy early in February 1961, that "we must have the energy and vision to lay sound foundations for meeting the problems which will result from the steady growth of our urban areas." They applauded many points of his more lengthy discussion of urban problems in a message on March 9. But the new editor of *American City*, William S. Foster, who had succeeded Harold S. Buttenheim after his retirement in 1956, was in several respects disappointed. The President's proposal of federal backing for 40-year mortgages, with no down payments, to spur the construction of houses by moderate-income families and of cooperative and low-rental projects for low-income families, was fine, but his call for an additional 100,000 public housing units was not sufficient, Foster declared, since each of several large metropolises would need that many. His promise of greater freedom to local housing authorities was welcomed, particularly in the matter of design, as was the promise of greater assistance for planning, but Kennedy had failed to endorse metropolitan-wide planning and area redevelopment, Foster noted, and his call for the creation of a Department of Housing and Urban Affairs revealed that he had failed to grasp the urgent need for a broadly conceived Department of Urban Affairs able to tackle all the urgent metropolitan problems.[2]

How best to rally support for metropolitan causes was the concern of many civic leaders. Alfred Willoughby, editor of the

National Civic Review (as the old *National Municipal Review* had been renamed in 1959), saw the crucial "Battlefields of 1961" to be in twelve state capitals where the legislative apportionment was most seriously out of line. Numerous studies, such as one on the "Devaluation of the Urban and Suburban Vote," prompted by the appearance of the 1960 Census Reports, amply documented the continued dominance of the dwindling rural population. The repeated refusals of the legislatures in several states to adopt equitable redistricting laws, despite the pledges of both parties, as in Maryland in 1960, and in face of the decrees of state judges, as in Minnesota and Washington, finally persuaded the federal courts to accept the challenge.[3]

When the Supreme Court announced its decision in *Baker v. Carr,* a Tennessee apportionment case decided on March 26, 1962, urban leaders everywhere rejoiced. Convinced of its "tremendous implications," editor Willoughby gathered and republished comments from numerous journals across the land. In the process he discovered that the decision had left many questions unanswered, was open to varied interpretations, and failed to prescribe judicial remedies. Numerous redistricting suits were nevertheless filed, in Maryland and Georgia in April and in a dozen more states within another month. The National Municipal League, securing a Ford Foundation grant to maintain a clearinghouse service on legislative reapportionment, scheduled a series of monthly articles in its *Civic Review* starting in September, but the early reports proved disappointing.[4]

Reapportionment battles raged in many state capitals during the next few years. In several cases, when the courts ordered special legislative sessions to redistrict the state, leaders of the dominant but threatened faction adopted compromise measures that so gerrymandered the districts as to prolong their control or made only token concessions to the principle of equality. The voters rejected some of these proposals and the courts set others aside; even in a few states where the courts endeavored to supply a redistricting formula, as in Alabama, the situation remained confused. When, however, the Council of State Governments launched a move for the adoption of three amendments to limit the authority of the federal courts in this field, editor Willoughby warned that it was counseling suicide for the states. The National Municipal League devoted most of its annual conference at Detroit, in November 1962, to the apportionment question. One session, focusing on the benefits to be derived by the states as their governments became more truly representative, featured a report of the Advisory Commission on Intergovernmental Relations, which reviewed the steps taken in all but three states to recognize the peculiar status of their metropolitan areas.[5]

Yet the advocates of the "new civil right" of an equal vote made few tangible gains until the Supreme Court, in February 1964, more clearly reaffirmed its "one man one vote" principle first enunciated two years before in *Gray* v. *Sanders,* a Georgia case. In a rapid succession of decisions that spring, the Court invalidated the districts of almost a third of the state legislative houses and extended its standards in *Reynolds* v. *Sims* to state senate districts and in *Wesberry* v. *Sanders* to Congressional districts as well. Numerous congressmen joined the protest movement at this point. But when the courts in response to an Illinois case directed that the state elections there in 1964 be held on a statewide at-large basis, other legislatures tackled the problem in greater earnest. Kentucky, responding to a suit brought by citizens of Louisville, successfully redistricted both houses to the full satisfaction of urban and rural voters, both white and black. In Alabama and elsewhere in the Deep South the resistance of the rural districts to reapportionment began to crumble as the civil rights campaign for Negro registration gained headway in these areas. In the North—Michigan and New York, for example—some legislative leaders endeavored to divide the urban, particularly the central-city, vote among districts hopefully controlled by suburban majorities, but their schemes frequently miscarried. By January 1966, when thirty-four states were pressing forward with the task, increasing to forty the number that appeared satisfactorily redistricted, the *National Civic Review* could conclude that the "Apportioning Woes [are] Nearing [a] Conclusion."[6]

While the Warren court, impelled in some measure by the civil-rights stand it had earlier assumed on the race question and supported in the South by fears of the voting power of rural Negroes, was pressing its campaign in behalf of equality for the metropolitan voter, the Kennedy administration was opening still other frontiers for metropolitan advance. The water pollution control act of July 1961 increased the funds available for such studies and for limited aid in such projects from $3 million to $5 million. The new housing act of that year was still more venturesome. It not only promised an additional $2 billion over the next four years for urban renewal but raised the ratio of federal grants to two-thirds of the costs for land acquisition and project planning and extended the latter provision to include some related metropolitan planning. Moreover, in response to suburban pressures ably marshaled by Senator Harrison A. Williams of New Jersey, the housing act increased to $75 million the funds available for mass-transportation planning and included modest provisions for open-space planning and acquisition, a new field of federal support.[7]

President Kennedy's keen interest in the arts prompted him, at Arthur Schlesinger's suggestion, to engage August Heckscher, "to conduct an inquiry 'without fanfare' into the resources, possibilities and limitations of national policy in relation to the arts." Heckscher's report, submitted in the spring of 1963, recommended the independent establishment of an Advisory Council on the Arts to integrate federal activities in this field and the organization of a National Arts Foundation to promote the work. The President, who promptly created the Council by executive decree, was also interested in the move to preserve the architectural qualities of the Lafayette Square area in Washington and soon became involved in plans for the city as a whole.[8] While his assassination cut short any broader application of these interests, Kennedy's concern for the cultural aspects of cities in general was revealed by his support of a proposed revision of the Library Services Act of 1956. The administration-backed Comprehensive Education Bill, of January 1963, incorporated many of the recommendations of the American Library Association. It proposed an extension of federal grants to city and university libraries and subsidies for library training programs. When the original bill was divided into sections, the portion dealing with public libraries proposed an increase in the federal appropriation for library services to $25 million, plus an additional $30 million to assist in the construction of library buildings. Although these measures failed to pass that year, the federal appropriations for library services in rural areas were maintained at the full quotas of $7.5 million annually and helped alert central-city libraries to serve formerly neglected suburban districts by the purchase of bookmobiles and by the provision of cataloguing and book-buying services to struggling libraries in neighboring towns and rural areas.[9]

Numerous federal agencies developed new services in direct collaboration with municipalities. The U.S. Public Health Service, for example, cooperated with the Milwaukee Health Department in an investigation of pollution on its lakefront. John Nolan, Jr., a leading planning consultant, accepted direction of transportation planning under the Housing and Home Finance Agency and soon had a demonstration project under way at Detroit in which the city, state, and federal authorities collaborated in an electronic installation of television, radar, computers, and signal lights to synchronize the flow of traffic on one of its expressways and double its capacity. In similar fashion Montgomery County in Pennsylvania secured federal support for an experimental effort to promote the use of parking at commuter train stops as an alternative to driving into Philadelphia.[10]

By far the most significant federal-city development in the first Kennedy year was the appointment of a President's Committee on Juvenile Delinquency. The committee, created in response to pressure for a new effort in behalf of teen-age youths in the city streets, soon launched a number of research and demonstration projects in various metropolises. As director, David Hackett, a special assistant to Attorney General Robert F. Kennedy, was greatly influenced by the contentions of Professors Cloward and Ohlin, in *Delinquency and Opportunity* published in 1960, that urban youths needed opportunities to achieve self-confidence by making their own decisions and that slum communities needed support in developing their own solutions. The President's Committee soon launched a project on the Lower East Side in New York City called Mobilization for Youth and persuaded Professor Kenneth Clark of Columbia to lead a research project in Harlem to determine the proper methods for an attack on the problems of urban poverty. The Haryou project, as it was called, was one of a number of efforts in New York and other cities sponsored in 1962 by the President's Committee in preparation for a broader attack on poverty in the years ahead.[11]

To direct these cooperative efforts and supply a balanced federal leadership, President Kennedy recommended the creation of a properly staffed department of urban affairs. "In a few short decades," he advised Congress in January 1962, "we shall be a nation of vastly expanded population, living in expanded urban areas in housing that does not exist, moving about by means of systems of urban transportation that do not now exist. The challenge is great and," he added, "the Federal Government must act to carry out its proper role of encouragement and assistance to state and local governments in solution to these problems." Although the proposed name, Department of Housing and Urban Affairs, placed chief emphasis on that major problem, the President's message indicated his awareness of the broader aspects of the department's tasks:

> The present and future problems of our cities are as complex as they are manifold. There must be expansion: but orderly and planned expansion, not explosion and sprawl. Basic public facilities must be extended ever further into the areas surrounding urban centers. . . . The scourge of blight must be overcome, and the central cores of our cities, with all their great richness of economic and cultural wealth, must be restored to lasting vitality. . . . We neglect our cities at our peril, for in neglecting them we neglect the nation.[12]

But Kennedy's support of the proposed department was secondary to his commitment in another field, civil rights, and the link he chose to make between the two temporarily blocked the department's creation. Since, in his view, housing and civil rights were crucial problems for the new department, he determined to appoint Robert C. Weaver, head of the Housing and Home Finance Agency and the highest ranking Negro in the federal service, as the new Secretary with full Cabinet rank. When news of that decision reached some of his Southern supporters in Congress, the prospects for an early passage of the enabling act fluctuated. Several representatives endeavored to persuade him to choose another appointment, but the President refused to reconsider and the bill was defeated in the House Rules Committee.[13] Some urban advisers questioned the wisdom of sacrificing the department to the civil rights cause, yet this convergence of issues was destined to be the most significant that the New Frontier would reveal.

• *Metropolitan Organization and Planning*

If, as some critics charged, the President's grasp of the metropolitan problem was deficient, his shortcoming was widely shared. Few saw the situation as clearly as Robert H. Connery and Richard H. Leach. After a careful study "of one federal program after another" they concluded that "the approach of the national government to urban problems has been not only piecemeal, but, with few exceptions, through the cities. The new pattern of urban settlement is in the metropolitan community, and it is only through using a metropolitan approach that real progress can be made." [14] Even the Conference of Mayors, the most vigorous spokesman for the big cities, had failed to champion this larger cause. Possibly the National Municipal League, with its more diversified membership and broader commitment, was a more logical agency to press the reform, but its causes were so numerous that this one, though earnestly accepted, was unsuccessfully promoted.[15]

The decision, of course, was not for the President or any federal authority to make, not even for the cities as legally constituted. It required a broader agreement and determination to cooperate than any of the 212 metropolitan areas had yet developed among their numerous municipalities and incorporated districts. The negative vote cast in the fifties against proposed federations, as well as consolidations, were matched in the early sixties—at Durham, North Carolina, and Richmond, Virginia—before Nashville and Davidson County accepted a compromise merger plan. That second success in a decade prompted two additional Tennessee metropolises, Memphis and Chattanooga, and San Antonio in Texas to consider consolidation with their counties, but again the proposals were voted down, as were new compromise measures for a third and fourth time at Seattle and St. Louis, respectively.[16]

Because of this impasse, the Advisory Commission on Intergovernmental Relations acquired an unexpected opportunity for leadership. Established by act of Congress in 1959 in response to a recommendation of the President's earlier Kestnbaum Commission, it was the sole survivor of the several study groups of the Eisenhower period and, limited to a small staff, its prospects for influence appeared dim. Yet with Frank Bane, a distinguished municipal scholar, as chairman, and a wide representation of governors, congressmen, mayors, and other governmental officials on its 25-man board, the commission prepared a number of reports designed to point the way for improved intergovernmental relations. Its first concern was with state and federal contacts, but in 1961, after some of President Kennedy's Cabinet appointees had taken their places on the board, notably Abraham A. Ribicoff and Arthur Goldberg, the commission issued several reports dealing with metropolitan problems. One on "Governmental Structure, Organization and Planning in Metropolitan Areas" outlined and cited examples of ten possible approaches to the problem.[17]

Yet Thomas H. Reed, who, as Luther Gulick remarked, had "worked harder and more productively on problems of metropolitan government than any other man," was not satisfied with the "arsenal of remedial weapons" presented by the Advisory Commission. In "A Call for Plain Talk," delivered at the annual conference of the National Municipal League in December 1962, he pleaded for a nationwide campaign under the slogan "Self-government for Metropolitan Areas." After reviewing the limitations of the several compromise approaches—the special-function districts, interunit contracts, voluntary cooperation, regional planning councils, and others described by the Advisory Commission—he singled out for major emphasis its appeal to the state legislatures to supply more "workable machinery for the formulation and adoption of metropolitan government by the people affected." [18]

Among others who addressed that conference at Miami Beach, Robert C. Wood called for more than "the simple magnification in size of the present political and governmental system." The new metropolitan government should first of all, he maintained, be "policy-oriented"; secondly, it should seek "an infusion of talent at the research level, in the development stage, in the exercise of top-level executive power, in the recruitment of new career specialists," and, finally, it should seek "the coordination of these policy efforts through channels which maintain a metropolitan perspective." [19]

Scholars and municipal officials alike were busily assessing the various metropolitan approaches. A Denver study compared the accomplishments of Dade County's two-level metropolitan government with those of the Denver Inner-County Area Commission. Several research groups analyzed the procedures of the "Lakewood Plan" developed by Los Angeles County and praised its remarkable success in providing services under contract to the numerous suburbs of that sprawling complex. Although the city itself was not involved, the county functions had grown since 1954 to justify the employment, six years later, of 37,000 workers and a budget of $500 million. Since the elections were nonpartisan, the officials escaped the customary pressure for patronage and achieved a high standard of efficiency; some observers, however, deplored the low degree of democratic participation. Governor Edmund G. Brown's Commission on Metropolitan Area Problems proposed the formation of multipurpose districts for every metropolis in California, each to include the central city, and an authority at the state level to supervise their formation and to check new applications for incorporation. But again the legislature failed to act.[20]

More promising, in the opinion of Victor Jones, another established authority in the field, was the movement for the creation of official regional councils. The continued activity of some of the pioneer councils, notably in the Detroit, Philadelphia, and Washington areas, had prompted the formation of additional bodies of this sort at Baltimore and San Francisco in 1961. These agencies appeared, to Jones, to point the way for useful development in the sixties. Mayor Wagner successfully revived his former Metropolitan Regional Council, and others now appeared in the Los Angeles, Seattle, Atlanta, and three lesser metropolitan areas. This increased interest prompted the Advisory Commission to make a special study of their structure and activities.[21]

Yet these official councils, dependent as they were on reaching a consensus among unequal parties, had, in the experience of Robert Warren, research director for Seattle's Metropolitan District Authority, limited value. He was more impressed by the numerous services Los Angeles County was able to supply under its Lakewood Plan. Since, in his opinion, all efforts to achieve a rationalized form of metropolitan government had failed, even in Dade County where much confusion persisted, Warren proposed "A Municipal Service Market Model of Metropolitan Organization." Under this plan each local subdivision would contract for such services as it desired and perform or neglect others as it chose. If the metropolitan community as a whole wished to upgrade services, it could employ a grants-in-aid policy to spur the laggard districts, but it would normally depend on open-market practices to satisfy the wants of the region.[22]

This practical scheme brought a prompt and indignant rejoinder from Norton E. Long of Brandeis University. In a forceful article in the *Journal* of the American Institute of Planners, "Citizenship or Consumership in Metropolitan Areas," he urged that the larger objectives of metropolitan citizenship be kept in view. "The future of the city," he declared, "lies in our capacity to develop a political philosophy of the self-governing community that can inform the fragmented mass of the metropolitan area with a meaningful common political life. The metropolitan area that succeeds in creating a political form and a philosophy and leadership to go with it will ensure the survival of local self-government and the emergence of a new age of great cities in the United States." [23]

The question of goals was of course a perennial concern of planners, particularly regional planners. Volunteer regional planning associations and variously appointed official councils had appeared in at least sixty-three metropolitan districts by 1962. Most of them had limited staffs with only research and advisory functions, yet they sometimes exerted promotional and educational influence. The outstanding model, the regional economic study of the New York area by a large team of scholars assembled by Raymond Vernon of Harvard for the Regional Plan Association of New York and jointly backed by the Rockefeller Brothers Fund and the Ford Foundation, had been completed in the late fifties. On the appearance of the last of its nine publications, a summary volume by Vernon in 1960, numerous scholars hastened to assess the work. As Frederick Gutheim of Washington put it, these volumes not only helped the reader, "as no other body of data, to see the metropolitan region as a whole," but they also revealed the "inadequacy of metropolitan government." [24]

No other regional planning group attempted such a comprehensive study, but several launched new research efforts. Foundations were ready to back these programs when initiated by volunteer agencies, as in San Antonio, and federal funds were available to support official regional planning bodies. Indeed the prospect of securing federal grants-in-aid stimulated the formation of several regional planning commissions, and the Advisory Commission hastened to recommend that such official bodies be created in every metropolitan district and be asked to comment on all area programs requesting grants-in-aid before they could be approved in order to promote regional coordination. The commission also urged the states to authorize the establishment of these agencies and to give them adequate authority.[25]

Several progressive states were in fact moving in this direction. Twenty-five had authorized the formation of regional councils, and Colorado, Oregon, and Wisconsin launched new statewide studies of metropolitan problems. When Governor Brown finally secured the passage in 1963 of a modified provision for the creation not only of a Local Agency Formation Commission in each county and Regional Planning District Councils where desired, but also a statewide Coordinating Council on Urban Affairs, the state of Washington promptly adopted the last provision. Governor Elbert N. Carvel of Delaware, in an address before the National Municipal League in 1962, declared, "The states must take a positive lead in helping to meet urban problems." His own State Planning Board, created the year before, was not only empowered but directed to work closely with city planning groups and also to use the research services of a Division of Urban Affairs developed under a Ford grant at the University of Delaware.[26]

Some of the new state programs reflected the impact of the re-apportionment movement; others represented a revival of the postwar planning and development efforts. In Minnesota the creation of the Twin-City Metropolitan Planning Commission, with members from seven counties as well as the two cities, was supported by some to quiet the urban demand and by others to strengthen it and provide regional coordination.[27] In Hawaii, Alaska, and New Jersey earlier economic-development agencies assumed regional planning functions in the early sixties. Boston, after a 10-year struggle, finally secured legislative authorization in 1963 for a Metropolitan Planning Council of twenty-one persons to be appointed by the governor from the city and its twenty suburbs.[28]

The effort to staff these state and regional agencies as well as the city planning and redevelopment commissions placed an increasing strain on the profession. Despite the flood of graduates from the many universities that now offered courses in the field, many planners had little training, and leaders in the profession became concerned lest the poor quality of some of the work would further weaken the planners' limited influence. Several of the centers for urban studies offered special seminars and conducted regional workshops in an endeavor not only to upgrade the performance of staff workers in the field but also to try out and perfect new analytical tools and to formulate and debate appropriate goals.[29]

The Brookings Institution in Washington took the initiative in organizing a series of seminars on urban decision making and planning in numerous cities. Its program, jointly sponsored in each case by a local college, generally as a part of its extension service, drew a score or more community leaders, both public and private, with several social scientists from regional institutions and urban experts from a greater distance together for ten weekly conferences on crucial metropolitan problems. The directors of this experiment assembled and reproduced an extensive volume of scholarly and journalistic commentaries on each topic and induced many of the busy participants to do their homework before each weekly session, in Cincinnati, Baltimore, Lansing, Newark, and Memphis among other cities in 1961 and later years.[30]

Impressed by the opportunities for increased scholarly and citizen cooperation in the field, Robert Gutman and David Popenoe, of the Urban Studies Center at Rutgers University, produced a special issue of the *American Behavioral Scientist* on "Urban Studies." After a suggestive review of recent writings in the field, they dealt respectively with the research and educational possibilities and included an extended discussion of a proposed extension program in urban studies by John E. Bebout, director of the Rutgers Center, and a brief consideration of the potential contributions of science to city planning by John Dyckman of the Institute for Urban Studies at the University of Pennsylvania.[31]

Development in metropolitan planning thus reflected a convergence of federal, state, and local efforts and of practical and scholarly interests as well. In an attempt to evaluate the comprehensive planning that several of the regional bodies were undertaking, William S. C. Wheaton, director of the Institute of Urban and Regional Development at Berkeley, made a careful comparison of two of the best of the recently completed master plans, those of Washington and Denver. They provided, he reported, rival models, one for radial-corridor development and the other for controlled peripheral ring expansion, yet neither, as far as he could determine, had made a basic study of the relative desirability of these patterns. To support a more probing analysis, the Institute of Planners devoted the November 1965 issue of its *Journal* to a "Symposium on Programming and the New Urban Planning." [32]

Indeed, in the opinion of some of the younger planners, fresh from the interdisciplinary planning schools and graduate institutes at more than a score of major universities, much of the master planning that enjoyed a new vogue in metropolitan centers in the early sixties was of limited value. If it was not actually utopian in the tradition of Howard, Mumford, and the Goodmans, it was in large part deductive in a design sense, as William Petersen, a Berkeley sociologist, described the activity in a provocative article in the *Journal* of the American Institute of Planners. Even when inductive techniques were employed they suffered, he declared, from "the notion that the physical factors are the key determinants of all others." This "physical bias," as David Farbman, another critic, characterized the deficiencies of a hundred master plans, resulted, in Petersen's view, from the failure to see that "planning concerns process and not state," that "it pertains not to some idealized future but to the mode of moving from the present," and that "the relevant skills are not exclusively architecture, landscape architecture, sanitation engineering, and the like . . . but rather the full range of the social sciences." In addition, in Paul Davidoff's view, planning should reflect the pluralism of the metropolis by giving full consideration to the aspirations of ethnic and other special-interest groups as well as to the civic and economic character of the community.[33]

• *The Metropolis in Turmoil*

If city planners in the mid-sixties were awakening to the importance of social as well as economic and other aspects of the metropolis and were ready to consult the social scientists, it was a result, at least in part, of their experience with housing and urban-renewal projects during the previous decade. In spite of the constructive revisions of 1954 and 1956, these federal programs, from which much was anticipated, had been so complicated by a converging historical development—the crowding of Negroes into the central cities—that the bright prospects of eradicating the slums were giving way to the dismaying reality of rioting in the streets. The Workable Programs, for which local planners had gladly accepted federal grants, required more than a patchwork of model designs of high-rise apartments and business blocks set in spacious plazas, or of garden apartments and well-landscaped row houses. Even the requirement of a more detailed economic analysis, both of the blighted neighborhood and of the broader community's financial resources to carry its share of the cost, was not a great obstacle, especially not after New York City administrators had successfully introduced the use of computers. But the problems of relocating the displaced slum dwellers, particularly those who were colored, and of winning resident participation in the planning of these projects were proving increasingly difficult. Long before professors of planning began to talk about the need for plural planning and for the insights of social science, urban-renewal project directors in several metropolises were turning to social workers and citizen associations for help in this trying situation.[34]

Several promising demonstrations of the possibility of making urban renewal a program of social as well as physical rehabilitation, as in New Haven, Pittsburgh, and elsewhere, were already at hand in 1961 when President Kennedy named Dr. Robert Weaver director of the Housing and Home Finance Agency. Fully aware of the primary importance of this phase of the renewal program, he determined to enforce the requirement of citizen participation by delaying approval of the Workable Programs in a score of cities until evidence of the activity of citizen committees was produced. He agreed with William L. Slayton, director of the renewal program, that citywide committees would suffice where total-clearance projects were proposed, provided adequate plans for the resettlement of the displaced were submitted; but he insisted on resident participation when a neighborhood was to be rehabilitated, not cleared. The community renewal program, authorized in 1959, was only getting under way, and the agency endeavored in the early sixties to promote its wider application. By the end of June 1963 over 45,000 buildings were approved for rehabilitation to supply some 107,000 dwelling units in widely scattered renewal projects. One venture by a nonprofit group in Chicago, which received support for the rehabilitation of several scattered apartment blocks in various parts of the city, supplied a model for similar groups in other metropolises and soon presented new demands for federal funds.[35]

Many standard urban-renewal projects had made rapid progress in site clearance by the early sixties only to encounter difficulties in finding developers. Yet Newark among others had finally surmounted these obstacles, and by 1962 a Senate Subcommittee on Housing reported that "81 urban renewal projects had been completed, 548 more were in various stages of project execution, and

384 were in the planning stage." As Charles Abrams pointed out in citing this report, the designation "completed" "means simply that the land has been disposed of and a financial settlement made by the federal government for its acquisition," yet a sufficient number were in fact finished and open for occupancy to reveal the new problems of tenant selection and rental collection. Some projects defaulted, as in Detroit where one designed by Mies Van der Rohe had to be reorganized, but others proved successful and spurred new public and private redevelopment efforts in Cleveland, Baltimore, and Philadelphia as well as New Haven, in San Francisco, Detroit, and Chicago as well as Newark—to mention only a few where projects of special distinction were contributing to a civic revival.[36]

These accomplishments, however, were clouded by the continuing protests of those displaced and of many who urged their cause. The publication in 1962 of *The Urban Villagers* by Herbert J. Gans, which depicted the plight of the poor second-generation Italians who were uprooted from their depressed neighborhood in Boston's West End and scattered to many parts of the city in order to make way for a modern redevelopment of the district for high-rise luxury apartments, posed the dilemmas of urban renewal in a vivid fashion. A follow-up study of a large sample of the 2500 families displaced from the West End revealed that most of them had improved their housing but at a higher cost. Yet their limited advantages contrasted sharply with the hardships suffered by the Negro inhabitants of some renewal areas elsewhere. Chester Hartman, who made this study, concluded, after tabulating the findings of thirty-three other relocation studies, that the resettlement program "has been only an ancillary component of the renewal process," and that efforts in the 1960's to improve this work faced mounting difficulties.[37]

The failures, of course, were at the local level and in some cases reflected the eagerness of municipal and private developers to clear decaying inner-city sites; in other cases they revealed the wider community's resistance to a dispersed resettling of the displaced Negroes. In any event, many reformers who had insisted on local autonomy for urban-renewal projects now began to call for more rigid federal supervision of relocation programs. Others protested that the central cities alone could not master this problem, even under strict federal direction, and that the states should extend their urban-renewal authority to cover the entire metropolitan area so that resettlement of some of the inner-city poor could be made on cheap land in the suburbs.[38]

One federal response was increased emphasis on the rehabilitation of old neighborhoods. In some cities, Providence, for example, the Community Welfare Council assumed leadership in selecting appropriate neighborhoods, identifying the social deficiencies to be corrected, and spurring the community to action. In others, a settlement house provided the focus for community renewal and in some cases took the initiative in supplying new housing to replace the dilapidated structures removed by spot clearance. A non-profit Neighborhood Improvement Corporation, organized in San Francisco by the Mission Neighborhood Centers, Inc., to perform this function with federal backing under the 1961 Act, became a model for similar efforts elsewhere. But the chief task was to stimulate community participation in the rehabilitation effort, and here a score of neighborhood centers scattered from Boston to San Francisco performed a valuable service.[39]

Freedom House, established in the Washington Park area of Boston in 1949, was a noteworthy example. A resident effort from the start, its volunteer directors had formed more than a score of block associations to promote local improvements in the fifties, and it was from these groups that the first requests for federal aid arose in 1958, two years before John J. Collins, the new mayor of Boston, moved to establish the Boston Redevelopment Authority to supervise such programs. With full support from its Negro and white residents, Washington Park became the city's pioneer neighborhood rehabilitation project. To implement the program, Freedom House contracted with Action for Boston Community Development, a citywide organization formed as a result of a Ford Foundation grant for the promotion of neighborhood participation in social planning. With an enlarged staff, Freedom House sponsored 120 block-association meetings and several neighborhood hearings on proposed improvements. A preliminary plan, incorporating some of their suggestions, was unveiled late in 1961, and after further public hearings and many conferences a revised final plan received community support in January 1963. City, state, and federal approval followed and, on May 10, Dr. Weaver arrived to take part in ground-breaking ceremonies for the erection of Academy Homes, a 202-unit project to supply relocation homes for residents during the rehabilitation of their own houses.[40]

In some cities historic preservation societies joined the drive for community renewal. Earlier restoration projects, in Philadelphia, Washington, and several other places, received a new impetus from the renewal program. An Old Philadelphia Development Corporation undertook the restoration of the Society Hill area in that city, and with the College Hill Demonstration Project in Providence, completed in 1959, provided a strong incentive for new efforts in Mobile, Little Rock, and New Haven, to mention only three. These projects added a new dimension to the community-renewal program. Their goal of preserving buildings of historic and architectural interest helped to sustain the neighborhood's prestige and fostered efforts to restore its social as well as its physical amenities. And in the process of working together for the improvement of old neighborhoods, some poor residents and some wealthy patrons of the arts acquired a new sense of metropolitan citizenship.[41]

Although the initiative remained with the local communities, the emphasis placed by the federal agency on rehabilitation brought applications from ninety such projects by April 1963. All but one of the five largest metropolises and one-third of all central cities over 250,000 were engaged in this program. A major tool in this effort was code enforcement, and a decision by the federal authorities to require strict compliance with its regulations in this respect brought improvements in the enforcement of building, plumbing, electrical, and housing codes in many cities. In some cases, however, the difficulties encountered in these law-enforcement efforts prompted a renewed drive for total-clearance projects.[42]

As the number of clearance projects mounted, particularly in the downtown areas, local and national architectural societies displayed an increased concern for improved design standards. President Kennedy's interest in the arts prompted him to call a Conference on Aesthetic Responsibility at which the need for local efforts of this sort in every metropolis was stressed. But again a dilemma appeared as pressure developed in many towns for the employment of one or another of the nation's leading architects— Van der Rohe, I. M. Pei, Yamasaki, among others—limiting the opportunities of their local associates. To promote a wider recognition and utilization of architectural talent, the Public Housing Authority joined with the American Institute of Architects and the National Association of Housing and Redevelopment Officials in sponsoring regional design seminars in six widely scattered metropolises.[43]

Business leaders as well as architects and construction companies were becoming increasingly interested in the redevelopment of blighted inner-city areas. In spite of protests that the program had originally been adopted to assure improved housing to slum dwellers, Congress in 1961 increased the portion of the renewal funds available for nonresidential use from 10 to 30 per cent. This action gave federal approval and support to many downtown development schemes and spurred the reconstruction of extensive portions of Philadelphia and Boston, among other cities.[44] The need obviously was there but, in the opinion of Bernard J. Frieden, most such projects should be left to private investors, for only those that were economically sound as commercial ventures would prove successful as renewal projects. After a careful study of the market for residential and commercial facilities in New York, Los Angeles, and Hartford, he found the shortage so great in the first two that private reconstruction of the slums was justified there, though not in Hartford where even urban renewal would, in his view, be a mistake.[45]

Private investors were in fact launching many downtown ventures, some of far greater cost than the renewal projects. Here the development corporations, such as the Downtown Council in Minneapolis, the Citizens Progress, Inc., of Wichita, and several old established bodies, notably the Citizens League of Greater Cleveland, provided effective leadership. Sometimes enterprising merchants teamed up for the occasion, as in Rochester, where the McCurdy and the Forman brothers engaged Victor Gruen to build

Midtown Plaza.[46] Most of these groups, however, welcomed the assistance the federal government extended for planning not only within the central district but also throughout the market area. The Area Redevelopment Administration, established under the 1961 Act, proved especially helpful in some economically depressed cities, such as Altoona, Pennsylvania, Burlington, Vermont, and Helena, Arkansas. In the large metropolitan centers the business leaders were also becoming increasingly concerned with air pollution and welcomed the passage of the Clean Air Act in 1963, which provided additional assistance to state and city agencies battling this problem.[47]

Most of the downtown and inner-city redevelopment efforts, both public and private, were complicated by another circumstance that was now acquiring explosive characteristics. As the migration of Negroes to the cities continued, it fanned out in the sixties to reach many communities previously but slightly affected. Few central cities over 100,000 in population failed to attract a sizable influx of nonwhites, and those few were for the most part places of stagnation or slow growth, such as Scranton and New Bedford in the Northeast and Duluth in the Midwest. In dynamically growing metropolises, like Rochester and Syracuse in New York, San Francisco and San Bernardino in California, where Negroes, previously few in number, had reached 5 per cent by 1960, they now approached or exceeded a tenth of the central-city totals. In many larger centers, whose heavy industries or geographic location had earlier attracted large contingents, the increase was not so dramatic, but in most places the cluster of nonwhite settlements adjoining the business district was threatening to encircle it.[48]

The final cause in every case was the larger ring of white residents and the resistance many of them maintained to the outward spread of Negro settlement. Because of their increasing numbers, the density and more especially the percentages of nonwhites in the inner city were mounting and, aggravated by their general poverty, threatened the economic vitality of the central commercial districts. Yet, when the civic and business leaders endeavored to save the city's central core by employing urban-renewal powers to clear nearby slums and replace them with high-rise luxury apartments, they inevitably aggravated the Negro's housing problems and forged still another link between the metropolis and the federal government.[49]

The mounting demand of Negroes for more and better housing and the rising protest of civil rights advocates finally prompted Kennedy, in November 1962, to issue his long-contemplated executive order banning discrimination against Negroes in public housing and in all projects erected with federal assistance. That action not only called for a careful check of the rental practices of all urban-renewal projects but also focused attention again on the American city's most serious problem—not its slums but the plight of its inner-city residents.[50]

If the welfare of the residents of urban slums still seemed somewhat remote to most Americans in the fall of 1962, the situation changed dramatically during the following year. The efforts of biracial committees and human relations commissions in some 300 cities and towns had awakened many whites to the nature of the problem, but the reforms they had effected in some places—opening parks to all races and accepting token integration in the schools —seemed hopelessly inadequate to thousands of young Negroes in Southern and border towns who had engaged in numerous "sit-ins" and "freedom rides" after the initial success of the bus boycott in Montgomery in 1958. By these methods they had already desegregated some lunch counters and stores and won other concessions in various places, but it was early in April 1963 when Dr. King, leader of the Southern Christian Leadership Conference, selected Birmingham as the site for an intensified nonviolent demonstration against racial discrimination in employment and services that the Negro revolution began to engulf the cities of the South.[51]

The rapid succession of civil rights crises that summer did not all spring from an urban base, yet together they raised issues that soon brought throngs of demonstrators into the streets of Detroit as well as Nashville, obstructed traffic in 800 cities and towns North and South, and finally assembled a quarter of a million zealous participants for the great March on Washington on August 28, 1963. Their demand was for jobs and freedom "now." Of course the freedom and the jobs they wanted were local, but, with everybody else, the Negroes looked increasingly to the federal government to guarantee their rights in these and other respects. A new civil rights act would help, and Kennedy, who had recommended such a bill in February and submitted a first draft in June, now pressed for its adoption. Hoping to secure equal public accommodations for Negroes and to safeguard their other social and political rights, he posed the issue in terms that were both lofty and practical. "We are confronted with what is essentially a moral issue," he declared. "The fires of frustration and discord are burning in every city, North and South, where legal remedies are not at hand. Redress is sought in the streets, in demonstrations, parades and protests, which create tensions and threaten violence." The President hoped, by a new law, to provide effectively legal remedies.[52]

Demonstrations, parades, and protests multiplied as the bill made slow progress in committee hearings. Many white sympathizers in the North were surprised at the range of frustrations displayed by inner-city residents that summer and fall. Boycotts in Philadelphia, Chicago, and New York against department stores that refused to hire Negroes; rent strikes in Harlem and a few other places to compel landlords to supply heat and proper maintenance; mass picketing at construction jobs and other worksites where Negroes were denied employment in San Francisco and elsewhere; school boycotts against de facto segregation in New York and other cities marked the widening spread of the Negro revolution. In the North as well as in the South, the civil rights question came to a focus in the cities, but in most cases remedial action there depended on state and federal decisions.[53]

If even token integration made but slow progress in Southern cities because of opposition at the state level, de facto segregation was progressively aggravated in the North because of the resistance of the suburbs to Negro settlement. Alerted by the testimony of Dr. Kenneth Clark that de facto segregation in the North was as injurious to the Negro child as enforced segregation in the South, Dr. James E. Allen, Jr., among other educational leaders in the North, endeavored to correct the situation there. As commissioner of education in New York, Dr. Allen requested all school superintendents in the state to submit by September 1, 1963, a description of any local discriminatory practices or conditions and a plan for their eradication. Every community in the Empire State and many elsewhere debated the integration question with new interest that summer and fall.[54]

The debate became more intense with each passing month. As boards of education in New York State communities, such as White Plains and Rochester, and in responsive cities elsewhere, notably New Haven and Berkeley, laid plans for open enrollment or experimented with the pairing of predominantly Negro with predominantly white school districts, as at Princeton, the latent fears and hostilities of many white citizens burst into the open. William L. Miller, running for alderman of the 15th Ward in New Haven, was surprised to discover that the key local issues were national issues, such as school integration and housing. He had never heard of the "busing" problem and when it was described he assumed that it concerned only the school commissioners, but shortly after his election Miller found himself in the midst of a battle over the realignment of the school district boundaries.[55]

In similar fashion Mayor Henry W. Maier of Milwaukee, who had been working for three years to link the county's metropolitan development projects with a social development program for inner-city residents, discovered that fall that some of his Negro supporters had joined a group of pickets organized by CORE for a sit-in at his office to force him to remove a hostile county official. The mayor of Milwaukee was no more successful in resolving his inner-city problems than President Kennedy was in pressing for the adoption of the Civil Rights Act, but there was no longer any doubt that the two issues were closely related. Indeed these historic trends had so converged that on hearing the tragic news of Kennedy's assassination in hostile Dallas, many shocked citizens assumed that it was the act of vengeful segregationists.[56]

• *Metropolitan Ferment and the "Great Society"*

Humiliated by the outrage perpetrated in one of the proudest centers of the New South, some Southern leaders were ready, with

Lyndon B. Johnson, for a more constructive approach to the civil rights question. An earlier tragedy in another Southern city, Birmingham, had, as his biographers, Evans and Novak, reported, "ruled out any further compromise, in Johnson's view." Not only was the new President ready and determined to press the civil rights bill to successful enactment, but he was soon to make the neglect of the inner-city slums a major target in his plans for the "Great Society." [57] With untiring zeal and matchless skill he pressed one metropolitan program after another on Congress and with a few exceptions saw them move to final passage. Yet the consensus he sought and in part achieved never fully encompassed the mass of urban Negroes. Indeed the Negro revolution acquired a new zeal and leadership of its own in 1964 and boldly challenged the best efforts of the metropolis and the Great Society.

Determined to win public confidence, Johnson assured the former leaders of Kennedy's New Frontier of his support of their programs and relentlessly prodded Congress for their enactment. He sought first a budget with a sharp tax reduction to stimulate the economy, a policy advocated by Walter Heller, chairman of the Council of Economic Advisers, and a matter of major concern to the cities. With its passage, he tackled the crucial civil rights issue. He insisted on the acceptance of all portions of the strengthened bill, including the fair employment practices clause added in the House Judiciary Committee shortly before Kennedy's assassination. Capitalizing on the emotional reaction to that tragedy, he declared in his first address to the Congress, "no memorial oration or eulogy could more eloquently honor President Kennedy's memory than the earliest possible passage of the civil rights bill for which he fought so long." That speech on November 27 was, however, only the start of a lengthy campaign in which a record-breaking filibuster continued into June, but the final version of the bill retained all the major provisions intact. Not content with this victory, the new President pressed for the enactment that summer of other Kennedy proposals. These included an act long advocated by metropolitan leaders—federal aid for mass transit demonstration projects—and the more significant antipoverty program.[58]

According to his biographers, President Johnson began to talk about the Great Society in March, three months after his first call for a "War on Poverty." By that date he was ready to name Sargent Shriver as director of the proposed Office of Economic Opportunity and to launch the long campaign for the drafting and enactment of a suitable act. The mayors and welfare officials of New York, Detroit, and San Francisco, among other cities, were soon flying to Washington to testify on the needs of the urban poor and on imaginative techniques for their relief. There was no dearth of suggestions. Job training programs in Detroit, nursery schools in Cleveland, neighborhood center activities in Los Angeles and Chicago, and many more received attention. The most influential contributions were made by three demonstration projects launched a year or two before in New York by President Kennedy's Committee on Juvenile Delinquency. Mobilization for Youth, with a community action program in operation, Haryou, with its research findings almost ready for release, and ACT (the Associated Community Teams), backed by Congressman Adam Clayton Powell, each provided significant leads. Two other experimental programs in the encouragement of participation by poor inner-city residents —at Oakland and New Haven, both backed by generous Ford Foundation grants—attracted special interest. As the debate continued through July and into August, a new urgency advanced its cause with the outbreak of riots in Harlem and Brooklyn, even in affluent Rochester. Johnson may have made the fortunes of this bill his "mission," as his biographers maintain. He insisted on its passage as a measure of confidence in his leadership, but for many in Congress and for hundreds of thousands in urban and rural slums it had larger implications and a heartening promise.[59]

No racial outbreak was more unexpected or more disillusioning than that at Rochester in late July 1964. A prosperous city, with one of the lowest unemployment rates in the country and with possibly the highest per capita contribution to welfare agencies, it had a Human Rights Commission and a state SCAD office, both to assure fair employment opportunities to all. Its neighborhood centers had active workers in the streets and its churches as well as its schools were earnestly facing the problems brought on by a recent and rapid influx of Negroes. Its administration had only the year before created a Police Advisory Board, the second in the land, to hear any complaints of brutality against the police. Yet the incident that triggered the riot was the dispatch of police dogs to help suppress a minor disturbance at a street dance in a crowded slum area on a hot Friday night. Astonished by the unexpected violence, the police displayed great restraint and eventually, aided by state militia, contained the rioting. Three days later and after a heavy rain they brought the disturbance to an end, but not without great property losses and four accidental deaths.[60]

Congressman Frank Horton from Rochester's affluent east side district was as nonplused as any other citizen. "Rochester's shock is not without shame," he told his fellow congressmen after the violence had subsided. He could not explain "the weekend's bloodshed and havoc" but he did plead for aid in the "quest for racial peace." And when the roll call came on the antipoverty measure a few days later, he cast one of the twenty-two Republican votes for its passage.[61]

The antipoverty program was not a direct response to the inner-city riots of the summer of 1964, but it was a response to the problems and the social-economic distress that had produced the riots. And one of its provisions, calling for the enlistment of the poor in programs of self-help and neighborhood rehabilitation, set the tone for much of the reconstruction undertaken in Rochester and other riot-torn cities in the next year. In Oakland, where the pioneer Gray Areas Program was launched with a Ford grant in 1962, local civic leaders and social agencies had supplied the initiative; in New Haven, where the second and more successful project was undertaken, it was an imaginative mayor and the president of the school board who jointly took the lead; in each case, however, the effort was to induce participation at all levels of programing and action by the inner-city residents. And less than a month after the passage of the Economic Opportunity Act, Mayor James Cavanaugh of Detroit, assisted by Governor George W. Romney and by Sargent Shriver, was preparing to inaugurate a similar community action program, one of the first of 400 to be undertaken in the next half year as a part of the Great Society's War on Poverty.[62]

President Johnson thus had an urban program under way well before the election. The party platforms adopted that summer further drew the line between the opponents and the advocates of federal action. Whereas the Republicans deplored the fact that "local and state responsibility have given way to regimentation, conformity, and subservience to central power," the Democrats declared that "no government at any level can properly complain of violation of its powers, if it fails to meet its responsibilities." Barry Goldwater's many attacks on crime and corruption had an antiurban tone and anti-Negro connotations that failed to win favor in the cities. This coupled with his record of opposition to the Civil Rights Act, contributed to his humiliating defeat. Johnson's sweeping victory in all but six Southern states, and in three of the four major metropolises in those states, gave him an unprecedented majority in Congress and paved the way for further legislative triumphs.[63]

President now in his own right, Johnson stressed the urban aspect of his program in his State of the Union message in January. "To begin to think, work and plan for the development of entire metropolitan areas," the country needed, he declared, a Department of Housing and Urban Development. Events had moved so rapidly, both in the cities and in Congress, that neither that compound name nor the probable appointment of Dr. Weaver as secretary now seemed an unsurmountable obstacle.[64] While awaiting the measure's passage, the President spoke out in favor of increased aid to cities for improvements in their water and sanitary facilities and for acquisition of open-space land. These and other provisions were progressively gathered into the framework prepared for the new department. So many conflicting interests were in fact involved that the bill was not finally passed until September, and the appointment of Weaver was delayed until January 1966.[65]

This long delay did not, however, prevent numerous accomplishments during the interim. An amendment to the housing act in the previous year had authorized federal grants-in-aid to support code enforcement in renewal areas, a constructive response to critics of the earlier bulldozer tactics. In addition to promoting rehabilitation projects, the Housing and Home Finance Agency processed the first eleven applications for mass-transit aid that spring. It also pressed for the adoption of a two-pronged measure authorizing rent subsidies to help low-income families find accommodations to fit their needs in nonprofit projects, and creating a "rent-certificate" program to enable housing authorities to lease private properties when the demand for public housing could not be met easily by new construction. This program, following a demonstration project in New Haven, also permitted housing authorities to move into areas of the city where a new project might be blocked. On signing the Act in August, President Johnson gave one of the pens to Mayor Lee, who promptly used it to apply for the first grant under the new subsidy.[66]

The creation of the new Department of Housing and Urban Development would not, as the editor of the *American City* warned, solve all the problems. There were many tasks that the cities and the federal government could not tackle without state assistance, and Governor Romney of Michigan urged the states to asume their proper responsibilities in order to avoid the threat of national centralization. Frank Bane, chairman of the Advisory Commission on Intergovernmental Relations, had been stressing this need for several years; in 1965 he proposed that the federal government channel all grants-in-aid through the states, where they were administratively organized to distribute it, and otherwise directly to the cities as a prod to states to reform. Only a few states, notably California, were ready to perform the function, but John Anderson, Jr., former Republican governor of Kansas, accepted appointment as director for the new Citizens Conference on State Legislatures with the hope that, as the effects of reapportionment appeared, these bodies would develop staffs and programs to serve their fragmented metropolitan communities.[67]

Not all were in agreement, however, on the objectives of that service. The National Municipal League, which had secured a Ford grant to undertake a five-year research project to explore opportunities for state technical assistance to cities, named its former president, Dean Cecil Morgan of the Tulane Law School, as director of these studies. Governor Warren E. Hearner of Missouri created a State Department of Urban Affairs to undertake such technical assistance, as boards in New York and Kentucky as well as Michigan, among others, were already doing. But this was not sufficient, in the opinion of Senator Joseph D. Tydings of Maryland, who deplored the failure of the states to assist their metropolises in achieving an identity and an effective voice of their own. California's Coordinating Council on Urban Problems was one of the few positive moves in this direction and, with Governor Brown's other reform agencies, promoted the internal coordination of its rapidly expanding metropolitan communities. Elsewhere, as James Reston observed at Detroit in June 1966, "The Governors of the American states almost sound these days as if they were going the way of the modern kings." [08]

Unable to await state action, the cities and the federal government were boldly moving ahead. The antipoverty administration created regional offices to supervise state programs where they appeared and to promote and supervise local community projects as well. It soon had groups of Volunteers in Service to America (VISTA) working in Baltimore, Miami, and Hartford; Neighborhood Youth Corps and Job Corps in New York, Chicago, and Newark, among other cities, and Head Start projects in over 2,000 communities. The Economic Development Act of 1965, authorizing the expenditure of $3.5 billion to assist in the rejuvenation of depressed areas, encompassed rural areas and small towns as well; its first report listed 1280 municipalities, counties, and reservations as eligible for support when proper projects were presented.[69]

Enterprising mayors, like Richard Lee of New Haven, with imaginative projects ready to launch, could get more than their city's share since federal officials needed successful demonstrations to supply models and inspiration for projects elsewhere.[70] But the resistance the antipoverty efforts encountered in some communities produced many delays. The announced policies of promoting resident participation, creating neighborhood organizations, and hiring nonprofessionals wherever possible sometimes brought these new agencies into conflict with old welfare institutions or with neighborhood organizations sponsored independently, particularly those promoted by Saul Alinsky's Industrial Areas Foundation.[71]

Renewed rioting in the summer of 1965, and again in 1966, spurred efforts to develop an effective leadership among the poor.

The National Council of Churches, recently reawakened to the problems of the city that had given birth to its predecessor, the Federal Council of Churches in 1908, prodded and assisted local Federations of Churches in several metropolises to raise considerable sums, $100,000 for two years in Rochester, for example, to engage Alinsky's aid in organizing the Negro districts. His strategy was to provoke slum dwellers to work off their frustrations by outspoken attacks on "the power structure"; his training program in Chicago taught prospective slum leaders how to organize a local power group of their own by obstructing and if possible seizing control of community efforts in their neighborhoods. Whether these tactics would reach and involve the unorganized men and women at the bottom remained uncertain, although some observers hailed TWO, the Woodlawn Organization in Chicago, as a successful demonstration. "FIGHT" (for Freedom, Integration, God, Honor, and Today) in Rochester and other Alinsky offspring of the sixties were still too young to stand judgment on this count, but they did from the start create an animated dialogue between the new leaders they produced and those community representatives who had previously made an effort to tackle the problems of the slums. Where "the revolt against welfare colonialism," as Charles E. Silberman and Frank Reissman among others characterized the movement, failed to secure a share of the antipoverty funds (as the Harlem Youth Development program, better known as Haryou and somewhat similar in tactics but not associated with Alinsky, did in New York City) it generally required a new expression of confidence in substantive form from the churches, as in the case of both TWO and FIGHT, but the will to give the effort a full trial remained strong.[72]

The federal government's call for neighborhood organization and participation, in both the antipoverty and urban-renewal fields, had many and varied results. In most places the poor were "represented" by leaders selected by the officials, and the participation was minimal; in some places, however, block clubs organized by a settlement house or an antipoverty worker developed sufficient strength to provide indigenous leadership and to undertake programs of neighborhood improvement and social involvement, notably at Richmond, California, where the Community Development Project reported the integration and rejuvenation of a former blighted district without the displacement of its residents. Similar efforts occurred in other communities, sometimes with very promising results, in New Haven's Wooster Square and San Francisco's St. Francis Square redevelopment projects, for example. But frequently the struggle for power among old and new leaders or between rival organizations so divided the community that it provided a fertile field for spontaneous outbursts of frustration, despair, and anger, as at Watts in 1965, which was only the most appalling of at least a score of urban riots in that and the succeeding year.[73]

One in Atlanta, in September 1966, was especially revealing. Mayor Ivan Allen, Jr., had distinguished himself as a supporter of civil rights, one of the few of official standing in the South, and also as an eager applicant for federal aid in urban-renewal and antipoverty programs. Negro votes had helped on two occasions to elect him, and he enjoyed the confidence of the Atlanta Summit Leadership Conference, which had drawn representatives of most of the city's Negro organizations into frequent policy and programing discussions with white leaders. Yet when a police officer wounded a Negro in an attempt to arrest him for a suspected car theft, a militant leader of the Student Nonviolent Coordinating Committee ("Snick"), dispatched a sound truck through the streets, spreading the call for a demonstration of "Black Power," and a riot erupted. By his prompt intervention at the scene, Mayor Allen was able to calm the furor and to assure a disciplined restoration of order that night; he was also able to maintain it, five days later, when a white segregationist shot and killed a Negro in another Atlanta slum area by quickly arresting the suspect and charging him with murder. Mayor Allen received wide acclaim, including some from local Negro leaders, for his forthright valor, but he was only, in his own opinion, vindicating the character of Atlanta The fact that 44 per cent of the city's residents were colored, many of them Atlanta-born homeowners and respected if still segregated members of the middle class, gave the several Negro communities of Atlanta a stability that helped to check irresponsible action. Mayor Allen, after castigating the current leadership of Snick as "the backwash of the civil rights movement," hastened to declare, as soon as quiet was restored, that much still needed to be done to improve conditions in the Negro districts. Recognizing the futility of an appeal to the state, he promptly launched a study to determine whether any federal programs of possible assistance had been overlooked.[74]

There was of course another and more traditional method of exerting pressure, and many Negroes found it when they discovered that their votes carried considerable weight in tightly contested elections. The registration campaigns pressed in most cities and in many rural counties in the South increased the number of Negroes eligible to vote in 1964 to approximately 6 million. An estimated 4.5 million turned out on election day that November, giving Johnson, in spite of his Southern origins, perhaps 95 per cent of their votes. The effect in several cities was most welcome to the Democrats and helped to elect, in addition to many whites, a number of Negroes as aldermen, supervisors, district attorneys, judges, representatives to state legislatures, and even to the House of Congress. A Negro almost won election as mayor of Cleveland, and another ran second among the commissioners elected in Dayton and as a result became deputy mayor. Still another, Robert C. Henry, elected a commissioner, was chosen by his fellow commissioners to serve as mayor of Springfield, Ohio. Several Negroes elected as school commissioners or to other boards found themselves chosen to serve as chairman or president. Indeed throughout the North the readiness of whites to give Negroes a share in the responsibilities of government resulted in the election or appointment of some 1,500 to official posts in 1964.[75] *

Despite fears that the widespread evidence of a "backlash" of white resentment against Negro violence would produce a relaxation in the attack on the slum problem, neither the federal government nor most urban administrators showed signs of weakening. New experiments in school integration and new programs for rejuvenating the slums appeared in several cities. When, for example, one Rochester suburb invited a busload of children from the inner-

* Several Negroes triumphed at the polls in 1967, including Carl B. Stokes as mayor of Cleveland.

city districts to attend its primary schools in September 1965, suburban towns elsewhere debated similar proposals, and a year later five in the environs of Hartford launched such a program on a larger scale. Some 10,000 teachers and other college graduates enrolled in the newly formed National Teachers Corps that summer to accept assignments in "poverty pockets" where local school districts requested supplementary instructors.[76] Mayor John V. Lindsay invited two of Mayor Lee's ablest assistants, Mitchell Sviridoff and Edward Logue, to make reorganization studies of New York City's poverty and housing programs and then pressed both to move to New York to direct them. Sviridoff accepted, but Logue, who three years earlier had responded to a similar appeal from Boston, was skeptical of Lindsay's ability to get sufficient federal support to do the job required in that metropolis and returned to Boston to continue his well-launched programs for its reconstruction.[77]

Doubts of the federal government's will and ability to meet the full challenge began to mount after the election of 1966. Not only was Johnson's majority considerably reduced but the soaring costs of the Vietnam war threatened to divert the funds needed for the war on poverty. Yet the federal government, which had assumed new grants-in-aid programs—nine in 1964, and seventeen in 1965 —was not prepared to abandon the field. It had made new friends by its support, for example, for urban trails for the use of cyclists and horseback riders as well as hikers in metropolitan areas, and by its encouragement to art galleries, museums, and libraries. While federal aid to the arts was granted indirectly, by creating a National Foundation on the Arts and the Humanities in 1965 and under the Elementary and Secondary School Act a year later, and consisted chiefly of support for planning and programing of educational projects, Johnson's endorsement of Kennedy's library bill had brought its passage in 1964 and increased the federal aid available each year to $55 million for urban as well as rural libraries.[78]

Although some reports on the antipoverty programs were critical, others were laudatory, and few suggested any relaxation of effort. Indeed the sessions of the Conference of Mayors in June and of the League of Cities in December brought earnest appeals for continued federal support. Two series of hearings on urban needs by Senator Abraham Ribicoff's subcommittee produced an outpouring of demands from mayors, administrators, and the executives of urban-focused agencies protesting against rumored cuts in appropriations for the cities. The federal government, they maintained, would have to gird itself to expend huge sums to eliminate poverty in America and to rebuild the decaying cores of its metropolises in the years ahead.[79]

Other voices protested that the federal government could not alone be expected, nor should it be allowed, to assume full responsibility for the joint tasks of rebuilding the cities and abolishing poverty. The Committee for Economic Development called upon the states to modernize their local governmental structures in order to increase efficiency and permit metropolitan communities to act as responsible units in the solution of their problems. Responding to these and other pressures, nine states, some with reapportioned legislatures, established new state planning agencies and seven granted local bodies power to engage in regional planning. A detailed review of planning legislation in 1964 and 1965 revealed a widespread awakening by the states to the need for responsible leadership in metropolitan and regional redevelopment. Some champions of private enterprise maintained, on the other hand, that the great corporations and private builders also had opportunities to seize and responsibilities to assume if the nation was to preserve its traditional freedoms. Several leading firms, notably the U.S. Gypsum Company in Harlem, and the Smith, Kline and French Laboratories in Philadelphia, remodeled their old factories and renovated adjoining tenements in order to supply new jobs in their slum areas and to spur the rehabilitation of these neighborhoods to the profit of all concerned.[80]

More spectacular still was the new-towns movement in which Robert E. Simon and James L. Rouse seized a dramatic lead. Reston, the model city started by Simon in 1963 on an open site 18 miles from Washington, was partially ready for occupancy by the summer of 1966. Meanwhile Community Research and Development, Inc., founded by Rouse, had launched construction at the first of a cluster of nine villages planned as the satellite city of Columbia, Maryland, between Baltimore and Washington. These

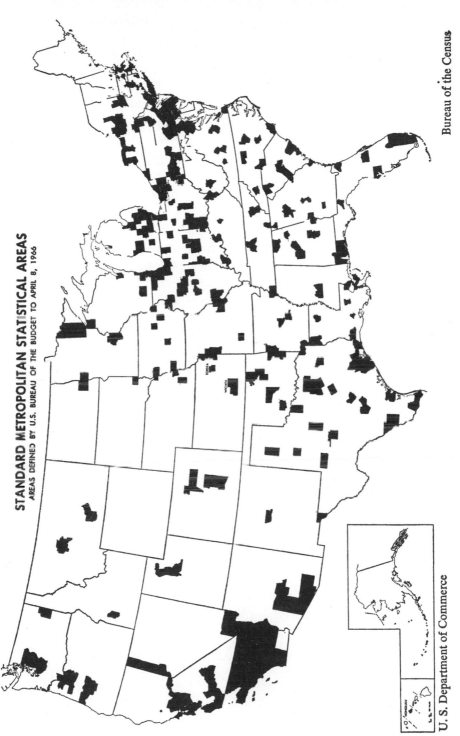

STANDARD METROPOLITAN STATISTICAL AREAS

AREAS DEFINED BY U.S. BUREAU OF THE BUDGET TO APRIL 8, 1966

Bureau of the Census

U. S. Department of Commerce

multimillion-dollar projects were only the most spectacular of several score started or proposed by private builders across the country.[81]

Excited by these developments and spurred by the difficulties many cities were encountering in redevelopment efforts, numerous planners and civic leaders pressed for federal aid for the new-town movement. A group called the Committee for National Land Development Policy opened headquarters in Chicago to promote the location and development of twenty-five new core cities and to enlist industrial and federal backing.* In Washington, however, where the lobbyists of several cities had opened permanent offices, and where for years the Conference of Mayors and the old American Municipal Association, renamed the League of Cities in 1964, with a dozen other national civic bodies had maintained staffs, and where the International City Managers' Association now also established an office, the broader interests of existing cities commanded first attention. And when Congress passed the Demonstration Cities Act, in October 1966, it gave major emphasis to demonstration projects for the restoration of blighted districts in old central cities and included support for new-town developments as a corollary.[82]

A more significant corollary, in the opinion of Professor Wheaton of Berkeley, was the inclusion of a metropolitan-areas demonstration program. A primary objective of the act was to encourage communities to coordinate all aspects of their redevelopment projects, and this provision extended the area of coordination to entire metropolitan districts. It followed and strengthened a clause in the Housing and Urban Redevelopment Act of the previous year, which supported regional planning. Now, in addition, the Department of Housing and Urban Development was empowered to require a review of all applications for assistance beyond the central

* Curiously enough, no one noted the interesting fact that more new metropolises were emerging by natural processes of urban growth than the new-town developers were seriously projecting. Thus the 212 Standard Metropolitan Statistical Areas of 1960 increased to 228 by April 1966, with one or more in every state, except Vermont, Wyoming, and Alaska, as the adjoining map will show. This represented an addition of 88 metropolises in the quarter century since 1940 when the 50,000 minimum for the central city was adopted.

cities by an official regional council or planning board. Not only did Mayor Lindsay hasten to reactivate New York's Metropolitan Regional Council but Detroit moved to strengthen its Supervisors Inter-County Commission and the appropriate officials in a score of lesser metropolises took steps to create or revive similar councils. Moreover, the National Association of Counties devoted the entire program at its 31st Annual Conference at New Orleans in July to the discussion of metropolitan planning. The prime objective was to control sprawl and make "the boundless city," as Robert C. Wood described it, more livable.[83]

In a period when the plight of the inner city, the mounting despair of its residents, and the fragmentation of the metropolis commanded attention in every daily issue of the urban press and in innumerable periodicals, this tentative formulation of what President Johnson called "Creative Federalism" was a promising start. It would prove disillusioning, Wheaton among others warned, if adequate funds were not forthcoming, but new organizations both public and private were girding to forestall that possibility. One was the Joint Council on Urban Development formed by the urban lobbyists at Washington; another was the Democratic Study Group organized by urban representatives in Congress.[84] Still another was Urban America, Inc., established in the hot summer of 1965 by a merger of the old American Planning and Civic Association with the younger and more richly endowed Action Council for Better Cities. Designed as a promotional as well as a research group, it secured grants from Ford and other foundations to distribute "seed money" to promising projects and to undertake technical cost and planning studies on a wide range of urban problems. To head the staff it engaged William L. Slayton, previously the chief urban-renewal administrator and familiar on that account not only with the procedures and the possibilities in government but also with the agencies and the needs of every city in the land. If a coordination of public and private, federal, state, and local energies was possible, Slayton and his 50-member staff should, his backers believed, help to achieve it. With a number of new civic and promotional groups in widely scattered metropolises, such as LEAP, organized to supply Leadership and Education for the Advancement of Phoenix, it displayed great hopes for the future of the city and relied with confidence on the new research techniques perfected in a host of urban laboratories and institutes across the land.[85]

- ● *Toward a Federal Synthesis*

Urban and national leaders alike were turning to the scholars for help. In spite of rumblings of anti-intellectualism, the prestige of the research scholar reached a new high in the early sixties. Urban surveys in every field were employing university professors as research directors—in planning and housing, in public health and welfare, even in business and government. Moreover, in almost every case the leaders, hoping to achieve a consensus, adopted an interdisciplinary approach. Aided by computers, they applied new statistical techniques and developed new comparative standards. Under the weight of evidence, several formerly pervasive theories crumbled and gave way to new hypotheses. Yet in the process many old dilemmas reappeared and with several new ones complicated the search for a synthesis.

In contrast with earlier decades, when sociologists held the lead in urban analysis, political scientists assumed the initiative in the sixties. As the march of events quickened, in the reapportionment battles, in the many and varied efforts to reach effective decisions in metropolitan districts, and in the new crisis created by the Negro revolution, scholars were challenged to provide both a meaningful theory and programs for action. It soon became apparent that the old power-structure thesis would no longer explain these developments. With the publication in 1961 of Professor Dahl's probing volume on *Who Governs?* and in succeeding years of other products of the Yale study of New Haven's politics, notably Nelson Polsby's *Community Power and Political Theory,* the enervating concept of a small control group of manipulators or decision makers gave way to the vision of a pluralistic society more congenial to the nation's democratic tenets. Some scholars, refusing to discredit the earlier findings of Hunter and his followers, agreed with Lawrence D. Mann, who viewed these contrasting systems as the extremes in a spread of community power arrangements that extended from autocracy in Atlanta to democracy in New Haven. One difficulty here was that no point on the continuum was fixed, as a later study of Atlanta demonstrated, when M. Kent Jennings of the Brookings Institution found a plural pattern of power groups there, with links by the early sixties to Negro power groups as well.[86]

Professor Dahl and the other members of the Yale group could accept this amplification of their analysis since it merely extended the range of possible power groups. The key factor was the quality of leadership developed in each city and in the varied aspects of its life. Numerous scholars studied patterns of decision making in housing, in central-city and regional planning, in urban redevelopment, both public and private, even in social planning, and Edward C. Banfield and James I. Wilson at Harvard summarized, in *City Politics*, the findings of a team of researchers in more than a score of cities across the land. Mayor Maier of Milwaukee added some illuminating suggestions from the viewpoint of an experienced urban official concerning the strategy and the tactics of leadership. Edward Sofen among others studied the strategy requirements of the more complicated governmental structure in Miami and Dade County. Roscoe C. Martin in *The Cities and the Federal System* explored the developing relationships in functional areas, such as aviation, between local and national authorities.[87]

Even this pluralistic consensus did not long stand unchallenged, however. A major defect of this analysis, in the opinion of Professor Walker of Michigan, was its assumption that an effective decision-making structure was the primary objective. Political science should be equally concerned, he believed, with an analysis of the implications of "the political inactivity of the average citizen" and also with a study of "social movements which appear on the periphery of the organized political system." His categorization of Dahl, Polsby, and others as proponents of an "elitist theory" of government brought a sharp rejoinder from Dahl, who denied that his descriptive analysis of the plural structure of decision making in New Haven provided a normative answer to the question: Who should govern? The debate concerned government and the metropolis at many points, but we can only note here that both of these scholars recognized the need for more study of the role in a democracy of massive protest movements such as those represented by the Negro revolution in the city.[88]

These problems raised questions that political scientists alone could not resolve and prompted a number of interdisciplinary symposia and publications. Thus the Tamiment Institute and *Daedalus* held a joint seminar in the Poconos in the spring of 1960 to hear and debate papers by distinguished representatives of several disciplines. Their contributions, edited by Lloyd Rodwin and published as *The Future Metropolis* in 1961, provided an illuminating review of the urban situation. Another book compiled and published that year by Oliver P. Williams and Charles Press, *Democracy in Urban America,* supplied pertinent selections from many writers on the subject. Still another, edited by Philip Olson, made an eclectic approach to *America as a Mass Society.* No issues were resolved by these volumes, least of all by the last one, which endeavored only to assemble the opposing arguments, but its most striking passage, a paraphrase of Karl Marx in the introduction of a paper by Edward Shils—"A specter is haunting sociologists. It is the specter of 'mass society,' "—could not properly have been published a year later, for this "phantasm" evaporated as the Negro revolution swept from city to city in 1964 and after.[89]

Several sociologists gave close attention to these quasi-political aspects of the metropolis. Professor Scott Greer of Northwestern University devoted several books to the subject, notably one entitled *The Emerging City: Myth and Reality.* After dismissing the mass-society concept as too pessimistic and characterizing much of the early sociological analysis as "cumulative" but static and "not a complete explication," he described the transformation of the city into the metropolis as a "continuing process" affecting residents of the cities and the "carrying society" in progressive degrees as the "scale" of that society expanded. He saw the urban community as providing the integrating environment needed to distribute the inevitable tension between the dynamic larger society and the primary family group. As a minor social system, the urban community, in his analysis, needed a "polity" to supply full scope to the "community actors" and to enable them to make necessary adjustments and possible contributions to the larger society. The two other types of urban individuals, the "isolates" and the "neighbors," could find an adequate or at least a satisfying range of opportunities in a part of a city or in a suburb—a "community of limited liability" as Greer, borrowing a Janowitz concept, assessed it; but only a fully articulated metropolis could answer the needs of a mature member and citizen of the larger society.[90]

Several sociologists wrote comprehensive volumes in the urban field. Some, produced as texts to fill the needs of the increasing number of college courses on this subject, reviewed and attempted to integrate the work of earlier scholars. Leonard Reissman, however, took a more critical view of the contributions of his predecessors and assigned each to a limited category in his typology of urban studies. Deploring the "myth" that cities were failures, since their dramatic growth had demonstrated their continued appeal to mankind, he identified four factors—urbanization, industrialization, the emergence of a middle class, and the birth of nationalism —that, when properly weighted, supplied a typology with which to classify national societies. His analysis in *The Urban Process,* like that of Professor Greer, reached beyond the single urban community to encompass the larger society it was helping to shape; he also recognized, with some other sociologists, the historical dimensions of that process.[91]

Yet, as if to prove the importance of the historical dimension, each of these volumes and several others on the city, written before the Negro revolution, appeared a bit outdated after its eruption. Morton Grodzins, who had commented perceptively on "The Great Schism of Population" in a 1959 book, was quoted by Williams and Press and cited by others, but the full implication of the situation for sociology was scarcely recognized.[92] A veritable flood of books in the middle sixties filled the gap—books by "action" as well as ecological sociologists, clinical as well as educational psychologists, social as well as economic historians, forthright as well as painstaking journalists, articulate as well as sensitive offspring of the slums. Some were powerful firsthand documents, notably Claude Brown's *Manchild in the Promised Land;* others made a more objective analysis, *Negroes in the Cities* by the Taeubers, for example; still others, such as Dr. Kenneth Clark's *Dark Ghetto,* combined emotional intensity with scientific insight.[93]

Several related studies of a somewhat broader character also contributed to an understanding of the Negro revolution. Stanley Lieberson's *Ethnic Patterns in American Cities* and *Beyond the Melting Pot* by Nathan Glazer and Daniel P. Moynihan were outstanding, as was *Delinquency and Opportunity* by Richard Cloward and Lloyd Ohlin. Frank Reissman and others assembled pithy articles by sixty scholars in a compendium on *Mental Health and the Poor*. But most comprehensive of all was *The Negro American,* edited by Parsons and Clark, and reproduced in large part from two recent issues of *Daedalus*. "Nothing is of greater significance to the welfare and vitality of this nation than the movement to secure equal rights for Negro Americans," declared President Johnson in the Foreword to this volume, which assembled the relevant wisdom of some thirty distinguished scholars. Here for the first time Talcott Parsons, dean of theoretical sociologists, viewed the Negro's struggle for "Freedom Now" as an integral part of the evolving "societal community" in America. Not only did he link it with the nation's history of increasing ethnic diversity and cultural pluralism, he also related it to the country's rural-urban trends and saw the future of the American metropolis and the promise of the Federal Union as bound up with the fortunes of this crucial movement.[94]

The more practical aspects of urban redevelopment had meanwhile focused the attention of many economists, too, on the city. In the fifties development groups in several metropolises had engaged research teams to prepare economic-base studies and central business district reports; while several of these served a promotional purpose, a critical review by John Rannells of Philadelphia revealed in 1961 the need for a stronger body of tested theory to coordinate this effort. The Ford Foundation made a grant of $350,000 that year to Resources for the Future, Inc., to support its projected studies of urban economics. Economists on the staffs of urban institutes at several universities pressed for the acquisition of additional computers and the establishment of data-processing centers. Soon a number were in operation, at Rutgers and Syracuse as well as at the Universities of Oklahoma and Wisconsin, among others, and in 1961 some of their directors formed an Urban and Regional Information Systems Association to coordinate their work.[95]

With the increased volume of data, the pressure for the development of an adequate theory mounted. Several scholars were in fact making significant contributions. Richard L. Meier of the Joint Center in Cambridge produced a tentative draft of *A Communications Theory of Urban Growth* that attracted keen interest and pointed the way for systematic data collection and analysis in new areas.[96] Wilbur R. Thompson of Wayne State University in Detroit made a more comprehensive attack on the problem in *A Preface to Urban Economics*. Backed by Resources for the Future, he took full advantage of the scholarly talent assembled by its Committee on Urban Economics and produced a volume that supplied not only models and formulae for charting metropolitan growth trends but also patterns and guidelines for data collection on many aspects of the urban economy. He provided for the measurement of public as well as private contributions to the economy and explored the possibility of weighting shifts in national policy and world trends.[97]

The practical value of such technological advances was unquestioned, but planners had the additional tasks of measuring preferences and determining goals. We have previously noted some of the dilemmas they faced in seeking to coordinate the plans of neighboring districts; equally difficult, however, was the determination of design and scale. The long struggle of the advocates of new towns and integral neighborhoods seemed to be winning a consensus of approval when the publication by Jane Jacobs of her polemical volume, *The Death and Life of Great American Cities,* in 1961 challenged the basic tenets of the movement. A resident and admirer of Greenwich Village, an aging district in old Manhattan, she made a strong case for the vitality and charm of its variegated street life in contrast to the planned order and quiet of the spaciously landscaped new towns advocated by Mumford, Stein, and their followers. Stunned by the totality of Mrs. Jacobs's criticism

and by the popular response it evoked, community planners nevertheless rallied to defend the burgeoning new cities and even projected "New Towns Intown," as one developer put it.[98]

The controversy directed attention to a new effort to test the
merits of rival urban designs. A volume by Ansel M. Strauss,
Images of the American City, posed some of the questions. Geographers, long concerned with determining and preserving the advantages of urban as well as transport sites, contributed to the
analysis. But the impact of Jean Gottman's monumental volume,
Megalopolis, which depicted the emergence of one vast urbanized
region extending without a break from Boston (eventually from
Portland, Maine) to Washington and Baltimore (eventually to
Richmond, Virginia), was to quicken the search for an acceptable
design for communities of more limited size. Victor Gruen expressed the judgment of an imaginative but practical architect and
planner when he stressed, in his volume on *The Heart of Our
Cities*, the imperative necessity of restoring the vitality and convenience of the central business districts by freeing them for
pedestrian use and enjoyment.[99]

Many architects as well as planners and social scientists joined
the debate over the ideal city. Two profusely illustrated volumes,
Face of the Metropolis, by Martin Meyerson and associates, and
Man-Made America: Chaos or Control, by Christopher Tunnard
and Boris Pushkarev, displayed some of the achievements as well
as some of the hazards of metropolitan growth. Richard E. Gordon
and others attacked the suburban sprawl in *The Split-Level Trap*,
while S. D. Clark accused critics of the suburbs of selecting only
abnormal models for analysis. Several volumes presented technical
studies of the housing market, the space requirements of houses
and yards, and the adequacy of housing projects. All the papers
delivered at the fourth annual forum of Resources for the Future
in 1962 and edited by Lowden Wingo, Jr., in *Cities and Space:
The Future Use of Urban Land*, displayed "the current scientific
ethos," as Robert Gutman observed in a review. They were, he
reported, more concerned with urban problems than with urban
designs and recognized the planner's obligation to prepare alternate
choices for the public.[100]

Even the policy of drafting alternate plans and surrendering to others the final decision left to the planners ample scope for creative work. Some were content to apply the traditional patterns, occasionally in imaginative combinations, fitting them neatly into the given space; others, however, were intrigued by the possibility of employing the newer techniques of the social sciences to determine the correct solution for planning dilemmas. Harvey S. Perloff, director of the regional studies program of Resources for the Future, was a proponent of this latter approach. He had organized an interdisciplinary planning seminar at Pittsburgh in 1958 at which distinguished sociologists, economists, and political scientists as well as planners had read and discussed papers analyzing the structure, organization, and growth processes of the metropolis. Their major objective, as revealed in the printed version of the papers and comments, edited and published by Perloff in 1961 under the title *Planning and the Urban Community,* was to identify possible areas for fruitful research and to determine the planner's educational needs.[101]

Scholars at a dozen active centers of urban studies were eagerly pursuing these objectives. Many of these men served in addition as consulting editors on one or another of a half dozen journals dealing wholly or in part with urban affairs. Both the *National Civic Review* and *Land Economics* gave increased attention to their book review sections and featured critical articles on urban problems by academic scholars. Three new publications, *Nation's Cities,* established in 1963 by the National Municipal Association, *Trans-action,* launched in November that year as a Community Leadership Project of Washington University in St. Louis, and the *Urban Affairs Quarterly,* which made its appearance late in 1965, provided a continuing and critical discussion of urban problems and developments for officials, teachers, and scholars. But it was in the *Journal* of the American Institute of Planners that the major controversies raged, often achieving an interdisciplinary sophistication unrivaled even in the more academic reviews. A succession of able editors boldly sought contributions from the leading proponents of varied interpretations and produced frequent special editions compiled by distinguished guest editors on particular aspects of the planner's functions. The need for more scholarly training based on more systematic research was constantly stressed.[102]

In further pursuance of both objectives, a few years later, a group of scholars at the University of California in Berkeley undertook to make "a systematic examination of the underlying concepts about the metropolitan community" of interest to planners. As summarized by John W. Dyckman, newly arrived chairman of the Berkeley Center for Planning and Development, the six major contributors to the symposium on *Explorations into Urban Structure* were in full agreement only on the inadequacy of the planner's conventional wisdom and the need for further explorations. Yet none of the "intellectual constructs" they examined seemed applicable to the "open system" faced by practical planners. After probing the distinctions between spatial and functional concepts of urban communities, recognizing the interdependence of public and private decisions and developmental efforts and emphasizing the dynamic character of the urban growth process, they tended in varying ways to pull back from an acceptance of social-structure controls over urban goals and procedures. Dyckman, at least, welcomed the pluralism detected by some scholars and seized upon Norton Long's concept of the city as an ecology of games to conclude by counseling planners to share the decision making in their game with politicians, economists, and artists where their fields impinged, and, as urged by Professor Wheaton, one of the contributors and formerly one of the architects of the community renewal program, to consult with the residents and citizens affected whenever they could be involved.[103]

But choices concerning the ideal size, character, and arrangement of the metropolis also required a consideration of psychological and other cultural factors. Numerous scholars were already exploring this field, and Dr. Leonard J. Duhl, a psychiatrist on the staff of the National Institute of Mental Health, assembled contributions from some thirty of them for his comprehensive volume on *The Urban Condition*. Duhl and his colleagues did not attempt to answer the questions of what size, what degree of complexity, and what kind of administrative structure are desirable—their object was to develop "a new way of viewing complexity, of viewing bigness and unravelling confusion." With occasional expressions of regret, they recognized that man's urban communities were becoming ever larger and more complex and required a "reconciliation between the 'social-irrational' man and his instincts . . . and the 'economic' or 'rational' man . . . who uses the strength of his ego to control the environment." Several of Duhl's contributors considered the place and character of political action in the metropolis, and Harvey S. Perloff, among others, analyzed social-planning and community-action programs. While most scholarly writers now hesitated to express judgment on the merits of neighborhood life, Lawrence Haworth made it an essential ingredient in his definition of *The Good City*.[104]

Another scholarly study of the community is of particular interest here because its conceptual analysis provides a striking parallel to my own treatment of the metropolis. Roland L. Warren combined academic and field experience in a rigorous application of social-system analysis to community studies. The community, as he defined it, was a social as well as a spatial entity and could have varying degrees of autonomy, service and psychological identity, and integration. By demonstrating that urban communities varied from each other and changed in time within each of these dimensions, Warren was able to construct an analytical graph. And by charting the positions of several sample communities at various dates on the graph he discovered that American cities had moved from a state of considerable autonomy and strong local identity toward one of interdependence and subordination to the national society. Much historical data, as we have seen, supports this conceptualization and also buttresses his further thesis that America experienced a "great change" in the second quarter of the present century when many local or "horizontal" community ties became weak and the national or "vertical" ties became dominant.[105]

Warren's study not only opened new vistas for historical sociology; it also provided theoretical guidelines for community organizers. His analysis had little to say about the techniques of organization but offered suggestive hints for action sociologists on the timing and direction of community efforts. Thus it was the weakened character of local community bonds, which he regarded as the social price paid for urbanization, that stimulated recurring attempts at community development. Here again the experience of the social-center and social-unit movements of the middle and late teens as well as the neighborhood organization programs of the fifties and sixties illustrate and are partially explicated by Warren's theoretical analysis.

The number and variety of scholarly studies and journalistic descriptions of the metropolis almost defied comprehension; fortunately, however, a few books supplied a general approach. Philip Hauser and Leo Schnore provided, in *The Study of Urbanization,* a comprehensive review of the literature on the city in a series of bibliographical essays by experts in economics, sociology, political science, geography, and history and other essays on the research opportunities in each field. Mitchell Gordon summarized the shocking aspects of more than a dozen urban problems in a paperback account, *Sick Cities.* York Willbern, director of the Bureau of Government Research at Indiana University, related some of the maladies, in a slender volume, *The Withering Away of the City,* to the rapid urbanization of metropolitan regions and their failure to achieve a comparable development in the political and fiscal fields. John Bollens and Henry Schmandt assembled and organized the findings of scholars in several disciplines in their comprehensive volume, *The Metropolis: Its People, Politics and Economic Life.*[106]

But it was Professor Gulick who most successfully placed the contemporary urban situation in national perspective. More closely involved in urban developments than any other scholar during the previous four decades, he spoke from rich experience and with a sure grasp of the mounting volume of research when in 1961 he delivered the four lectures later published under the title *The Metropolitan Problem and American Ideas.* With great clarity he reviewed the local urban problems that have become national concerns; noted the dilemmas involved in the choices between private and public action and among local, state, and national responsibility; and posed the challenges that have become progressively more insistent—to develop neighborhoods of human proportions, political entities of metropolitan dimensions, and a cooperative three-cornered federalism to avoid a national centralization and achieve a dynamic regional diversity and growth.[107]

Historians in increasing numbers were likewise contributing to the study of the city. A few additional metropolises attracted urban biographers, Kansas City and Washington, for example, and new books appeared on Boston, New York, Chicago, and Rochester. Several historians tackled specific urban topics, notably Richard Wade in *Slavery in the Cities* before the Civil War; Roy Lubove in *The Progressives and the Slums* before 1917; John W. Reps in *The Making of Urban America,* a revealing study of city planning in the colonial and early national periods; and Gilbert Osofsky in *Harlem: The Making of a Ghetto: 1890–1930.* Constance M. Green, who published two distinguished volumes on Washington, also produced a second summary account of *The Rise of Urban America.* Other scholars compiled historical source books on American cities in an endeavor to weave together the scattered strands of the nation's urban development. My own earlier volume, *The Urbanization of America, 1860–1915,* had a similar objective.[108]

The Urban History Group, formed in 1953 to foster these studies, issued occasional newsletters and continued to hold annual meetings. At its 1961 session in Washington the members discussed a critical charge by Eric Lampard of Wisconsin that they had failed to make significant application of the more probing technique of the social sciences to the study of urban history. A few historians were, however, already exploring that possibility, as Charles N. Glaab revealed in an updated bibliographical survey of their work. Thus Sam B. Warner at Harvard made use of a computer in charting the course of suburban trends in post-Civil War Boston, and Glaab and A. Theodore Brown incorporated social-science concepts in their new comprehensive volume, *A History of Urban America.* Historians welcomed the opportunity to participate in some of the interdisciplinary institutes on the city. One such conference, sponsored by the Joint Center at Cambridge, focused its full attention on the role of "The City in History." Although not in attendance, Lewis Mumford and his new book by that title were frequently mentioned at its sessions, which ranged almost as widely throughout the world's history as that brilliantly written volume itself.[109]

If most of these efforts failed to achieve the conceptual break-through some social scientists desired and gave but slight attention to the emerging metropolis, they did testify to the increased aware-ness of the city that has swept progressively through intellectual circles in America during the past five decades. It therefore seems appropriate that a historian, while awaiting the development of more scientific techniques, should at least observe, as I have at-tempted to do in these chapters, what many in other fields have been saying for years, that the nation and its cities have together, in the past half century, experienced basic transformations in their character and relationships, and that this historic process has de-veloped sufficient stress to forge a new entity best described as Metropolitan America.

To recapitulate: We have seen how the mushrooming cities of the early 1910's grew in number, size, and complexity and devel-oped problems that prompted them to seek broader powers and larger resources. We have also seen how the tentative early re-lationships between the cities and the federal government, born of the First World War, waned during the twenties as the resurgent cities struggled hopefully to achieve metropolitan character and autonomy; and how these relationships again waxed during the thirties when the Depression disclosed the fiscal inadequacies of the cities and revealed their economic interdependence with the rest of the nation. We have further seen how the early appeals for federal assistance became more cautious as the threat of na-tional control and centralization appeared; how the cities renewed their efforts to achieve a metropolitan polity and a sound fiscal base; and how the states resisted these moves even during the Eisenhower years when the national government reasserted its federal character and prodded, or at least admonished, the states to assume their full responsibilities and to strengthen those of their urban communities.

We have noted that these developments, stemming in part from internal urban growth, were also conditioned by extraneous his-toric events—wars and depressions and technological changes. We have also noted how the break in the flow of immigrants during the First World War prompted Northern cities to seek a fresh supply of labor in the South; how that new migration offered an escape for an oppressed people, which they continued to enjoy in the twenties; and how their much larger migration, in response to the more acute labor demands of industry in the Second World War, has since increased and now confronts cities North and South with social and moral challenges that are part of the nation's heritage, thus binding the fate of its cities more firmly with that of the nation as a whole.

We have observed the attempts of innumerable civic leaders, local and national, to meet the challenges presented by the mushrooming communities in their respective historical and geographical settings. We have observed their efforts to develop organizations capable of formulating and implementing programs on local, state, and national levels; we have followed the fluctuating influence of reformers like Harold S. Buttenheim, Richard S. Childs, Clarence Stein, Thomas Adams, Lewis Mumford, Clarence Perry, Paul Betters, and of mayors like Daniel W. Hoan, Murray Seasongood, Fiorello H. LaGuardia, and managers like Clarence A. Dykstra, L. P. Cookingham, Clarence E. Ridley, and the rising fortunes of their successors in various fields, Frank Bane, Robert C. Weaver, Richard Lee, Martin Luther King.

We have also seen the emergence of a host of social scientists, as diversified as were Robert E. Park, Luther H. Gulick, Catherine Bauer Wurster, Saul Alinsky. In our attempt to follow the evolution of their theories we have seen that the questions they asked tended to spring from the contemporary situation and that the concepts they produced supplied at least a tentative rationalization or ideology for the period. Thus we have seen the Chicago school's ecological theories of the expansive twenties give way, in emphasis, to the class-structure theories of the depressed thirties, to the power-structure theories of the forties, and to the pluralism of the fifties; but we have also seen the earlier concepts revived and reinterpreted to produce a sense of historic depth and to contribute to the prevailing social-systems analysis that now again supplies a theoretical accompaniment in harmony with the converging metropolitan and national developments in both the social and political spheres.

This of course is not a full account of the rise of Metropolitan America. Many aspects of its history have been neglected or noted only in passing. The economic factors in particular call for extensive research; fortunately, with their new techniques and analytical concepts, scholars in that field will soon be able to add greatly to our understanding both of metropolitan growth and of its relation to the national economy. In the political field many historical gaps in our knowledge remain, especially the vital linkage between agitation and action, but already the Brookings Institution, among other bodies, is engaged in such research. And of the growth of metropolitan culture very little has been said—very little in fact is known, for, in spite of the voluminous materials and numerous studies available, scholars have scarcely begun to interpret this aspect of American history. I have noted some details in each of these and other facets of the emerging metropolises, especially in my early chapters, but I have progressively narrowed the account with each decade in order to follow those strands of metropolitan growth that were drawing it ever more deeply into the stream of national history. If, to some, the city's history now appears submerged in that larger stream, we can only answer that the character of the nation's internal history has in the process been so completely transformed that it requires a full appreciation of the role of the metropolis.

As we bring this account to an end in December 1966, the daily papers are full of stirring events involving the cities and hints concerning the future of Metropolitan America. A Senate subcommittee hearing, the first ever held on the welfare of the cities, has just drawn to a close with a mass of significant testimony awaiting analysis. Another distant war has grown apace, commanding an increased share of the nation's resources, and threatens to cripple the federal government's mounting attack on urban slums and to stall its broader war on poverty. The recent elections have encouraged a number of state governors to flourish their standards, but whether they propose, with Rockefeller in New York, to offer leadership in a new advance for the cities, or with Reagan in

California, to sound a retreat on the home front, remains obscure. Meanwhile the Negro revolution, reaching into every city and school district in the land and raging fitfully in the central cores of many metropolises, poses a challenge that will test the intelligence of all scholarly disciplines, prove the stamina of the federal system, and help to determine the quality of Metropolitan America.

NOTES

CHAPTER 1

1. U.S. *Census* (1910), Pop. I: 73–78.
2. Blake McKelvey, *The Urbanization of America: 1860–1915* (New Brunswick, N. J., 1963), pp. 234–252; N. S. B. Gras, *An Introduction to Economic History* (New York, 1922), pp. 281–329.
3. *Ibid.;* U.S. *Census* (1910), VIII: 87–91; U.S. *Census of Manufactures* (1947), pp. 37–39, Table 4, includes data for 1919; McKelvey, *op. cit.,* pp. 49–52.
4. U.S. *Census* (1910), Pop. I: 79; U.S. *Census* (1920), Pop. I: 63–75; U.S. *Census* (1930), Pop. II: 16–19.
5. Gras, *op. cit.,* pp. 292–329; U.S. *Census* (1920), Pop. I: 63–75; U.S. *Census of Manufactures* (1947), p. 21; C. Warren Thornthwaite, *Internal Migration in the U.S.* (Washington, 1934), pp. 29–30.
6. Paul H. B. d'Estournelles de Constant, *America and Her Problems* (New York, 1915); Bayrd Still, *Mirror for Gotham* (New York, 1956), pp. 257–263.
7. Stephen Graham, *With Poor Immigrants to America* (New York, 1914), pp. 123–140; George Birmingham [James O. Hannay], *From Dublin to Chicago* (New York, 1914), pp. 149–176; G. K. Chesterton, *What I Saw in America* (New York, 1922); Philip Gibbs, *People of Destiny* (New York, 1920), pp. 53–65; Clare Sheridan, *My American Diary* (New York, 1922), p. 358.
8. Gibbs, *op. cit.,* pp. 68–85; W. L. George, *Hail Columbia* (New York, 1921), pp. 161–171, 185–222. Foreign travelers had long been interested in the metropolitan spread of such cities as Philadelphia and Boston, see Still, *op. cit.,* pp. 127–129, 175, 178, 212, 267–268; Alfred Kazin, *A Walker in the City* (New York, 1951); Graham R. Taylor, *Satellite Cities* (New York, 1915).
9. Gras, *op. cit.,* p. 329; Theodore Dreiser, *A Book about Myself* (New York, 1922), pp. 20, 451; Morton and Lucia White, *The Intellectual Versus the City* (Cambridge, 1962), pp. 131–135, 179–182.
10. Allen Eaton, ed., *A Bibliography of Social Surveys* (New York, 1930),

pp. xvi–xxx; Walter T. Arndt, *The Emancipation of the American City* (New York, 1917), pp. 73–135; *National Municipal Review,* January 1916, pp. 24–37; April 1916, pp. 211–219, 222–241; July 1916, pp. 395–402; Frank M. Stewart, *A Half-Century of Municipal Reform* (Berkeley, 1950), pp. 140–141.

11. Arndt, *op. cit.,* p. 35; Committee on Metropolitan Government, *The Government of Metropolitan Areas in the U.S.* (National Municipal League, New York, 1913), pp. 256–271.

12. *National Municipal Review,* May 1917, pp. 445–446.

13. Edith E. Wood, *Slums and Blighted Areas in the U.S.* (Washington, 1935), pp. 27–55; Roy Lubove, *The Progressives and the Slums: Tenement House Reforms in New York City, 1890–1917* (Pittsburgh, 1962); *National Municipal Review,* April 1916, pp. 349–351.

14. *American City,* XII (1915), pp. 197, 203, 321–325; XIII (1915), pp. 93–100, 291–298; XV (1917), pp. 508–511; Roy Lubove, *Community Planning in the 1920's* (Pittsburgh, 1963), pp. 5–15.

15. John Nolan, "Twenty Years of City Planning Progress in the U.S.: 1907–1927," ASPO *Newsletter,* June-July and August 1966; *American City,* XVII (1917), pp. 32–34.

16. *American City,* XII (1915), pp. 432–439, 445; XIII (1915), pp. 175–179; Eaton Manufacturing Co., *A Chronicle of the Automobile Industry in America: 1893–1946* (Cleveland, 1946), pp. 35–39; Merrill Denison, *The Power to Go* (New York, 1956), p. 288; *Historical Statistics of the U.S.* (1949), p. 146.

17. S. J. Makielski, Jr., *The Politics of Zoning: The New York Experience* (New York, 1966), pp. 7–40; *American City,* July 1919, pp. 1–3; *National Municipal Review,* May 1917, pp. 325–348; May 1918, pp. 244–254; Forbes B. Hays, *Community Leadership: The Regional Plan Association of New York* (New York, 1965), p. 8; Werner Z. Hirsch, ed., *Urban Life and Form* (New York, 1963), pp. 44–53.

18. *National Municipal Review,* 1916, pp. 315–316, 501, 638–642; 1917, pp. 110, 519, 520.

19. *American City,* XII (1915), pp. 110–113; (1917), pp. 407–415; *National Municipal Review,* April 1915, pp. 286–290; September 1918, pp. 487–493; Stewart, *op. cit.,* pp. 110–148.

20. Norman N. Gill, *Municipal Research Bureaus* (Washington, 1944), pp. 12–29; *National Municipal Review,* October 1916, p. 637.

21. Bayrd Still, *Milwaukee, The History of a City* (Madison, 1948), pp. 521–528.

22. Arndt, *op. cit.,* pp. 240, 252.

23. U.S. *Census* (1920), I: 45; H. D. Hamilton, *Legislative Apportionment, Key to Power* (New York, 1964), p. 18.

24. Ernest S. Bogart and J. M. Mathews, *The Modern Commonwealth* [Centennial History of Illinois, Vol. V] (Chicago, 1922), pp. 203–205; Alexander C. Flick, ed., *History of New York State* (New York, 1935), VII: 216–217, 233.

25. J. M. Mathews, "Municipal Representation in State Legislatures," *National Municipal Review,* XII (1923), pp. 135–141; Stewart, *op. cit.,* pp. 53–54, 60, 76, 91–92; R. S. Childs, *Civic Victories* (New York, 1952), pp. 83–91, 134–152, 262–263.

26. *Ibid.,* pp. 242–251; A. R. Hatton, "The Ashtabula Plan," *National Municipal Review,* V (1916), pp. 57–63.

27. *National Municipal Review,* March 1917, pp. 202–206.

28. *American City*, XII (1915), pp. 337–338; XIV (1916), pp. 572–574; *National Municipal Review*, IV (1915), pp. 281–285; V (1916), pp. 496–498; Stewart, *op. cit.*, pp. 137–138; Blake McKelvey, *Rochester, The Quest for Quality: 1890–1925* (Cambridge, 1956), [cited below as *Rochester III*] pp. 95, 102, 106.

29. Wilbur C. Phillips, *Adventuring for Democracy* (New York, 1940), pp. 143–285; *National Municipal Review*, VI (1917), pp. 125–126; IX (1920), pp. 553–559.

30. *National Municipal Review*, VIII (1919), pp. 468–470; IX (1920), pp. 156–160; *American City*, XIV (1916), pp. 468–470; William J. Norton, *The Cooperative Movement in Social Work* (New York, 1927), pp. 35–99; Scott M. Cutlip, *Fund Raising in the United States* (New Brunswick, 1965), pp. 64–79.

31. *National Municipal Review*, VI (1917), pp. 366–368; Arthur Durham, *Community Welfare Organization* (New York, 1958), pp. 75–77.

32. J. B. Andrews, "American Cities and the Prevention of Unemployment," *American City*, XIV (1916), pp. 117–121; Waldo G. Leland and N. D. Mereness, *Introduction to the American Official Sources for the Economic and Social History of the World War* (New Haven, 1926), p. 342.

33. *Historical Statistics of the U.S.: 1798–1945*, p. 33.

34. Rupert B. Vance, *All These People, The Nation's Human Resources in the South* (Chapel Hill, 1945), pp. 112–120, see tables 21 and 26; T. J. Woofter, Jr., *Negro Problems in Cities* (New York, 1928), pp. 26–30; U.S. *Census* (1910), I: 172, 178–180, 207–213.

35. Frederick G. Detweiler, *The Negro Press in the U.S.* (Chicago, 1922), pp. 6–15; George E. Haynes, *The Trend of the Races* (New York, 1922), pp. 23–62.

36. Woofter, *op. cit.*, pp. 37–39, 52–70; Birmingham, *op. cit.*, pp. 159–167.

37. Gunnar Myrdal, *An American Dilemma* (New York, 1962 ed.) pp. 742–744; Woofter, *op. cit.*, pp. 38–51.

38. Gilbert Osofsky, "Progressivism and the Negro: New York, 1900–1915," *American Quarterly*, Summer 1964, XVI: 153–167; Myrdal, *op. cit.*, pp. 742–744, 812–838.

39. Emmett J. Scott, *The Negro Migration During the War* (Carnegie Endowment for International Peace, New York, 1920), pp. 29–71; Louise V. Kennedy, *The Negro Peasant Turns Cityward* (New York, 1930), pp. 24–53, and *passim;* Elliott M. Rudwick, *Race Riot in East St. Louis July 2, 1917* (Carbondale, Ill., 1964), pp. 16–26; Chicago Commission on Race Relations, *The Negro in Chicago: A Study of Race Relations and a Race Riot* (Chicago, 1922), p. 86.

40. Rudwick, *op. cit.*, pp. 27–57, 74–132; *The Negro in Chicago, op. cit.*, pp. 71–78.

41. Scott, *op. cit.*, pp. 128–129, 134–138; Woofter, *op. cit.*, p. 325; *National Municipal Review*, VI: 281–292.

42. Scott, *op. cit.*, pp. 95–99, 119–125, 129–131, 141–151; St. Clair Drake and H. R. Cayton, *Black Metropolis* (New York, 1945), pp. 64–65; "The Negro in Hartford," *Hartford Times*, Nov. 26, 1963, Supplement, pp. 4–6; *The Negro in Chicago*, pp. 94–103, 145–148.

43. Drake and Cayton, *op. cit.*, pp. 58–59; Scott, *op. cit.*, pp. 152–174; Haynes, *op. cit.*, pp. 159–163; Myrdal, *op. cit.*, pp. 842–850; Woofter, *op. cit.*, pp. 76–77.

44. *National Municipal Review*, September 1917, pp. 575–576; Kennedy,

op. cit., pp. 127–128; *Survey*, May 4, 1918; January 4, 1919, pp. 455–461; John Hope Franklin, *From Slavery to Freedom* (New York, 1956 ed.), pp. 464–466.

45. Harold F. Gosnell, *Negro Politicians, The Rise of Negro Politics in Chicago* (Chicago, 1935), pp. 153–205; *The Negro in Chicago*, pp. 145–356; Drake and Cayton, *op. cit.*, pp. 54–63.
46. Scott, *op. cit.*, pp. 103–118; *The Negro in Chicago*, pp. 357–400.
47. *The Negro in Chicago*, pp. 1–52.
48. *The Negro in Chicago*, pp. xx, 2, 53–78; Myrdal, *op. cit.*, pp. 745, 1392; Drake and Cayton, *op. cit.*, pp. 69–74; Constance McLaughlin Green, *Washington Capital City, 1879–1950* (Princeton, 1963), pp. 266–268; Arthur I. Waskow, *From Race Riot to Sit-In, 1919 and the 1960's* (New York, 1966), pp. 20–120, 304–307; Franklin, *op. cit.*, pp. 469–478.
49. U.S. *Census* (1920), II: 47, 55, 79; Alain Locke, ed., *The New Negro: An Interpretation* (New York, 1925), pp. 309–311, 333–340; Thomas Reed Powell, "Constitutionality of Race Segregation," *Columbia Law Review*, XVIII (February 1918), pp. 146–152; *American City*, April 1916, p. 356; August 1918, pp. 151–157; Franklin, *op. cit.*, pp. 489–511.
50. Childs, *op. cit.*, p. 90; *National Municipal Review*, January 1918, p. 105; September 1918, pp. 487–489.
51. *American City*, July 1917, pp. 470–471; March 1918, pp. 204–207. Rochester's drive in May brought in $4,838,093 from 117,064 subscribers, see Blake McKelvey, *Rochester, The Quest for Quality: 1890–1925* (Cambridge, 1956), p. 303; Cutlip, *op. cit.*, pp. 110–153.
52. Waldo G. Leland and N. D. Mereness, *Introduction to the American Official Sources for the Economic and Social History of World War* (New Haven, 1926), pp. 36–50; *National Municipal Review*, July 1917, pp. 449–453; September 1918, pp. 472–482; *American City*, May 1917, pp. 453–470.
53. *American City*, May 1917, p. 499; June 1917, pp. 584–586; January 1918, pp. 157–159; Gerd Korman, "Americanization at the Factory Gate," Industrial and Labor Relations *Review*, April 1965, pp. 399–400.
54. *National Municipal Review*, July 1917, pp. 465–468; March 1918, p. 221; November 1918, p. 562; Preston W. Slosson, *The Great Crusade and After: 1914–1928* (New York, 1930), pp. 63–71.
55. Thomas A. Frothingham, *The American Reinforcement in the World War* (New York, 1927), pp. 46–50; Hugh S. Johnson, *The Blue Eagle from Egg to Earth* (New York, 1935), pp. 73–87.
56. Grosvenor B. Clarkson, *Industrial America in the World War: 1917–1918* (New York, 1923), pp. 241–242; *American City*, May 1918, pp. 465–469; July 1918, pp. 14–15; Leland and Mereness, *op. cit.*, pp. 57–72; Charles A. Otis, *Here I Am* (Cleveland, 1951), pp. 122–123, 162; Bernard M. Baruch, *American Industry in the War* (New York, 1941), pp. 40–42.
57. Benedict Crowell and Robert F. Wilson, *The Armies of Industry* (New Haven, 1921), I: 51–55; *American City*, April 1918, pp. 331–336; *National Municipal Review*, 1918, pp. 289–291, 334–335.
58. *American City*, February 1918, pp. 97–100; September 1918, p. 194; January 1919, pp. 23–24; February 1919, p. 179; *National Municipal Review*, November 1918, pp. 553–560.
59. *National Municipal Review*, January 1919, pp. 3–15, 22, 49–52.
60. *American City*, January 1919, pp. 23–25; March 1919, pp. 211–214; April 1919, pp. 326–328, 417–421.

61. Harry Barnard, *Independent Man: The Life of Senator James Couzens* (New York, 1958), pp. 109–138; quote from p. 122; William P. Lovett, *Detroit Rules Itself* (Boston, 1930), pp. 45–49, 118, 138–144.
62. Lewis Mumford, "Attacking the Housing Problem on Three Fronts," *Nation,* September 6, 1919, pp. 332–333.
63. N.Y. Conference of Mayors, *Proceedings* (1919), pp. 29–33; Norman Gill, *op. cit.,* pp. 12–21.
64. John M. Glenn, L. Brandt, and F. E. Anderson, *Russell Sage Foundation: 1907–1946* (New York, 1947), pp. 17–25; Louise C. Wade, *Graham Taylor: Pioneer for Social Justice: 1851–1938* (Chicago, 1964), pp. 164–185; Frank J. Bruno, *Research in Social Work* (New York, 1957), pp. 140–143; Roy Lubove, *The Professional Altruist: The Emergence of Social Work as a Career: 1880–1930* (Cambridge, 1965).
65. Emmett J. Scott, *Negro Migrations During the War* (New York, 1920); George E. Haynes, *The Trend of the Races* (New York, 1922); *The Negro in Chicago: A Study of Race Relations and a Race Riot* (Chicago, 1922); Lewis, *Planning the Modern City* (New York, 1916, 1922, 1943, 1949); Charles Zueblin, *American Municipal Progress* (New York, 1916).
66. Robert E. Park, "The City: Suggestions for the Investigation of Human Behavior in the City Environment," *American Journal of Sociology,* March 1915, pp. 577–612; Maurice R. Stein, *The Eclipse of Community; An Interpretation of American Studies* (Princeton, 1960), pp. 13–31.
67. Theodore Dreiser, *The Color of a Great City* (New York, 1923); T. V. Smith and Leonard D. White, eds., *Chicago, An Experiment in Social Science Research* (Chicago, 1929), pp. 1–18; Ernest W. Burgess and D. J. Bogue, eds., *Contributions to Urban Sociology* (Chicago, 1964), pp. 1–7; Bernard C. Borning, *The Political and Social Thought of Charles A. Beard* (Seattle, 1962), pp. 64–138.

CHAPTER 2

1. *New York Times,* December 20, 1920, p. 1; January 16, 1921, II: 2; Literary Digest, October 29, 1921, p 10; December 3, 1921, p. 10. Immigration restriction and the depression held the population to 150,697,000 in 1950, and the food problem was one of surplus.
2. U.S. Bureau of the Census, *Historical Statistics of the U.S.: 1789–1945* (Washington, 1949), p. 33; "Crisis in Demobilization," *New Republic,* V. 18 (1919), pp. 81–84; "The Negro Laborer and the Immigrant," *Survey,* May 14, 1921, pp. 209–210.
3. Carey McWilliams, *Southern California Country* (New York, 1936); Remi Nadeau, *Los Angeles, From Mission to Modern City* (New York, 1960); Arthur Feiler, *America Seen Through German Eyes* (New York, 1928), pp. 18–24.
4. U.S. Bureau of the Census, *The Growth of Metropolitan Districts in the U.S.: 1900–1940* (Washington, 1947), pp. 33–45; Glenn E. McLaughlin, *The Growth of American Manufacturing Areas* (Pittsburgh, 1938), pp. 50–74.
5. *The Growth of Metropolitan Districts,* pp. 33–45, Miami, Los Angeles, San Diego, St. Petersburg, and Atlantic City.
6. Amos H. Hawley, *Human Ecology* (New York, 1950), p. 376; Carter Goodrich, *et al., Migration and Economic Opportunity* (New York, 1936), pp. 119, 287–392; McLaughlin, *op. cit.,* pp. 97–104.

7. Leo Wolman and Gustav Peck, "Labor Groups in the Social Structure," *Recent Social Trends* (New York, 1933), II: 805, 817, 820, 829; Irving Bernstein, *The Lean Years: A History of the American Worker: 1920–1933* (Boston, 1960), pp. 55–70.

8. M. Aurousseau first distinguished between the basic and nonbasic industries, those producing for export and those for local maintenance, in an article published in the *Geographical Review* (1921), p. 574; see a review of the development of this distinction in Harold M. Mayer and C. F. Kohn, eds. *Readings in Urban Geography* (University of California, 1959), pp. 87–99. See also Wilbur R. Thompson, *A Preface to Urban Economics* (Baltimore, 1965), pp. 27–50.

9. George E. Mowry, *The Urban Nation: 1920–1960* (New York, 1965) pp. 1–17; A. M. Schlesinger, Jr., *The Crisis of the Old Order* (Cambridge, 1957), pp. 73–76; Bernstein, *op. cit.*, pp. 70–75.

10. *Growth of Metropolitan Districts*, pp. 27–32; Goodrich, *Migration and Economic Opportunity*, pp. 344–392.

11. John Higham, *Strangers in the Land* (New Brunswick, 1955), pp. 264–311; Isaac A. Hourwich, *Immigration and Labor: The Economic Aspects of European Immigration to the U.S.* (New York, 1922); Robert A. Divine, *American Immigration Policy* (New Haven, 1957), pp. 1–10. In an unpublished paper on "The Klan," Kenneth T. Jackson describes the influence of the KKK in Chicago in the early 1920's.

12. Higham, *op. cit.*, pp. 312–316; Preston W. Slosson, *The Great Crusade and After: 1914–1928* (New York, 1930), pp. 292–300; McKelvey, *Rochester*, III: 350–353.

13. Higham, *op. cit.*, pp. 316–330; Slosson, *op. cit.*, pp. 299–308; Divine, *op. cit.*, pp. 10–18, 26–51. The heated debates between 1927 and 1929 over the application of the national origins provision, which did not take effect until 1929, reflected ethnic rather than urban-rural rivalries.

14. *Historical Statistics of the U.S.*, pp. 29, 30, 31, 33; Thornthwaite, *Internal Migration in the U.S.*, pp. 3, 12–13, 26–32; Rupert B. Vance, *All These People* (Chapel Hill, 1945), pp. 26–28, 33, 111–123.

15. Niels Carpenter, "Migration Between City and Country in the Buffalo Metropolitan Area," in N. E. Humes, ed., *Economics, Sociology, and the Modern World* (Cambridge, 1935), p. 273; Vance, *op. cit.*, pp. 111–123.

16. Gilbert Osofsky, *Harlem: The Making of a Ghetto: Negro New York, 1890–1930* (New York, 1965), pp. 105–158; St. Clair Drake and H. R. Cayton, *Black Metropolis* (New York, 1945), pp. 60–90; Henderson H. Donald, "The Urbanization of the American Negro," *Studies in the Science of Society* (New Haven, 1937), pp. 180–200. See also Chester Rapkin and W. G. Grisby, *The Demand for Housing in Racially Mixed Areas* (Berkeley, 1960), pp. 11–12.

17. U.S. *Census* (1930), Pop. II: 18, 32, 34, 65–66; Paul Levinson, *Race, Class, and Party* (New York, 1932), pp. 132–146.

18. Harlan P. Douglass, *The Suburban Trend* (New York, 1925), p. 5; Sam B. Warner, *Street-car Suburbs* (Cambridge, 1965).

19. William Dobriner, *The Suburban Community* (New York, 1958), p. 5; Douglass, *op. cit.*, pp. 38–122; Merrill Denison, *The Power to Go* (New York, 1956), p. 288.

20. *Growth of Metropolitan Districts*, pp. 33–45; McLaughlin, *op. cit.*, pp. 128–133, 186–190; George W. Hilton and John F. Due, *The Electric Interurban Railways in America* (Stanford University, 1960).

21. *Growth of Metropolitan Districts,* p. 15.
22. *American City,* October 1920, pp. 351–354; June 1923, pp. 556–558; *Rochester Herald,* October 28, 1922.
23. *American City,* April 1922, p. 387; June 1922, pp. 583–586; October 1924, p. 330; *National Municipal Review,* July 1924, pp. 386–387; November 1924, p. 664.
24. *American City,* December 1922, pp. 496–500; June 1924, pp. 612–615; March 1926, p. 307; City Planning, April, 1927, pp. 101–107.
25. *Architectural Record,* July 1920, pp. 53–74, 121–135; December 1920, pp. 531–534; *American City,* July 1920, pp. 26–30; September 1923, pp. 290–291; *National Municipal Review,* October 1920, pp. 620–622; January 1921, p. 10; Edith E. Wood, *Slums and Blighted Areas in the U.S.* (Washington, 1935), pp. 27–61.
26. Roy Lubove, *Community Planning in the 1920's: The Contributions of the Regional Planning Association of America* (Pittsburgh, 1964), pp. 31–36; *Report of the Housing Committee of the New York State Reconstruction Commission* (Albany, 1920); Clarence Stein, "The New York State Regional Plan," *City Planning,* July 1925, pp. 110–112.
27. *Architectural Record,* December 1920, pp. 531–534; *Housing Betterment,* November 1922, pp. 314–318, 340–341, 351–374; July 1923, pp. 278–294; November 1923, pp. 383–385; June 1926, pp. 73–93; *National Municipal Review,* May 1924, pp. 283–287.
28. Edith E. Wood, *op. cit.,* pp. 36–63; Edith Abbott, *Tenements of Chicago* (Chicago, 1936); *National Municipal Review,* December 1920, pp. 762–765; October 1921, p. 502; September 1923, p. 559; June 1924, pp. 374–376; John R. Riggleman, "Building Cycles in the U.S. 1875–1932," *American Statistical Association Journal,* June 1933, pp. 174–183.
29. Lubove, *op. cit.,* pp. 115–116; Thomas Adams, *The Building of the City* [Regional Plan of New York and its Environs, Part II] (New York, 1931); Forbes B. Hays, *Community Leadership: The Regional Plan Association of New York* (New York, 1965), pp. 1–21.
30. Adams, *op. cit.,* pp. 75–76, 195–219; Lubove, *op. cit.,* pp. 115–119; *American City,* May 1928, pp. 107–108; July 1928, pp. 92–95.
31. *National Municipal Review,* February 1921, pp. 111–116; November 1926, pp. 644–650, 663–664; October 1928, pp. 567–577; June 1929, pp. 359–363; September 1930, p. 581; *American City,* January 1926, pp. 1–9; September 1926, pp. 314–315; June 1929, p. 113; September 1929, p. 130.
32. Lubove, *op. cit.,* pp. 36–38, 77–79; *National Municipal Review,* April 1926, p. 245; July 1926, pp. 381–385; *American City,* July 1926, pp. 620–622; State Commission on Housing and Regional Planning, *Report, New York Legislative Documents* (1924), No. 43, pp. 1–103; (1926), No. 40, pp. 1–47; State Housing Board Report, *New York Legislative Documents* (1927), No. 95, pp. 1–97.
33. Lubove, *op. cit.,* pp. 31–33, 38–44; Clarence Stein, *Toward New Towns for America* (Liverpool, 1951), pp. 12–21.
34. Stein, *op. cit.,* pp. 22–69; Lubove, *op. cit.,* pp. 49–50, 55–58; *National Municipal Review,* June 1926, pp. 330–336.
35. Lubove, *op. cit.,* pp. 58–66; *American City,* March 1925, pp. 277–281; Stein, *loc. cit.*
36. Lubove, *op. cit.,* pp. 50–54, 69–72; *American City,* November 1928, pp. 149–152; October 1929, p. 160; November 1929, pp. 116–122.

37. *National Municipal Review,* July 1928, pp. 435–436; September 1928, p. 522; November 1928, p. 715; Adams, *op. cit.,* pp. 78, 93, 134, 195–219.
38. *American City,* September 1929, p. 130; October 1929, p. 163; November 1929, p. 95.
39. Roy S. MacElwee, *Port Development* (New York, 1926); *American City,* January 1919, pp. 1–9, 27–37, 127–219; April 1919, pp. 326–328; May 1919, pp. 419–421; November 1923, pp. 485–490; President's Conference on Unemployment, *Report* (1921), pp. 63–100.
40. *Historical Statistics of Cities* (1929), p. 170; *American City,* January 1921, pp. 22–23; April 1921, p. 376; February 1923, pp. 107–108, 139–140.
41. *American City,* May 1923, pp. 499–501; June 1923, pp. 611–612; July 1923, pp. 18–20; January 1926, p. 25; *National Municipal Review,* January 1928, pp. 5–6; December 1930, p. 861.
42. *American City,* April 1924, pp. 360–361; December 1924, p. 588; April 1926, p. 435; January 1929, pp. 156–157.
43. *American City,* March 1922, pp. 267–269; January 1923, pp. 77–79; March 1926, pp. 543–544; February 1929, pp. 132–133; *National Municipal Review,* April 1923, pp. 180–185.
44. *National Municipal Review,* October 1919, pp. 581–583; June 1921, p. 12; November 1926, pp. 644–650; August 1929, pp. 517–522; Emerson P. Schmidt, *Industrial Relations in Urban Transportation* (Minneapolis, 1937), pp. 48–50, 66–69; *American City,* February 1929, pp. 81–82.
45. *American City,* June 1920, pp. 602–608; August 1922, p. 138; September 1930, pp. 109–110.
46. *American City,* October 1929, p. 161; November 1929, p. 154; February 1930, pp. 151–152.
47. *American City,* March 1919, pp. 253–256; June 1920, pp. 513–514; July 1920, pp. 14–16; April 1922, p. 334; February 1926, p. 191; January 1929, p. 138.
48. *American City,* May 1914, pp. 342, 494; February 1921, pp. 168–170, 217–219; April 1921, p. 447; October 1923, pp. 347–353; November 1923, pp. 479–482; December 1928, pp. 53–56, 72.
49. *American City,* July 1919, pp. 20–24; July 1920, pp. 107–109; *National Municipal Review,* March 1923, pp. 123–126; February 1926, pp. 104–107.
50. *National Municipal Review,* September 1926, pp. 510–515; August 1927, p. 548; March 1928 (Supplement), pp. 180–194.
51. *American City,* March 1922, pp. 209–212; *National Municipal Review,* February 1923, pp. 77–82; January 1930, p. 70; Frederick J. Adams and Gerald Hodge, "City Planning Instructions in the U.S. The Pioneer Days, 1900–1930," *American Institute of Planners, Journal,* February 1965, pp. 43–51.
52. *National Municipal Review,* May 1924, pp. 318–319; September 1924, pp. 485–488; November 1924, p. 666; June 1925; S. J. Makielski, Jr., *The Politics of Zoning: The New York Experience* (New York, 1966), pp. 41–50.
53. Nelson P. Lewis, *Planning the Modern City* (New York, 1922), p. 28; *American City,* November 1922, pp. 405–406.
54. *American City,* April 1925, pp. 381–384; October 1925, pp. 349–354; November 1927, pp. 577–579.
55. *American City,* November 1927, pp. 580–582; *National Municipal*

Review, October 1930, pp. 681–704; *City Planning,* January 1932, pp. 1–15; John Nolan, "Twenty Years of City Planning Progress in the U.S.: 1909–1927," ASPO *Newsletter,* June, July and August 1966.

56. *National Municipal Review,* January 1923, pp. 16–19; December 1923, p. 735.

57. *National Municipal Review,* September 1921, pp. 474–479; June 1924, pp. 257–365; July 1927, pp. 462–466; *American City,* November 1929, pp. 94–95; February 1930, pp. 142–144; *City Planning,* April 1926, p. 97; July 1929, pp. 141–162.

58. MacElwee, *op. cit.,* pp. 50–51; *American City,* April 1923, pp. 363–364, 377–378; September 1924, pp. 219, 225; June 1925, pp. 644–647, 652–653; *National Municipal Review,* May 1924, pp. 319–320; June 1928, pp. 167, 344; Constance M. Green, *Washington, Capital City, 1879–1950* (Princeton, 1963), pp. 286–287; National Municipal League, *The Government of Metropolitan Areas in the U.S.* (New York, 1930); *City Planning,* July 1928, pp. 231–232.

59. *National Municipal Review,* June 1921, pp. 327–330.

60. *American City,* September 1920, p. 261; McKelvey, *Rochester, The Quest for Quality* (Cambridge, 1956) [cited below as *Rochester* III], p. 376.

61. *American City,* September 1922, p. 260; December 1924, p. 558; February 1930, p. 107; *National Municipal Review,* November 1924, p. 661; April 1928, p. 250; July 1934, p. 390; Thomas F. Campbell, *Freedom's Forum: The City Club 1912–1962* (Cleveland, 1963).

62. *National Municipal Review,* January 1923, pp. 50–52; November 1924, p. 661; *American City,* May 1923; Campbell, *op. cit.,* pp. 31–36; see also "Proceedings of the 18th Annual Meeting of the Government Research Association" (Mimeograph Copy, New York, 1929), pp. 27, 129–131, for a list of such organizations in 1928.

63. *National Municipal Review,* January 1917, pp. 128–129; July 1917, pp. 523–524; May 1923, pp. 227–229, 239–242; February 1928, pp. 106–112; January 1927, p. 38; *American City,* April 1922, p. 348; March 1927, p. 394.

64. *National Municipal Review,* April 1923, pp. 165–167, 176; November 1923, pp. 639–640; December 1924, p. 727; April 1925, pp. 207–208; December 1925, pp. 712–721; June 1928, pp. 357–358; March 1929, pp. 203–220; May 1929, p. 351.

65. *National Municipal Review,* November 1925, pp. 663–667; January 1928, pp. 13–15; January 1925, pp. 16–21; March 1929, pp. 203–220; May 1929, pp. 289–299; September 1929, pp. 549–554; Norman N. Gill, *Municipal Research Bureaus* (Washington, 1944), pp. 17–21.

66. *National Municipal Review,* August 1926, pp. 465–471; February 1929, pp. 70–75; Charles P. Taft, *City Management: The Cincinnati Experiment* (New York, 1933), pp. 25–194; George M. Harris, *Westward to the East* (London, 1935), pp. 40–50; Ralph A. Straetz, *PR Politics in Cincinnati* (New York, 1958).

67. *National Municipal Review,* December 1925, pp. 715–721; January 1928, p. 1; June 1928, pp. 357–364; July 1929, pp. 464–470; Campbell, *op. cit.,* pp. 35–36.

68. Bayrd Still, *Milwaukee, The History of a City* (Madison, 1948), pp. 546–547, 559–561; *National Municipal Review,* January 1926, pp. 5–8; July 1934, p. 390; *American City,* December 1925, p. 585; May 1929, pp. 96–99; September 1930, pp. 87–98.

69. *National Municipal Review,* November 1923, pp. 691–692; December

1926, p. 731; January 1921, p. 67; January 1928, p. 1; December 1930, p. 862; *American City,* January 1929, pp. 108–110; July 1929, p. 470.

70. *City Planning,* January 1927, pp. 2–15; April 1927, pp. 87–95; *National Municipal Review,* February 1924, pp. 106–108.

71. *National Municipal Review,* May 1923, pp. 263–264; *American City,* May 1926, pp. 527–528; *Housing Betterment,* December 1925, pp. 355–358; March 1926, pp. 207–213; September 1929, p. 215; *City Planning,* April 1925, pp. 5–7.

72. *Housing Betterment,* September 1929, p. 215. Other cities listed here included Cleveland, Detroit, Los Angeles, Milwaukee, Toledo, and Minneapolis and St. Paul; Albany, Dallas, Portland and San Francisco reported regional planning efforts in the *National Municipal Review,* June 1926, pp. 344–347; Green *op. cit.,* pp. 284–288; *American City,* July 1926, p. 103; January 1929, pp. 114–116; *City Planning,* July 1925, pp. 110–112; July 1926, pp. 208–210; N.Y. State, Niagara Frontier Planning Board, *Reports,* 1926–1946.

73. *American City,* July 1924, p. 32; *National Municipal Review,* January 1927, pp. 118–126; *City Planning,* July 1926, pp. 208–210.

74. *National Municipal Review,* September 1926, pp. 518–522; June 1929, pp. 426–427; July 1929, p. 431; August 1929, pp. 529–532; October 1929, pp. 603–609.

75. *National Municipal Review,* January 1923, p. 41; March 1923, pp. 105, 135–141; December 1924, pp. 678–683; October 1925, pp. 600–603; July 1929, p. 491; *American City,* March 1925, pp. 267–268.

76. Howard D. Hamilton, ed., *Legislative Apportionment: Key to Power* (New York, 1964), pp. 19–22, quoting from *Fergus* v. *Marks,* 321 Ill. (1926).

77. *National Municipal Review,* May 1924, pp. 288–293; October 1928 (Supplement), pp. 619–658; *American City,* January 1927, p. 1; November 1927, pp. 575–576.

78. Harold E. Stearns, ed., *Civilization in the U.S.* (New York, 1922), pp. 10, 12, 17, 286–287.

79. Charles Merz, *The Dry Decade* (Garden City, N.Y., 1931), pp. 51–56, 163–180; Andrew Sinclair, *Prohibition, the Era of Excess* (Boston, 1962), pp. 178–192; E. H. Sutherland and C. E. Gehlke, "Crime and Punishment," *Recent Social Trends,* II: 1118–1120, 1124–1135; Slosson, *op. cit.,* pp. 112–129.

80. Carroll H. Wooddy, *The Growth of the Federal Government, 1915–1932* (New York, 1934), pp. 97–104; Merz, *op. cit.,* pp. 158–207; Sinclair, *op. cit.,* pp. 192–219.

81. Sinclair, *op. cit.,* pp. 242–416; George E. Mowry, *The Urban Nation: 1920–1960* (New York, 1965), pp. 53–65; Bernstein, *op. cit.,* pp. 75–82.

82. Lloyd Lewis, *Chicago, The History of Its Reputation* (New York, 1929), pp. 441–472; Victor S. Yarror, "Crime and Political Corruption in Chicago," *National Municipal Review,* June 1926, pp. 317–320; Sinclair, *op. cit.,* pp. 221–229; E. W. Burgess and D. J. Bogue, eds., *Contributions to Urban Sociology* (Chicago, 1964), pp. 559–576.

83. *National Municipal Review,* October 1923, pp. 586–591, 706–712; September 1926, pp. 560–561; June 1930, pp. 391–397; *American City,* January 1923, pp. 1–3; March 1927, p. 387; May 1927, pp. 665–667; September 1930, pp. 111–114; *Literary Digest,* June 1, 1929, pp. 5–7.

84. Allen Churchill, *The Improper Bohemians: A Recreation of Greenwich Village in Its Heyday* (New York, 1959), pp. 150–285; Bernard

Duffey, *The Chicago Renaissance in American Letters* (East Lansing, 1954), pp. 134–137; Mrs. Florence Older, *San Francisco: Magic City* (New York, 1961), pp. 172–175.

85. Lawrence A. Cremin, *The Transformation of the School* (New York, 1961), pp. 202–207, 221–224, 240–248, 277–280; Green, *op. cit.,* pp. 340–351.
86. Cremin, *op. cit.,* pp. 154, 275–276, 280–290, 296–303; U.S. Bureau of Education, *Biennial Survey* (1928), pp. 96–97; U.S. Commissioner of Education, *Report* (1922), pp. 101–127; Blake McKelvey, *Rochester*, III: 8–85, 102–105; *ibid.,* IV: 46–48; Slosson, *op cit.,* pp. 320–330.
87. Clarke A. Chambers, *Seedtime of Reform* (Minneapolis, 1963), pp. 29–58; McKelvey, *Urbanization of America, 1860–1915*, pp. 150–151, 243, 270–273.
88. Chambers, *op. cit.,* pp. 48–58; *Recent Social Trends*, II: 774–780; *Annals of the American Academy of Political and Social Science*, September 1929, pp. 80–97; Herbert H. Lou, *Juvenile Courts in the United States* (Chapel Hill, 1927), pp. 23–25.
89. Scott M. Cutlip, *Fund Raising in the United States* (New Brunswick, 1965), pp. 212–238, 323; Roy Lubove, *The Professional Altruist: The Emergence of Social Work as a Career: 1880–1930* (Cambridge, 1965), pp. 118–221; *American City*, February 1926, p. 177; January 1929, pp. 125–126; Green, *op. cit.,* pp. 317–327; McKelvey, *Rochester*, IV: 39–41; Chambers, *op. cit.,* pp. 116–128; *Recent Social Trends*, II: 1180–1218.
90. Green, *op. cit.,* pp. 314–336; *National Municipal Review*, June 1928, pp. 327–328; August 1929, p. 546.
91. *American City*, August 1925, pp. 194–196; August 1926, pp. 162–165; March 1927, pp. 373–375; October 1927, p. 475; *Hartford Times*, November 26, 1963, A 10–12; Levinson, *op. cit.,* pp. 132–146.
92. *National Municipal Review*, June 1927, p. 350; December 1927, pp. 748–751; Detroit Bureau of Municipal Research, *The Negro in Detroit* (Detroit, 1926).
93. *National Municipal Review*, May 1928, pp. 261–264; Harold F. Gosnell, *Negro Politicians, The Rise of Negro Politics in Chicago* (Chicago, 1955); Ralph J. Bunche, "The American City as a Negro Political Laboratory," *Proceedings of the Annual Meeting of the Government Research Association* (Mimeographed, New York, 1928), pp. 53–64.
94. T. V. Smith and L. D. White, eds., *Chicago: An Experiment in Social Science Research* (Chicago, 1929); Ernest W. Burgess and D. I. Bogue, eds., *Contributions to Urban Sociology* (Chicago, 1964), pp. 1–10; Clifford Shaw, *et. al., Delinquency Areas* (Chicago, 1929); Nels Anderson, *The Hobo* (Chicago, 1923); Frederick M. Thrasher, *The Gang* (Chicago, 1927).
95. Ernest W. Burgess, "The Growth of the City: An Introduction to a Research Project," *Pub. of American Sociological Society* (1924), pp. 85–97; Harvey W. Zorbaugh, *The Gold Coast and the Slum* (Chicago, 1929).
96. Burgess and Bogue, *op. cit.,* pp. 591–641; A. B. Hollinghead, "Community Research," *American Soc. Review*, April 1947, pp. 136–142.
97. Jesse F. Steiner, *The American Community in Action* (New York, 1928); Konrad Bercovici, *Around the World in New York* (New York, 1929); *American City*, February 1924, p. 125; March 1927, pp. 287–

293; June 1928, pp. 144–146; Clarence A. Perry, *Ten Years with the Community Center Movement* (New York, 1921); Louis Wirth, *The Ghetto* (Chicago, 1928); Maurice R. Stein, *The Eclipse of Community* (Princeton, 1960), pp. 13–46.

98. Robert and Helen Lynd, *Middletown* (New York, 1929); M. Aurousseau, "The Distribution of Population," *Geographical Review* (1921), p. 574; Robert M. Haig, "Towards an Understanding of the Metropolis," *Quarterly Journal of Economics,* February 1926, pp. 403–420; American Sociological Society, *Proceedings* (1925); Mildred Hartsough, *The Twin Cities as a Metropolitan Market* (Minneapolis, 1925); *Regional Survey of New York and Its Environs* (1929).

99. Philip M. Hauser and L. F. Schnore, eds., *The Study of Urbanization* (New York, 1965), pp. 123–124; Leonard Reissman, *The Urban Process* (Glencoe, 1964), pp. 39–68; *National Municipal Review,* May 1928, p. 310; R. T. Donald, "Political Science and the Study of Urbanism," American Political Science *Review,* June 1957, pp. 491–509.

100. Slosson, *op. cit.,* pp. 347–358; W. A. Dill, *Growth of Newspapers in the U.S.* (Lawrence, Kansas, 1928), pp. 29–76.

101. Slosson, *op. cit.,* pp. 387–393; *Recent Social Trends,* pp. 973, 988; U.S. Department of Commerce, *Commercial and Government Radio Stations of the U.S.* (Washington, 1930), pp. 164–169.

102. Dill, *op. cit., pp.* 76–77; *Sales Management Magazine,* September 27, 1930; David M. Potter, *People of Plenty* (Chicago, 1954), p. 169.

103. John H. Mueller, *The American Symphony Orchestra* (Bloomington, 1951); Jesse F. Steiner, *Americans at Play* (New York, 1933), pp. 9–28; *Recent Social Trends,* p. 994; *American Art Annual* (1925), pp. 31–62; *National Municipal Review,* October 1928, p. 578.

104. *Recent Social Trends,* pp. 991–995; *National Municipal Review,* May 1922, pp. 128–130; September 1924, pp. 242–244; September 1928, pp. 114–118; July 1932, pp. 422–423.

105. Gilbert Seldes, *The Seven Lively Arts* (New York, 2nd ed., 1957), pp. 137 and *passim.*

106. Lewis Mumford, *Sticks and Stones* (New York, 1924), pp. 153–235.

CHAPTER 3

1. Dexter M. Keezer and Stacy May, *The Public Control of Business* (New York, 1930).

2. *Historical Statistics of the U.S.: 1789–1945,* pp. 33, 38.

3. Conrad Tauber, *The Changing Population of the U.S.* (A Census Monograph, Washington, 1958), pp. 99–108; Rupert B. Vance, *All These People* (Chapel Hill, 1945), pp. 126–131.

4. Broadus Mitchell, *Depression Decade: From New Era Through New Deal, 1929–1941* (New York, 1947), pp. 91–99.

5. *National Municipal Review,* April 1929, pp. 281–282; May 1930, pp. 289–292; *American City,* April 1930, pp. 113–114; Arthur D. Gayer, *Public Works in Prosperity and Depression* (New York, 1935), pp. 178–182.

6. *American City,* November 1930, p. 104; May 1931, pp. 143–144; *National Municipal Review,* May 1931, pp. 277–281; July 1931, pp. 402–406; September 1931, pp. 513–517; November 1931, pp. 633–635, 677–678.

7. *National Municipal Review,* November 1930, pp. 740–743; December

1931, p. 683; *American City,* December 1930, p. 85; *City Managers Yearbook* (1932), pp. 30–33, 73–101.
8. *American City,* January 1930, pp. 159–169; December 1930, p. 149; January 1931, p. 5; Irving Bernstein, *The Lean Years: A History of the American Worker: 1920–1933* (Cambridge, 1960), pp. 247–302.
9. E. P. Hayes, *Activities of the President's Emergency Committee for Employment* (Concord, N.H., 1936), pp. 50–57, 96–106; *City Managers Yearbook* (1932), pp. 81–94; Bernstein, *op. cit.,* pp. 302–311.
10. Scott M. Cutlip, *Fund Raising in the U.S.: Its Role in American Philanthropy* (New Brunswick, 1965), pp. 304–307; Clarke A. Chambers, *Seedtime of Reform: American Social Service and Social Action: 1918–1933* (Minneapolis, 1963), pp. 193–194, 196–200; Mitchell, *op. cit.,* pp. 99–104.
11. *American City,* May 1930, pp. 133–134; Cutlip, *op. cit.,* p. 307; *National Municipal Review,* December 1931, pp. 689–691.
12. Blake McKelvey, *Rochester,* IV: 56–67; *American City,* January 1932, pp. 119–120; Gayer, *op. cit.,* pp. 193–198, 424–436.
13. *American City,* June 1932, p. 51; December 1932, pp. 5, 47–48; January 1933, p. 49; *National Municipal Review,* February 1932, pp. 78–79, 88–93, 152–156.
14. *National Municipal Review,* November 1931, pp. 630–634; April 1932, pp. 267–281; November 1932, pp. 628–638; January 1933, p. 3; February 1933, pp. 51–54.
15. *National Municipal Review,* July 1932, p. 462; October 1932, p. 618; April 1933, pp. 162–167; *American City,* August 1932, pp. 80–83; November 1932, pp. 47–48; February 1933, p. 5; McKelvey, *Rochester,* IV: 68–71; Richard D. Lunt, *The High Ministry of Government: The Political Career of Frank Murphy* (Detroit, 1965), pp. 28–50; American Municipal Association, *Proceedings* (1932), pp. 137–148; Robert H. Connery and Richard H. Leach, *The Federal Government and Metropolitan Areas* (Cambridge, 1960), pp. 65, 74–76, 85; Howard Zim, *LaGuardia in Congress* (Ithaca, N.Y., 1958), pp. 175–230.
16. Mitchell, *op. cit.,* pp. 126–133; Bank failures that numbered 642 in 1929, 1,345 in 1930, 2,298 in 1931, dropped to 1,456 in 1932 after the formation of the National Credit Corporation, but the plight of the remaining banks seemed everywhere most precarious.
17. *National Municipal Review,* April 1933, pp. 174–178; Charles E. Gilbert, "National Political Alignments and the Politics of Large Cities," *Political Science Quarterly,* March 1964, pp. 26–31; E. E. Robinson, *The Presidential Vote: 1896–1932* (Stanford, 1934). Of the 136 metropolises, 43 voted Democratic for the first time since 1916, 23 continued their earlier Democratic support. See also Samuel Eldersveld, "The Influence of the Metropolitan Party Pluralities in Presidential Elections Since 1920," *American Political Science Review,* (1949), pp. 1195–1202; Samuel Lubell, *The Future of American Politics* (New York, 1952), pp. 34–35, 50.
18. *American City,* February 1933, pp. 43–44; May 1933, pp. 5, 35; *National Municipal Review,* March 1933, pp. 118–119, 125–128; April 1933, pp. 160–161, 197–198; U.S. Conference of Mayors, *City Problems of 1934* (Chicago, 1935), pp. vi, 1–7.
19. Schlesinger, *The Age of Roosevelt,* I: 451; *American City,* May 1933, p. 35; June 1933, p. 5.
20. *National Municipal Review,* April, 1933, pp. 157–158, 194; June 1933,

pp. 259–260; July 1933, pp. 310–312; August 1933, pp. 358–365, 374–388; September 1933, pp. 406–443.

21. *National Municipal Review,* January 1933, pp. 12–15, 23; *American City,* October 1933, p. 3; November 1933, p. 45; *Municipal Year Book* (1935), pp. 188–190.

22. *American City,* August 1933, p. 35; November 1935, pp. 49–50; December 1933, p. 5; *City Problems for 1934,* pp. 85–88.

23. *American City,* January 1934, p. 5; Schlesinger, *Age of Roosevelt,* II: 263–281; American Municipal Association, *Proceedings* (1933), pp. 349–351.

24. Schlesinger, *op. cit.,* II: 1–23; *National Municipal Review,* April 1933, pp. 174–178; Mitchell, *op. cit.,* pp. 133–139, 314–320; *Municipal Year Book* (1935), pp. 154–162.

25. Clarke A. Chambers, *op. cit.,* pp. 211–250; Frances Perkins, *The Roosevelt I Knew* (New York, 1946), pp. 150–153, 174–196; George E. Mowry, *The Urban Nation: 1920–1960* (New York, 1965), pp. 90–112.

26. Hugh S. Johnson, *The Blue Eagle from Egg to Earth* (New York, 1935), pp. 163–270; Schlesinger, *op. cit.,* II: 87–151, 385–396; Perkins, *op. cit.,* pp. 197–255; Charles R. Walker, *American City* (New York, 1937), p. 88–128; Irving Bernstein, *The New Deal Collective Bargaining Policy* (Berkeley, 1960), pp. 29–39.

27. *American City,* January 1932, p. 102; August 1932, p. 72; September 1932, p. 82; *Housing,* March 1932, pp. 32–34, 43; October 1932, pp. 165, 184–186, 193–195; *National Municipal Review,* February 1933, pp. 55–58, 85–113; President's Conference on Home Building and Home Ownership, *Home Ownership, Income, and Type of Dwelling* (Washington, 1931), pp. 69–75; Timothy L. McDonnell, *The Wagner Housing Act* (Chicago, 1957), pp. 26–28.

28. Mitchell, *op. cit.,* pp. 331–334; *American City,* June 1933, pp. 5, 75; August 1933, p. 37; September 1933, p. 73; November 1933, p. 5; December 1933, pp. 68–71; January 1934, pp. 5, 44; *Housing,* June 1933, pp. 65–116; June 1934, pp. 145–176; McDonnell, *op. cit.,* pp. 29–39.

29. McDonnell, *op. cit.,* pp. 39–43; *American City,* January 1934, pp. 73–75; February 1934, pp. 75–77; May 1934, p. 5; June 1934, p. 110; July 1934, p. 79; September 1934, p. 99; October 1934, p. 5; Carter Goodrich, *Migration and Economic Opportunity* (Philadelphia, 1936), p. 639; Martin Meyerson, Barbara Terrett, and Wm. L. C. Wheaton, *Housing, People, and Cities* (New York, 1962), pp. 222–226; Hal Burton, *The City Fights Back* (New York, 1954), pp. 161–164.

30. National Association of Housing Officials, *A Housing Program for the U.S.* (Chicago, 1934); McDonnell, *op. cit.,* pp. 72–82; *Housing Officials Year Book* (1935), pp. 37–43.

31. *National Municipal Review,* February 1934, pp. 107–109; June 1934, pp. 296–298; Mitchell, *op. cit.,* pp. 314–321, 451, 453.

32. *National Municipal Review,* June 1934, pp. 313–332; August 1934, pp. 415–419, 423.

33. *American City,* May 1934, p. 5; October 1934, p. 39; Charles Garrett, *The LaGuardia Years* (New Brunswick, 1961), pp. 178–187; *City Problems of 1935,* pp. 1–19.

34. *American City,* December 1934, p. 5; January 1935, p. 5; February 1935, p. 5; A. M. Schlesinger, Jr., *The Politics of Upheaval* [*The Age of Roosevelt,* III] (New York, 1960), pp. 235–270, 343–351.

35. *American City*, June 1935, p. 42; November 1935, p. 73; December 1935, p. 5; December 1939, pp. 81–83; Mitchell, *op. cit.*, pp. 318–320; Schlesinger, III: 264–268; *Annals*, January 1940, pp. 44–52.

36. *American City*, January 1937, p. 62; Dixon Wechter, *The Age of the Great Depression* (New York, 1948), pp. 260–270.

37. Hallie Flanagan, *Arena* (New York, 1940); Susan E. Salitan, "The Federal Theatre Project," Ms. at Smith College (1964); Charles and Mary Beard, *America in Midpassage* (New York, 1939), pp. 632–638, 770–800.

38. Charles Abrams, *The City Is the Frontier* (New York, 1965), pp. 239–243; *National Municipal Review*, October 1931, pp. 592–594; Clarence S. Stein, *Toward New Towns for America* (Chicago, 1951), pp. 15–20, 101–110; George A. Warner, *Greenbelt: The Cooperative Community* (New York, 1954); *American City*, November 1935, p. 63; May 1936, pp. 59–61; August 1936, pp. 46–49; *City Planning*, October 1931, pp. 261–263; Lester G. Seligman and E. E. Cornwell, eds., *New Deal Mosaic: Roosevelt Confers with the National Emergency Council, 1933–1936* (Eugene, Ore., 1965), pp. 483, 488, 497.

39. Schlesinger, *The Age of Roosevelt* III: 371–373, 385–400; *Housing Officials Year Book* (1935), pp. 1–36; (1936), pp. 28–34, 191–212; see the excellent summary of the judicial prospects for public housing in Abrams, *op. cit.*, pp. 244–249.

40. Joseph G. Rayback, *A History of American Labor* (New York, 1959), pp. 346–355; Mitchell, *op. cit.*, pp. 268–295; David Brody, "The Emergence of Mass Production Unionism," in John Braman and Others, *Change and Continuity in Twentieth Century America* (Ohio University Press, 1964), pp. 221–242; Bernstein, *Collective Bargaining Policy*, pp. 84–128.

41. Fred Whitney, *Government and Collective Bargaining* (New York, 1951), pp. 210–232.

42. Howard S. Kaltenborn, *Governmental Adjustment of Labor Disputes* (Chicago, 1943), pp. 171–186, 202–217; William L. Nunn's three articles in *National Municipal Review*, March, April, and December 1940, pp. 174–177, 248–252, 784–791; *City Problems* (1936), pp. 122–128; (1937), pp. 67–74.

43. Mitchell, *op. cit.*, pp. 277–300; Rayback, *op. cit.*, pp. 336–340; Chalmers, *op. cit.*, pp. 255–267; Seba Eldridge, *Development of Collective Enterprise* (University of Kansas, 1943), pp. 338–347.

44. *American City*, February 1936, pp. 5, 97–98; April 1936, pp. 45, 62; January 1937, p. 5; *City Problems* (1936), pp. 1–16 (1937), pp. 1–13.

45. Eldersveld, *loc. cit.*, p. 1196; *Statistical Abstracts of the U.S.* (1937), p. 150; *National Municipal Review*, May 1941, pp. 264–267; Schlesinger, III: 426–428; Gilbert Osofsky, *Harlem, the Making of a Ghetto* (New York, 1966), p. 243; Mowry, *op. cit.*, pp. 114–116; Lubell, *op. cit.*, pp. 46–50.

46. McDonnell, *op. cit.*, pp. 88–114; *American City*, May 1935, p. 67; October 1935, p. 5; February 1936, p. 81; May 1936, p. 5.

47. McDonnell, *op. cit.*, pp. 115–402; *American City*, January 1937, pp. 45–48; February 1937, p. 54–55; September 1937, p. 5; February 1938, p. 5; *National Municipal Review*, July 1938, pp. 375–376; *City Problems* (1937), pp. 117–131, 137–138; Abrams, *op. cit.*, pp. 241–246.

48. Edith E. Wood, *Slums and Blighted Areas in the U.S.* (Washington, 1935), pp. 36–65; *American City*, April 1938, p. 93; August 1938, p.

5; November 1938, p. 99; *Housing Officials Year Book* (1939), pp. 206–208, 211–216, lists 33 local housing councils.

49. *National Municipal Review,* April 1937, pp. 206–207; February 1939, p. 55.

50. *American City,* August 1938, p. 5; November 1938, pp. 87–89; *National Municipal Review,* June 1939, pp. 420–422; *Housing Officials Year Book* (1940), pp. 217 ff.

51. *American City,* October 1934, pp. 41–42; April 1935, p. 65; January 1937, pp. 62, 77–79; July 1937, p. 105; January 1938, p. 5; July 1938, p. 5; January 1939, pp. 62–65; June 1939, p. 5; October 1939, pp. 99–101. See the extended bibliography of Work-relief Project Reports in Robert A. Walker, *The Planning Function in Urban Government* (Chicago, 1941); *City Problems* (1940), pp. 32–40.

52. *National Municipal Review,* August 1936, pp. 452–464; "Federal Services to Municipal Governments," Brookings Institution *Leaflets* (Washington, 1934); National Resources Committee, *Urban Government* (1939) I: 64–65; *Annals,* May 1965, p. 16–22.

53. *National Municipal Review,* December 1934, pp. 656–657; December 1935, p. 663.

54. George M. Harris, *Westward to the East: The Record of a World Tour in Search of Local Government* (London, 1935); *Municipal Year Book* (Chicago, 1934).

55. *American City,* November 1934, p. 39; July 1936, p. 50; *National Municipal Review,* June 1936, pp. 347–353; November 1938, p. 553; McKelvey, *Rochester,* IV: 94–103.

56. *National Municipal Review,* February 1934, pp. 100–103; January 1940, pp. 6–9; *American City,* July 1937, p. 105; Larry M. Elison, *The Finances of Metropolitan Areas* (Ann Arbor, 1964), pp. 81–84, 97–98.

57. Elison, *op. cit.,* p. 156, see table; *National Municipal Review,* April 1938, pp. 187–196, 203, 208; May 1940, pp. 296–300.

58. *American City,* October 1930, pp. 89–92; January 1932, p. 84; November 1933, p. 65; January 1934, p. 73; October 1934, pp. 41–42; May 1937, pp. 50–51; August 1937, pp. 45–47; February 1938, p. 30; *City Planning,* July 1932, p. 171; October 1932, pp. 229–234; Works Progress Administration, *Index of Research Projects* (Washington, 1939), I: 280–281.

59. Forbes B. Hays, *Community Leadership* (New York, 1965), pp. 1–31; *American City,* September 1930, p. 100; March 1931, pp. 127–128; May 1931, pp. 116–118; April 1935, pp. 85–87; *National Municipal Review,* May 1932, pp. 296–297; Lubove, *op. cit.,* pp. 107–114; Constance Green, *Washington,* II: 286–288; Harold M. Lewis, *County and Regional Planning Organizations in New York State* (Albany, 1936).

60. Lubove, *op. cit.,* pp. 115–122; Lewis Mumford, "The Plans of New York I," *New Republic,* June 15, 1932, pp. 123–124; Thomas B. Adams, *The Building of the City* [Regional Plan of New York and Its Environs, Vol. II] (New York, 1931).

61. *New Republic,* July 6, 1932, pp. 207–210; *American City,* April 1935, pp. 85–87; Frank Lloyd Wright, *When Democracy Builds* (Chicago, 1945), pp. 56–60; Forbes B. Hays, *op. cit.,* pp. 18–21, 28–36.

62. Stein, *op. cit.,* pp. 83–91, 169–207; *American City,* April 1934, p. 31; August 1934, p. 73; Norman Beckman, "Federal Long-Range Planning: The Heritage of the National Resources Planning Board, AIP *Journal,*" May 1960, pp. 89–91.

63. *American City,* July 1937, pp. 55–58; August 1937, p. 71; April 1938, pp. 87–89; June 1938, pp. 37–39; August 1939, pp. 35, 44–45; Philip H. Cornick, *Premature Subdivision and Its Consequences* (New York, 1938).

64. *National Municipal Review,* May 1931, pp. 256–257; June 1931, pp. 386–387; February 1937, p. 97; March 1938, pp. 129–137; December 1939, p. 827–831; Malcolm E. Jewell, ed., *The Politics of Reapportionment* (New ʹork, 1962), p. 6 and *passim.*

65. *National Municipal Review,* October 1934, pp. 502, 505–513; April 1935, p. 66; October 1935, pp. 512–514, 537; December 1935, pp. 699, 702; April 1939, pp. 279–286; Council of State Governments, *The States and the Metropolitan Problem* (Chicago, 1956), pp. 72–87.

66. *Ibid.,* pp. 124–126; *American City,* October 1936, pp. 71–75; *Municipal Year Book* (1935), pp. 128–135; (1936), pp. 135–139. *See also* John T. Bollens, *Special District Governments in the United States* (Berkeley, 1957).

67. *National Municipal Review,* May 1936, pp. 290–292; March 1939, p. 205; November 1939, pp. 757, 763; May 1940, pp. 291–295; *Municipal Year Book* (1940), pp. 128–135.

68. N. M. Gill, *Municipal Research Bureaus* (Washington, 1944), pp. 21–25; *National Municipal Review,* May 1933, p. 251 (a list of 33 bureaus); March 1939, p. 205; *American City,* October 1934, p. 40; October 1938, p. 91.

69. *American City,* June 1931, pp. 81–84; March 1937, pp. 7, 85–87; May 1937, p. 7; March 1938, pp. 47–48; November 1939, pp. 35–36; Winston W. Crouch and B. Dinerman, *Southern California Metropolis* (Los Angeles, 1963), pp. 46–47.

70. See the excellent discussion of these developments in Roscoe C. Martin, *The Cities and the Federal System* (New York, 1965), pp. 83–92.

71. Merrill Denison, *The Power to Go* (New York, 1956), p. 288.

72. National Conference on City Planning, *City Problems of Town, City and Region* (Philadelphia, 1931), pp. 35 and ff. New York City, not included in this table, was in a class by itself. In 1939, after consolidating its rapid-transit lines under two boards, it reported a total passenger load for the year of 1,852,944,000, more than three times the number carried by all steam roads in America. See *National Municipal Review,* November 1940, pp. 728–735.

73. *American City,* January 1930, p. 129; July 1930, pp. 107–108; November 1932, pp. 64–66; July 1935, p. 79; January 1936, pp. 53–56; March 1939, pp. 49–51; August 1939, pp. 51–55; Southern California Planning Institute, *A Review of Developments,* II (1960), p. 127.

74. *American City,* November 1929, p. 100; August 1935, p. 61; January 1936, pp. 95–97; March 1937, pp. 89–91; June 1937, pp. 99–101; October 1937, pp. 71–72.

75. *National Municipal Review,* February 1936, pp. 72, 85, 91–96; November 1936, pp. 680–757; December 1938, p. 616; Frederick C. Mosher, *City Manager Government in Seven Cities* (Chicago, 1940); Garrett, *The LaGuardia Years,* pp. 86, 230–243; Frederick Shaw, *The History of the New York City Legislature* (New York, 1954), pp. 188–210.

76. *American City,* February 1932, p. 80; August 1939, p. 59; Albert Lepawsky, *The Judicial System of Metropolitan Chicago* (Chicago, 1932), p. 20.

77. *American City,* July 1929, pp. 13–134, 154; August 1937, pp. 62–63;

May 1939, pp. 77–79; *National Municipal Review,* December 1934, pp. 650–653; May 1938, pp. 530–535; July 1940, pp. 448–450; Edward L. Thorndike, *Your City* (New York, 1939); *Municipal Year Book* (1937), pp. 137–144.

78. *American Journal of Sociology* (1938), pp. 1–24; *Recent Social Trends* (New York, 1933), I: 443–496; National Resources Committee, *Our Cities, Their Roles in the National Economy* (Washington, 1937); Nels Anderson and E. C. Lindeman, *Urban Sociology* (New York, 1928); L. L. Bernard, ed., *The Field Methods of Sociology* (New York, 1934).

79. Milla A. Alihan, *Social Ecology* (New York, 1938), pp. 208–222; Maurice R. Davie, "The Pattern of Urban Growth," in G. P. Murdock, ed., *Studies in the Science of Society* (New Haven, 1937), pp. 133–161.

80. Robert and Helen Lynd, *Middletown in Transition* (New York, 1937); W. Lloyd Warner and Paul S. Lunt, *The Social Life of a Modern Community* [Yankee City Series I] (New Haven, 1941). See the analysis of these and other researches by Maurice R. Stein, *The Eclipse of Community* (Princeton, 1960), pp. 13–70; and Leonard Reissman, *The Urban Process: Cities in Industrial Societies* (Glencoe, 1964).

81. H. H. McCarty, *Industrial Migration in the U.S.* (Iowa City, 1930); Robert E. Dickinson, "The Metropolitan Regions of the U.S.," *Geographical Review* (1934), pp. 278–296. See also John W. Alexander, "The Basic-Nonbasic Concept of Urban Economic Functions," *Economic Geography,* July 1954; Homer Hoyt, *One Hundred Years of Land Values in Chicago* (Chicago, 1933) and *The Structure of Growth in Residential Neighborhoods in American Cities* (Washington, 1939).

82. Charles E. Merriam, S. D. Pratt, and A. Lepawsky, *The Government of the Metropolitan Region at Chicago* (Chicago, 1933); Harold Gosnell, *Machine Politics: Chicago Model* (Chicago, 1937); Caroline F. Ware, *Greenwich Village: 1920–1930* (Boston, 1935); Allison Davis and Others, *Deep South* (Chicago, 1941); Robert Faris and H. W. Dunham, *Mental Disorders in Urban Areas* (Chicago, 1939); Caroline F. Ware, ed., *The Cultural Approach to History* (Columbia, 1940), pp. 228–243.

83. A. M. Schlesinger, *The Rise of the City: 1878–1898* (New York, 1933); *ibid.,* "The City in American History," Mississippi Valley *Historical Review* (1940), pp. 43–66; reprinted with added bibliography in *ibid., Paths to the Present* (New York, 1949), pp. 210–233, 297–299. See William Diamond, "On the Dangers of an Urban Interpretation of History," in Eric F. Goldman, *Historiography and Urbanization: Essays . . . in Honor of W. Stull Holt* (Baltimore, 1941), pp. 91–103 ff.

84. See the discussion of these and other writers of the period in Dixon Wecter, *The Age of the Great Depression* (New York, 1948), pp. 262–266; John W. Aldridge, *After the Lost Generation* (New York, 1951), pp. 12–81; Maxwell Geismar, *The Last of the Provincials* (Cambridge, 1943), pp. 361–380, and *Writers in Crisis* (Cambridge, 1961), pp. 144–146, 169–183, 263–268; David A. Shannon, *Between the Wars: America, 1919–1941* (Boston, 1965), pp. 198–201; Blanche H. Gelfant, *The American City Novel* (Norman, Okla., 1954), pp. 175–196; Hugh M. Gloster, *Negro Voices in American Fiction* (New York, 1965), pp. 222–240.

85. Wecter, *op. cit.,* pp. 236–241, 261–267; Charles and Mary Beard, *America in Midpassage* (New York, 1939), pp. 652–744; Howard Taubman, *The Making of the American Theatre* (New York, 1965), pp. 227–237.

86. The Beards, *op. cit.*, pp. 595–632, 717–742.
87. See the bibliography in McKelvey, *Urbanization of America* (New Brunswick, 1963), pp. 333–357.
88. Harland Bartholomew, *Urban Land Use* (Cambridge, 1932); Henry Wright, *Re-housing Urban America* (New York, 1935); Clarence Perry, *Housing for the Machine Age* (New York, 1939); Edith E. Wood, *Recent Trends in American Housing* (New York, 1931) and *Slums and Blighted Areas in the U.S.* (Washington, 1935); Frank Lloyd Wright, *Modern Architecture* (Princeton, 1931), *The Disappearing City* (New York, 1932), and *Architecture and Modern Life* (New York, 1932).
89. John Burchard and A. B. Brown, *The Architecture of America: A Social and Cultural History* (Boston, 1961), pp. 398–401; *American City*, May 1934, p. 64; December 1934, p. 56; *American Magazine of Art*, April 1943, pp. 183–188.
90. Beard, *op. cit.*, pp. 770–800.
91. *American City*, April 1931, p. 127; November 1931, p. 105; November 1932, p. 76; August 1938, pp. 49–50; McKelvey, *Rochester*, IV: 107–108; Leon Carnovsky and Lowell Martin, eds., *The Library in the Community* (Chicago, 1944), pp. 40–58.
92. Garrett, *op. cit.*, pp. 178–189; Hays, *op. cit.*, pp. 55–62; S. J. Makielski, Jr., *The Politics of Zoning: The New York Experience* (New York, 1966), pp. 48–66.
93. Lewis Mumford, *The Culture of Cities* (New York, 1938), pp. 1–12 and *passim*.
94. *Ibid.*; see also Leonard Reissman's discussion of Mumford in Reissman, *op. cit.*, pp. 62–68.
95. Mumford, *op. cit.*, pp. 358–366, 400–401.
96. *Municipal Year Book* (1936–1940); each volume contains an article on "Federal-City Relations" for the year by Mallery, as well as a current list of the leagues and associations engaged in the movement; (1937), pp. 3–12; *City Problems of 1938–1939*, pp. 2–7; *City Problems of 1940*, pp. 8–15, 47–53.

CHAPTER 4

1. *City Problems of 1940*, pp. 9–22, 24–86.
2. Edwin A. Cottrell, "A Year of Defense Preparation," and Roy H. Ousley, "Federal-City Relations in 1940," *Municipal Year Book* (1941), pp. 1–10, 96–108; *National Municipal Review*, October 1939, pp. 742–744.
3. *National Municipal Review*, September 1940, p. 573; July 1941, pp. 427–429; *American City*, January 1941, p. 5, 13; February 1941, pp. 5, 37–38; *Municipal Year Book* (1942), pp. 1–4, 204–214, 317–334.
4. David Hinshaw, *The Home Front* (New York, 1943), pp. 30–45.
5. Mildred H. Gillie, *Forging the Thunderbolt* (Harrisburg, 1947), pp. 180–181; *Business Week*, November 28, 1942; *National Municipal Review*, June 1941, p. 361; Robert H. Connery and Richard H. Leach, *The Federal Government and Metropolitan Areas* (Cambridge, 1960), pp. 39–41; Levin H. Campbell, Jr., *The Industry-Ordnance Team* (New York, 1946), pp. 1–34.
6. Scott M. Cutlip, *Fund Raising in the U.S.* (New Brunswick, 1965), pp. 397–418; *American City*, January 1942, pp. 35–51; February 1942, pp. 35–39.

7. Marvin W. Schlegel, *Conscripted City: Norfolk in World War II* (Norfolk, 1951), pp. 78–87, 254–258.
8. John Burchard and Albert Bush-Brown, *The Architecture of America: A Social and Cultural History* (Boston, 1961), pp. 405–406; Schlegel, *op. cit.*, pp. 20–88; Robert Havighurst and H. G. Morgan, *The Social History of a War-Boom Community* (New York, 1951); McKelvey, *Rochester*, IV: 127, 139, 151; *National Municipal Review*, March 1942, pp. 163–164; *American City*, June 1941, p. 5; *City Problems of 1942*, pp. 7–22.
9. Schlegel, *op. cit.*, pp. 219–296; Green, *Washington*, II: 477–487; McKelvey, *Rochester*, IV: 131–152; *National Municipal Review*, January 1942, pp. 1–5; March 1942, pp. 136–142; June 1942, pp. 336–338; *American City*, April 1941, p. 71; December 1941, pp. 44–46; January 1942, p. 103.
10. U.S. Civilian Production Administration, *Industrial Mobilization for War* (Washington, 1947), I: 93–184, 231–272; *American City*, August 1942, pp. 38–39; *National Municipal Review*, June 1943, pp. 321–325; September 1943, pp. 456–458, Connery and Leach, *op. cit.*, pp. 39–41, 147–199.
11. U.S. *Census* (1950), P–A 1: 66–69; Philip M. Hauser, *Changing Markets: Changes of a Geographic Nature in Wartime* (Washington, 1943), Mimeographed pamphlet, pp. 8–14; William C. Hallenbeck, *American Urban Communities* (New York, 1951), pp. 62–65, 588–590; Robert A. Will, "Federal Influence on Industrial Location: How Extensive?" *Land Economics*, February 1964, pp. 49–55.
12. *American City*, September 1943, p. 83; February 1945, pp. 78–79; May 1945, pp. 85–86; St. Clair Drake and H. R. Cayton, *Black Metropolis* (New York, 1945), p. 90; John Hope Franklin, *From Slavery to Freedom* (New York, 1956 ed.), pp. 564–567.
13. Robert Shogan and Tom Craig, *The Detroit Race Riot* (Philadelphia, 1964), pp. 25–110; Franklin, *op. cit.*, pp. 580–582; Myrdal, *An American Dilemma*, p. 568.
14. Paul F. Wendt, *Housing Policy—The Search for Solutions* (Berkeley, 1962), pp. 152–155; *American City*, February 1942, pp. 67–69; March 1942, pp. 69, 136–142; May 1943, pp. 46, 75; July 1943, pp. 42–43.
15. *American City*, May 1941, p. 35; November 1942, pp. 35–37; April 1943, p. 5; *National Municipal Review*, February 1943, pp. 63–67, 97; *Municipal Year Book* (1943), pp. 334–336. Connery and Leach, *op. cit.*, pp. 143–147; Norman Beckman, "Federal Long-Range Planning: The Heritage of the National Resources Planning Board," AIP *Journal*, May 1960, pp. 89–97.
16. Roscoe C. Martin, Frank J. Munger, and Others, *Decisions in Syracuse* (Bloomington, 1961), pp. 47–74; *National Municipal Review*, February 1943, p. 104; June 1943, pp. 334–335.
17. *American City*, March 1943, pp. 42–43; May 1943, p. 37; June 1943, p. 72; *National Municipal Review*, July 1943, p. 393; *Municipal Year Book* (1944), pp. 7, 317–319; Hal Burton, *The City Fights Back* (New York, 1954), pp. 185–195; Theodore Brown, *The Politics of Reform* (Kansas City, 1958), pp. 359–389. See also Jeanne R. Lowe, *Cities in a Race with Time* (New York, 1967), pp. 110–148.
18. *American City*, October 1943, p. 41; December 1943, pp. 37–39; 53–58; *National Municipal Review*, February 1944, 66–69, 103–105; March 1944, pp. 155–156.

19. *National Municipal Review,* February 1945, pp. 91–94; *Journal of* American Institute of Planners, Autumn 1944, pp. 1–27; April-June 1945, pp. 25–29.
20. *American City,* March 1945, pp. 5, 80–82, 91–92; July 1945, pp. 72–74; October 1945, pp. 93–94; *National Municipal Review,* May 1945, pp. 223–229.
21. *National Municipal Review,* November 1945, p. 521; April 1946, pp. 172–176.
22. *American City,* January 1945, pp. 5, 125; March 1945, p. 17; September 1945, pp. 96–97; February 1946, p. 69; June 1946, p. 77.
23. Lewis Mumford, *City Development: Studies in Disintegration and Renewal* (New York, 1945), pp. 18, 177, 190–197; *Journal* of the American Institute of Planners, Summer 1945, pp. 36–40.
24. *American City,* May 1941, p. 69; December 1941, pp. 39, 71; May 1943, pp. 47–49; April 1944, pp. 95–97; May 1944, p. 55; July 1944, p. 115; September 1944, pp. 83–85; February 1946, pp. 79–80; *Journal* of the A.I.A., Autumn 1944, pp. 18–27; *Housing Year Book* (1944), pp. 11–14; Burton, *op. cit.,* pp. 10–15.
25. Forbes B. Hays, *Community Leadership* (New York, 1965), pp. 70–94; *American City,* July 1944, pp. 70–71; *National Municipal Review,* July 1943, p. 384–385; AIA *Journal,* April-June 1945, pp. 25–29; Charles Abrams, *The City Is the Frontier* (New York, 1965), pp. 95–98; S. J. Makielski, Jr., *The Politics of Zoning* (New York, 1966), pp. 63–75.
26. *Proceedings* of the National Conference on Post-War Housing (New York, 1944), pp. 5–99.
27. *Ibid.,* pp. 100–119.
28. AIA *Journal,* February 1945, pp. 51–53; April 1945, pp. 135–138; October 1946, pp. 159–168.
29. *National Municipal Review,* September 1945, pp. 376–380; December 1945, p. 587; January 1946, pp. 23–24. See also John E. Pearson, "The Significance of Urban Housing in Rural-Urban Migration," *Land Economics,* August 1963, pp. 231–239.
30. *National Municipal Review,* October 1945, pp. 453–455; October 1946, pp. 453–456; *Journal* of the A.I.A., February 1946, pp. 67–70; McKelvey, *Rochester,* IV: 182, 188; Burton, *op. cit.,* pp. 128–136; Robert J. Mowitz and Deil S. Wright, *Profile of a Metropolis: A Case Book* (Detroit, 1962), pp. 13–20.
31. *National Municipal Review,* January 1943, pp. 17–20; *Municipal Year Book* (1948), pp. 278–282.
32. Green, *Washington,* II: 490–494; *National Municipal Review,* February 1942, pp. 117–118; *American City,* April 1942, pp. 68–70.
33. *National Municipal Review,* June 1947, p. 329; *American City,* June 1947, p. 5; *Housing Year Book* (1949), pp. 300–308; (1950), pp. 318–324; *New York Times,* May 13, 1947, 24:1: Ashley A. Ford and Hilbert Fefferman, "Federal Urban Renewal Legislation," *Law and Contemporary Problems,* Autumn 1960, pp. 641–653.
34. *Municipal Year Book* (1948), pp. 278–282; (1949), pp. 302–307; (1950), pp. 318–324; *National Municipal Review,* July 1949, pp. 324–327; *American City,* October 1947, pp. 96–98; June 1949, pp. 84–85; August 1949, pp. 93–94; October 1949, pp. 79–81; AIA *Journal,* December 1947, pp. 245–250; *Planning and Civic Comment,* March 1950, pp. 28–32; Coleman Woodbury, ed., *Urban Redevelopment: Problems and*

Practices (Chicago, 1953), pp. 332–370; Ford and Fefferman, *op. cit.,* pp. 643–650. *See also* Richard O. Davies, *Housing Reform During the Truman Administration* (Columbia, Mo., 1966), which appeared after this section had been written.
35. *Municipal Year Book* (1950), pp. 318–324; Paul F. Wendt, *Housing Policy, The Search for a Solution* (Berkeley, 1962), pp. 163–165, 190–202; Woodbury, *op. cit.,* pp. 226–228, 409–420.
36. *American City,* June 1943, p. 5; August 1949, p. 83; December 1949, p. 131; AIA *Journal,* Spring 1948, pp. 15–23, 35–36; Summer 1948, pp. 38–43; Karl E. and Alma F. Taeuber, *Negroes in Cities* (Chicago, 1965), pp. 38–40, 119; Woodbury, *op. cit.,* pp. 353–370; see also St. Clair Drake and Horace R. Cayton, *Black Metropolis* (New York, 1945).
37. Franklin, *From Slavery to Freedom,* pp. 593–595; *American City,* February 1945, pp. 78–79; Morton Grodzins, *The Metropolitan Area as a Racial Problem* (Pittsburgh, 1959).
38. *American City,* May 1947 , pp. 271–272; August 1947, pp. 125–127; September 1947, pp. 115–116; September 1948, pp. 141–142, 155; Shelly *v.* Kraemer, 68 U.S. Supreme Court, 836; Rupert B. Vance and N. J. Demerath, eds., *The Urban South* (Chapel Hill, 1954), pp. 210–214; Woodbury, *op. cit.,* pp. 226–228.
39. *National Municipal Review,* November 1947, pp. 558–564; April 1948, pp. 210–211; *American City,* May 1947, pp. 71, 90–91; October 1947, pp. 86–88; June 1949, pp. 84–85; AIA *Journal,* Autumn 1945, pp. 25–26; Spring 1947, pp. 29–32; Spring 1948, p. 23–28; *Municipal Year Book* (1948), pp. 284–285; Burton, *op. cit.,* pp. 11–12.
40. See reference to note 36 and March 1948, pp. 94–96, 120; AIA *Journal,* December 1947, pp. 245–250; *American City,* September 1948, pp. 108–109; Spring 1949, pp. 11–16; *National Municipal Review,* May 1948, pp. 248–251; July 1949, pp. 324–327; Burton, *op. cit.,* pp. 106–113.
41. U.S. *Census* (1950), Pop. I: 29, 69, 76; Betty Tableman, *Governmental Organization in Metropolitan Areas* (Ann Arbor, 1951), pp. 3–10; Taeuber, *op. cit.,* pp. 153.
42. *American City,* January 1947, pp. 82–83; *National Municipal Review,* January 1946, pp. 4–8; December 1949, pp. 571–574; August 1948, pp. 82–84; AIA *Journal,* August 1947, pp. 73–80; Summer 1948, pp. 4–9; July 1948, pp. 371–376; Martin and Munger, *op. cit.,* pp. 42–46.
43. U.S. *Census of Manufactures* (1947), pp. 37–39; National Security Resources Board, *National Security Factors in Industrial Location* (Washington, 1948); Hallenbeck, *op. cit.,* pp. 588–590; Woodbury, *op. cit.,* pp. 225–288.
44. Charles E. Gilbert, "National Political Alignments and the Politics of Large Cities," *Political Science Quarterly,* March 1964, pp. 25–51; Samuel J. Eldersveld, "The Influence of Metropolitan Party Pluralities in Presidential Elections Since 1920," *American Political Science Review,* XLII (1949), pp. 1189–1206; Samuel Lubell, *The Future of American Politics* (New York, 1951), pp. 168–170, 211–220.
45. Lorin Peterson, *The Day of the Mugwump* (New York, 1961); *City Problems* (1943–1944), pp. 47–70.
46. This subject merits a thorough study, but see *National Municipal Review,* November 1940, pp. 720–723; June 1941, pp. 376–377; September 1941, p. 530; November 1941, pp. 633–637; December 1943,

p. 616; January 1944, pp. 40–41; October 1946, pp. 477–488; Blake McKelvey, "A History of the City Club of Rochester," *Rochester History*, IX, October 1947; Thomas F. Campbell, *Freedom's Forum: The City Club [of Cleveland] 1912–1962* (Cleveland, 1963).

47. *National Municipal Review*, November 1940; July 1940, pp. 459–466; September 1940, pp. 575–584; November 1940, pp. 720–723; June 1941, pp. 335–340; *Municipal Year Book* (1948), pp. 220–223; Winston W. Crouch and B. Dinerman, *Southern California Metropolis* (Berkeley, 1963), pp. 191–203.

48. *National Municipal Review*, April 1941, pp. 211–216; July 1941, pp. 400–408; Thomas H. Reed, *City Growing Pains* (New York, 1942); Victor Jones, *Metropolitan Government* (Chicago, 1942).

49. *National Municipal Review*, April 1944, pp. 197–198; June 1944, pp. 277–282; March 1946, pp. 111–112; Crouch and Dinerman, *op. cit.*, pp. 111, 119–202, 220–221, 375, 389.

50. *The Boston Contest of 1944:* Prize Winning Programs (Boston, 1945); *Planning and Civic Comment*, April 1945, pp. 1–11; January 1948, pp. 5–8; *National Municipal Review*, January 1945, pp. 30–31; March 1946, p. 114; October 1946, pp. 451–452; February 1947, p. 93; March 1948, p. 172; December 1949, pp. 615–616; December 1950, pp. 543–544; *Municipal Year Book* (1948), pp. 1–3; *American City*, November 1948, pp. 90–93; John C. Bollens, *Special District Governments in the U.S.* (Berkeley, 1957), pp. 54–64; Council of State Governments, *The States and the Metropolitan Problem* (Chicago, 1956), pp. 26–123; Tableman, *op. cit.*, pp. 11–75, 140–166; U.S. Bureau of Census, *Governmental Units Overlaying City Areas* (Washington, 1947).

51. *Planning and Civic Comment*, April 1949, pp. 18–20; Crouch and Dinerman, *op. cit.*, pp. 167–168, 280–286; *American City*, February 1949, pp. 88–90; A. Theodore Brown, *The Politics of Reform: Kansas City's Municipal Government: 1925–1950* (Community Studies 116, Kansas City, 1958), pp. 313–341.

52. *National Municipal Review*, (1947), pp. 2–7; January 1948, pp. 7–9, 59; May 1949, pp. 212–214; *Municipal Year Book* (1949), pp. 4–5, 195–196, 202; Larry M. Elison, *The Finances of Metropolitan Areas* (Ann Arbor, 1964), pp. 81–84, 97–98.

53. *National Municipal Review*, February 1941, pp. 73–79; May 1943, pp. 223, 256–257; December 1945, pp. 534–535; March 1946, pp. 115–120; April 1946, pp. 177–182; July 1946, pp. 350–354; May 1948, pp. 259–260; Robert B. McKay, *Reapportionment: The Law and Politics of Equal Representation* (New York, 1965), see summaries of the laws of each state in the Appendix.

54. McKay, *op. cit.*, pp. 66–70; Colgrove v. Green, 328, U.S. 549–556.

55. Gordon E. Baker, *Rural vs. Urban Political Power* (New York, 1955), pp. 11–26; *National Municipal Review*, July 1949, pp. 318, 355; November 1949, pp. 482–484.

56. William G. Colman, "The Role of the Federal Government," *Annals*, May 1965, pp. 23–34; *National Municipal Review*, February 1947, pp. 113; May 1947, pp. 240–246; July 1947, p. 420; February 1948, pp. 86–90; December 1949, pp. 551–555, 567; *American City*, August 1947, pp. 98–99; January 1949, pp. 84–85.

57. *American City*, July 1948, p. 68; *National Municipal Review*, January 1947, pp. 18–25; October 1948, pp. 471–479; November 1949, pp. 485–490.

58. *National Municipal Review,* March 1947, p. 122; September 1948, pp. 412–420; *Planning and Civic Comment,* July 1949, pp. 12–18; William D. Miller, *Mr. Crump of Memphis* (Baton Rouge, 1964); Martin Meyerson and Ed C. Banfield, *Politics, Planning and the Public Interest* (Glencoe, 1955), pp. 61–88.

59. Roscoe C. Martin, *The Cities and the Federal System* (New York, 1965), pp. 83–108, 115–119, see p. 97 for the LaGuardia quote; Connery and Leach, *op. cit.,* pp. 30–32.

60. R. B. Vance and N. J. Demerath, eds., *The Urban South* (Chapel Hill, 1954), pp. 180–200; *National Municipal Review,* February 1946, pp. 77–78.

61. *American City,* September 1947, pp. 121–122; November 1947, pp. 558–560; December 1947, pp. 635–636; Howard R. Lewis, *With Every Breath You Take* (New York, 1965), pp. 202–211; Burton, *op. cit.,* pp. 105–115.

62. Merrill Denison, *The Power to Go* (New York, 1956), p. 288; *American City,* May 1943, p. 55; January 1945, pp. 78–80; *National Municipal Review,* October 1946, pp. 465–469; John Bauer and Peter Costello, *Transit Modernization and Street Traffic Control* (Chicago, 1950).

63. *American City,* January 1945, pp. 5, 125; August 1947, p. 115; September 1947, p. 89; October 1947, pp. 135–137; March 1949, pp. 131–133; Connery and Leach, *op. cit.,* pp. 49–51.

64. Hope Tisdale, "The Process of Urbanization," *Social Forces,* XX (March 1942), pp. 311–316; August B. Hollingshead, "Community Research: Development and Present Conditions" *American Soc. Review,* XIII (April 1948), pp. 136–148; Maurice R. Stein, *The Eclipse of Community* (Princeton, 1960), pp. 278–279; Don J. Bogue, *The Structure of the Metropolitan Community* (University of Michigan, 1950); Amos H. Hawley, *Human Ecology* (New York, 1950), pp. 371–404.

65. Calvin F. Schmid, *Social Trends in Seattle* (University of Washington, 1944); Robert C. Angell, "The Social Integration of American Cities of more than 100,000 Population," *Amer. Soc. Review,* XII (June 1947), pp. 335–342; Angell, "The Moral Integration of Cities," *American Journal of Society,* July 1951, Part II.

66. Lloyd Warner and Paul S. Lunt, *Social Life in a Modern Community* (New Haven, 1941); Harold M. Hodges, *Social Stratification: Class in America* (Cambridge, 1964), pp. 11, 62–63.

67. Hodges, *op. cit.,* pp. 51–58, 64, 66–76; James West, *Plainsville U.S.A.* (New York, 1945); Cleveland Amory, *Proper Bostonians* (New York, 1947); E. Digby Baltzell, *The Philadelphia Gentlemen* (Glencoe, 1958). John P. Marquand, however, in *Timothy Dexter Revisited* (Boston, 1960), pp. 3–17, found the Warner thesis "dated" as far as Newburypart is concerned.

68. Hodges, *op. cit.,* pp. 64–66, 117–120; Warner and Associates, *Social Class in America* (Chicago, 1949); Warner and Associates, *Democracy in Jonesville* (New York, 1949); A. B. Hollingshead, *Elmtown's Youth* (New York, 1949); Allison Davis and Associates, *Deep South: A Social and Anthropological Study of Caste and Class* (Chicago, 1941).

69. Hodges, *op. cit.,* pp. 79–101; C. C. North and P. K. Hatt, "Jobs and Occupations: A Popular Evaluation," *Public Opinion News,* September 1947, pp. 3–13.

70. Cliver Cox, *Cast, Class, and Race* (Garden City, 1949); E. Gordon,

Erickson, *Urban Behavior* (New York, 1954), pp. 363–370; Gerhard E. Lenski, "American Social Classes: Statistical Strata or Social Groups?" *American Journal of Sociology,* September 1952, pp. 139–144; C. Wright Mills, "The American Business Elite: A Collective Portrait," *Journal of Economic History* IV (1945), Supplement, pp. 20–44; William Miller, "American Historians and the Business Elite," *Journal of Economic History* IX (1949), pp. 184–208.

71. Bessie L. Pierce, *A History of Chicago, II* (New York, 1940); Bayrd Still, *Milwaukee* (Madison, 1948); Blake McKelvey, "American Urban History Today," *American Historical Review,* July 1952, pp. 919–929; James W. Livingood, *The Philadelphia-Baltimore Trade Rivalry: 1780–1860* (Harrisburg, 1947); William Diamond, "On the Dangers of an Urban Interpretation of History," in Eric F. Goldman, ed., *Historiography and Urbanization* (Baltimore, 1941), pp. 67–108.

72. R. T. Daland, "Political Science and the Study of Urbanism," *American Political Science Review,* June 1957, pp. 491–509; Chauncey D. Harris, "The Functional Classification of Cities in the U.S.," *Geographical Review,* Vol. 33 (1943), p. 86–99; Robert E. Dickinson, *City, Region, and Regionalism* (London, 1947); Rupert B. Vance with Danielevsky, *All These People: The Nation's Human Resources in the South* (Chapel Hill, 1945).

73. John Dollard, *Caste and Class in a Southern Town* (New Haven, 1937); Robert Faris and W. H. Dunham, *Mental Disorders in Urban Areas* (Chicago, 1939); Stein, *op. cit.,* pp. 251–254; C. Schroeder, "Mental Disorders in Cities," *American Journal of Sociology,* Vol. 48 (1942), pp. 40–47; H. Harlan and J. Wherry, "Delinquency and Housing," *Social Forces,* Vol. 27 (1948), pp. 58–61.

74. Saul D. Alinsky, *Reveille for Radicals* (Chicago, 1946); Seba Eldridge, ed., *Development of Collective Enterprise* (Lawrence, Kansas, 1943); Gordon Hamilton, *Theory and Practice of Social Case Work* (New York, 1940); Harleigh Trecker, *Social Group Work: Principles and Practices* (New York, 1948); Roy Lubove, *The Professional Altruist: The Emergence of Social Work as a Career* (Cambridge, 1965), pp. 223–224; Kenneth L. M. Pray, *Social Work in a Revolutionary Age* (Philadelphia, 1949), pp. 19–52, 225–288; Harold L. Wilensky and Charles N. Lebeaux, *Industrial Society and Social Welfare* (New York, 1958), pp. 283–334.

75. Gunnar Myrdal, *American Dilemma* (New York, 1944), pp. 4, 294–317, 377–379, 670–700; Charles S. Johnson, *Patterns of Negro Segregation* (New York, 1943); R. C. Weaver, *The Negro Ghetto* (New York, 1948); E. F. Frazier, *The Negro in the U.S.* (New York, 1949); St. Clair Drake and H. R. Cayton, *Black Metropolis* (New York, 1945).

76. *Planning and Civic Comment,* October 1941, p. 18; Burchard and Bush-Brown, *op. cit.,* pp. 422, 428, 436, 439, 442, 447; José Luis Sert, *Can Our Cities Survive?* (Cambridge, 1942); Eliel Saarinen, *The City* (New York, 1943); Sigfried Giedion, *Space, Time, and Architecture* (Cambridge, 1942); Joseph Hudnut, *Architecture and the Spirit of Man* (Cambridge, 1949).

77. Lewis Mumford, *From the Ground Up* (New York, 1956), pp. 3–26.

78. Percival and Paul Goodman, *Communitas: Ways of Livelihood and Means of Life* (New York, 1947); David Riesman with Nathan Glazer and Ruel Denny, *The Lonely Crowd* (New York, 1950), 1953 ed., pp. 309, 348.

79. Wilbur C. Hallenbeck's *American Urban Communities*, published in 1951, revealed the considerable progress made by scholars since the earlier text by Stuart A. Queen and S. F. Thomas, *The City: A Study of Urbanism in the U.S.*, appeared in 1939.

CHAPTER 5

1. *American City*, January 1950, pp. 75–78; February 1950, pp. 82–83.
2. *American City*, January 1950, p. 77; *Municipal Year Book* (1954), p. 7.
3. U.S. *Census* (1960), Pop., I–A: 1–4, 1–11.
4. *Municipal Year Book* (1951), p. 33; (1953), pp. 33–36; (1957), p. 50; *National Municipal Review*, April 1952, pp. 182–186.
5. U.S. *Census* (1950), P–A 1: 65–76; (1960) I: xxii; *Municipal Year Book* (1951), pp. 32–33; (1961), pp. 57–63; John C. Bollens and Henry J. Schmandt, *The Metropolis: Its People, Politics, and Economic Life* (New York, 1965), p. 412 (for table).
6. U.S. *Census* (1960), Pop. I, Pt. I: xxxiii, 1–237; Harry Sharp and Leo F. Schnore, "The Changing Color Composition of Metropolitan Areas," *Land Economics*, May 1962, pp. 169–185; Bernard J. Frieden, *The Future of Old Neighborhoods* (Cambridge, Mass., 1964), pp. 13–19; Karl E. and Alma F. Tauber, "The Changing Character of the Negro Migration," *American Journal of Sociology*, January 1965, pp. 429–441.
7. *Municipal Year Book* (1961), pp. 36–37; Robert A. Will, "Federal Influence on Industrial Location: How Extensive?" *Land Economics*, February 1964, pp. 49–55.
8. *Municipal Year Book* (1951), pp. 1–7.
9. *American City*, July 1951, p. 95; April 1952, p. 5; January 1954, pp. 7–9; Robert H. Connery and Richard H. Leach, *The Federal Government and Metropolitan Areas* (Cambridge, 1960), pp. 41–47.
10. *Municipal Year Book* (1951), pp. 5–7; *American City*, July 1951, pp. 79–81; April 1952, p. 5.
11. *Municipal Year Book* (1951), pp. 3–4; (1952), pp. 6–7; *National Municipal Review*, February 1952, pp. 74–79.
12. Richard A. Scannon, ed., *America Votes* (New York, 1955, 1958), Vols. I and II; Charles E. Gilbert, "National Political Alignments and the Politics of Large Cities," *Political Science Quarterly*, March 1964, pp. 27, 41–42; Louis Harris, *Is There a Republican Majority: Political Trends, 1952–1956* (New York, 1954), pp. 123–124 and *passim*.
13. *Municipal Year Book* (1954), pp. 1–4; *National Municipal Review*, April 1954, pp. 174–181.
14. *National Municipal Review*, July 1950, p. 360; October 1950, pp. 445–449; March 1952, p. 159; July 1952, pp. 368–369; December 1952, p. 538; A. Theodore Brown, *The Politics of Reform, Kansas City's Municipal Government: 1925–1950* (Kansas City), pp. 393–400.
15. *Planning and Civic Comment*, December 1951, pp. 20–22; March 1952, pp. 19–23, 30–32; September 1954, pp. 1–14; *National Municipal Review*, April 1954, p. 211; May 1955, p. 273; May 1956, p. 254; February 1957, pp. 98–99; March 1957, pp. 153–154; November 1957, pp. 538–540; July 1958, p. 357. The Citizens Union of New York and the Citizens League of Cleveland both celebrated their 60th anniversaries in 1957 while the city or civic clubs of New York, Chicago, and Pittsburgh marked their semicentennials in the early fifties.

16. National Municipal Review, February 1956, pp. 91–92; May 1956, pp. 252–253; February 1957, pp. 98–99; *New York Times*, November 5, 1961. See the description of some of the organizations in Milwaukee by Henry J. Schmandt and William H. Standing, *Milwaukee: Metropolitan Study Commission* (Bloomington, Ind., 1965), pp. 32–40.
17. *American City*, January 1951, pp. 69–70; *National Municipal Review*, February 1956, pp. 72–73; July 1958, pp. 325–331.
18. *National Municipal Review*, May 1955, pp. 262–265; April 1958, p. 189; July 1958, pp. 325–331; Oliver B. Williams and C. Press, eds., *Democracy in Urban America: Readings* (Chicago, 1961), pp. 276–294.
19. *American City*, December 1951, pp. 86–87; May 1952, pp. 99–101; March 1953, pp. 118–122; *National Municipal Review*, June 1954, p. 300.
20. *American City*, June 1930, p. 5; August 1953, p. 94; December 1953, p. 11; *National Municipal Review*, June 1954, pp. 299, 300; March 1957, pp. 124–130; *Municipal Year Book* (1954), p. 39; John C. Bollens, *Special District Governments in the U.S.* (Berkeley, 1951), pp. 93–115.
21. *Municipal Year Book* (1954), pp. 1–3, 37; *National Municipal Review*, July 1953, pp. 326–330; May 1954, pp. 261–263; June 1954, p. 313.
22. *Planning and Civic Comment*, September 1954, pp. 1–5, 37–38; December 1954, pp. 31–32.
23. *Municipal Year Book* (1956), pp. 1–5; *National Municipal Review*, January 1954, p. 21; May 1955, pp. 278–279; William Anderson, The *Nation and the States* (Minneapolis, 1955), pp. 214–229.
24. *National Municipal Review*, September 1955, pp. 431–433; *Municipal Year Book* (1956), p. 34; Connery and Leach, *op. cit.*, pp. 118–120, 130.
25. *Municipal Year Book* (1956), pp. 34–37; (1957), pp. 44–46; *National Municipal Review*, December 1957, pp. 590–591; January 1958, pp. 30–33, 43–46; July 1958, p. 334; Schmandt and Standing, *op. cit.*, pp. 73–202; Metropolitan Community Studies, *Metropolitan Challenge* (Dayton, 1959).
26. *National Municipal Review*, June 1956, pp. 287–288; February 1957, pp. 89–104; April 1957, p. 219; November 1957, pp. 528–529; Government Affairs Foundation, *Metropolitan Communities: A Bibliography* (Chicago, 1956); Edwin A. Cottrell and Helen Jones, *The Metropolis: Is Integration Possible?* (Los Angeles, 1955).
27. John C. Bollens, ed., *Exploring the Metropolitan Community* (Berkeley, 1961); Henry J. Schmandt, Paul G. Steinbecker, and George D. Wendel, *Metropolitan Reform in St. Louis: A Case Study* (New York, 1961); Scott Greer, "Dilemmas of Action Research in the Metropolitan Problem," in Morris Janowitz, ed., *Community Political Systems* (Glencoe, 1961), pp. 185–206.
28. Edward Sofen, *The Miami Metro Experiment* (Bloomington, Ind., 1963), pp. 36–70; *National Municipal Review*, June 1957, pp. 305–307.
29. *National Municipal Review*, September 1956, pp. 396–398; April 1957, pp. 181–188; May 1958, pp. 235–237; September 1958, pp. 399–400; May 1959, p. 259; November 1959, p. 533.
30. *National Municipal Review*, April 1955, p. 198; September 1959, pp. 423–425.
31. *National Municipal Review*, October 1957, pp. 469–473; May 1959,

p. 260; July 1959, pp. 359–360; September 1959, pp. 426–427; December 1959, p. 590; James A. Norton, *The Metro Experience* (Cleveland, 1963).

32. *National Municipal Review,* October 1958, pp. 464–465; June 1959, pp. 313–314.

33. *National Municipal Review,* October 1955, pp. 466–468; January 1957, pp. 34–36; March 1957, pp. 124–130; October 1959, pp. 480–482.

34. Edward C. Banfield and Morton Grodzins, *Government and Housing in Metropolitan Areas* (New York, 1958), pp. 7–152; Robert H. Connery and R. H. Leach, *The Federal Government and Metropolitan Areas* (Cambridge, 1960), pp. 102–115.

35. *American City,* January 1951, p. 75; *National Municipal Review,* May 1954, pp. 235–242; July 1957, p. 376; *Planning and Civic Comment* September 1954, p. 1–5.

36. *National Municipal Review,* April 1952, pp. 182–186; June 1953, pp. 305–310; March 1957, p. 127; July 1957, pp. 376–377; October 1957, pp. 469–473; December 1957, pp. 570–575; March 1958, pp. 127–130; April 1959, pp. 198–200; Forbes B. Hays, *Community Leadership: The Regional Plan Association of New York* (New York, 1965), pp. 96–97, 113–117.

37. *National Municipal Review,* September 1958, pp. 397–399; *Planning and Civic Comment,* March 1959, pp. 28–30; June 1959, pp. 292–297; Connery and Leach, *op. cit.,* pp. 102–115.

38. *National Municipal Review,* February 1950, pp. 87–90; April 1954, pp. 174–181.

39. Larry M. Elison, *The Finances of Metropolitan Areas* (Ann Arbor, 1964), p. 81–98; *National Municipal Review,* January 1950, pp. 53–54; May 1950, pp. 255–256; January 1951, pp. 17, 23–38; May 1951, pp. 270, 275; March 1952, pp. 158; September 1952, pp. 212–214.

40. *Municipal Year Book* (1956), p. 1–4, 451–455; *American City,* August 1956, pp. 15–18, 165–166; White House Conference on Education, *A Report to the President* (Washington, 1956), pp. 97–99.

41. Lowdon Wingo, Jr., *Transportation and Urban Land* (Washington, 1961), pp. 1–4; *American City,* September 1956, pp. 130–132; October 1956, pp. 136–139; November 1956, pp. 138–141; January 1957, p. 11; *Municipal Year Book* (1957), pp. 2–4.

42. *National Municipal Review,* March 1957, pp. 149–151; May 1957, pp. 258–259; Adelaide K. Roeslein, *Sister Cities: The Road to Peace* (Long Beach, Calif., 1965).

43. Morton Grodzins, "The Federal System," in U.S. President's Commission on National Goals, *Goals for America* (New York, 1960), pp. 267–268; Edward C. Banfield and James I. Wilson, *City Politics* (Cambridge, 1963), p. 74, a list of federal grants-in-aid programs.

44. *Municipal Year Book* (1958), pp. 1–8; (1960), pp. 46–47; *National Municipal Review,* September 1957, pp. 394–400; March 1958, pp. 133–134; October 1958, p. 473; Roscoe C. Martin, *The Cities and the Federal System* (1965), pp. 115–119; Connery and Leach, *op. cit.,* pp. 30–34.

45. *Municipal Year Book* (1950), pp. 212–298; (1952), pp. 323–329; *American City,* January 1954, p. 9.

46. *American City,* July 1950, pp. 5, 111, 131, 155; August 1950, pp. 118–120; March 1955, pp. 126–131; Hal Burton, *The City Fights Back* (New York, 1954), pp. 185–195; John Rannells, *The Core of the City*

(New York, 1956), pp. 63–73; Coleman Woodbury, ed., *Urban Redevelopment: Problems and Practices* (Chicago, 1953), pp. 332–353; Robert J. Mowitz and D. S. Wright, *Profile of a Metropolis: A Case Book* (Detroit, 1962), pp. 20–79; Alan Altshuler, *The City Planning Process: A Political Analysis* (Ithaca, 1965), pp. 200–265. For an excellent account of the developments in Pittsburgh, see a new book by Jeanne R. Lowe, *Cities in a Race With Time* (New York, 1967), pp. 131–148.

47. *Municipal Year Book* (1951), pp. 292–300; (1952), pp. 325–328; *American City,* April 1950, pp. 133, 150; June 1950, p. 115.

48. Martin Meyerson and Edward C. Banfield, *Politics, Planning and the Public Interest* (Glencoe, 1955); Coleman Woodbury, ed., *The Future of Cities and Urban Redevelopment* (Chicago, 1953), pp. 377–383, 430–444, 455–467.

49. Woodbury, *Urban Redevelopment,* pp. 415–453; Mowitz and Wright, *op. cit.,* pp. 80–94; Martin Meyerson, Barbara Terrett and W. L. C. Wheaton, *Housing, People and Cities* (New York, 1962), pp. 78–81.

50. Harold Kaplan, *Urban Renewal Politics: Slum Clearance in Newark* (New York, 1963), pp. 15–26; *American City,* September 1951, pp. 110–111; November 1951, p. 103; December 1953, pp. 107–108; August 1954, pp. 92–94; September 1954, pp. 22, 118–119. See also Marvin B. Sussman, ed., *Community Structure and Analysis* (New York, 1959), pp. 134–204.

51. Woodbury, *Future of Cities,* pp. 16–25; Herbert J. Gans, *The Urban Villagers* (Glencoe, 1962); Charles Abrams, *The City Is the Frontier* (New York, 1965), pp. 78–90.

52. Davis McEntire, *Residence and Race* (Berkeley, 1960), pp. 293–296, 334–342; Abrams, *op. cit.,* pp. 86–92.

53. Housing and Home Finance Agency, *Annual Report* (Washington, 1955), pp. 405–408; *Housing and Redevelopment Directory* (1952–1953); *American City,* February 1951, pp. 110–111; January 1955, pp. 13, 141–143; *Municipal Year Book* (1956), pp. 309–312; *National Municipal Review,* April 1956, pp. 194–195.

54. *American City,* August 1956, pp. 135–136; April 1957, p. 19; *Municipal Book* (1958), pp. 272, 306 308, 314–322; *Planning and Civic Comment,* September 1957, p. 13.

55. Robert A. Dahl, *Who Governs: Democracy and Power in an American City* (New Haven, 1961), pp. 118–140; *National Civic Review,* March 1959, pp. 154–156; Nelson W. Polsby, *Community Power and Political Theory* (New Haven, 1963), pp. 72–79; William L. Miller, *The Fifteenth Ward and the Great Society* (Boston, 1966), pp. 149–166; Lowe, *op. cit.,* pp. 405–485.

56. Kaplan, *op. cit.,* p. 3; *Annals,* May 1965, p. 47; *American City,* March 1956, pp. 144, 199–201; June 1957, pp. 282–286; *Municipal Year Book* (1960), p. 313–316; *National Civic Review,* March 1959, p. 158; September 1959, pp. 399–413, 422. See also the Directory of Projects in Housing Finance Agency, *Annual Report* (1960), pp. 294–299.

57. Abrams, *op. cit.,* pp. 90–94, 106–108; *Planning and Civic Comment,* September 1952, p. 26; Catherine Bauer, "The Dreary Deadlock of Public Housing," *Architectural Forum,* May 1957, pp. 140–142, 220–222; Lowe, *op. cit.,* pp. 176–193.

58. Martin Meyerson, Barbara Terrett, and W. L. C. Wheaton, *Housing, People and Cities* (New York, 1962), pp. 316–335; Rockefeller

Brothers Fund, *Challenge to America: Its Economic and Social Aspects* (New York, 1958); John W. Dyckman and R. R. Isaacs, *Capital Requirements for Urban Development and Renewal* (New York, 1961), p. 93 and *passim*.
59. Davis McEntire, *Residence and Race* (Berkeley, 1960), pp. 323–328; *National Municipal Review*, December 1958, pp. 546–550; John C. Bollens, *Special District Governments in the U.S.* (Berkeley, 1957), pp. 116–131; Catherine Bauer Wurster, "Framework for an Urban Society," President's Commission on National Goals, *Goals for Americans* (New York, 1960), pp. 229–231.
60. McEntire, *op. cit.,* pp. 334–339; Robert C. Weaver, "Class, Race and Urban Renewal," *Land Economics*, August 1960, pp. 235–251.
61. George E. Mowry, *The Urban Nation: 1920–1960* (New York, 1965), pp. 244–247.
62. *U.S. Statistical Abstracts* (1965), pp. 25, 92; Frieden, *op. cit.,* pp. 12–46.
63. Harry Sharp and Leo F. Schnore, "The Changing Color Composition of Metropolitan Areas," *Land Economics*, May 1962, pp. 170–171; Karl E. and Alma F. Tauber, *Negroes in Cities* (Chicago, 1965), pp. 31–43, 57, 117; Rupert B. Vance and N. D. Demerath, eds., *The Urban South* (Chapel Hill, 1954), pp. 210–214.
64. Sofen, *op. cit.,* pp. 64–70; McEntire, *op. cit.,* pp. 9–101.
65. *Municipal Year Book* (1951), pp. 3–4; (1953), pp. 490–492; *American City*, February 1950, p. 97; Meyerson, Terrett, and Wheaton, *op. cit.,* pp. 79–80.
66. Vern Countryman, ed., *Discrimination and the Law* (Chicago, 1965), pp. 13–18, 21–28, 82–90; Anthony Lewis and the *New York Times, Portrait of a Decade: The Second American Revolution* (New York, 1964), pp. 15–24. Henry A. Bullock, "Urbanism and Race Relations," in Vance and Demerath, *op. cit.,* pp. 219–226.
67. Lewis, *op. cit.,* pp. 25–31; Brown v. Board of Education, 347 U.S. 483 (1954); *American City*, August 1954, p. 155; Bullock, *op. cit.,* p. 226.
68. Benjamin Muse, *The Years of Prelude: The Story of Integration Since the Supreme Court's 1954 Decision* (New York, 1964), pp. 1–51, 87–104; Countryman, *op. cit.,* pp. 51–63; Lewis, *op. cit.,* pp. 32–45.
69. Lewis, *op. cit.,* pp. 46–69; Muse, *op. cit.,* pp. 122–159.
70. Charles L. Weltner, *Southerners* (Philadelphia, 1966), pp. 20–35; Lewis, *op. cit.,* pp. 154, 168–170; Muse, *op. cit.,* pp. 56–72.
71. McEntire, *op. cit.,* pp. 262–263, 293–296, 319–323; *Municipal Year Book* (1956), pp. 445, 465–468; Countryman, *op. cit.,* pp. 80–85; Muse, *op. cit.,* pp. 84–85.
72. McEntire, *op. cit.,* pp. 299–314; *American City*, September 1954, p. 21.
73. McEntire, *op. cit.,* pp. 180–183; *American City*, August 1954, p. 155.
74. McEntire, *op. cit.,* pp. 199–212; Vincent J. Giese, *Revolution in the City* (Notre Dame, Ind., 1961); Luigi Laurenti, *Property Values and Race: Studies in Seven Cities* (Berkeley, 1960); L. K. Northwood and E. A. T. Barth, *Urban Desegregation: Negro Pioneers and Their White Neighbors* (Seattle, 1965); Chester Rapkin and William G. Grigsby, *The Demand for Housing in Racially Mixed Areas* (Berkeley, 1960); Thomas L. Gillette, "A Study of the Effects of Negro Invasion on Real Estate Values," *American Journal of Economics and Sociology*, January 1957, p. 151–161; Lewis, *op. cit.,* pp. 245–250; Muse, *op. cit.,* pp. 201–209.

75. Lewis, *op. cit.*, pp. 70–73; James Baldwin, *Nobody Knows My Name* (New York, 1961), pp. 102–116; Lewis Killian and Charles Grigg, *Racial Crisis in America: Leadership in Conflict* (Englewood Cliffs, N.J., 1964), pp. 45–129.
76. Lewis, *op. cit.*, pp. 70–73; L. D. Reddick, *Crusader Without Violence, A Biography of Martin Luther King, Jr.* (New York, 1959), pp. 112–145.
77. Franklin Frazier, *The Negro Church in America* (New York, 1963); pp. 71–81; Claude Brown, *Manchild in the Promised Land* (New York, 1965); Whitney M. Young, "Intergroup Relations and Social Work Practice," *Social Welfare Forum* (1960), pp. 146–153; U.S. *Census, Current Population Reports: Population Characteristics* (Series P 20, No. 150, April 1966), pp. 13–14; Saul Bernstein, *Youth on the Streets* (New York, 1964), pp. 58–183.
78. James V. Cunningham, *The Resurgent Neighborhood* (Notre Dame, Ind., 1965), pp. 133–135, 145–149; Isadore Seeman, "Social Welfare and Urban Renewal," *Social Welfare Forum* (1960), pp. 208–214; Lowe, *op. cit.*, pp. 463–483.
79. Alan Altshuler, *op. cit.*, pp. 60–70; Marvin B. Sussman, ed., *Community Structure and Analysis* (New York, 1959), pp. 173–207; Lowe, *op. cit.*, 485–522.
80. Altshuler, *op. cit.*, pp. 65–70; *Annals*, May 1964, pp. 74–77; *National Civic Review*, December 1959, p. 590.
81. *National Municipal Review*, June 1951, pp. 305–307; December 1952, pp. 565–566; September 1953, pp. 387–392, 402; September 1954, pp. 398–402; December 1955, pp. 571–575; May 1957, pp. 245–246; January 1958, p. 25; February 1958, p. 74; October 1958, p. 457; September 1959, pp. 415–416; George E. Baker, *Rural Versus Urban Political Power* (New York, 1955).
82. Connery and Leach, *op. cit.*, pp. 115–119, 129–134.
83. Connery and Leach, *op. cit.*, pp. 6–8, 27–30, 55–56; Howard R. Lewis, *With Every Breath You Take* (New York, 1965), pp. 202–211; *Municipal Year Book* (1958), pp. 331, 471.
84. U.S. President's Commission on National Goals, *Goals for Americans* (New York, 1960), pp. 225–248; Reddick, *op. cit.*, pp. 187–197.
85. C. Wright Mills, *The Power Elite* (New York, 1956). See also W. Lloyd Warner and J. C. Abegglen, *Big Business Leaders in America* (New York, 1955); Mabel Newcomer, *The Big Business Executive: The Factors That Made Him: 1900–1950* (New York, 1955); Suzanne Keller, "The Social Origins and Career Lines of Three Generations of American Business Leaders," University of Michigan Microfilm, 1953.
86. Floyd Hunter, *Community Power Structure* (Chapel Hill, 1953); Morton Grodzins, *The Metropolitan Area as a Racial Problem* (Pittsburgh, 1959).
87. Norton E. Long, "The Local Community as an Ecology of Games," *American Journal of Sociology*, November 1958, pp. 251–261; Gerhard E. Lenski, "American Social Classes: Statistical Strata or Social Groups?" *American Journal of Sociology*, September 1952, pp. 139–144; Robert A. Dahl, "Critique of the Ruling Elite Model," *American Political Science Review*, June 1958, pp. 463–469; Floyd Hunter, "Community Organization" in Vance and Demerath, *op. cit.*, p. 255; Roland J. Pelligrin and Charles H. Coates, "Absentee-owned Corporations and Community Power Structure," *American Journal of Sociol-*

ogy, March 1956; see William Kornhauser's analysis of the distinction between C. Wright Mills and David Riesman in "Power Elite or Veto Group?" in Reinhard Bendix and Seymour M. Lipset, eds., *Class, Status, and Power* (Glencoe, 2nd ed., 1966), pp. 210–218; see also William Spinard, "Power in Local Communities," *ibid.*, pp. 218–230.

88. Dahl, *loc. cit.;* Long, *loc. cit.;* see the critical analysis of the Hunter and Mills thesis in Nelson W. Polsby, *op. cit.* See also Charles Press, *Main Street Politics: Policy Making at the Local Level* (East Lansing, Mich., 1962), for a full and illuminating survey of the periodical literature on this subject during the 1950's.

89. Morris Janowitz, *The Community Press in an Urban Setting* (Glencoe, 1952); Morris Janowitz, ed., *Community Political Systems* (Glencoe, 1961), pp. 13–17; *Publishers Weekly*, December 1947, p. 2,750.

90. Maurice R. Stein, *The Eclipse of Community* (Princeton, 1960), pp. 275, 297–303; C. Wright Mills, *The Sociological Imagination* (New York, 1959). See also Seymour M. Lipset and Reinhard Bendix, *Social Mobility in Industrial Society* (University of California, 1959), pp. 102–104, 114–143, 158–159.

91. Max Weber, *The City* [translated and edited by Don Martindale and Gertrude Neuwirth] (Glencoe, 1958), pp. 9–62.

92. Eshref Shevky and Marilyn Williams, *The Social Areas of Los Angeles: Analysis and Typology* (Los Angeles, 1949); Wendell Bell, "Social Areas: Typology of Urban Neighborhoods," in Marvin B. Sussman, ed., *Community Structure and Analysis* (New York, 1959), pp. 65–69; Scott Greer and Ella Kube, "Urbanism and Social Structure: A Los Angeles Study," *ibid.*, p. 106; Eshref Shevky and Wendell Bell, *Social Area Analysis* (Stanford, Calif., 1955).

93. Williams and Press, *op. cit.*, pp. 125–133; Stein, *op. cit.*, pp. 192–226; William M. Dobriner, ed., *The Suburban Community* (New York, 1958), pp. 209–224; William H. Whyte, *The Organization Man* (New York, 1956), pp. 281–297, *passim;* Auguste C. Spectorsky, *The Exurbanites* (New York, 1958).

94. Samuel Pratt, "Metropolitan Community Development and Change in Sub-center Economic Functions," *American Sociological Review* (August 1957), pp. 434–440; Bennett M. Berger, *Working-Class Suburb: A Study of Auto Workers in Suburbia* (Berkeley, 1960).

95. William M. Dobriner, ed., *The Suburban Community* (New York, 1958), pp. 375–382 and *passim.*

96. Robert C. Wood, *Suburbia: Its People and Their Politics* (Boston, 1958).

97. G. Edward Janosik, "Suburban Balance of Power," *American Quarterly*, Summer 1955, pp. 123–141; Wood, *op. cit.*, pp. 139–153, 199–212.

98. Howard L. Green, "Hinterland Boundaries of New York City and Boston in Southern New England," *Economic Geography*, October 1955, pp. 283–300; *National Municipal Review*, March 1957, pp. 158–159; Jean Gottman, *Megalopolis: The Urbanized Northeastern Seaboard of the U.S.* (New York, 1961). See also Walter Isard, *Methods of Regional Analysis: An Introduction to Regional Science* (New York, 1960).

99. Harold M. Mayer and Clyde F. Kohn, eds., *Readings in Urban Geography* (Chicago, 1959); Charlton F. Chate, "Today's Urban

Regions," *National Municipal Review*, June 1956, pp. 274–280; Gunnar Alexandersson, *The Industrial Structure of American Cities* (Lincoln, Nebr., 1956); Albert J. Reiss, Jr., "The Functional Specialization of Cities," *Municipal Year Book* (1957), pp. 54–68; Otis D. Duncan and A. J. Reiss, Jr., *Social Characteristics of Rural and Urban Communities: 1950* (New York, 1956); Victor Jones and Andrew Collver, "Economic Classification of Cities and Metropolitan Areas," *Municipal Year Book* (1959), pp. 67–77; F. Stuart Chapin and Shirley F. Weiss, eds., *Urban Growth Dynamics in a Regional Cluster of Cities* (New York, 1962).

100. Robert M. Fisher, ed., *The Metropolis in Modern Life* (New York, 1955), pp. 66–79; University of Pennsylvania *Law Review*, February 1957; American Academy of Political and Social Sciences, *Annals*, November 1957.

101. Fisher, *op. cit.*, pp. 85–123; *Annals*, November 1957, pp. 30–38, 112–122; University of Pennsylvania *Law Review*, February 1957, pp. 489–514.

102. *National Municipal Review*, January 1955, pp. 55–56; June 1956, pp. 287–288; June 1958, p. 302.

103. Christopher Tunnard and Henry Hope Reed, *American Skyline: The Growth and Form of Our Cities and Towns* (Boston, 1955); Wilfred Owen, *The Metropolitan Transportation Problem* (Washington, 1956) and *Cities in the Motor Age* (New York, 1959); Martin Meyerson and Edward C. Banfield, *op. cit.*

104. Vance and Demerath, *op. cit.*, pp. ix–x, and *passim*.

105. Clarence S. Stein, *Toward New Towns for America* (Chicago, 1951); Robert A. Nisbet, *The Quest for Community* (New York, 1953); John Rannells, *op. cit.*; Fred K. Vigman, *Crisis of the Cities* (Washington, 1955).

106. Bessie L. Pierce, *Chicago*, III (New York, 1957); Blake McKelvey, *Rochester, The Quest for Quality: 1890–1925* (Cambridge, 1956); Carl Bridenbaugh, *Cities in Revolt* (New York, 1955); Richard C. Wade, *The Urban Frontier* (Cambridge, 1959); Bayrd Still, *Mirror for Gotham* (New York, 1956); Constance McLaughlin Green, *American Cities in the Growth of the Nation* (London, 1957); Frank M. Stewart, *A Half Century of Municipal Reform* (Berkeley, 1950); John Higham, *Strangers in the Land* (New Brunswick, 1955); Charles Garrett, *The LaGuardia Years* (New Brunswick, 1961).

107. Frank P. Zeidler, "Urbanism and Government: 1957–1977," *Annals*, November 1957, pp. 74–81. For a discussion of the cause of his frustrations, see Schmandt and Standing, *op. cit.*

108. Wallace S. Sayre, "Urbanism and Government, 1957–1977: A Rejoinder," *Annals*, November 1957, pp. 82–85.

CHAPTER 6

1. William Buckman, "Politics and Federalism: Party or Anti-Party?" *Annals*, May 1965, pp. 107–111; Theodore H. White, *The Making of the President: 1960* (New York, 1961), pp. 350–365; Richard M. Scammon, ed., *Who Votes: 1960* (Pittsburgh, 1962).

2. *American City*, April 1961, p. 7; *New York Times*, March 10, 1961.

3. *National Civic Review*, January 1961, pp. 4–5; February 1961, pp. 70–75; Paul T. David and R. Eisenberg, "Devaluation of the Urban and

Suburban Vote" (Bureau of Public Administration, Richmond, Va., 1961); William C. Havard and Loren P. Beth, *The Politics of Misrepresentation: Rural-Urban Conflict in the Florida Legislature* (Louisiana State University); Malcolm E. Jewell, *The Politics of Reapportionment* (New York, 1962), pp. 1–44 and *passim*.

4. Jewell, *op. cit.*, pp. 36–44; *National Civic Review*, May 1962, pp. 244–250; June 1962, pp. 317–321; July 1962, pp. 349, 373–377; September 1962, p. 441; October 1962, pp. 500–507; Howard D. Hamilton, ed., *Legislative Apportionment: Key to Power* (New York, 1964), pp. 32–55.

5. *National Civic Review*, December 1962, pp. 623–625; January 1963, pp. 30–33; March 1963, pp. 153–157; January 1964, pp. 6–13; Andrew Hacker, *Congressional Districting: The Issue of Equal Representation* (rev. ed., Washington, 1964), pp. 22–38; Hamilton, *op. cit.*, pp. 59–123.

6. Hacker, *op. cit.*, pp. 37–47, 122–133; *National Civic Review*, April 1963, pp. 184–187, 204–207; May 1964, pp. 239–240; July 1964, pp. 352–357, 377–378; November 1964, pp. 530–534; February 1965, pp. 99–100; September 1965, pp. 413–421; November 1965, pp. 555–565; January 1966, pp. 29–34; Hamilton, *op. cit.*, pp. 127–169.

7. *Planning and Civic Comment*, September 1961, pp. 15, 21–22; Edward C. Banfield and James Q. Wilson, *City Politics* (Cambridge, 1963), p. 74; Michael N. Danielson, *Federal-Metropolitan Politics and the Commuter Crisis* (New York, 1965), pp. 137–179.

8. Arthur M. Schlesinger, Jr., *A Thousand Days: John F. Kennedy in the White House* (Boston, 1965), pp. 733–738.

9. *The Browker Annual* (1963), pp. 123–143; (1964), pp. 111–113; Daniel Hawthorne, *Public Libraries for Everyone* (New York, 1961), pp. 44–181; U.S. Department of Health, Education, and Welfare, *Indicators*, July 1966, pp. 3–7.

10. *American City*, April 1963, p. 85; *Planning and Civic Comment*, March 1962, pp. 19–20; *National Civic Review*, October 1962, pp. 482–485; March 1963, pp. 126–127, 131.

11. Richard A. Cloward and Lloyd E. Ohlin, *Delinquency and Opportunity: A Theory of Delinquent Gangs* (Glencoe, Ill., 1961), pp. 139–142, 211; Kenneth B. Clark, *Dark Ghetto: Dilemmas of Social Power* (New York, 1965), pp. xiii–xx, 39–41; Herbert Krosney, *Beyond Welfare: Poverty in Supercity* (New York, 1966), pp. 3–55.

12. Maxwell Meyerson, *Memorable Quotations of John F. Kennedy* (New York, 1965), pp. 250–251.

13. Theodore C. Sorensen, *Kennedy* (New York, 1965), pp. 481–482; Richard E. Neustadt, "Kennedy in the Presidency: A Premature Appraisal," *Political Science Quarterly*, September 1964, pp. 324–329.

14. Robert H. Connery and Richard H. Leach, *The Federal Government and Metropolitan Areas* (Cambridge, 1960), p. 58.

15. *Ibid.*, pp. 69–81.

16. *American City*, March 1961, p. 7; *National Civic Review*, January 1962, p. 34; June 1962, pp. 326–328; September 1962, pp. 449–450; December 1962, pp. 630–632; July 1964, pp. 385–386.

17. Advisory Commission on Intergovernmental Relations, *Governmental Structure, Organization, and Planning in Metropolitan Areas* (Washington, 1961).

18. Luther Halsey Gulick, *The Metropolitan Problem and American Ideas* (New York, 1962), p. 124; Thomas H. Reed, "A Call for Plain Talk,"

National Civic Review, March 1962, pp. 119–228, quotes from pp. 120 and 125.

19. Robert C. Wood, "There Are Many Roads," *National Civic Review,* March 1962, pp. 129–134, and 174 for quotes.

20. *National Civic Review,* January 1961, pp. 38, 40–42; March 1961, pp. 149–150; September 1961, pp. 434–435; March 1962, pp. 139–142. See also Scott Greer, *Metro-politics: A Study of Political Culture* (New York, 1963), and James A. Norton, *The Metro Experience* (Cleveland, 1963) for comparative studies of the campaigns for metropolitan reorganization in Miami, St. Louis, and Cleveland.

21. American Institute of Planners, *Journal,* August 1960, pp. 201–223; *National Civic Review,* January 1962, pp. 31–33; June 1962, pp. 302–308; *Municipal Year Book* (1964), pp. 57–59; Advisory Commission on Intergovernmental Relations, *Metropolitan Councils of Government* (Washington, 1966).

22. Robert Warren, "A Municipal Service Market Model of Metropolitan Organization," AIP *Journal,* August 1964, pp. 193–203.

23. Norton E. Long, "Citizenship or Consumership in Metropolitan Areas," AIP *Journal,* February 1965, pp. 2–6.

24. Raymond Vernon, *Metropolis: 1985* (Cambridge, 1960); Forbes B. Hays, *Community Leadership: The Regional Plan Association of N.Y.* (New York, 1965), pp. 97–103; AIP *Journal,* February 1961, pp. 91–97; May 1961, p. 15; *National Civic Review,* July 1962, pp. 389–390, 397; *Municipal Year Book* (1964), pp. 59–60.

25. *Municipal Year Book* (1964), pp. 59–60; AIP *Journal,* August 1963, p. 160; *Planning and Civic Comment,* December 1962, pp. 35–40; Banfield and Wilson, *op. cit.,* pp. 189–203.

26. *National Civic Review,* July 1962, pp. 384–390; December 1962, pp. 609–612; September 1963, pp. 452–453; *Municipal Year Book* (1964), pp. 53–54. See also Ira M. Heyman, "Annual Legislative Review— Planning Legislation: 1963," AIP *Journal,* August 1964, pp. 247–254.

27. *National Civic Review,* January 1963, pp. 38–39; February 1965, pp. 73–78; May 1965, pp. 269–270; see also Alan Altshuler, *The City Planning Process: A Political Analysis* (Ithaca, 1965), for an able discussion of the problems and accomplishments in that city.

28. AIP *Journal,* November 1961, pp. 325–331; *National Civic Review,* December 1963, pp. 615–616.

29. Robert Gutman and David Popenoe, eds., "Urban Studies," *American Behavioral Scientist,* February 1963, pp. 4–62; *Planning and Civic Comment,* December 1962, pp. 39–40; Banfield and Wilson, *op. cit.,* pp. 192–196; Altshuler, *op. cit.,* pp. 292–296; Harvey S. Perloff, ed., *Planning and the Urban Community* (Pittsburgh, 1961); Werner Z. Hirsch, ed., *Urban Life and Form* (New York, 1963); see also Sam B. Warner, ed., *Planning for a Nation of Cities* (Cambridge, 1966).

30. The Brookings Institution Advanced Study Program, *The Urban Policy Conferences* (Leaflet, Washington, 1963).

31. Robert Gutman and David Popenoe, eds., "Urban Studies: Present Trends and Future Prospects in an Emerging Academic Field," *American Behavioral Scientist,* February 1963, pp. 4–62.

32. AIP *Journal,* November 1963, pp. 250–254; November 1965, pp. 282–374.

33. Paul Davidoff, "Advocacy and Pluralism in Planning," AIP *Journal* November 1965, pp. 331–338; William Petersen, "On Some Meanings

of Planning," AIP *Journal*, May 1966, pp. 130–143; David Farbman, "A Description, Analysis and Critique of the Master Plan," quoted by Davidoff, *loc. cit.*, p. 338; *American Behavioral Scientist*, February 1963, pp. 56–62.

34. *American Behavioral Scientist*, February 1963, pp. 47–48; James I. Wilson, "Planning and Politics: Citizen Participation in Urban Renewal," AIP *Journal*, November 1963, pp. 242–249; David A. Grossman, "The Community Renewal Program," AIP *Journal*, November 1963, pp. 264–265.

35. Robert C. Weaver, *The Urban Complex: Human Values in Urban Life* (New York, 1964), pp. 97–121; *Journal of Housing*, September 30, 1963, pp. 430–482; Community Progress, Inc., *Community Action Program Review* (New Haven, 1965).

36. Charles Abrams, *The City Is the Frontier* (New York, 1965), pp. 99, 106, 159 and *passim;* Harold Kaplan, *Urban Renewal Politics: Slum Clearance in Newark* (New York, 1963), pp. 184–191; Scott Greer, *Urban Renewal and American Cities* (Indianapolis, 1965), pp. 81–86; AIP *Journal*, February 1965, pp. 7–12.

37. Herbert J. Gans, *The Urban Villagers, Group and Class in the Life of Italian-Americans* (Glencoe, 1962); Chester Hartman, "The Housing of Relocated Families," AIP *Journal*, November 1964, pp. 266–279.

38. Abrams, *op. cit.*, pp. 67, 138–154; Greer, *op. cit.*, pp. 78–81, 165–174; see also James I. Wilson, ed., *Urban Renewal: The Record and the Controversy* (Cambridge, 1966), pp. 189–582.

39. Fern M. Colburn, *The Neighborhood and Urban Renewal* (New York, 1963), pp. 20–95; Elizabeth Wood, "Social Welfare Planning," *Annals*, March 1964, pp. 119–128.

40. Dorothy Gazzolo, ed., "Citizen Participation," *Journal of Housing*, No. 8, 1963, pp. 435–439 and *passim;* James I. Wilson, "Planning and Politics: Citizen Participation in Urban Renewal," AIP *Journal*, *loc. cit.*

41. Urban Renewal Administration, *Historic Preservation Through Urban Renewal* (Washington, 1963); Grossman, *op. cit.*, pp. 262–263; see also Jeanne R. Lowe, *Cities in a Race With Time* (New York, 1967), pp. 341–351; Anthony Bailey, "Through the Great City," *The New Yorker*, August 5, 1967, pp. 35–50.

42. AIP *Journal*, November 1963, p. 262; September 1966, pp. 289–298; Weaver, *op. cit.*, pp. 99–100.

43. Abrams, *op. cit.*, pp. 157–159; Weaver, *op. cit.*, pp. 123–135; David B. Carlson, "Urban Renewal: A New Face on the American City," *Architectural Forum*, August 1963, pp. 80–85.

44. Clifford C. Ham, "Urban Renewal: A Case Study in Emerging Goals in an Intergovernmental Setting," *Annals*, May 1965, pp. 44–51; Ernest Haverman, "Rebirth of Philadelphia," *National Civic Review*, November 1962, pp. 538–543; Victor Gruen, *The Heart of Our Cities* (New York, 1964), pp. 321–325.

45. Bernard J. Frieden, *The Future of Old Neighborhoods* (Cambridge, 1964); citizens of resurgent Hartford will probably detect a different mistake. The dramatic success of Constitution Plaza in Hartford appears to refute Frieden's calculations as far as that city is concerned.

46. *National Civic Review*, July 1961, pp. 345–348, 387; June 1962, p. 336; Gruen, *op. cit.*, pp. 300–320.

47. AIP *Journal*, November 1964, pp. 287–295; *National Civic Review*,

May 1965, pp. 279–280; Committee on Economic Development, *Community Economic Development Efforts, Five Case Studies* (New York, 1964); *Municipal Year Book* (1964), pp. 52–53. See also Oscar H. Steiner, *Downtown, U.S.A.* (Dobbs Ferry, N.Y., 1964).

48. U.S. *Census*, Population (1960), *Selected Area Reports, Standard Metropolitan Statistical Areas, Final Report* PC (3)–1D; *ibid.*, Current Population Reports, *Population Estimates*, Series P–25, pp. 345, 347; *U.S. News and World Report*, February 21, 1966, pp. 72–73; March 7, 1966, pp. 50–52; Alan K. Campbell and Associates, *The Negro in Syracuse* (Syracuse, 1964), pp. 1–9, 20–38. I am venturing to project the nonwhite growth rates of the 1950's in to the 1960's on the basis of their regional growth rates and the growth rates of the individual cities.

49. Raymond Vernon, *The Myth and Reality of Our Urban Problems* [Mimeographed] (Cambridge, 1962), pp. 40–51; Kaplan, *op. cit.*, pp. 96–113, 147–164; Glen H. Beyer, *Housing and Society* (New York, 1965), pp. 338–345; Greer, *op. cit.*, pp. 129–141. See the papers by Gunnar Myrdal and John Dyckman in Warner, ed., *op. cit.*, pp. 3–42.

50. Schlesinger, *op. cit.*, pp. 938–939; Sorensen, *op. cit.*, pp. 480–482; AIP *Journal*, November 1963, p. 263; Congressional Quarterly Service, *Revolution in Civil Rights* (Washington, 1965), pp. 3, 16–17, 38.

51. Lewis Killian and Charles Grigg, *Racial Crisis in America: Leadership in Conflict* (Englewood, N.J., 1964), pp. 45–129; Arthur I. Waskow, *From Race Riot to Sit-In: 1919 and the 1960's* (Garden City, N.Y., 1966), pp. 232–236; Arthur J. Levin, "Official Human Relations Commissions," *Municipal Year Book* (1964), pp. 251–262; Sorensen, *op. cit.*, pp. 488–491; see also David Stahl, F. B. Sussman and L. B. Bloomfield, eds., *The Community and Racial Crisis* (New York, 1966).

52. Sorensen, *op. cit.*, pp. 492–506; Waskow, *op. cit.*, pp. 235–244, 254. See *Revolution in Civil Rights*, p. 39, for the Kennedy quote.

53. Waskow, *op. cit.*, pp. 238–246; Charles E. Silberman, *Crisis in Black and White* (New York, 1964), pp. 139–144, 201–214, 238–243.

54. Nathan Glazer, "School Integration Policies in Northern Cities," AIP *Journal*, August 1964, pp. 178–193; Kenneth B. Clark, *op. cit.*, pp. 111–153; Silberman, *op. cit.*, pp. 285–307; *Revolution in Civil Rights*, p. 78, a table on desegregation in Southern states; Benjamin Muse, *Ten Years of Prelude* (New York, 1964), pp. 201–240.

55. "Racial Imbalance in the Rochester Public Schools," *Report to the Commissioner of Education* (Rochester, September 1963); Glazer, *loc. cit.*, pp. 185–188; William Lee Miller, *The Fifteenth Ward and the Great Society* (Boston, 1966), pp. 3–8, 15–16, 50–65; Robert A. Dentler, "Barriers to Northern School Desegregation," in Talcott Parsons and Kenneth Clark, eds., *The Negro American* (Boston, 1966), pp. 472–489.

56. Henry W. Maier, *Challenge to the Cities: An Approach to a Theory of Urban Leadership* (New York, 1966), pp. 43–70; Schlesinger, *op. cit.*, pp. 967–977, 1020–1025; Sorensen, *op. cit.*, pp. 749–750; Warren Leslie, *Dallas, Public and Private* (New York, 1964), pp. 213–224.

57. Rowland Evans and Robert Novak, *Lyndon B. Johnson: The Exercise of Power* (New York, 1966), pp. 376–380 ff.

58. Walter H. Heller, *New Dimensions of Political Economy* (Cambridge, 1966), pp. 35–40; Evans and Novak, *op. cit.*, quote on pp. 350, 368–380; *Revolution in Civil Rights*, pp. 39–67; *American City*, August

1964, p. 7; George M. Smerk, *Urban Transportation: The Federal Role* (Bloomington, Ind., 1965), pp. 140–176.

59. Evans and Novak, *op. cit.*, pp. 426–434; *Congressional Record*, July 1964, pp. 16,611–16,624, 16,973; August 1964, pp. 18,268–18,275, 18,558–18,611; *American City*, March 1964, pp. 154, 156, 159; April 1964, p. 7.

60. *American City*, September 1964, p. 7; Waskow, *op. cit.*, pp. 255–262; Desmond Stone, "Rochester Riots: A Scar or a Spur?" *Rochester Times-Union*, September 1964; Dean Harper, "Aftermath of a Long Hot Summer," *Trans-action*, July-August 1965.

61. *Congressional Record*, July 27, 1964, pp. 16,973–16,974; August 7, 1964, p. 18,634.

62. *National Civic Review*, September 1962, pp. 424–428; December 1964, pp. 605–606; *Journal of Housing*, June 1965, pp. 296–305; Krosney, *op. cit.*, pp. 55, 69, 145–147.

63. William Buchanan, "Politics and Federalism: Party or Anti-Party?" *Annals*, May 1965, p. 112; Theodore H. White, *The Making of the President: 1964* (New York, 1965), pp. 294–406.

64. *Business Week*, March 6, 1965, pp. 32–34; *National Civic Review*, February 1965, p. 101.

65. *National Civic Review*, April 1965, pp. 209–211; *American City*, April 1965, p. 7; *New York Times*, September 10, 1965; January 14, 1966.

66. *Municipal Year Book* (1965), p. 357; *American City*, February 1965, p. 7; November 1965, p. 6; *National Civic Review*, April 1965, p. 216; December 1965, pp. 586–593; Miller, *op. cit.*, pp. 215–230.

67. *American City*, November 1965, p. 6; *National Civic Review*, March 1965, pp. 126–130, 157; June 1965, pp. 321–325; January 1966, pp. 8–13; Henry C. Hary, "The Dawn of Community-Defining Federalism," *Annals*, May 1965, pp. 147–153.

68. *National Civic Review*, May 1965, pp. 233–234; January 1966, pp. 5–7, 13; May 1966, pp. 278–279; *Harper's Magazine*, March 1966, pp. 71–78; *New York Times*, June 24, 1966.

69. "Poverty War Reviewed," *Journal of Housing*, June 1966, pp. 296–305; *National Civic Review*, January 1966, p. 45.

70. Miller, *op. cit.*, pp. 147–159 ff.

71. Sanford L. Kravitz, "Community Action Programs: Past, Present and Future," *American Child*, November 1965, pp. 1–6; Janet and Thomas Reiner, "Urban Poverty," AIP *Journal*, August 1965, pp. 261–166; James I. Wilson, "Planning and Politics: Citizen Participation in Urban Renewal," AIP *Journal*, November 1963, pp. 246–249.

72. Silberman, *op. cit.*, pp. 308–358; Krosney, *op. cit.*, pp. 69–96; Harper, *op. cit.*, Warren C. Haggstrom, "The Power of the Poor," in Frank Reissman and Associates, eds., *Mental Health of the Poor* (Glencoe, 1964), pp. 205–222; Frank Reissman, "The New Anti-Poverty Ideology," *Poverty and Human Resources Abstracts*, I:4 (1966), pp. 5–16; Kenneth B. Clark, *op. cit.*, pp. xiii–xiv, and *passim;* New York Times, April 10, 1966; October 9, 1966; for the origins of the Council of Churches see Blake McKelvey, *Urbanization of America: 1860–1915* (New Brunswick, N.J., 1963), pp. 165–166, 268–270.

73. J. Clarence Davies, *Neighborhood Groups and Urban Renewal* (New York, 1966), pp. 131–146 ff.; James V. Cunningham, *The Resurgent Neighborhood* (Notre Dame, Ind., 1965), pp. 23–42, *passim;* see also the review of this book by Walter Thabit, AIP *Journal*, May 1966,

pp. 181–182; Weaver, *op. cit.*, pp. 126, 133–137; Miller, *op. cit.*, pp. 210–212; *New York Times*, November 1965; *Newsweek*, December 13, 1965, p. 29; PHR *Abstracts*, I, No. 4, p. 79; *U.S. News and World Report*, August 15, 1960, pp. 36–37; August 22, 1966, p. 10; *Business Week*, December 17, 1966, pp. 162–166; editors of *Ebony, The Negro Handbook* (Chicago, 1966), pp. 82–92.

74. Reese Cleghorn, "Allen of Atlanta Collides with Black Power and White Racism," *New York Times Magazine*, October 16, 1966, pp. 32–33, 134–140.

75. *The Negro Handbook* (1966), pp. 280–283, 429–470; *National Municipal Review*, February 1966, pp. 94–96. See also Abie Miller, *The Negro and the Great Society* (New York, 1965), pp. 195–209.

76. *Rochester Times-Union*, September 8, 1965; July 31, 1966; *New York Times*, July 31, 1966; December 7, 1966.

77. *Business Week*, December 1965, pp. 35–38; November 1966, pp. 152–154; *New York Times*, May 1, 1966; December 7, 1966.

78. See Norman Beckman's review of Martin, *The Cities and the Federal System* in *American Political Science Review*, June 1966, pp. 399–400; *Annals*, May 1965, pp. 21–22, 28–29; *New York Times*, July 23, 1966; John C. Frantz and Nathan M. Cohen, "The Federal Government and Public Libraries: A Ten Year Partnership, 1957–1966," U.S. Department of Health, Education, and Welfare, *Indicators*, July 1966, pp. 2–11; July 1966, pp. 3–7.

79. *New York Times*, November 30, 1966; December 8, 1966.

80. *National Civic Review*, March 1965, pp. 162–163; Committee for Economic Development, *Modernizing Local Government to Secure a Balanced Federalism* (New York, 1966); Norman Beckman and Page L. Ingraham, "Planning Legislation: 1964–1965," AIP *Journal*, September 1966, pp. 300–317.

81. William H. Whyte, *Cluster Development* (New York, 1964); *New York Times*, February 17, 1964; *Harper's Magazine*, December 1965, pp. 85–94; *Business Week*, August 20, 1966, pp. 101–110. See also Bailey, *loc. cit.*, pp. 50–60.

82. *Rochester Times-Union*, June 30, 1966; "The City Lobbyists Head for Washington," *Business Week*, July 9, 1966, pp. 89–96; American Society of Planning Officials, *Newsletter*, November 1966, p. 119; *American City*, March 1966, p. 12.

83. "Community Development Law Passes," *Journal of Housing*, November 1966, pp. 563–570; "Comments on the Demonstration Cities Program," AIP *Journal*, November 1966, pp. 366–376; *National Civic Review*, September 1965, pp. 436–438; June 1966, pp. 325–330; July 1966, pp. 401–403; *New York Times*, September 10, 1966; October 10, 1966; *Rochester Democrat and Chronicle*, July 31, 1966.

84. *National Civic Review*, May 1966, p. 294; *Business Week*, July 1966, p. 93; AIP *Journal*, November 1966, p. 368; Heller, *op. cit.*, pp. 117–172.

85. "The City's Own Pressure Group," *Business Week*, October 1, 1966, pp. 158–160; ASPO *Newsletter*, November 1966; *National Civic Review*, May 1965, pp. 276–380; Scott Keyes, *Urban and Regional Studies at U.S. Universities* (Baltimore, 1964).

86. Robert Dahl, *Who Governs?* (New Haven, 1961); Nelson W. Polsby, *Community Power and Political Theory* (New Haven, 1963); Lawrence D. Mann, "Studies in Community Decision-Making," AIP *Journal*,

February 1964, pp. 58-65; M. Kent Jennings, "Planning and Community Elites in Two Cities," AIP *Journal,* February 1965, pp. 62-68; M. Kent Jennings, *Community Influentials: The Elite of Atlanta* (Glencoe, 1964). See also Wallace S. Sayre and Nelson W. Polsky, "American Political Science and the Study of Urbanization" in Philip M. Hauser and Leo F. Schnore, eds., *The Study of Urbanization* (New York, 1965), pp. 115-156.

87. Peter H. Rossi and Robert A. Dentles, *The Politics of Urban Renewal: The Chicago Findings* (Glencoe, 1961); Edward C. Banfield and James I. Wilson, *City Politics* (Cambridge, 1963); Henry W. Maier, *op. cit.;* Edward Sofen, *The Miami Metro Experiment* (Bloomington, 1963); Daniel R. Grant, "Metro Politics and Professional Political Leadership: The Case of Nashville," *Annals,* May 1964, pp. 72-83; Daniel R. Grant, "Metro's Three Faces," *National Civic Review,* June 1966, pp. 317-324; Roscoe C. Martin, *op. cit.* (New York, 1965). See also *Annals,* May 1954, for three articles on politics in the city.

88. Jack L. Walker, "A Critique of the Elitist Theory of Democracy," *American Political Science Review,* June 1966, pp. 285-295, see p. 391 for quote; Robert A. Dahl, "Further Reflections on 'The Elitist Theory of Democracy,' " *ibid.,* pp. 296-305.

89. Lloyd Rodwin, ed., *The Future Metropolis* (New York, 1961); Oliver P. Williams and Charles Press, eds., *Democracy in Urban America: Readings* (Chicago, 1961); Philip Olson, ed., *America as a Mass Society* (Glencoe, 1963), quote from p. 30; see also Warner, ed., *op. cit.*

90. Scott, Greer, *The Emerging City: Myth and Reality* (Glencoe, 1962); see also Greer, *Metro-Politics: A Study of Political Culture* (New York, 1963).

91. Leonard Reissman, *The Urban Process: Cities in Industrial Societies* (Glencoe, Ill., 1964). See also James M. Beshers, *Urban Social Structures* (Glencoe, 1962); John Siryamaki, *The Sociology of Cities* (New York, 1964); Gideon Sjoberg, "Theory and Research in Urban Sociology," Hauser and Schnore, *op. cit.,* pp. 157-190.

92. Morton Grodzins, "The Great Schism of Population," in Williams and Press, *op. cit.,* pp. 62-70.

93. Saul Bernstein, *Youth on the Streets* (New York, 1964); Claude Brown, *Manchild in the Promised Land* (New York, 1965); Kenneth Clark, *op. cit.,* Michael Harrington, *The Other America: Poverty in the United States* (Baltimore, 1963); Nathaniel Hentoff, *Our Children Are Dying* (New York, 1966); Joseph P. Lyford, *The Airtight Cage* (New York, 1966); Abie Miller, *op. cit.;* [Daniel Moynihan] *The Negro Family: The Case for National Action* (U.S. Department of Labor, Washington, 1965); Charles E. Silberman, *op. cit.;* Robert Tebbel, *The Slum Makers* (New York, 1963); Karl and Alma Taeuber, *Negroes in Cities* (Chicago, 1965).

94. Stanley Lieberson, *Ethnic Patterns in American Cities* (Glencoe, Ill., 1963); Nathan Glazer and Daniel P. Moynihan, *Beyond the Melting Pot* (Cambridge, 1964); Richard A. Cloward and Lloyd E. Ohlin, *Delinquency and Opportunity: A Theory of Delinquent Gangs* (Glencoe, 1961); Scott Greer, *Urban Renewal and American Cities* (Indianapolis, 1965); Talcott Parsons and Kenneth B. Clark, eds., *The Negro American* (Boston, 1966), pp. xix-xxviii, 709-754. This recent book has appeared too late for full incorporation in my study but many of its significant articles confirm and supplement portions of my analysis.

Frank Reissman, Jerome Cohen, Arthur Pearl, eds., *Mental Health and the Poor* (Glencoe, 1964).

95. John Rannells, "Approaches to Analysis," AIP *Journal*, February 1961, pp. 17–24; see also 10–16, 88–90; *National Civic Review*, March 1961, p. 162; John E. Bebout and Ronald J. Grele, *Where Cities Meet: The Urbanization of New Jersey* (Princeton, 1964); *Land Economics*, February 1961, pp. 51–58; February 1962, pp. 67–70; Ralph W. Pfouts, ed., *The Technique of Urban Economic Analysis* (West Trenton, 1960); *National Civic Review*, June 1966, pp. 345–346.

96. Richard L. Meier, *A Communications Theory of Urban Growth* (Cambridge, 1962).

97. Wilbur R. Thompson, *A Preface to Urban Economics* (Baltimore, 1965). See also C.E.D., *Community Economic Development Efforts: Five Case Studies* (New York, 1964); AIP *Journal*, May 1965, *passim;* J. R. Meyer, J. F. Kain, and M. Wohl, *The Urban Transportation Problem* (Cambridge, 1965); Walter Y. Oi and Paul W. Shuldimer, *An Analysis of Urban Travel Demands* (Evanston, Ill., 1962); Wilbur R. Thompson, "Urban Economic Growth and Development in a National System of Cities," in Hauser and Schnore, *op. cit.,* pp. 431–490.

98. Jane Jacobs, *The Death and Life of Great American Cities* (New York, 1961); Harvey S. Perloff, "New Towns Intown," AIP *Journal*, May 1966, pp. 155–162.

99. Ansel M. Strauss, *Images of the American City* (Glencoe, 1961); François C. Vigier, "An Experimental Approach to Urban Design," AIP *Journal*, February 1965, pp. 21–31; *National Civic Review*, June 1962, pp. 343–344; December 1965, pp. 618 623; Lowden Wingo, Jr., *Transportation and Urban Land* (Washington, 1961); Jean Gottman, *Megalopolis: The Urbanized Northeastern Seaboard of the U.S.* (New York, 1961); Victor Gruen, *The Heart of Our Cities* (New York, 1964), pp. 297–339; Harold M. Mayer, "A Survey of Urban Geography," in Hauser and Schnore, *op. cit.,* pp. 81–114. See also the excellent description of the Boston to Washington "Megalopolis" by Anthony Bailey, "Through the Great City," *The New Yorker*, July 22, 29, August 5, 1967.

100. Martin Meyerson and Others, *Face of the Metropolis* (New York, 1963); Christopher Tunnard and Boris Pushkarev, *Man-Made America: Chaos or Control* (New Haven, 1963); Richard E. Gordon and Katherine and Max Gunther, *The Split-Level Trap* (New York, 1961); S. D. Clark, *The Suburban Society* (Toronto, 1966); William G. Grigsby, *Housing Markets and Public Policy* (Philadelphia, 1963); Serge Chermayeff and Christopher Alexander, *Community and Privacy* (Garden City, N.Y., 1963); Daniel Wildner and Others, *The Housing Environment and Family Life* (Baltimore, 1962); Lowden Wingo, Jr., *Cities and Space: The Future Use of Urban Land* (Baltimore, 1962); AIP *Journal*, August 1965, pp. 247–276.

101. Harvey S. Perloff, ed., *Planning and the Urban Community* (Pittsburgh, 1961).

102. *Urban Affairs Quarterly* lists 55 urban studies institutes in its first issue, December 1965, pp. 87–90, but only a dozen were staffed for research activities.

103. Melvin C. Webber, John W. Dyckman, Donald S. Foley, Albert Z. Guttenberg, William L. C. Wheaton, and Catherine Bauer Wurster, *Explorations into Urban Structure* (Philadelphia, 1964). See also F.

Stuart Chapin, Jr., "Foundations of Urban Planning," in Werner Z. Hirsch, ed., *Urban Life and Form* (New York, 1963), pp. 217–248.

104. Leonard J. Duhl, ed., *The Urban Condition: People and Policy in the Metropolis* (New York, 1963), p. viii; Lawrence Haworth, *The Good City* (Bloomington, Ind., 1963); J. Clarence Davies, III, *Neighborhood Groups and Urban Renewal* (New York, 1966); John Mays, *Growing Up in the City* (London, 1964).

105. Roland L. Warren, *The Community in America* (Chicago, 1963).

106. Hauser and Schnore, *op. cit.*, Mitchell Gordon, *Sick Cities: Psychology and Pathology of American Urban Life* (Baltimore, 1963); York Willbern, *The Withering Away of the City* (Birmingham, 1964); John C. Bollens and Henry J. Schmandt, *The Metropolis: Its People, Politics and Economic Life* (New York, 1965).

107. Luther Halsey Gulick, *The Metropolitan Problem and American Ideas* (New York, 1962).

108. A. Theodore Brown, *Frontier Community: Kansas City to 1870* (Columbia, Mo., 1963); Charles N. Glaab, *Kansas City and the Railroads* (Madison, 1962), and *The American City: A Documentary History* (Homewood, Ill., 1963); Constance M. Green, *Washington, Village and Capital, 1800–1878* (Princeton, 1962), *Washington, Capital City, 1879–1950* (Princeton, 1963), and *The Rise of Urban America* (New York, 1965); Roy Lubove, *The Progressives and the Slums: Tenement House Reform in New York City: 1890–1917* (Pittsburgh, 1962); and *Community Planning in the 1920's* (Pittsburgh, 1963); Blake McKelvey, *Rochester: An Emerging Metropolis: 1925–1961* (Rochester, 1962); and *The Urbanization of America: 1860–1915* (New Brunswick, N.J., 1963); Gilbert Osofsky, *Harlem: The Making of a Ghetto: Negro New York 1890–1930* (New York, 1965); John W. Reps, *The Making of Urban America* (Princeton, 1965); Richard Wade, *Slavery in the Cities: The South 1820–1860* (New York, 1964); see also Allen F. Davis, "The American Historian vs. The City," *Social Studies,* March and April 1965, for a more complete bibliography.

109. Charles N. Glaab, "The Historian and the American City: A Bibliographical Survey," in Hauser and Schnore, *op. cit.*, pp. 53–80; Urban History Group, *Newsletter* 1–23 (1953–); Eric F. Lampard, "American Historians and the Study of Urbanization," *American Historical Review,* October 1961, pp. 49–61; Sam B. Warner, *Streetcar Suburbs: The Process of Growth in Boston, 1870–1900* (Cambridge, 1963); Charles N. Glaab and A. Theodore Brown, *A History of Urban America* (New York, 1967); Oscar Handlin and John Burchard, eds., *The Historian and the City* (Cambridge, 1963); Lewis Mumford, *The City in History* (New York, 1961); see also Asa Briggs, *Victorian Cities* (London, 1963), one of the best of a number of able studies of European cities.

BIBLIOGRAPHICAL NOTE

It is of course too early to prepare a bibliographical guide of lasting value in the metropolitan field, for important new studies and significant documents are constantly appearing and will quickly date any listing. Several, indeed, have come from the press in the few months that have elapsed since the completion of this study. Moreover the current issues of a half-dozen urban and scholarly journals are producing articles of timely interest in the field. It may prove helpful, nevertheless, to name some of the more useful bibliographical guides that are already available and to suggest how scholars can readily keep up to date in this rapidly developing field of study.

At present, the most comprehensive survey of the literature is *The Study of Urbanization,* edited by Philip M. Hauser and Leo F. Schnore and published in 1965. It contains able chapters on the work of historians by Charles N. Glaab, of geographers by Harold M. Mayer, of political scientists by Wallace S. Sayre and Nelson Polsby, of sociologists by Gideon Sjoberg, and of economists by Raymon Vernon and Edgar M. Hoover. Some materials missed under this disciplinary approach are covered in Scott Keyes, *Urban and Regional Studies at U.S. Universities* (Baltimore, 1964), in David R. Grant, *Metropolitan Surveys: A Digest* (Chicago, 1958), and by Robert Gutman and David Popenoe, "Urban Studies," *American Behavioral Scientist,* February 1963. In the field of planning two recent publications supply broad reviews of the works in progress, Sam B. Warner, Jr., Ed. *Planning for a Nation of Cities* (Cambridge, 1966) and several articles in the November 1965 issue of the AIP *Journal.* Sam B. Warner's volume on *Street Car Suburbs* (Cambridge, 1965) contains a useful discussion of the use of public, particularly national, documentary sources.

Other recent publications in the several academic fields contain bibliographies of a comprehensive character. A few in the realm of history merit special mention here. "A Selection of Works Relating to the History of Cities," by Philip Dawson and Sam B. Warner, Jr., provided a useful bibliography for the volume on *The Historian and the City* edited by Oscar Handlin and John Burchard. The extended bibliography in my earlier book on *The Urbanization of America: 1860–1915* supplied a more detailed listing of resources on the history of American cities. The most comprehensive of several bibliographical articles is that of Allen F. Davis on "The American Historian vs. The City" published in two parts in *The Social Studies* for March and April 1965. Periodic issues of The Urban History Group *Newsletter,* now published by the Department of History of the University of Wisconsin-Milwaukee, provide a helpful listing of new articles and books in the field of urban history. Readers of the present volume will have noted that the last section in each of my chapters endeavors to place the historical and other writings of urban students of its decade in perspective, and my footnotes for those sections will supply a convenient guide.

A few books that have grasped the significance of the increased interrelatedness of metropolitan and federal developments merit special note. Robert H. Connery and Richard H. Leach, *The Federal Government and Metropolitan Areas* (Cambridge, 1960) one of the New York Metropolitan Regional studies, makes a broad approach to its topic. Roscoe C. Martin, *The Cities and the Federal System* (New York, 1965), sees the mounting need for intergovernmental cooperation and traces its development in several fields, especially in airport construction. Michael N. Danielson, *Federal Metropolitan Politics and the Commuter Crisis* (New York, 1965) analyzes developments in that practical field. Advisory Commission on Intergovernmental Relations, *Metropolitan America: Challenge to Federalism* (Washington, 1966), reviews the many fields of federal and metropolitan involvement. William L. Miller, *The Fifteenth Ward and the Great Society* (Cambridge, 1960) discovers and develops the broader implications inherent in local political controversies in one inner-city ward.

Students interested in following these developments in a time sequence will find a wealth of pertinent detail in the successive issues of a dozen periodicals. My own heavy reliance, especially in the 1920's and 1930's, on the *American City* (1909–) and the *National Municipal Review* (1912–1958), renamed the *National Civic*

Review (1958–), is clearly evident in my footnotes. Other more specialized publications include the City Managers *Yearbook* (1915–1934), succeeded by the *Municipal Year Book* (1935–); *Land Economics* (1924–); *City Planning* (1925–1934), succeeded by *Planning and Civic Comment* (1935–1965); *Housing Betterment* (1922–1933), *Housing Yearbook* (1935–1949), *Journal of Housing* (1941–); and the *Journal* of the American Institute of Planners (1935–). Among several recently established publications that focus on the metropolis are *Nation's Cities* launched in 1963 by the American Municipal Association, now the National League of Cities; *Trans-action* started that year by Washington University in St. Louis; the *Urban Affairs Quarterly* founded in 1965, and the Poverty and Human Resources *Abstracts* issued jointly in 1966 by the University of Michigan and Wayne State University. The book review sections and the lists of related reports and publications that regularly appear in several of these journals, notably in the AIP *Journal,* are as useful to the student as the reviews in the more academic journals.

INDEX

Abbott, Edith, 45
Abrams, Charles, 216
Adams, Thomas, 45, 46, 101, 116, 251
Addams, Jane, 30
Advisory Committee on Intergovernmental Relations, 156, 157, 161, 203, 208, 210, 211, 228
Advisory Council on the Arts, 204
Afro-American, 17
Air pollution, 187, 220
Airports, 52, 90, 105, 115, 120, 127, 141, 142, 156, 157, 168, 187
Akron, 5, 10, 33, 34, 35, 51, 58
Albuquerque, 123, 163
Alihan, Milla A., 109
Alinsky, Saul D., 148, 149, 229, 230, 251
Allen, Ivan, Jr., Mayor of Atlanta, 231
Allen, James E., Jr., 222
Altoona, 220
Amalgamated Clothing Workers of America, 48
American City, 24, 28, 55, 59, 69, 79, 83, 167
American Council To Improve Our Neighborhoods (ACTION), 164, 171, 172, 185, 237
American Friends Service Committee, 182
American Institute of Architects, 130, 219
American Municipal Association, 82, 84, 105, 156, 166, 167, 171, 236
American Planning and Civic Association, 158, 159, 237

Americanization movement, 78
Anderson, John, Jr., 228
Anderson, Nels, 70, 108
Anderson, William, 62
Andrews, John B., 15
Angell, Robert C., 145
Anti-poverty measures, 226, 229
Apartment houses, 42, 134
Architects, 87, 130, 149, 196–197, 219, 244
Architecture, 75, 114
Arndt, Walter T., 9, 12
Art Commissions, 74
Artists' Projects, (WPA), 114
Ashtabula, 13
Association of Metropolitan Regional Organizations, 161, 164
Atlanta: cited, 4, 20, 42, 48, 131, 139, 154, 165, 180, 181, 190, 210, 239; described, 231
Atlantic City, 33
Austin, 97
Automobiles, 11, 42, 46, 48, 52, 106, 143

Baker, Newton D., 9, 23
Baker vs. Carr, 202
Baltimore: cited, 4, 7, 8, 13, 54, 60, 62, 74, 95, 135, 147, 172, 179, 209; charities of, 24; redevelopment in, 49, 134, 216; planning, 124, 169; politics of, 157; studied, 213
Baltimore Housing Authority, 97
Bane, Frank, 196, 208, 228, 251
Banfield, Edward C., 164, 189, 197, 239
Bankers, 82, 89